Cavendish
Publishing
Limited

EMPLOYMENT LAW

TITLES IN THE SERIES

Administrative Law

Child Law

Civil Liberties

Commercial Law

Company Law

Constitutional & Administrative Law

Contract Law

Criminal Law

Criminal Litigation & Sentencing

Criminology

Employment Law

English Legal System

Equity & Trusts

Evidence

Family Law

International Trade Law

Jurisprudence

Land Law

Landlord and Tenant

Law of Tort

Public International Law

Revenue Law

'A' Level Law - Paper 1

'A' Level Law - Paper 2

Lecture notes...

Cavendish
Publishing
Limited

EMPLOYMENT LAW

Michael Jefferson, MA (Oxon), BCL
Lecturer in Law
The University of Sheffield

First published in Great Britain 1994 by Cavendish Publishing
Limited, The Glass House, Wharton Street, London WC1X 9PX
Telephone: 0171-278 8000 Facsimile: 0171-278 8080

© Jefferson, M 1995
First edition 1994
Second edition 1995

British Library Cataloguing in Publication Data

Jefferson, Michael
Employment Law - (Lecture Notes Series)
I Title II Series
344.2041125

ISBN 1 85941 162 2
Cover photograph by Jerome Yeats
Printed and bound in Great Britain

Preface

In some areas of law two editions of a text in two calendar years would have to be justified or excused. However, the rapid development of employment law over the last 18 months necessitates a new edition of this book. Changes have been revolutionary in the field of sex discrimination, which now pervades the whole of individual labour law. The House of Lords' decision in *ex p EOC* has been particularly influential, leading to changes affecting part-time workers especially in relation to continuity and unfair dismissal, and who would have seen 20 years ago that express contractual terms such as mobility clauses would have been struck down as being indirectly discriminatory (see *Meade-Hill v The British Council*)? The law on discrimination on the grounds of pregnancy will shortly have to be rewritten when the House of Lords gets round to *Webb v EMO*. The Transfer Regulations ('TUPE') continue to exercise ever-baleful fascination for practitioners and students. The Court of Session had to intervene to put the law back on track after a decision of the Employment Appeal Tribunal sitting in Scotland (see *Stirling DC v Allen*) but there is an interesting if strange English EAT decision stating that no limitations such as the two-year qualifying period apply when claiming unfair dismissal in connection with a transfer (see *Milligan v Securicor*). TUPE (which will need to be amended when the EC concludes its discussions on how to bring the 1977 Acquired Rights Directive into the 1990s) and the procedure for handling redundancies are set for change as a result of two ECJ judgments. Elsewhere there has been an anti-employee decision in unfair dismissal – which is sometimes called a mature jurisdiction – (see *Duffy v Yeomans* in the Court of Appeal) and an astonishing anti-union decision in the Lords (see the *Associated* cases discussed in Chapter 16). We continue to live in interesting times.

As part of its drive towards deregulation (what Davies and Freedland call 'derigidification') the government has abrogated the law on unfair selection for redundancy in breach of an agreed procedure or customary agreement, another anti-collective bargaining measure. It continues to oppose draft directives on workers' rights and has exercised the opt-out under the Protocol to the Maastricht Treaty. It also promises to consolidate individual employment law just as it did to collective labour law in 1992. The halcyon days when we could talk about s 57(3) of EP(C)A may be numbered.

I have striven to concentrate on the major case-law developments while retaining the old favourites. The book stands or falls by its organisation of material within a strong framework. That structure is preserved into the second edition. The book contrives to deal with topics generally covered on an employment law course. Some topics such as Sunday trading I have deliberately not considered. At the time of writing the Disability Discrimination Bill was under discussion, and no attempt has been made to incorporate its provisions.

I know that the book is read by consultants, FE lecturers and advisers as well as by students. I hope that the second edition will continue to be read by all these constituencies and that readers will inform me of my sins of commission and omission.

I have endeavoured to state the law as at 1 June 1995. I have also been able to refer to the *North Yorkshire Dinner Ladies'* case (reported in August).

Michael Jefferson
St Barnabas' Day 1995

Outline Table of Contents

Preface   *v*

Table of Cases   *xi*

Table of Statutes   *xxxi*

1   **MODERN EMPLOYMENT LAW**   1

    1.1   Ideological conflict   1
    1.2   An industrial relations theory   2
    1.3   The law and industrial relations   3
    1.4   Policies continuing   13
    Summary of Chapter 1   15

2   **INSTITUTIONAL MATTERS**   17

    2.1   Institutions   17
    2.2   Tribunals   18
    2.3   Other institutions of English employment law   21
    2.4   Membership of the European Community   29
    Summary of Chapter 2   41

3   **FORMATION OF THE CONTRACT OF EMPLOYMENT**   43

    3.1   Employment contracts are contracts   43
    3.2   Who is an employee?   44
    3.3   The tests   46
    3.4   'Labels'   55
    3.5   Special types of workers   58
    3.6   Law or fact?   61
    3.7   Who are the employers?   62
    3.8   General criticism   62
    Summary of Chapter 3   65

4   **THE COMMON LAW OF CONTRACT**   67

    4.1   Common law contract   67
    4.2   Offer and acceptance   67
    4.3   Infancy   67
    4.4   Illegality   68
    4.5   Form: in writing   71
    4.6   Written statement   72
    4.7   Express terms   76
    4.8   Restraint of trade   79
    4.9   Implied terms   83
    4.10   Variation   97
    4.11   Payment of wages   98
    Summary of Chapter 4   101

5   **EQUAL PAY**   103
   5.1   Equal pay: introduction   103
   5.2   Effect of EC law   114
   5.3   Critique   119
   Summary of Chapter 5   121

6   **DISCRIMINATION ON THE GROUNDS OF SEX OR RACE**   123
   6.1   Introduction: basic approach   123
   6.2   Coverage: effect and width   124
   6.3   Grounds   125
   6.4   Definition   126
   6.5   Scope   139
   6.6   Exceptions   142
   6.7   Procedure   145
   6.8   Remedies   146
   6.9   Differences from equal pay   150
   Summary of Chapter 6   153

7   **TERMINATION OF THE CONTRACT OF EMPLOYMENT
        AT COMMON LAW**   155
   7.1   Termination without dismissal   155
   7.2   Termination by dismissal   162
   Summary of Chapter 7   173

8   **COMMON ISSUES IN REDUNDANCY PAYMENTS
        AND UNFAIR DISMISSAL**   175
   8.1   Statutory claims   175
   8.2   Policy   177
   8.3   Qualifications   177
   8.4   The effective date of termination   181
   8.5   Continuity   182
   8.6   Dismissal   187
   Summary of Chapter 8   191

9   **REDUNDANCY PAYMENTS**   193
   9.1   Introduction   193
   9.2   Misconduct   193
   9.3   Definition of redundancy   194
   9.4   Suitable employment unreasonably refused   199
   9.5   Trial periods   200
   9.6   Time off   201
   9.7   Redundancy procedure   202
   Summary of Chapter 9   211

10   UNFAIR DISMISSAL: THE GENERAL APPROACH   213

   10.1 Introduction   213
   10.2 Written reasons   213
   10.3 Reason for dismissal   215
   10.4 After-discovered reasons   216
   10.5 Potentially fair reasons: burden of proof   217
   10.6 Reasonableness   222
   Summary of Chapter 10   247

11   UNFAIR DISMISSAL – PARTICULAR PROBLEMS   249

   11.1 Introduction   249
   11.2 Automatically unfair   249
   11.3 Automatically fair   258
   11.4 Industrial pressure   263
   Summary of Chapter 11   265

**12   REDUNDANCY PAYMENTS AND
       UNFAIR DISMISSAL REMEDIES**   267

   12.1 Coverage   267
   12.2 Redundancy payments   267
   12.3 Unfair dismissal   270
   Summary of Chapter 12   285

13   TRANSFER OF UNDERTAKINGS   287

   13.1 Introduction   287
   13.2 Laws   289
   13.3 Trade unions   299
   Summary of Chapter 13   303

14   TRADE UNIONS   305

   14.1 Coverage   305
   14.2 Definition   305
   14.3 Legal status of unions   307
   14.4 Restraint of trade   308
   14.5 Listing   308
   14.6 Independence   309
   14.7 Recognition   311
   14.8 Collective bargaining information: duty to provide   312
   14.9 Time off   316
   14.10 Political fund   319
   Summary of Chapter 14   325

15   TRADE UNION GOVERNANCE   327

  15.1   Introduction   327
  15.2   Association and dissociation   327
  15.3   Union rules   330
  15.4   'Bridlington': the principles   336
  15.5   Unjustifiable discipline   340
  15.6   Ballots   343
  Summary of Chapter 15   347

16   INDUSTRIAL ACTION   349

  16.1   Coverage   349
  16.2   Collective agreements   349
  16.3   Effect on employment contracts   350
  16.4   Restricted strikes   351
  16.5   Liability for action   353
  16.6   Immunity   362
  16.7   Impermissible purpose   366
  16.8   Secondary action   367
  16.9   Strike ballot   368
  16.10   Citizen's and member's right   371
  16.11   Vicarious liability   372
  16.12   Damages   375
  16.13   Injunctions   375
  16.14   Picketing   378
  Summary of Chapter 16   385

Recommended Reading List   387

Index   393

Table of Cases

Abernethy v Mott, Hay & Anderson [1974] ICR 323; IRLR 213........................10.3.1
Adda International Ltd v Curcio [1976] ICR 407; IRLR 425 ....12.3.20
Addis v Gramophone Co [1909] AC 488; [1908-10] All ER Rep 1 ....7.2.13
Addison v Babcock FATA Ltd [1988] QB 280; [1987] 2 All ER 784 ....12.3.24
Addison v London Philharmonic Orchestra [1981] ICR 261 ....3.3.5
Adlington v British Bakeries (Northern) Ltd [1989] ICR 438; IRLR 218 ....14.9.1
Ainsworth v Glass Tubes Ltd [1977] ICR 757; IRLR 45 ....5.1.3
Air Canada v Lee [1978] ICR 1202; IRLR 392 ....9.5.1
Airfix Footwear Ltd v Cope [1978] ICR 1210; IRLR 396.....................3.3.18, 3.3.22
Albion Shipping Agency v Arnold [1982] ICR 22; [1981] IRLR 525 ....5.1.14
Alidair Ltd v Taylor (see Taylor v Alidair Ltd)
Allen v Cannon Hygiene Ltd [1995] IRLB 514 ....6.4.23
Allen v Flood [1898] AC 1, [1895-99] All ER Rep 52 ....6.2, 16.5.10, 16.5.22
Amalgamated Society of Boilermakers v George Wimpey & Co Ltd
  [1977] IRLR 95 ....9.7.10
Amalgamated Society of Railway Servants v Osborne
  [1910] AC 87; 79 LJ Ch 87 ....14.10
American Cyanamid Co v Ethicon Ltd [1975] AC 396; 1 All ER 504 ....4.8.14,
                                                                      16.13.2, 16.13.5
Amies v ILEA [1977] 2 All ER 100; ICR 308 ....5.2
Amos v Max-Arc Ltd [1973] ICR 46; IRLR 285.......................................9.3.3
Anglia Regional Co-operative Society v O'Donnell (1994) 27 May, EAT 655/91..........9.4.1
Annandale Engineering v Samson [1994] IRLR 59 ....4.4.3
Arbeiterwohlfahrt der Stadt Berlin v Bötel [1992] IRLR 423 ....5.2.1
Arden v Bradley [1994] IRLB 490 ....4.9.19
Argent v Minister of Social Security [1968] 1 WLR 1749; 3 All ER 208................3.3.1
Arnold v Beecham Group Ltd [1982] ICR 744; IRLR 307 ....5.1.7
Associated British Ports v Palmer [1993] IRLR 337, ICR 101;
  [1995] ICR 406, 2 WLR 754...11.2.8, 15.2.5
Associated British Ports v Transport and General Workers Union
  [1989] 1 WLR 939; 3 All ER 822..16.5.10, 16.13.2
Associated Newspapers Group Ltd v Flynn (1970) 10 KIR 17........................16.6.11
Associated Newspapers Ltd v Wilson [1993] IRLR 337;
  [1995] ICR 406, 2 WLR 354...11.2.8, 15.2.5
Association of Patternmakers and Allied Craftsmen v Kirvin Ltd
  [1978] IRLR 318; 13 ITR 446 ....9.7.5
Association of Scientific, Technical and Managerial Staffs v Parkin
  [1984] ICR 127; [1983] IRLR 448 ....14.10.2
Association of Scientific, Technical and Managerial Staffs v Hawker
  Siddeley Aviation Ltd [1977] IRLR 418 ....9.7.10
Association of University Teachers v University of
  Newcastle- upon-Tyne [1987] ICR 317; [1988] IRLR 10 ....9.7.16
Atkinson (Octavius) & Sons Ltd v Morris [1989] ICR 431; IRLR 158...............10.6.37
Attridge v Jaydees Newsagents Ltd (1980) EAT 603/79................................4.4
Attwood v Lamont [1920] 3 KB 571 ....4.8.8
Austin Rover Group Ltd v Amalgamated Union of Engineering
  Workers (Technical and Supervisory Section) [1985] IRLR 162...................16.13.6
Aziz v Trinity Taxis Ltd [1989] QB 463; [1988] 2 All ER 860.......................6.4.23

BBC v Beckett [1983] IRLR 43..8.6.4
BL Cars Ltd v Brown [1983] ICR 143; IRLR 193.....................................6.4.19
BMK Ltd v Logue [1993] ICR 601; IRLR 477 ....8.4.1
Bailey v B P Oil (Kent Refinery) Ltd [1980] ICR 642; IRLR 287....................10.6.4
Baker v Cornwall County Council [1990] ICR 452; IRLR 194.........................6.7.1
Baker v Rochdale Health Authority [1994] IRLB 502 ....5.1.14
Baldwin v British Gas Corporation [1995] IRLR 139................................7.2.4
Banerjee v City & East London Area Health Authority [1979] IRLR 147.............10.5.10

Bank voor Handel en Scheepvaart NV v Slatford [1953] 1 QB 248;
   [1952] 2 All ER 956..3.3.9
Barber v Guardian Royal Exchange Assurance Group Ltd
   [1991] 1 QB 344; [1990] 2 All ER 660 ....5.1.10, 5.1.17, 5.2.1, 5.2.2,
                                              5.2.5, 5.2.7, 6.6.6
Barber v NCR Manufacturing Ltd [1993] IRLR 95 ....5.1.15
Barclays Bank plc v Kapur [1991] 2 AC 355, 1 All ER 646.......................................6.7
Barclays Bank plc v Young [1994] IRLB 492...6.4.20
Barley v Amey Roadstone Corp Ltd (No 2) [1978] ICR 190;
   [1977] IRLR 299 ....12.3.20
Barratt Developments (Bradford) Ltd v Union of Construction
   Allied Trades & Technicians [1978] ICR 319; [1977] IRLR 403.......................9.7.7, 9.7.10
Barretts & Baird (Wholesale) Ltd v Institute of Professional Civil
   Servants [1987] IRLR 3..16.5.18
Bass Leisure Ltd v Thomas [1994] IRLR 104 ....9.3.6
Beaverbrook Newspapers Ltd v Keys [1978] ICR 582; IRLR 34 ....16.6.11, 16.13.4
Beetham v Trinidad Cement Ltd [1960] AC 132; 1 All ER 274...............................16.6.6
Begacem v Turkish Delight Kebab House (1988) EAT 471/87 ....4.4.3
Bentley Engineering Co Ltd v Crown [1976] ICR 225; IRLR 146...............................8.5.13
Benveniste v University of Southampton [1989] ICR 617; IRLR 122......................5.1.14
Berriman v Delabole Slate Ltd [1985] ICR 546; IRLR 305......................................13.2.21
Berwick Salmon Fisheries Co Ltd v Rutherford [1991] IRLR 203.............................8.5.13
Bessenden Properties Ltd v Corness [1977] ICR 821n; [1974] IRLR 338.....................12.3.35
Bhudi v IMI Refiners Ltd [1994] ICR 307; IRLR 204 ....2.4.4, 6.4.14, 6.9
Bick v Royal West of England School for the Deaf [1976] IRLR 326 ....6.3.2
Bigham v GKN Kwikform [1992] ICR 113, IRLR 4 ....11.3.7
Bilka-Kaufhaus GmbH v Weber von Hartz
   [1986] ECR 1607; 2 CMLR 701....................................5.1.16, 5.2.1, 6.4.20
Birch v National Union of Railwaymen [1950] Ch 602; 2 All ER 253......................14.10.6
Birch v University of Liverpool [1985] ICR 470; IRLR 165..7.1.14
Birds Eye Walls Ltd v Roberts [1994] ICR 338; IRLR 29 ....5.2.3
Birmingham Optical plc v Johnson [1995] ICR 459...8.3.10
Blaik v Post Office [1994] IRLR 280..5.2
Bliss v South East Thames Regional Health Authority [1987] ICR 700;
   [1985] IRLR 308 ....7.2.13
Blue Circle Staff Association v Certification Officer
   [1977] 1 WLR 239; 1 All ER 145 ....14.6.3
Board of Governors of St Matthias Church of England School v Crizzle
   [1993] IRLR 472, ICR 401 ....6.4.20
Bork (P) International A/S v Foreningen af Arbejdsledere i Danmark
   [1988] ECR 3057; [1990] 3 CMLR 701 ....13.2.6, 13.2.12
Boston Deep Sea Fishing & Ice Co v Ansell (1888) 39 Ch D 339;
   [1886-90] All ER Rep 65 ....7.2.7, 10.4
Bowaters Containers Ltd v McCormack [1980] IRLR 50..10.5.8
Boxfoldia Ltd v National Graphical Association (1982)
   [1988] ICR 752; IRLR 383..16.3.1
Boychuk v H J Symons Holdings Ltd [1977] IRLR 395 ....10.5.3
Bracebridge Engineering Ltd v Darby [1990] IRLR 3 ....4.9.19, 6.4.10
Bradley v National and Local Government Officers Association
   [1991] ICR 359; IRLR 159..15.5.4
Braund (Walter) (London) Ltd v Murray [1991] ICR 327; IRLR 100.........................12.3.22
Breen v Amalgamated Engineering Union [1971] 2 QB 175;
   1 All ER 1148 ....15.3.1
Brekkes Ltd v Cattel [1972] Ch 105; [1971] 1 All ER 1031......................................16.5.19
Brennan v J H Dewhurst Ltd [1984] ICR 52; [1983] IRLR 357 ....6.5.1
Briggs v North Eastern Education and Library Board [1990]
   IRLR 181 ....6.4.13

Brimelow v Casson [1924] 1 Ch 302; [1923] All ER Rep 40 ....16.5.12
British Aircraft Corp v Austin [1978] IRLR 332 ....8.6.4
British Airways Engine Overhaul Ltd v Francis [1981] ICR 278; IRLR 9 ....11.2.2
British Association of Advisors and Lecturers in Physical Education v
    National Union of Teachers [1986] IRLR 497 ....14.2.1
British Broadcasting Corporation v Dixon [1979] QB 546; 2 All ER 112.........................7.1.12
British Broadcasting Corporation v Hearn [1977] 1 WLR 1004;
    [1978] 1 All ER 111...16.6.9
British Coal Corp v Cheesbrough [1990] 2 AC 256; 1 All ER 641
    (also called NCB v Cheesbrough)..12.2.4
British Coal Corporation v Smith [1994] IRLR 342;, ICR810 ....5.1.3, 5.1.4, 5.1.14,
                                                                                       5.1.15, 5.1.16, 5.2.1
British Gas plc v Sharma [1991] ICR 19; IRLR 101 ....6.7.1, 6.8.3
British Home Stores Ltd v Burchell [1980] ICR 303n; [1978] IRLR 379.........................10.6.1
British Labour Pump Ltd v Byrne [1979] ICR 347; IRLR 94 ....10.6.31
British Leyland (UK) Ltd v McQuilken [1978] IRLR 245 ....4.9.37
British Railways Board v Paul [1988] IRLR 20 ....5.1.2
British Railways Board v National Union of Rail, Maritime and Transport
    Workers (1992) 17 September..16.11.2
British Transport Commission v Gourley [1956] AC 185; 3 All ER 786.........................7.2.16
British United Shoe Machinery Co Ltd v Clarke [1978] ICR 70;
    [1977] IRLR 297 ....12.3.21
Britool Ltd v Robert [1993] IRLR 481 ....11.2.2
Bromley v H & J Quick Ltd [1988] ICR 623; IRLR 249 ....5.1.8
Brook v London Borough of Haringey [1992] IRLR 478 ....6.4.13
Brooks v British Telecommunications plc [1992] ICR 414; IRLR 66 ....8.3.5
Broome v DPP [1974] AC 587; 1 All ER 314 ....16.14.3, 16.14.18,
                                                                                       16.14.19, 16.14.21
Brown v JBD Engineering Ltd [1993] IRLR 568 ....8.6.4
Brown v Rentokil Ltd [1995] IRLR 211 ....6.5.4
Brown v Stockton-on-Tees Borough Council [1989] AC 20;
    [1988] 2 All ER 129..10.6.39
Brown v Stuart Scott & Co Ltd [1981] ICR 166 ....10.2.2
Browning v Crumlin Valley Collieries Ltd [1926] 1 KB 522; 95 LJKB 711.....................4.9.13
Burgess v Bass Taverns Ltd [1994] IRLB 499..11.2.4
Burdett-Coutts v Hertfordshire CC [1984] IRLR 91 ....4.10.1
Burrett v West Birmingham Health Authority [1994] IRLR 7 ....6.4.3

CGB Publishing v Killey [1993] IRLR 520 ....11.2
Cabaj v Westminster City Council [1994] IRLR 530..10.6.20
Calder v H Kitson Vickers Ltd [1988] ICR 365 ....3.8
Calder v Rowntree Mackintosh Confectionery Ltd [1993] IRLR 212,
    ICR 811 ....5.1.14
Caledonian Mining Co Ltd v Bassett [1987] ICR 425; IRLR 165 ....7.1.14
Camellia Tanker Ltd SA v International Transport Workers'
    Federation [1976] ICR 274; IRLR 190..16.5.8
Campey & Sons v Bellwood [1987] ICR 311 ....11.3.6
Cannell v Council of the City of Newcastle-upon-Tyne [1994] IRLB 493 ....8.5.13
Capper Pass Ltd v Lawton [1977] QB 852; 2 All ER 11..5.1.5
Cardiff Women's Aid v Hartup [1994] IRLR 390 ....6.5.1
Carlill v Carbolic Smokeball Co [1893] 1 QB 256; 62 LJQB 257 ....4.2
Carlin v St Cuthbert's Co-operative Association Ltd [1974] IRLR 188 ....10.3.1
Carlson v Post Office [1981] ICR 343; IRLR 158...11.2.7
Carrington v Helix Lighting Ltd [1990] ICR 125; IRLR 6 ....6.7.3
Carrington v Therm-A-Stor Ltd [1983] 1 WLR 138; 1 All ER 796.................................11.2.3
Carron Co v Robertson 1967 SC 273; 2 ITR 484...9.4.1
Carter v The Law Society [1973] ICR 113; 117 SJ 116 ....14.2.3

Cassidy v Minister of Health [1951] 2 KB 343; 1 All ER 574 ....3.3.7
Catamaran Cruisers v Williams [1994] IRLR 386 ....3.4.1, 10.5.8
Chakki v United Yeast Co Ltd [1982] ICR 140; 2 All ER 446 ....7.1.10
Chant v Aquaboats Ltd [1978] 3 All ER 102; ICR 643 ....11.2.3
Chaplin v Leslie Frewin (Publishers) Ltd [1966] Ch 71;
   [1965] 3 All ER 764...4.3
Chapman v Goonvean and Rostowrack China Clay Co Ltd
   [1973] 1 WLR 678; 2 All ER 1063...9.3.7, 9.3.8
Cheall v Association of Professional, Executive, Clerical and
   Computer Staff [1983] AC 180; 1 All ER 1130..15.4
Chubb Fire Security Ltd v Harper [1983] IRLR 311 ....10.5.8
Churchill v Yeates & Son Ltd [1983] ICR 380; IRLR 187 ....8.3.10
City and Hackney Health Authority v Crisp [1990] ICR 95; IRLR 47.......................12.3.4
City of Bradford Metropolitan Council v Arora [1991] 2 QB 507;
   3 All ER 545 ....6.8.2
Civil Service Union v Central Arbitration Committee [1980] IRLR 135....................14.8.4
Clarke v Chadburn (No 2) [1985] 1 WLR 78; 1 All ER 211...15.3.7
Clarke v Heathfield (No 2) [1985] ICR 606 ....16.13.7
Clarke v Eley (IMI) Kynoch Ltd [1983] ICR 165; [1982] IRLR 131 ....6.4.13, 6.4.14, 6.4.20
Clarks of Hove Ltd v Bakers' Union [1978] 1 WLR 1207;
   [1979] 1 All ER 152...9.7.5
Clement-Clarke International Ltd v Manley (1979) IRLIB 145;
   EAT 219/79 ....12.3.33
Clouston & Co v Corry [1906] AC 122; [1904-7] All ER Rep 685 ....7.2.6
Clymo v Wandsworth London Borough Council [1989] IRLR 241;
   2 CMLR 577 ....6.4.13, 6.4.20
Coates v Modern Methods and Materials Ltd [1983] QB 192;
   [1982] 2 All ER 946..11.3.4
Coker v Diocese of Southwark [1995] ICR 563..3.5.2
Cole v Fred Stacey Ltd [1974] IRLR 73; 9 ITR 11..4.4
Cole v Midland Display Ltd [1973] IRLR 73 ....4.9.32
Coleman v Magnet Joinery Ltd [1974] ICR 46; IRLR 343 ....6.4.9
Coleman v Skyrail Oceanic Ltd [1981] ICR 864; IRLR 398...12.3.6
Collier v Sunday Referee Publishing Co Ltd [1940] 2 KB 647;
   4 All ER 234 ....4.9.15
Collins v Hertfordshire County Council [1947] KB 598 ....3.3.4, 3.3.8, 3.3.11
Coloroll Pension Trustees Ltd v Russell [1995] ICR 179;
   [1994] IRLR 586..5.2.1, 5.2.2
Colwyn Borough Council v Dutton [1980] IRLR 420..11.4
Commercial Plastics Ltd v Vincent [1965] 1 QB 623;
   [1964] 3 All ER 546..4.8.6
Commission of the European Communities v United Kingsom (two cases)
   [1994] IRLR 392; 1 CMLR 345 ....9.7.1, 9.7.10, 9.7.16, 13.1.3,
                                                                                        13.3, 13.3.3, 13.3.5
Commission for Racial Equality v Dutton [1989] QB 783; 1 All ER 306 ....6.4.18
Condor v Barron Knights [1966] 1 WLR 87; 110 SJ 71..7.1.6
Construction Industry Training Board v Labour Force Ltd
   [1970] 3 All ER 220;9 KIR 269 ....3.5.10
Construction Industry Training Board v Leighton
   [1978] 2 All ER 723; IRLR 60 ....4.6.6
Conway v Wade [1909] AC 506; [1908-10] All ER Rep 344..16.6.10
Cook (James W) & Co (Wivenhoe) Ltd v Tipper
   [1990] ICR 716; IRLR 386..8.3.10
Coral Leisure Group Ltd v Barnett [1981] ICR 503; IRLR 204...4.4.2
Corby v Morrison [1980] ICR 564; IRLR 218 ....4.4, 4.4.2
Cort (Robert) & Son Ltd v Charman [1981] ICR 816; IRLR 437 ....8.4.1
Costa v ENEL [1964] ECR 585; CMLR 425..2.4.1

Council of the Isles of Scilly v Brintel Helicopters Ltd [1995]
  ICR 240; IRLR 6..13.2.5, 13.2.7
Courtaulds Northern Spinning Ltd v Moosa [1984] ICR 218; IRLR 43 ....12.3.24, 12.3.31
Courtaulds Northern Spinning Ltd v Sibson [1988] ICR 451; ....
  IRLR 305...4.9.1, 4.9.3, 8.6.3
Cowley v Manson Timber Ltd [1995] ICR 367; IRLR 153 ....12.3.5
Crawford v Swinton Insurance Brokers Ltd [1990] ICR 85; IRLR 42 ....13.2.21
Cresswell v Inland Revenue Board [1984] 2 All ER 713; ICR 508 ....4.9.23
Crofter Hand Woven Harris Tweed Co Ltd v Veitch [1942] AC 435;
  1 All ER 142 ....16.5.20
Crompton v Truly Fair (International) Ltd [1975] ICR 359; IRLR 250 ....8.5.15
Crown Suppliers (PSA) v Dawkins [1993] ICR 517; IRLR 284 ....6.3.3
Cuthbertson v AML Distributors [1975] IRLR 228..4.6.6

Daddy's Dance Hall A/S v Foreningen af Arbejdsledere i Danmark
  2 CMLR 517; [1988] IRLR 315..13.2.6, 13.2.11
Dalton v Burton's Gold Medal Biscuits Ltd [1974] IRLR 45 ....10.6.11
Danfoss (see Handels-og)
Darnell v UK Case No 34/1992/379/453 ....2.2.1
Davidson v Pillay [1979] IRLR 275 ....4.4.3
Davies v Presbyterian Church of Wales [1986] 1 WLR 323;
  1 All ER 313 ....3.5.2, 3.6
Davis Contractors Ltd v Fareham Urban District Council
  [1956] AC 696; 2 All ER 145 ....7.1.2
Davis v New England College of Arundel [1977] ICR 6...............................3.3.10, 3.3.18, 3.4.2
De Francesco v Barnum (1890) 45 Ch D 430;
  [1886-90] All ER Rep 414 ....4.3
De Souza v Automobile Association [1986] ICR 514; IRLR 103.................................6.4.19
Deane v London Borough of Ealing [1993] ICR 329; IRLR 209 ....6.8.2
Defrenne v Belgium [1971] ECR 445; [1974] 1 CMLR 494 ....5.2.3
Defrenne v SABENA (No 2) [1976] ECR 455; ICR 547..2.4.2, 5.2.1
Dekker v Stichting Vormingscentrum voor Junge Volwassenen-Plus
  [1992] ICR 325; [1991] IRLR 27 ....6.5.4
Delaney v Staples [1992] 1 AC 687; 1 All ER 944 ....4.11.4
Derwent Coachworks v Kirby [1995] ICR 48; [1994] IRLR 639 ....12.3.31
Devine v Designer Flowers Wholesale Florist Sundries Ltd
  [1993] IRLR 517 ....12.3.26
Devis (W) & Sons Ltd v Atkins [1977] AC 931; 3 All ER 40........................7.2.7, 10.4, 10.4.1,
                                                                              10.6, 12.3.17, 12.3.32
Devonald v Rosser [1906] 2 KB 728; [1904-7] All ER Rep 988 ....4.9.13
Deyong v Shelburn [1946] KB 227; [1946] 1 All ER 226 ....4.9.17
Dibro Ltd v Hore [1990] ICR 370; IRLR 129..5.1.12
Dimbleby & Sons Ltd v National Union of Journalists
  [1984] 1 WLR 427; 1 All ER 751 ....16.6.4, 16.6.5
Dines v Initial Health Care Services Ltd [1995] ICR 11; [1994] IRLR 336 ....13.2.7
Discount Tobacco and Confectionery Ltd v Armitage [1990] IRLR 15.......................15.2.5
Dixon v British Broadcasting Corp
  (see British Broadcasting Corp v Dixon)
Dobie v Burns International Security (UK) Ltd [1985] 1 WLR 43;
  [1984] 3 All ER 333..10.5.8
Doughty v Rolls Royce plc [1992] IRLR 126, ICR 538...2.4.3
Downer v Onyx (UK) Ltd [1995] 1 CMLR 559 ....2.4
Drake v Morgan [1978] ICR 56; [1977] Crim LR 739..15.3.4
Driver v Cleveland Structural Engineering Ltd [1994] ICR 372; IRLR 636 ....11.2.2
Dryden v Greater Glasgow Health Board [1992] IRLR 469 ....8.6.4
Drym Fabricators Ltd v Johnson [1981] ICR 274 ....3.5.5

Duffy v Yeomans & Partners Ltd [1995] ICR 1; [1994] IRLR 642 ....10.6.4, 10.6.6, 10.6.7
Dugdale v Kraft Foods Ltd [1977] ICR 48; IRLR 368 ....5.1.6
Duke v GEC Reliance [1988] AC 618; ICR 339 ....2.4.3, 2.4.4
Dunk v George Waller & Son Ltd [1970] 2 QB 163; 2 All ER 630 ....7.2.12
Dunlop Ltd v Farrell [1993] ICR 885...12.3.21
Duport Steels Ltd v Sirs [1980] 1 WLR 142; 1 All ER 529 ....16.6.10

Eagland v British Telecommunications plc [1992] IRLR 323,
    [1993] ICR 644 ....4.9.6
East Lindsey District Council v Daubney [1977] ICR 566; IRLR 181 ....10.6.26
Eaton Ltd v King [1995] IRLR 75 ....10.6.37
Eaton Ltd v Nuttall [1977] 1 WLR 549; 3 All ER 1131 ....5.1.6, 5.1.8
EC Commission v UK [1982] ICR 578; IRLR 333 ....2.4.6, 5.1.9
Edwards v Society of Graphical and Allied Trades [1971] Ch 354;
    [1970] 3 All ER 689 ....14.4.1, 15.3.13
Egg Stores (Stamford Hill) Ltd v Leibovici [1977] ICR 260;
    [1976] IRLR 376 ....7.1.6
Electrical & Engineering Association v Ashwell-Scott Ltd
    [1976] IRLR 319 ....9.7.4
Electrical, Electronic Telecommunications and Plumbing Union v
    Times Newspapers Ltd [1980] 1 All ER 1097 ....14.3.2
Electrolux Ltd v Hutchinson [1976] IRLR 410...5.1.5
Emerald Construction Ltd v Lowthian [1966] 1 WLR 691;
    1 All ER 1013 ....16.5.11
Enderby Town Football Club Ltd v Football Association Ltd
    [1971] Ch 591; 1 All ER 215 ....15.3.12
Enderby v Frenchay Health Authority [1992] IRLR 15................................5.1.15, 5.1.16, 5.1.17,
                                                                                                                        6.4.14, 6.4.18
Enessy Co SA v Minoprio [1978] IRLR 489 ....12.3.6
Equal Opportunities Commission v Robertson [1980] IRLR 44.................................6.5.2
Esterman v National and Local Government Officers Association
    [1974] ICR 625; [1975] 1 KILR 179..15.3.3
Etherson v Strathclyde Regional Council [1992] ICR 579; IRLR 392.......................5.1.2
European Chefs (Catering) Ltd v Currell (1970) 6 ITR 37 ....9.3.9
Express & Star Ltd v National Graphical Association (1982)
    [1986] ICR 589; IRLR 222..16.11.4
Express Newspapers Ltd v McShane [1980] AC 672; 1 All ER 65 ....16.6.10

Faccenda Chicken Ltd v Fowler [1987] Ch 117; [1986] 1 All ER 617 ....4.9.26
Factortame v Secretary of State for Transport [1991] 1 AC 603;
    1 All ER 70..2.4.1
Falconer v ASLEF [1986] IRLR 331 ....16.5.5, 16.5.18, 16.10.1

Faust v Power Packing Casemakers Ltd [1983] ICR 292; IRLR 117 ....11.3.3, 11.3.9
Fentiman v Fluid Engineering Products Ltd [1991] ICR 570; IRLR 150 ....12.3.24
Ferguson v John Dawson & Partners (Contractors) Ltd
    [1976] 1 WLR 1213; 3 All ER 817..3.4.2, 3.4.4, 3.4.5
Fisscher v Voorhuis Hengelo BV [1994] IRLR 662 ....5.2.1
Fitch v Dewes [1921] 2 AC 158; All ER Rep 13...4.8.6
Fitzgerald v Hall, Russell & Co Ltd [1970] AC 984;
    [1969] 3 All ER 1140..8.5.13
Fitzpatrick v British Railways Board [1992] ICR 221;
    [1991] IRLR 376 ....11.2.2
Ford Motor Co Ltd v AUEFW [1969] 2 QB 303; 2 All ER 481..................................4.9.35
Ford v Warwickshire CC [1983] AC 71; 1 All ER 753 ....8.5.13
Foss v Harbottle (1843) 2 Hare 461, 67 ER 189 ....15.3.8

Foster v British Gas plc [1991] 1 QB 405; ICR 84 ....2.4.3
Francovich v Italian Republic [1992] IRLR 84 ....2.4.5
Freemans plc v Flynn [1984] ICR 874; IRLR 486 ....12.3.6
Fuller v Stephanie Bowman (Sales) Ltd [1977] IRLR 87 ....9.4.2
Futty v D & D Brekkes Ltd [1974] IRLR 130 ....8.6.1

Gale v Northern General Hospital NHS Trust [1994] IRLR 292 ....13.2.4
Gallacher v Department of Transport [1994] ICR 967; IRLR 231 ....11.2.7
Galt (Procurator Fiscal) v Philp [1984] IRLR 156 ....16.14.8
Garland v British Rail Engineering Ltd [1983] 2 AC 751; 2 All ER 402 ....5.2.1
Garrard v A E Southey & Co [1952] 2 QB 174; 1 All ER 597 ....3.7.1
Gascol Conversions Ltd v Mercer [1974] ICR 420; IRLR 155 ....4.6.9, 4.6.10, 4.9.40
Geest Line v Wright [1995] IRLB 513 ....8.3.4
General and Municipal Workers' Union v Wailes Dove
    Bitumastic Ltd [1977] IRLR 45 ....9.7.3
General Aviation Services (UK) Ltd v Transport and General
    Workers' Union [1985] ICR 615; [1986] IRLR 224 ....16.6.11
General Billposting Co Ltd v Atkinson [1909] AC 118;
    [1908-10] All ER Rep 619 ....4.8.10, 4.8.11
George v Beecham Group [1977] IRLR 43 ....12.3.9
Gill v El Vino Co Ltd [1983] QB 425; IRLR 206 ....6.4.6
Gimber (W) & Sons Ltd v Spurrett (1967) 2 ITR 308 ....9.3.10
Ging v Ellward (Lancs) Ltd (1978) [1991] ICR 222n; 13 ITR 265 ....12.3.24
Gorictree Ltd v Jenkinson [1985] ICR 51; [1984] IRLR 391 ....13.2.18, 13.2.20
Gould v Minister of National Insurance [1951] 1 KB 731;
    1 All ER 368 ....3.3.5
Gouriet v Union of Post Office Workers [1978] AC 4357;
    [1977] 3 All ER 70 ....16.4.1
Governing Body of the Northern Ireland Hotel and Catering College
    v National Association of Teachers in Further and Higher Education
    [1995] IRLR 83 ....9.7.2
Government Communications Staff Federation v CO [1993]
    ICR 163; IRLR 260 ....14.6.3
Greater Glasgow Health Board v Carey [1987] IRLR 484 ....6.4.13
Greater Manchester Police Authority v Lea [1990] IRLR 372 ....6.4.16, 6.4.20
Green & Son (Castings) Ltd v ASTMS [1984] ICR 352; IRLR 135 ....9.7.8
Green-Wheeler v Onyx (UK) Ltd [1993] IRLB 484 ....8.5.18, 13.2.10
Greenaway Harrison Ltd v Wiles [1994] IRLR 380 ....4.10.1, 8.6.3
Greencroft Social Club and Institute v Mullen [1985] ICR 451 ....6.4.15
Greig v Insole [1978] 1 WLR 302; 3 All ER 449 ....16.5.12
Griffin v London Pension Funds Authority [1993] ICR 564; IRLR 248 ....5.2
Griffin v South West Water Services Ltd [1995] IRLR 15 ....2.4.3, 9.7.9, 9.7.16
Griffiths v Buckinghamshire County Council [1994] ICR 265 ....4.9.37
Gunton v Richmond-upon-Thames London Borough Council
    [1980] ICR 755; 3 All ER 577 ....7.2.25, 7.2.28

Haberman-Beltermann v Arbeiterwohlfahrt [1994] IRLR 364 ....6.5.4
Hadden v University of Dundee Students' Association
    [1985] IRLR 449 ....13.2.7
Haden Ltd v Cowen [1982] IRLR 314 ....9.3.6
Hadmor Productions Ltd v Hamilton [1983] 1 AC 191;
    [1982] 1 All ER 1042 ....16.5.16, 16.5.19, 16.6.6
Hall v Lorimer [1994] 1 WLR 209; IRLR 171 ....3.3.18
Hamish Armour v ASTMS [1979] IRLR 24 ....9.7.5
Hampson v Department of Education and Science
    [1989] ICR 179; [1990] All ER 25 (CA) 6.4.20

Handels-og Kontorfunktionaernes Forbund i Danmark v Dansk
 Arbejdgiverforening [1989] ECR 3199; IRLR 532..................5.2.6, 6.5.4
Hannah Blumenthal (The) [1983] 1 AC 854; 1 All ER 34 ....7.1.2
Hardwick v Leeds Area Health Authority [1975] IRLR 319...............4.9.7, 10.6.26
Hare v Murphy Bros [1976] ICR 603; 3 All ER 940............................7.1.9
Harris & Russell Ltd v Slingsby [1973] 3 All ER 31; ICR 454...................7.2.2
Harrison v Kent County Council [1995] ICR 434 ....15.2.2, 15.2.5
Harrison Bowden Ltd v Bowden [1994] ICR 186 ....13.2.9, 13.2.10
Harvard Securities plc v Younghusband [1990] IRLR 17........................10.2.1
Haseltine Lake & Co v Dowler [1981] ICR 222; IRLR 25.......................7.2.2
Haughton v Olau Lines (UK) Ltd [1986] 1 WLR 504; 2 All ER 47 ....6.2.1
Hawker Siddeley Power Engineering Ltd v Rump [1979] IRLR 425 ....4.7
Hayes v Malleable Working Men's Club and Institute
 [1985] ICR 1; IRLR 367..6.5.4
Hayward v Cammell Laird Shipbuilders Ltd [1988] AC 894;
 2 All ER 257 ....5.1.10, 5.1.17, 5.2.1
Heatons Transport (St Helens) Ltd v Transport and General
 Workers Union [1973] AC 15; [1972] 3 All ER 101 ....15.3.2, 16.11.5
Hellyer Bros v McLeod [1987] 1 WLR 728; ICR 526............................3.3.21
Hertz v Aldi Marked K/S [1991] IRLR 31 (= the Handels-og case) 5.2.6, 6.5.4
Hewcastle Catering Ltd v Ahmed [1992] ICR 626; [1991] IRLR 473 ....4.4.4
Hickman v Maisey [1900] 1 QB 752; 69 LJQB 511...........................16.14.15
Hiles v Amalgamated Society of Woodworkers [1968] Ch 440;
 [1967] 3 All ER 70...15.3.3
Hill (RF) Ltd v Mooney [1981] IRLR 258...........................4.9.10, 8.6.4
Hill v CA Parsons & Co [1972] 1 Ch 305; [1971] 3 All ER 1345 ....7.2.26
Hill Samuel Investment Services Group Ltd v Nwauzu [1994] IRLB 567.............6.2
Hillyer v Governors of St Bartholomew's Hospital
 [1909] 2 KB 820; WN 188 ....3.2.3
Hilton International Hotels (UK) Ltd v Faraji [1994] ICR 259;
 IRLR 267 ....12.3.26
Hilton International (UK) Ltd v Protopapa [1990] IRLR 316......................8.6.4
Hindle Gears Ltd v McGinty [1984] IRLR 477 ....11.3.4, 11.3.9
Hindle v Percival Boats Ltd [1969] 1 WLR 174; 1 All ER 836 ....9.3.7
Hitchcock v Post Office [1980] ICR 100 ....3.3.19
Hogg v Dover College [1990] ICR 39............................4.10.2, 8.6.3
Hollister v National Farmers' Union [1979] ICR 542; IRLR 238...................10.5.8
Home Counties Dairies Ltd v Skilton [1970] 1 WLR 526;
 1 All ER 1227 ....4.8.8
Home Office v Holmes [1984] ICR 678; IRLR 299 ....6.4.13, 6.4.14, 6.4.19
Hopkins v National Union of Seamen [1985] ICR 268; IRLR 157 ....15.3.3
Hopkins v Norcros plc [1994] ICR 11; IRLR 18..............................7.2.17
Horizon Holidays Ltd v Grassi [1987] ICR 851; IRLR 371 ....12.3.24
Horsey v Dyfed County Council [1982] ICR 755; IRLR 395 ....6.4.8
Hotson v Wisbech Conservative Club [1984] ICR 859; IRLR 422 ....10.3.2
Hough v Leyland DAF Ltd [1991] ICR 696; IRLR 194.............................9.7.6
Howard v Pickford Tool Co Ltd [1951] KB 417, 95 SJ 44.......................7.2.28
Huddersfield Parcels Ltd v Sykes [1981] IRLR 115............................10.6.37
Hugh-Jones v St John's College, Cambridge [1979] ICR 848...............3.5.3, 6.6.4
Hughes v DHSS [1985] AC 776; IRLR 263 ....8.3.5
Huntley v Thornton [1957] 1 WLR 321; 1 All ER 234 ....16.5.20, 16.6.9
Hurley v Mustoe [1981] ICR 490; IRLR 208 ....6.4.5
Hutchinson v Enfield Rolling Mills Ltd [1981] IRLR 318...........10.6.26, 12.3.31
Hyland v JH Barker (Northwest) Ltd [1985] ICR 861, IRLR 403....................4.4

Ibex Trading Co Ltd v Walton [1994] ICR 907; IRLR 564 ....13.2.10, 13.2.18

Iceland Frozen Foods Ltd v Jones [1983] ICR 17; [1982] IRLR 439 ....10.6.2, 10.6.4
Igbo v Johnson Matthey Chemicals Ltd [1986] ICR 505; IRLR 215 ....7.1.15, 8.6.2
Ingram v Foxon [1984] ICR 685; [1985] IRLR 5 ....12.3.1
Initial Services Ltd v Putterill [1968] 1 QB 396; [1967] 3 All ER 145 ....4.9.28
Insitu Cleaning Co Ltd v Heads [1995] IRLR 4 ....6.4.10
International Sports Co Ltd v Thomson [1980] IRLR 340 ....10.6.24
Irani v Southampton & South West Hampshire HA
    [1985] ICR 590; IRLR 203 ....7.2.26
Ironmonger v Movefield Ltd [1988] IRLR 461 ....7.1.18
Irvine v Prestcold Ltd [1981] ICR 777; IRLR 281 ....6.8.3
Isle of Wight Tourist Board v Coombes [1976] IRLR 413...4.9.19

James v Eastleigh Borough Council [1990] 2 AC 751; 2 All ER 607......................................6.4.8
Jeetle v Elster [1985] ICR 389; IRLR 227...8.5.15
Jenkins v Kingsgate (Clothing Productions) Ltd: EAT:
    [1981] 1 WLR 1485; ICR 715; ECJ: [1981] 1 WLR 972; ICR 592 ....5.1.14, 5.1.18, 5.2.1
Jennings v Westwood Engineering Ltd [1975] IRLR 245 ....3.2.3
Joel v Cammell Laird [1969] ITR 206 ....4.9.39
Johnson v Nottinghamshire Combined Police Authority
    [1974] 1 WLR 358; 1 All ER 1082 ....9.3.7
Johnstone v BBC Enterprises Ltd [1994] ICR 180 ....11.2.7
Johnstone v Bloomsbury Health Authority [1992] 1 QB 333;
    [1991] 2 All ER 293 ....4.9.3, 4.9.16
Jones v Associated Tunnelling Co Ltd [1981] IRLR 477 ....4.10.2
Jones v Gwent County Council [1992] IRLR 521 ....7.2.27
Jones v University of Manchester [1993] ICR 474; IRLR 218 ....6.4.16
Jowett (Angus) & Co Ltd v NUTGW [1985] ICR 646;
    [1985] IRLR 326 ....13.2.13

Katsikas v Konstantinidis [1993] IRLR 179...13.1.3
Kavanagh v Hiscock [1974] 1 QB 600; 2 All ER 177 ....16.14.2
Kearney v Whitehaven Collieries Ltd [1893] 1 QB 700..4.4.5
Kelly v National Society of Operative Printers' Assistants
    (1915) 84 LJKB 2236; 31 TLR 632 ....15.3.4
Kelman v Care Services Ltd [1995] ICR 260 ....13.2.5
Kenny v South Manchester College [1993] IRLR 265, ICR 934 ....13.2.7
Kent County Council v Gilham [1985] ICR 227; IRLR 14 ....10.2.1, 10.5.10
Kent County Council v Gilham (No 2) [1985] ICR 233...10.6.4
Kentish Bus and Coach Co Ltd v Quarry [1994] EAT 287/92...9.5
Kidd v DRG (UK) Ltd [1985] ICR 405; IRLR 190...6.4.16, 6.4.20
King v Great Britain-China Centre [1992] ICR 566; [1991] IRLR 513 ....6.7.1
Kirby v Manpower Services Commission [1980] ICR 420; IRLR 229...................................6.4.19
Kirklees MBC v Wickes Building Services [1993] AC 27;
    [1992] 3 All ER 717...2.4.5
Kowalska v Freie und Hansestadt Hamburg [1992] ICR 29;
    [1990] IRLR 447 ....5.2.3, 5.3

Ladbroke Racing Ltd v Arnott [1983] IRLR 154 ....10.6.12
Lambeth London Borough v Commission for Racial Equality
    [1990] ICR 768; IRLR 231 ....6.6.3
Landsorganisationen i Danmark v Ny Molle Kro [1989] ICR 330;
    IRLR 37 ....13.2.6
Langston v AUEW [1974] 1 WLR 185; 1 All ER 980..4.9.15
Langston v AUEW (No 2) [1974] ICR 510; IRLR 182 ....12.3.6
Lansing Linde Ltd v Kerr [1991] 1 WLR 251; 1 All ER 418...................................4.8.14, 16.13.5
Lanton Leisure Ltd v White [1987] IRLR 119 ....8.4.2

Laverack v Woods of Colchester Ltd [1967] 1 QB 278;
    [1966] 3 All ER 683..7.2.14
Lawrence David Ltd v Ashton [1991] 1 All ER 385; [1989] ICR 123.....................4.8.14
Laws v London Chronicle (Indicator Newspapers) Ltd
    [1959] 1 WLR 698; 2 All ER 285..3.1, 4.9.21, 4.9.34
Lawton v BOC Transhield Ltd [1987] 2 All ER 608; ICR 7.................................4.9.33
Lee v Chung [1990] ICR 409; IRLR 236..3.3.22, 3.6
Lee v Lee's Air Farming Ltd [1961] AC 12; [1960] 3 All ER 420.............................3.5.7
Lee v Showmen's Guild of Great Britain [1952] 2 QB 329;
    1 All ER 1175 ....15.3.3, 15.3.6
Lees v Arthur Greaves (Lees) Ltd [1974] 2 All ER 83; ICR 501...........................7.1.14
Leigh v National Union of Railwaymen [1970] Ch 326;
    [1969] 3 All ER 1249...15.3.6
Lenehan v Union of Construction, Allied Trades and Technicians
    [1991] ICR 378; IRLR 78 ....15.6.6
Lesney Products & Co Ltd v Nolan [1977] ICR 235; IRLR 77.............................9.3.7
Leverton v Clwyd County Council [1989] AC 706; 1 All ER 78.................5.1.4, 5.1.17
Lewis v E Mason & Sons [1994] IRLR 4 ....11.3.3, 11.3.4
Lewis v Motorworld Garages Ltd [1986] ICR 157; [1985] IRLR 465.....................8.6.4
Lister v Romford Ice and Cold Storage Co Ltd [1957] AC 555;
    1 All ER 125 ....4.9.24
Litster v Forth Dry Dock and Engineering Co Ltd
    [1990] 1 AC 546; [1989] 1 All ER 1134.....................2.4.4, 13.2.10, 13.2.12,
                                                                                13.2.13, 13.2.14, 13.2.21
Lloyds Bank Ltd v Secretary of State for Employment
    [1979] 1 WLR 498; 2 All ER 573...8.5.13
Lock v Connell Estate Agents [1994] ICR 983; IRLR 444....................................12.3.35
London Borough of Wandsworth v National Association of
    Schoolmasters/Union of Women Teachers [1993] IRLR 344 ....16.6.11
London Fire & Civil Defence Authority v Betty [1994] IRLR 384..................10.6.27
Longden v Ferrari Ltd [1994] ICR 443; IRLR 157..13.2.10
Longley v National Union of Journalists [1987] IRLR 109 ....15.3.7
Lonrho Ltd v Shell Petroleum Co Ltd (No 2) [1982] AC 173;
    [1981] 2 All ER 456 ....16.5.10, 16.5.20
Lonrho plc v Fayed [1992] 1 AC 448; [1991] 4 All ER 961 ....16.5.20
Lord Advocate v de Rosa [1976] 1 WLR 946; 2 All ER 849 ....8.5.16
Lowson v Percy Main & District Social Club Institute Ltd
    [1979] ICR 568; IRLR 227 ....10.2.2
Luce v Bexley London Borough Council [1990] ICR 591; IRLR 422....................14.9.4
Lumley v Wagner (1852) [1843–60] All ER Rep 368; 21 LJ Ch 898..........4.8.13, 7.2.24
Lyon v St James Press Ltd [1976] ICR 413; IRLR 215 ....11.2.2
Lyons (J) & Sons v Wilkins [1896] 1 Ch 811; 65 LJ Ch 601 ....16.14.7

Macarthys Ltd v Smith [1980] ECR 1275; ICR 672..................................5.1.4, 5.2
McCausland v Dungannon District Council [1993] IRLR 583..............................6.4.15
Macer v Abafest Ltd [1990] ICR 234; IRLR 137.............................8.5.17, 13.2.22
MacLelland v National Union of Journalists [1975] ICR 116.............................15.3.4
McLory v Post Office [1992] ICR 758; [1993] 1 All ER 457 ....4.9.3
McMeechan v Secretary of State for Employment [1995] ICR 444 ....3.5.10
Malik v Bank of Credit and Commerce International SA
    [1995] IRLR 370 ....7.2.13
Mandla v Dowell Lee [1983] 2 AC 548; 1 All ER 1062...............6.3.3, 6.4.17, 6.4.20
Manifold Industries Ltd v Sims [1991] ICR 504; IRLR 242.................................11.3.3
MANWEB v Taylor [1975] ICR 185; IRLR 60 ....10.6.23
Market Investigations Ltd v Minister of Social Security
    [1969] 2 QB 173; [1968] 3 All ER 732....................................3.3.18, 3.3.22

Marleasing v La Comercial Internacional de Alimentacion SA
   [1990] ECR 4135; [1992] 1 CMLR 305 ....2.4.4, 6.8.4
Marley Tile Co Ltd v Shaw [1980] ICR 72; IRLR 25 ....11.2.4
Marshall v Harland and Wolff Ltd [1972] 1 WLR 899; 2 All ER 715 ....7.1.6
Marshall v Southampton & South West Hants Area
   Health Authority [1986] ECR 723; ICR 335................................2.4.2, 2.4.3,
                                           5.2.1, 5.2.5, 5.2.7
Marshall v Southampton & South West Hants Area
   Health Authority (No 2) [1991] ICR 136; [1990] IRLR 481 (CA);
   [1993] IRLR 445, ICR 893 (ECJ) 5.1.2, 6.2,
                                         6.8.1, 6.8.4, 6.9.2
Martin v MBS Fastenings (Glynwed) Distribution Ltd
   [1983] ICR 511; IRLR 198...7.1.16
Massey v Crown Life Insurance Co [1978] 1 WLR 676; ICR 590 ....3.4.4, 3.4.5, 3.4.6
Maund v Penwith District Council [1984] ICR 143; IRLR 24................................11.2.6
Maxwell v Walter Howard Designs Ltd [1975] IRLR 77 ....7.1.6
McAlwane v Broughton Estate Ltd [1973] 2 All ER 299; ICR 470.........................7.1.14
McCarthy v APEX [1980] IRLR 335 ....14.10.6
McConnell v Bolik [1979] IRLR 422 ....4.4.3
McCormick v Horsepower Ltd [1981] 1 WLR 993; 2 All ER 746 ....11.3.4
McCrea v Cullen & Davison Ltd [1988] IRLR 30...9.3.9
McDowell v Eastern British Road Services Ltd [1981] IRLR 482..........................11.2.15
McKindley v William Hill (Scotland) Ltd [1985] IRLR 492.................................9.5.1
McLeod v Hellyer Bros [1987] 1 WLR 728, ICR 526......................................3.3.21
Meade v London Borough of Haringey [1979] 1 WLR 637;
   2 All ER 1016 ....16.5.10
Meade-Hill v The British Council [1995] IRLB 522 ....6.4.13
Mears v Safecar Security Ltd [1983] QB 54; [1982] 2 All ER 865 ....4.6.5, 4.6.6,
                                         4.9.6, 4.9.12
Mediguard Services Ltd v Thame [1994] ICR 751, IRLR 504................................5.2.3, 5.2.5
Meer v London Borough of Tower Hamlets [1988] IRLR 399...............................6.4.14
Melon v Hector Powe Ltd [1981] 1 All ER 313; ICR 43...................................8.5.15
Menzies v Smith & McLaurin Ltd [1980] IRLR 180.......................................14.9.4
Mercury Communications Ltd v Scott-Garner [1984] Ch 37;
   1 All ER 179 ....16.6.8
Meridian Ltd v Gomersall [1977] ICR 597; IRLR 425.....................................10.6.14
Merkur Island Shipping Corp v Laughton [1983] 2 AC 570;
   2 All ER 189..16.5.1, 16.5.6, 16.5.16, 16.5.19
Mersey Dock and Harbour Co v Verrinder [1982] IRLR 152 ....16.14.13
Mersey Docks & Harbour Board v Coggins & Griffith
   (Liverpool) Ltd [1947] AC 1; [1946] 2 All ER 345................................3.3.7, 3.7
Meyer Dunmore International Ltd v Rogers [1978] IRLR 167 ....10.6.10
Middlebrook Mushrooms Ltd v Transport and General
   Workers Union [1993] ICR 612; IRLR 232...16.5.18
Midland Cold Storage Ltd v Steer [1972] Ch 630; 3 All ER 941 ....14.2.1
Midland Plastics Ltd v Till [1983] ICR 118; IRLR 9 ....11.3.4
Miles v Wakefield Metropolitan DC [1987] AC 539; 1 All ER 1089..........................4.9.11
Miller v Hamworthy Engineering Ltd [1986] ICR 846; IRLR 461...............4.9.42, 4.10.1
Milligan v Securicor Ltd [1995] IRLR 288 ....13.2.22
Ministry of Defence v Cannock [1994] ICR 918; IRLR 509................................6.8.1
Ministry of Defence v Crook [1982] IRLR 488..14.9.1
Ministry of Defence v Jeremiah [1980] QB 87;
   [1979] 3 All ER 833 ....6.4.4, 6.4.6, 6.4.19, 6.8.3
Ministry of Defence v Sullivan [1994] ICR 193 ....6.8.1
Mitchell v Arkwood Plastics (Engineering) Ltd [1993] ICR 471 ....10.6.27
Mogul Steamship Co Ltd v McGregor Gow & Co
   [1892] AC 25; [1891-94] All ER Rep 263..16.5.20

Monie v Coral Racing Ltd [1981] ICR 109; [1980] IRLR 431 ....10.4.1
Montreal Locomotive Works Ltd v Montreal [1947] 1 DLR 161 ....3.3.15
Moon v Homeworthy Furniture (Northern) Ltd
  [1977] ICR 117; [1976] IRLR 298 ....9.3.5
Moorcock, The (1889) 14 PD 64; [1886-90] All ER Rep 530 ....4.9.4
Morgan v Fry [1968] 2 QB 710; 3 All ER 452 ....16.3.1, 16.5.15
Morgan v Manser [1948] 1 KB 184; [1947] 2 All ER 666 ....7.1.3
Morgan v West Glamorgan County Council [1995] IRLR 68 ....7.2.28
Morganite Electrical Carbon Ltd v Donne [1988] ICR 18;
  [1987] IRLR 363 ....12.3.26
Moroni v Firma Collo GmbH [1995] ICR 137; [1994] IRLR 130 ....5.2.1
Morris (Herbert) Ltd v Saxelby [1916] 1 AC 688;
  [1916-17] All ER Rep 305 ....4.8.2
Morrish v Henlys (Folkestone) Ltd [1973] 2 All ER 137; ICR 482 ....4.9.22, 12.3.31
Morton Sundour Fabrics Ltd v Shaw (1967) 2 KIR 1; 2 ITR 502 ....7.2.2
Moss v McLachlan [1985] IRLR 76; 149 JP 167 ....16.14.2
Muffett (SH) Ltd v Head [1987] ICR 1; [1986] IRLR 488 ....12.3.28
Mulcahy v R (1868) LR 3 HL 306 ....16.5.20
Murphy v Bord Telecom Eireann [1988] ECR 673; 1 CMLR 879 ....5.1.2
Murphy v Epsom College [1985] ICR 80; [1984] IRLR 271 ....9.3.9

NAAFI v Varley [1977] 1 WLR 149, 1 All ER 840 ....5.1.14
Nagarajan v Agnew [1994] IRLR 61 ....6.4.23, 6.5.3
Nagle v Feilden [1966] 2 QB 633; 1 All ER 689 ....15.3.13, 15.4.7
Nagy v Weston [1965] 1 WLR 280; 1 All ER 689 ....16.14.4
National and Local Government Officers Association v
  Courtney-Dunn [1991] ICR 784 ....15.5.4
National Coal Board v Galley [1958] 1 WLR 16; 1 All ER 91 ....4.8.15, 4.9.36, 16.3.1
National Coal Board v National Union of Mineworkers
  [1986] ICR 736; IRLR 439 ....4.9.37, 14.7.1
National Coal Board v Ridgway [1987] 3 All ER 582; ICR 641 ....11.2.7
National Heart and Chest Hospitals v Nambiar
  [1981] ICR 441; IRLR 196 ....10.4.1
National Union of Gold, Silver and Allied Trades v
  Albury Bros Ltd [1979] ICR 84; [1978] IRLR 504 ....14.7.2
National Union of Public Employees v General Cleaning
  Contractors [1976] IRLR 362 ....9.7.6
National Union of Teachers v Governing Body of St Mary's
  Church of England (Aided) Junior School [1995] ICR 317 ....2.4.3
National Union of Teachers in Further and Higher Education v
  Blackpool and the Fylde College [1994] IRLR 227 ....16.9.6
National Vulcan Engineering Insurance Group Ltd v Wade
  [1979] QB 132; [1978] 3 All ER 121 ....5.1.14
Neale v Hereford and Worcester County Council
  [1986] ICR 471; IRLR 168 ....10.6.4
Neath v Hugh Steeper Ltd [1995] ICR 158; [1994] 1 All ER 929 ....5.2.1
Nelson v British Broadcasting Corporation
  [1977] ICR 649; IRLR 148 ....4.7.4, 9.3.6
Nelson v BBC (No 2) [1980] ICR 110; [1979] IRLR 346 ....12.3.31
Nethermere (St Neots) Ltd v Gardiner [1984] ICR 612; IRLR 240 ....3.3.20
Newland v Simons & Willer (Hairdressers) Ltd
  [1981] ICR 521; IRLR 359 ....4.4, 4.4.3
News Group Newspapers Ltd v Society of Graphical and
  Allied Trades [1986] ICR 716; IRLR 227 ....16.14.14, 16.14.18
Newstead v Department of Transport [1988] 1 WLR 612; 1 All ER 129 ....5.2.3
Nicoll v Nocorrode Ltd [1981] ICR 348; IRLR 163 ....8.5.4
Nimz v Freie und Hansestadt Hamburg [1991] IRLR 222 ....5.2.6

Nokes v Doncaster Amalgamated Collieries Ltd [1940] AC 1014;
   3 All ER 549 ....13.2
Noone v North West Thames Regional Health Authority
   [1988] ICR 813; IRLR 195...6.7.1, 6.8.1
North Yorkshire County Council v Fay [1986] ICR 133;
   [1985] IRLR 247..10.5.8
North Yorkshire County Council v Ratcliffe [1994]
   ICR 810; IRLR 342...5.1.14
Northamptonshire County Council v Dattani [1994] IRLB 488.........................6.4.23
Norton Tool Co Ltd v Tewson [1973] 1 WLR 45; 1 All ER 183 ....13.3.23, 12.3.29, 12.3.31
Notcutt v Universal Equipment Co (London) Ltd
   · [1986] 1 WLR 641; 3 All ER 582 ....7.1.7
Nothman v Barnet LBC [1979] 1 WLR 67; 1 All ER 142...................................8.3.5
Nottingham County Council v Lee [1980] ICR 635; IRLR 284 ....9.3.9
NWL Ltd v Woods [1979] 1 WLR 1294; 3 All ER 614 ....14.2.2, 16.6.10, 16.13.2,
                                                                                      16.13.4, 16.13.5

O'Brien v Associated Fire Alarms Ltd [1968] 1 WLR 1916;
   [1969] 1 All ER 93 ....4.9.1, 4.9.21
O'Brienv Barclays Bank plc [1995] 1 All ER 438 ....8.3.5
O'Brien v Sim-Chem Ltd [1980] 1 WLR 1011; 3 All ER 132 ....5.1.7
O'Hare v Rotaprint Ltd [1980] ICR 94; IRLR 47..9.3.9
O'Kelly v Trusthouse Forte plc [1984] QB 90; [1983] 3 All ER 456 ....3.3.18, 3.3.21, 8.5.1
O'Laoire v Jackel International Ltd [1991] ICR 718..7.2.17
O'Neill v Merseyside Plumbing Co Ltd [1973] ICR 96; 8 ITR 122 ....9.3.6
Ojutiku v Manpower Services Commission [1982] ICR 661; IRLR 418 ....6.4.20
Oliver v J P Malnick & Co [1983] 3 All ER 795; ICR 708....................................3.5.3, 6.2
Orr v Vaughan [1981] IRLR 63...10.5.8
Ottoman Bank v Chakarian [1930] AC 277, 142 LJ 465....................................4.9.22
Outlook Supplies Ltd v Parry [1978] ICR 788; IRLR 12..................................5.1.14
Owen & Briggs v Oates [1990] IRLR 472...4.8.10

P & O European Ferries (Dover) Ltd v Byrne [1989] ICR 779;
   IRLR 254..11.3.6
PSM International plc v Whitehouse [1992] IRLR 279..4.8.14
Palmanor Ltd v Cedron [1978] ICR 1008; IRLR 303.................................8.6.4, 12.2.4
Palmer v Southend-on-Sea BC [1984] 1 WLR 1129; 1 All ER 945 ....8.3.10
Parsons & Sons Ltd v Parsons [1971] ICR 271; IRLR 117.................................3.5.8
Parsons v BNM Labatories Ltd [1964] 1 QB 95; [1963] 2 All ER 658 ....7.2.17
Paul v National and Local Government Officers Association
   [1987] IRLR 413...14.10.2, 15.6.1, 15.6.5
Pearse v Bradford Metropolitan Council [1988] IRLR 379................................6.4.16
Pearson v Kent CC [1992] ICR 20; IRLR 110...8.5.13
Pel Ltd v Modgill [1980] IRLR 142 ....6.4.24
Pepper v Webb [1969] 1 WLR 514; 2 All ER 216 ....7.2.6
Perera v Civil Service Commission (No 2) [1983] ICR 428; IRLR 166 ....6.4.14
Pertemps Group plc v Nixon [1994] IRLB 488 ....3.5.10
Peters (Michael) Ltd v Farnfield [1995] IRLR 190 ....
Photostatic Copiers (Southern) Ltd v Okuda [1995] IRLR 11............................13.1.3
Pickstone v Freemans plc [1989] AC 66; [1988] 2 All ER 803...................2.4.4, 5.1.13
Piddington v Bates [1961] 1 WLR 162; [1960] 3 All ER 660.............................16.14.2
Piggott Bros & Co Ltd v Jackson [1992] ICR 85; [1991] IRLR 309 ....10.6.5
Polentarutti v Autokraft Ltd [1991] ICR 757; IRLR 457 ....12.3.31
Polkey v A E Dayton Services Ltd [1988] AC 344;
   [1987] 3 All ER 974 ....10.6.6, 10.6.7, 10.6.27,
                                                                          10.6.31, 10.6.32, 10.6.33,
                                                                          10.6.34, 10.6.38, 10.6.40
Porcelli v Strathclyde Regional Council [1986] ICR 564; IRLR 134 ....6.4.10

Port of London Authority v Payne [1994] ICR 555; IRLR 9 ....12.3.6
Porter v Queen's Medical Centre [1993] IRLR 486...13.2.7, 13.2.20
Poussard v Spiers (1876) 1 QBD 410; 45 LJQB 621 ....7.1.6
Post Office v Unionof Communication Workers [1990] ICR 258;
    1 WLR 981...16.9.3, 16.9.7
Prestige Group, Re [1984] 1 WLR 335; ICR 473...2.3.3
Prestwick Circuits Ltd v McAndrew [1990] IRLR 191; SLT 654 ....4.9.3
Price v Civil Service Commission [1977] 1 WLR 1417;
    [1978] 1 All ER 1228...6.4.13, 6.4.17
Provident Financial Group plc v Hayward [1989] 3 All ER 298;
    ICR 690 ....4.9.15
Prudential Assurance Co Ltd v Lorenz (1971) 11 KIR 78..16.5.7

Qualcast (Wolverhampton) Ltd v Ross [1979] ICR 386; IRLR 98 ....12.3.6, 12.3.26
Quinn v Leathem [1901] AC 495; [1900-03] All ER Rep 1 ....16.5.20
Qureshi v LondonBorough of Newham [1991] IRLR 264..6.7.1

R v BBC ex p. Lavelle [1983] 1 WLR 23; 1 All ER 241 ....7.2.27
R v British Coal Corporation ex p Price [1993] ICR 720; [1994] IRLR 72 ....9.7.4
R v British Coal Corporation ex p Vardy [1993] ICR 720; IRLR 104....................................9.7.6
R v Central Arbitration Committee ex p BTP Tioxide Ltd
    [1981] ICR 843; [1982] IRLR 60 ....14.8
R v Crown Prosecution Service ex p Hogg [1995]
    The Times 14 Apri...7.2.25
R v East Berkshire Health Authority ex p Walsh [1985] QB 152;
    [1984] 3 All ER 425...7.2.25
R v Jones [1974] ICR 310; 59 Cr App R 120 ....16.14.7
R v Mansfield Justices, ex p Sharkey [1985] QB 613; 1 All ER 193...............................16.14.10
R v Secretary of State for Employment ex p EOC...
    [1995] 1 AC 1; [1994] 1 All ER 910 ....2.3.3, 2.4.1, 2.4.5, 5.2.3, 5.3,
                                                                          6.1, 6.4.20, 7.2.25, 8.3.2
R v Secretary of State for Employment ex p Seymour-Smith
    [1994] IRLR 448..2.4.5, 6.4.20, 8.3.2
R S Components Ltd v Irwin [1974] 1 All ER 41; [1973] ICR 535.......................................10.5.8
RSPCA v Cruden [1986] ICR 205; IRLR 83 ....12.3.31
Radford v National Society of Operative Printers;
    Graphical and Media Personnel [1972] ICR 484; 116 SJ 695 ....15.3.6, 15.3.9
Rainey v Greater Glasgow Health Board [1987] AC 224;
    1 All ER 65 ....5.1.14, 5.1.15, 5.1.16,
                                                                                  5.1.17, 6.4.20
Rank Xerox Ltd v Churchill [1988] IRLR 280 ....4.9.3, 9.3.6
Rank Xerox (UK) Ltd v Goodchild [1979] IRLR 185 ....10.4.1
Rankin v British Coal Corporation [1993] IRLR 70 ....5.1.11, 6.2
RAO v Civil Aviation Authority [1994] ICR 495; IRLR 240...12.3.31
Rask v ISS Kantineservice A/S [1993] IRLR 133...13.2.7
Rasool v Hepworth Pipe Co Ltd [1980] ICR 494; IRLR 88 ....11.3.3
Ratcliffe v North Yorkshire County Council [1995] 3 All ER 597, IRLR 439 ....5.1.14, 5.1.18
Rayware Ltd v Transport and General Workers' Union
    [1989] 1 WLR 675; 3 All ER 583 ....16.14.18
Read (Richard) (Transport) Ltd v National Union of
    Mineworkers (South Wales Area) [1985] IRLR 67...16.13.6
Ready Mixed Concrete (South East) Ltd v Minister of
    Pensions & National Insurance [1968] 2 QB 497; 1 All ER 433..................3.3.6, 3.3.9, 3.3.14,
                                                                          3.3.15, 3.3.16, 3.3.17
Redmond (Dr Sophie) Stichtung v Bartol [1992] IRLR 366...13.2.5
Reed Packaging Ltd v Boozer [1988] ICR 391; IRLR 333....................................5.1.15, 5.1.17
Reid v Rush & Tompkins Group plc [1989] 3 All ER 228; IRLR 265 ....4.9.16

Reigate v Union Manufacturing Co (Ramsbottom) Ltd
[1918] 1 KB 592; [1918-19] All ER Rep 143...4.9.3
Reilly v R [1934] AC 176; 150 LT 384 ....3.5.11
Rely-a-Bell Burglar & Fire Alarm Co Ltd v Eisler
[1926] Ch 609; 95 LJ Ch 345..7.2.24
Rex Stewart Jeffries Parker Ginsberg Ltd v Parker [1988] IRLR 483...............................4.8.10
Richards v National Union of Mineworkers [1981] IRLR 247......................................14.10.2
Ridge v Baldwin [1964] AC 40; [1963] 2 All ER 66..7.2.25
Rigby v Ferodo Ltd [1988] ICR 29; [1987] IRLR 516....................4.9.41, 4.10.1, 7.2.28
Rinner-Kühn v FWW Spezial-Gebäudereinigung GmbH
[1987] IRLR 493 ....5.2.1
Roadchef Ltd v Hastings [1988] IRLR 142 ....12.3.24
Robb v London Borough of Hammersmith and Fulham
[1991] ICR 514; IRLR 72...7.2.27
Roberts v Birds Eye Walls Ltd [1991] ICR 43; IRLR 19 ....5.2.2
Robertson v British Gas Corp [1983] ICR 351; IRLR 302 ....4.6.10, 4.9.41
Robertson (Charles) (Developments) Ltd v White[1995] ICR 349.............10.6.7, 12.3.31
Robertson v Magnet Ltd (Retail Division) [1993] IRLR 512.......................................10.6.7
Robinson v British Island Airways Ltd [1978] ICR 304;
[1977] IRLR 477 ....10.5.8
Roebuck v National Union of Mineworkers (Yorkshire Area) (No 2)
[1978] ICR 676 ....15.3.10
Rookes v Barnard [1964] AC 1129; 1 All ER 367 ....1.3.5, 6.8.1,
16.5.13, 16.5.14
Royle v Trafford BC [1984] IRLR 184...4.9.11
Rummler v Dato-Druck GmbH [1987] ICR 774; 3 CMLR 127.................................5.2.8

S & U Stores Ltd v Wilkes [1974] 3 All ER 301; ICR 645...12.2.4
Sagar v Ridehalgh [1931] 1 Ch 310; [1930] All ER Rep 288 ....4.9.7
St John Shipping Corp v Joseph Rank Ltd [1957] 1 QB 267;
[1956] 3 All ER 683..4.4
Salvesen v Simons [1994] ICR 409; IRLR 52..4.4.3
Samways v Swan Hunter Shipbuilders Ltd [1975] IRLR 190......................................4.9.7
Sanders v Ernest A Neale Ltd [1974] 3 All ER 327; ICR 565 ....9.3.1
Sandhu v Department of Education and Science [1978] IRLR 208;
13 ITR 314...10.5.6
Sartor v P & O European Ferries (Felistowe) Ltd [1992] IRLR 271.........................10.6.20
Saunders v Richmond-upon-Thames Borough Council [1978] ICR 75;
[1977] IRLR 362 ....6.5.1
Saunders v Scottish National Camps Ltd [1981] IRLR 277.......................................10.5.9
Scala Ballroom (Wolverhampton) Ltd v Ratcliffe [1958] 1 WLR 1057;
3 All ER 220 ....16.5.20
Scally v Southern Health & Social Services Board [1992]
1 AC 294; 4 All ER 563..4.9.9
Scarah v Fish Container Services Ltd [1995] IRLB 519 ....3.3.21
Schmidt v Spar- und Leihkasse der Früheren Ämter Bordesholm,
Kiel und Cronshagen [1995] ICR 237; [1994] IRLR 302..13.2.5
Scott (Thomas) & Sons (Bakers) Ltd v Allen [1983] IRLR 329 ....14.9.1
Scott v Coalite Fuels and Chemicals Ltd [1988] ICR 355; IRLR 131 ....7.1.16
Secretary of State for Employment v Associated Society of
Locomotive Engineers and Firemen (No 2)
[1972] 2 QB 455; 2 All ER 949...4.9.8, 4.9.31,
4.9.47, 16.3.1
Secretary of State for Employment v Cohen [1987] ICR 570;
IRLR 169..8.5.15
Secretary of State for Employment v Levy [1990] ICR 18;
[1989] IRLR 469 ....5.2.3

Secretary of State for Employment v Spence [1987] QB 179;
 [1986] 3 All ER 616 ....13.2.10, 13.2.12, 13.2.13
Seide v Gillette Industries Ltd [1980] IRLR 427 ....6.3.3, 6.4.7
Seligman (Robert) Corp v Baker [1983] ICR 770 ....13.2.5
Seligman and Latz Ltd v McHugh [1979] IRLR 130 ....12.3.35
Sennitt v Fysons Conveyors Ltd [1994] IRLB 498 ....9.4.1
Sharifi v Strathclyde Regional Council [1992] IRLR 259 ....6.8.1
Sheffield v Oxford Controls Co [1979] ICR 396; IRLR 133 ....7.1.16
Shepherd (FC) & Co Ltd v Jerrom [1985] ICR 552; IRLR 275 ....7.1.10
Sheppard v National Coal Board (1966) 1 KIR 101; 1 ITR 177 ....9.4.1
Sherard v Amalgamated Union of Engineering Workers
 [1973] ICR 421; IRLR 188 ....16.6.11
Shields v E Coomes (Holdings) Ltd [1978] 1 WLR 1408;
 [1979] 1 All ER 456 ....5.1.5
Shipping Co Uniform Inc v International Transport Workers'
 Federation [1985] ICR 245; IRLR 71 ....16.9.2
Shirlaw v Southern Foundries (1926) Ltd [1939] 2 KB 206;
 2 All ER 113 ....4.9.5
Short v Henderson Ltd (1946) 62 TLR 427; 115 LJPC 41 ....3.3.7, 3.3.13
Showboat Entertainment Centre Ltd v Owens
 [1984] 1 WLR 384; 1 All ER 836 ....6.4.21, 6.4.22
Sibson v UK [1993] The Times 17 May 15.2.1
Sim v Rotherham Metropolitan BC [1987] Ch 216;
 [1986] 3 All ER 387 ....4.9.6, 4.9.11
Simmons v Hoover Ltd [1977] QB 284; 1 All ER 775 ....7.2.5, 9.2.1,
                                                                                   16.3.1, 16.3.2
Sinclair v Neighbour [1967] 2 QB 279; [1966] 3 All ER 988 ....7.2.5
Singh v British Steel Corporation [1974] IRLR 131 ....4.9.42
Singh v Rowntree Mackintosh Ltd [1979] ICR 554; IRLR 199 ....6.4.20
Skillen v Eastwoods Froy Ltd (1966) 2 KIR 183; 2 ITR 112 ....12.2.4
Slaughter v C Brewer & Sons Ltd [1990] ICR 730; IRLR 426 ....12.3.34
Smith v Avdel Systems Ltd [1994] IRLR 602 ....5.2.2
Smith v City of Glasgow District Council [1987] ICR 796; IRLR 326 ....10.3.1
Smith v Hayle Town Council [1978] ICR 996; IRLR 413 ....11.2.6
Smith v Safeway plc [1995] ICR 472; IRLR 132 ....6.5.3
Smith, Kline and French Laboratories Ltd v Coates [1977] IRLR 220 ....12.3.35
Snowball v Gardner Merchant Ltd [1987] IRLR 397 ....6.4.10
Snoxell v Vauxhall Motors Ltd [1978] QB 11; [1977] 3 All ER 770 ....5.1.14
Soros v Davison [1994] ICR 590; IRLR 264 ....12.3.21
Sougrin v Haringey Health Authority [1992] ICR 650; IRLR 416 ....6.7
South Wales Miners' Federation v Glamorgan Coal Co Ltd
 [1905] AC 239; [1904-07] All ER Rep 211 ....16.5.12
South West Launderettes Ltd v Laidler [1986] ICR 455; IRLR 305 ....8.5.5
Sovereign Distribution Services Ltd v TGWU [1990] ICR 31;
 [1989] IRLR 334 ....9.7.6
Spencer v Gloucestershire County Council [1985] IRLR 393 ....9.4.2
Spencer v Paragon Wallpapers Ltd [1977] ICR 301; [1976] IRLR 373 ....10.6.26
Spijkers v Gebr. Benedik Abattoir CV [1986] 3 ECR 1119; 2 CMLR 296 ....13.2.5
Spring v Guardian Assurance plc [1994] 3 WLR 354; ICR 596 ....4.9.34
Squibb UK Staff Association v Certification Officer
 [1979] 1 WLR 523; 2 All ER 452 ....14.6.2
Sreekanta v Medical Relief Agency (Stoke-on-Trent) Ltd
 [1994] IRLB 498 ....3.5.10
Stadt Lengerich v Helmig [1995] IRLR 216 ....5.2.9
Staffordshire County Council v Black [1995] IRLR 234 ....5.1.18, 6.4.16
Stapp v Shaftesbury Society [1982] IRLR 326 ....7.2.12, 8.4.1

Star Newspapers Ltd v Jordan [1994] IRLB 493...4.9.4
Steel Stockholders (Birmingham) Ltd v Kirkwood [1993] IRLR 515................................12.3.21
Stevenson v Teesside Bridge and Engineering Ltd [1971] 1 All ER 296;
   10 KIR 53 ....4.9.1
Stevenson v United Road Transport Union [1977] 2 All ER 941;
   ICR 893 ....7.2.25
Stevenson, Jordan & Harrison Ltd v MacDonald & Evans
   [1952] 1 TLR 101; 69 RPC 10 ....3.3.8, 15.3.11
Stewart v Cleveland Guest (Engineering) Ltd [1994] IRLR 440..6.4.10
Stirling District Council v Allan [1995] IRLR 301 ....13.2.9
Strange (SW) Ltd v Mann [1965] 1 WLR 629; 1 All ER 1069 ....7.1.13
Stratford (JT) & Son Ltd v Lindley [1965] AC 269; [1964] 3 All ER 102 ....16.5.16, 16.6.69
Sunley Turriff Holdings Ltd v Thomson [1995] IRLR 184..13.2.5
Sutton and Gates (Luton) Ltd v Boxall [1979] ICR 67; [1978] IRLR 486...........................12.3.31
Sutton v Revlon Overseas Corp Ltd [1973] IRLR 173 ....9.3.9
System Floors (UK) Ltd v Daniel [1982] ICR 54; [1981] IRLR 475 ....4.6.8, 4.6.10

Talke Fashions Ltd v Amalgamated Society of Textile Workers and
   Kindred Trades [1978] 1 WLR 558; 2 All ER 649..9.7.10
Tanna v Post Office [1981] ICR 374 ....6.2
Tanner v Kean [1978] IRLR 110 ....8.6.1
Tarmac Roadstone Holdings Ltd v Peacock [1973] 1 WLR 594;
   2 All ER 485 ....12.2.2
Taylor v Alidair Ltd EAT: [1977] ICR 446; [1976] IRLR 420 CA:
   [1978] ICR 445; IRLR 82...7.2.6, 10.5.4, 10.6.23
Taylor v Kent County Council [1969] 2 QB 560; 2 All ER 1080 ....9.4.1
Taylor v National Union of Mineworkers (Derbyshire Area)
   [1985] IRLR 65; (No 3) [1985] IRLR 99 ....15.3.8
Taylor v National Union of Mineworkers (Yorkshire Area)
   [1984] IRLR 445..15.3.5, 15.3.7, 15.6.7, 16.10.3
TBA Industrial Products Ltd v Locke [1984] ICR 228; IRLR 48 ....12.3.24
Teesside Times Ltd v Drury [1980] ICR 338; IRLR 72...8.5.17
Ten Oever v Stichting Bedrijfspenstoenfonds [1995] ICR 74;
   [1993] IRLR 601 ....5.2.2
Tennants Textile Colours Ltd v Todd [1989] IRLR 3 ....5.1.11
Thames Television Ltd v Wallis [1979] IRLR 136..3.3.18, 3.4.2
Thomas v National Coal Board [1987] ICR 757; IRLR 451 ....5.1.6
Thomas v National Union of Mineworkers (South Wales
   Area) [1986] Ch 20; [1985] 2 All ER 1.....................................16.14.4, 16.14.7, 16.14.9, 16.14.12,
                                                                    16.14.13, 16.14.14, 16.14.19
Thompson v GEC Avionics Ltd [1991] IRLR 488 ....8.4.1
Thompson v Woodland Designs Ltd [1980] IRLR 423 ....11.3.3
Thomson (DC) & Co Ltd v Deakin [1952] Ch 646;
   2 All ER 361 ....16.5.1, 16.5.6, 16.5.8,
                                                                    16.5.9, 16.5.20

Ticehurst v British Telecommunications plc [1992]
   ICR 383; IRLR 219...4.9.31
Tickle v Governors of Riverview CF School (1994) COIT 32420/92....................................6.8.1
Timex Corp v Thomson [1981] IRLR 522..12.3.9
Tipper v Roofdec Ltd [1989] IRLR 419 ....8.5.3
TNT Express (UK) Ltd v Downes [1993] IRLR 432..11.3.1, 12.3.31
Todd v British Midland Airways Ltd [1978] ICR 959; IRLR 370.....................................8.3.4
Tomlinson v Dick Evans 'U' Drive Ltd [1978] ICR 639; IRLR 77.......................4.4.3, 4.4.4
Torquay Hotel Co Ltd v Cousins [1969] 2 Ch 106;
   1 All ER 522 ....16.5.4, 16.5.16,
                                                                    16.5.17, 16.6.9

Tottenham Green Under Fives' Centre v Marshall
 [1991] ICR 320; IRLR 162 ....6.6.3
Trafford v Sharpe & Fisher (Building Supplies) Ltd [1994]
 IRLR 325 ....13.2.20
Transport and General Workers' Union v Ledbury Preserves
 (1928) Ltd [1985] IRLR 412 ....9.7.4
Transport and General Workers' Union v Nationwide
 Haulage Ltd [1978] IRLR 143 ....9.7.6
Transport and General Workers' Union v Webber
 [1990] ICR 711; IRLR 462 ....15.5.1
Treganowan v Robert Knee & Co Ltd [1975] ICR 408; IRLR 247 ....10.5.9
Trotter v Forth Ports Authority [1991] IRLR 419; IRLR 170 ....7.2.4
Trussed Steel Concrete Co Ltd v Green [1946] Ch 115, 62 TLR 128 ....3.5.6
Tsoukka v Potomac Restaurants Ltd (1968) 3 ITR 259 ....12.2.4
Turiff Construction v Bryant (1967) 2 KIR 659; 2 ITR 292 ....4.6.8
Tynan v Balmer [1967] 1 QB 91; [1966] 2 All ER 133 ....16.14.4, 16.14.18
Tyne & Clyde Warehouses Ltd v Hamerton [1978] ICR 661;
 IRLR 66 ....3.4.2

Union of Construction, Allied Trades and Technicians v Brain
 [1981] ICR 542; IRLR 224 ....10.6, 10.6.4
Union of Shop, Distributive and Allied Workers v Leancut Bacon Ltd
 [1981] IRLR 295 ....9.7.5
Union of Shop, Distributive and Allied Workers v Sketchley Ltd
 [1981] ICR 644; IRLR 291 ....14.7
United Bank Ltd v Akhtar [1989] IRLR 507 ....4.9.3
Universe Tankships Inc of Monrovia v International Transport
 Workers' Federation [1983] 1 AC 366; [1982] 2 All ER 67 ....16.5.21, 16.6.9
University of Cambridge v Murray [1993] ICR 460 ....8.3.9
University of Central England v NALGO [1995] IRLR 81 ....16.9.3

Van Gend en Loos v Nederlandse Administratie der Belastingen
 [1963] ECR 1; CMLR 105 ....2.4.1
Vaughan v Weighpack Ltd [1974] ICR 261; IRLR 105 ....12.3.29
Vaux Breweries Ltd v Ward (1968) 3 ITR 385 ....9.3.4, 9.3.7, 9.3.9
Vokes Ltd v Bear [1974] ICR 1; [1973] IRLR 363 ....10.6.23
von Colson v Land Nordrhein-Westfalen [1986] Ch 20;
 [1985] ICR 886 ....2.4.4, 6.8.4

WAC Ltd v Whillock 1990 SLT 219; IRLR 23 ....4.8.9
Waddington v Leicester Council for Voluntary Service [1977]
 1 WLR 544; IRLR 32 ....5.1.2
Wadman v Carpenter Farrer Partnership [1993] IRLR 374 ....6.4.11
Waite v GCHQ [1983] 2 AC 714; 2 All ER 1013 ....8.3.5
Walker v Crystal Palace FC [1910] 1 KB 87; WN 225 ....3.3.7
Walker v Josiah Wedgwood & Sons Ltd [1978] ICR 744; IRLR 105 ....8.6.4
Walker v Northumberland County Council [1995] IRLR 35 ....4.9.16
Wall's Meat Co Ltd v Khan [1979] ICR 52; [1978] IRLR 499 ....8.3.10
Wandsworth London Borough Council v National Association
 of Schoolmasters [1994] ICR 81; [1993] IRLR 344 ....16.6.8
Ward, Lock & Co Ltd v Operative Printers' Assistants' Society
 (1906) 22 TLR 327 ....16.14.7
Way v Latilla [1937] 3 All ER 759 ....4.9.10
Webb v EMO Air Cargo (UK) Ltd [1993] 1 WLR 49;
 [1992] 4 All ER 929 ....2.1.1, 2.4.4, 6.4.20, 6.5.4,
                                                             6.5.5, 11.2.18
Weddel (W) & Co Ltd v Tepper [1980] ICR 286; IRLR 96 ....10.4.1, 10.6.1

West Midlands Co-operative Society Ltd v Tipton
  [1986] AC 536; 1 All ER 513 ....10.4.1
West Midlands Passenger Transport Executive v Singh
  [1988] 1 WLR 730; 2 All ER 873 ....6.7.4
Western Excavating (ECC) Ltd v Sharp [1978] QB 761;
  1 All ER 713 ....4.9.3, 8.6.3, 8.6.5
Wetstein v Misprestige Management Services Ltd
  (1993) EAT 523/91..6.4.15
Wheeler v Patel [1987] ICR 631; IRLR 211 ....13.2.20
White v Kuzych [1951] AC 585; 2 All ER 435 ....15.3.6
White v Reflecting Roadstuds Ltd [1991] ICR 733, IRLR 331 ....4.9.3
Whittaker v Minister of Pensions [1967] 1 QB 156;
  [1966] 3 All ER 531 ....3.3.10, 3.3.11
Wickens v Champion Employment [1984] ICR 365...3.3.22
Wignall v British Gas Corp [1984] ICR 716; IRLR 493 ....14.9.1
Wileman v Minilec Engineering Ltd [1988] ICR 318; IRLR 144 ....6.4.10
Williams v Compair Maxam Ltd [1982] ICR 156; IRLR 82.................10.6.35, 10.6.37, 10.6.38
Williams v Western Mail and Echo Ltd [1980] ICR 366;
  IRLR 222..11.3.4
Williams v National Theatre Board Ltd [1982] ICR 715; IRLR 377................11.3.7
Wilson v Maynard Shipbuilding Consultants AB
  [1978] QB 665; ICR 376...8.3.4
Wilson v National Coal Board [1980] NLJ 1146..7.2.17
Wilson v Racher [1974] ICR 428; IRLR 114 ....7.2.6
Wilsons & Clyde Coal Co Ltd v English [1938] AC 57;
  [1937] 3 All ER 628...4.9.16
Wiltshire Police Authority v Wynn [1981] 1 QB 95; [1980] ICR 649............3.5.3
Wishart v NACAB Ltd [1990] ICR 794; IRLR 393..4.2
Withers v Flackwell Heath Football Supporters Club [1981] IRLR 307.........3.3.12
Wood v York City Council [1978] ICR 840; IRLR 228....................................8.5.3
Woodhouse v Peter Brotherhood Ltd [1972] 2 QB 520; 3 All ER 91 ....8.5.15
Woods v W M Car Services (Peterborough) Ltd [1982] ICR 693; IRLR 413............4.9.19, 8.6.5
Wragg (Thomas) & Sons v Wood [1976] ICR 313; IRLR 145 ....9.4.2
Wren v Eastbourne Borough Council [1993] IRLR 425, ICR 955 ....13.2.7
Writers' Guild of Great Britain v BBC [1974] 1 All ER 574; ICR 234 ....14.2.3
Wyatt v Kreglinger & Fernau [1933] 1 KB 793; 102 LJKB 325......................4.8.5
Wylie v Dee & Co (Menswear) Ltd [1978] IRLR 103.....................................6.6.2

Yetton v Eastwoods Froy Ltd [1967] 1 WLR 104; [1966] 3 All ER 353 ....7.2.15
Yewens v Noakes (1880) 6 QBD 530; 50 LJKB 530...3.3.4
Yorkshire Blood Transfusion Service v Plaskitt [1994] ICR 74.......................5.1.14
Young v University of Edinburgh (1995) IRLB 513..5.1.4
Young, James and Webster v United Kingdom [1981] IRLR 408;
  [1982] 4 EHRR 38 ....15.2.1
Young & Woods Ltd v West [1980] IRLR 201 ....3.3.22, 3.4.6

Zarb v British & Brazilian Produce Co (Sales) Ltd [1978] IRLR 78......................8.5.5
Zucker v Astrid Jewels Ltd [1978] ICR 1088; IRLR 385 ....11.2.4

European Community Legislation

Treaties

Maastricht Treaty 1992,
  Social Chapter...2.4.7

Treaty of Rome, 1958
  Art 5 ....2.4.3, 2.4.4, 2.4.5
  Art 100...2.4.8
  Art 100A 2.4.8
  Art 117.................................,....................................2.4.7
  Art 118...2.4.7
  Art 118A 2.4.8
  Art 119 ....1.3.15, 2.4.1, 2.4.2,
                                            2.4.5, 2.4.7, 2.4.8,
                                            4.11.15, 5.1.9, 5.2,
                                            5.2.1, 5.2.3, 5.2.4,
                                            5.2.5, 6.6.6
  Art 169 ....2.4.5, 2.4.6, 5.3
  Art 170..2.4.6
  Art 177..2.1.1
  Art 189..2.4.2
  Art 235..2.4.8

Directives

'Acquired Rights',
  'Business Transfers'
  (77/187) 1.3.15, 1.3.17,
                                            2.4.2, 2.4.3, 13.2.3,
                                            13.2.12, 13.2.13

'Collective Redundancies'
  (75/129) 9.7.16

'Equal Pay'
  (75/117) 5.2.5, 5.2.6
  Art 7(1)(a) 5.2.7

'Equal Treatment'
  (76/207) 2.4.2, 2.4.3, 2.4.4,
                                            5.2.5, 6.1, 6.3.2,
                                            6.4.20, 6.6.8
  Art 6...6.8.4

'Framework'
  (89/391) 11.2.17, 11.2.23

'Insolvency' (80/987)
  Art 11...2.4.5

'Pregnant Workers'
  (92/85) 11.2.17

'Terms and Conditions'
  'Written Particulars' (91/533)..................2.4.3, 4.6.1

'Works Councils'
  (95/45)..24.7

Charter of Fundamental
  Social Rights 1989 ....2.4.7

Draft Directives

'Atypical Workers'...2.4.8

'Burden of Proof in Sex Discrimination'..............2.4.8

'Working Time' 2.4.8

'Part-time Workers' 2.4.8

'Paternity Leave' 2.4.8

Draft European Company Statute 2.4.7

Table of Statutes

European Community Legislation

...

Table of Statutes

United Kingdom Legislation

Companies Act 1985
 s 318 ....3.5.8

Consumer Protection Act 1987 ....16.12

Contracts of Employment Act 1963 ....1.3.5

Criminal Justice and Public Order Act 16.14.1

Criminal Law Act 1977
 s 1 ....16.4.2, 16.14.7
 s 5 ....16.14.7
 Pt II 16.4.2

Deregulation and Contracting
 Out Act 1994 ....2.2.1
 s 36(1) 11.2.11

Education Reform Act 1988 ....14.9.4

Emergency Powers Act 1920 ....16.4

Emergency Powers Act 1964 ....16.4

Employers' Liability
 (Defective Equipment) Act 1969 ....4.9.17

Employment Act 1980 ....16.8.1
 s 4 ....1.3.21, 15.4.1
 s 5 ....15.4.1
 s 6 ....1.3.20
 ss 11-12 ....1.3.20
 s 16 ....1.3.21
 s 17 ....1.3.21
 s 18 ....1.3.21
 s 19 ....1.3.20
 Sched 2 ....1.3.20

Employment Act 1982 ....14.8.6
 ss 10-14 ....1.3.21
 s 15 ....1.3.21
 Sched 2, para 3(3) 7.2.3

Employment Act 1989
 s 4 ....6.6.2
 s 9 ....1.3.17, 1.3.20
 s 10 ....1.3.20
 s 13 ....1.3.20, 4.6.3
 s 14 ....1.3.20
 s 15 ....1.3.20, 10.2.2
 s 16 ....8.3.5
 s 20(1) 1.3.20
 s 20(2) 1.3.20
 Sched 1 ....6.6.2

Employment Act 1990
 s 3 ....1.3.20
 s 4 ....1.3.21
 s 6 ....1.3.21

Employment Protection Act 1975 ....1.3.14, 9.7
 s 11 ....1.3.24
 ss 99-107 ....1.3.15
 Sched 11 ....1.3.24

Employment Protection
 (Consolidation) Act 1978 ....1.3.5, 4.9.13,
                                                    4.9.45, 5.2.3,
                                                    7.2.19, 8.1.4,
                                                    11.2.20, 12.1,
                                                    4.6.1
 s 1 ....4.6.1
 s 2A 4.6.3
 s 4 ....4.6.4
 s 11 ....4.6.5
 s 22A 11.2.23
 s 29 ....14.9.6
 s 31 ....9.6, 14.9.6
 s 31A 14.9.6
 s 33(3A), (3B) 4.5
 s 33(3)(d) 4.5
 s 38 ....11.2.7
 s 49 ....7.2.3, 7.2.4,
                                                    7.2.7, 11.2.20,
                                                    11.2.6
 s 49(2) 7.2.3
 s 49(3) 7.2.4
 s 49(4A) 7.2.3
 s 49(5) 7.2.7
 s 53 ....1.3.20, 7.27,
                                                    10.1, 10.2.1,
                                                    10.2.3, 10.2.4
 s 53(2A) 11.2.19
 s 53(3) 10.2.2
 s 53(4) 10.2.2
 s 54 ....2.3.1, 3.2.3,
                                                    10.2.4, 10.5
 s 55 ....8.4, 8.4.1
 s 55(2) 8.6
 s 55(2)(b) 7.1.11
 s 55(3) 7.1.17
 s 55(5) 8.4.2
 s 57(1)(b) 10.5.7, 10.5.8
 s 57(2)(a) 10.5.4
 s 57(2)(b) 10.5.3
 s 57(2)(c) 10.5.5, 10.5.8
 s 57(2)(d) 10.5.6
 s 57(3) 1.3.20, 10.6,
                                                    10.6.2, 10.6.3, 13.2.18
 s 57(4) 10.5.4

s 57A............................11.2.23, 11.2.24,
                                    11.3.8, 12.3.9
s 57A(1)..12.3.9
s 59...11.2.11, 11.3.8
s 59(1)(b)..........................11.2.11, 11.2.14
s 60...6.5.5, 11.2.17,
                                    11.2.19, 11.3.8
s 60A 4.6.5, 11.2.20, 11.2.21,
                                    11.2.22, 12.3.14
s 60A(4)(a)(i) 11.2.20
s 61....................................10.5.7, 10.5.8
s 63..11.4
s 64(1)(b)..............................5.2.1, 8.3.5
s 65..8.3.6
s 67..8.3.9
s 68..12.3.2
s 68(1)...12.3.1
s 69..12.3.5
s 69(2)..............................12.3.2, 12.7.11
s 69(4)...12.3.4
s 70(1)...............................12.3.7, 12.3.8
s 71..12.3.9
s 71(2)...12.3.9
s 71(2)(a)...12.3.40
s 71(2)(b)...12.3.9
s 71(4)...12.3.7
s 71(5)...12.3.10
s 72...12.3.15
s 72(2)...12.3.9
s 73...12.3.16
s 73(2)...12.3.15
s 73(7)...12.3.17
s 73(7A)...12.3.3
s 73(a)...12.3.17
s 74(1)...............................12.3.21, 12.3.32
s 74(3)...12.3.25
s 74(4)...12.3.35
s 74(6)...12.3.31
s 75A...12.3.43
ss 81-120...9.1
s 81..3.2.3
s 81(2)...................9.3.3, 9.3.5, 10.5.5
s 82..9.4
s 82(1)..8.3.5
s 82(2)..9.2, 9.2.1
s 83(2)..8.6
s 83(2)(b)...7.1.11
s 84(3)...9.5, 9.5.1
s 84(4)..9.5
s 84(5)..9.5
s 85(2)...7.1.17
s 90...8.4, 8.4.1
s 91(2)..9.3.2
s 92..9.2.2
s 92(1)...9.2.2, 9.2.3
s 92(3)..9.2.2

s 93..7.1.4
s 94..13.1.3
s 99(1)(c)..3.5.11
s 128..2.2.1
s 131..2.1.1
s 138(1)..3.5.11
s 138(3)..3.5.11
s 138(4)..8.3.3
s 138(7)..3.5.11
s 140..3.4.8, 8.6.2
s 140(1)...............................7.1.15, 7.1.16
s 141..8.3.4
s 142(1)..................4.5, 7.1.11, 8.3.8
s 142(2)..8.3.3
s 153(1)................3.3.1, 8.3.1, 8.5.13
s 153(4)..8.5.5
Sched 4..12.2.1
Sched 9
    para 2........................8.3.7, 11.3.10
Sched 12..7.1.1
Sched 13
    para 1.3..8.5.4
    para 9 ....8.5.13, 8.5.14, 12.3.1
    para 14(3)......................................8.5.2
    para 15...8.5.2
    para 17(2)...............8.5.15, 8.5.17, 8.5.18,
                                    13.2.2, 13.2.5
    para 17(3)-(5).............................8.5.15
    para 18 ....8.5.15, 8.15.18
    para 18A 8.5.15
Sched 14.......................12.2.2, 12.2.4,
                                    12.3.4, 14.9.2
    para 7..12.2.6

Equal Pay Act 1975..................1.3.15, 2.3.3, 5.1,
                                    5.1.1, 5.1.18, 5.2.3,
                                    5.2.9, 5.3, 6.4.3,6.4.23,
                                    6.6.6, 6.8.4,6.9, 6.9.1
s 1(1) 5.1.2
s 1(2)...5.1.5
s 1(2)(b)..5.1.7
s 1(2)(c)......................5.1.9, 5.1.13, 5.1.17
s 1(3)...............................5.1.14, 6.4.20
s 1(6)...5.1.4
s 1(6)(a)..5.1.1
s 2A(2)..5.1.12
s 2(1)...5.1.2
s 2(5)...5.1.2
s 6(1)(a)..5.1.1
s 6(1)(b)..5.1.1
s 6(1A)(b)..5.1.1

European Communities Act 1972
s 2(1) 2.4.1

European Communities
(Amendment) Act 1986.............................2.4.8

Health and Safety at
  Work Act 1974.......................................3.2.3, 4.9.17,
                                                  13.2.13
  s 7...4.9.31

Highways Act 1980
  s 137...16.4.3

Industrial Relations Act 1971....................1.3.9, 1.3.12,
                                           2.2.2, 16.2, 16.4

Industrial Training Act 1964.................................1.3.13

Law Reform
  (Frustrated Contracts) Act 1943.........................7.1.4

Local Government Act 1988
  ss 17-20...1.3.20

Merchant Shipping Act 1970
  s 1(1)..4.5

Offshore Safety (Protection against
  Victimisation) Act 1992.................................11.2.22

Patents Act 1977
  ss 39-40...4.9.30

Payment of Wages in Public
  Houses Prohibition Act 1883............................1.3.20

Police Act 1964
  s 51(3)..16.14.5

Post Office Act 1953
  s 58..16.4.1

Prices and Incomes Act 1966..............................1.3.13

Public Order Act 1986
  s 3..16.14.1
  s 4A..16.14.1
  ss 11-16..16.14.1

Race Relations Act 1976...........................1.3.12, 2.3.3,
                                            6.1, 6.1.1, 6.2,
                                        6.4.1, 6.4.2, 6.4.22,
                                          6.4.23, 6.5.5,
                                              6.6.3, 6.6.4,
                                              6.8.2, 6.9.1
  s 1(1)(a)..6.4.3, 6.4.21
  s 1(1)(b)..6.4.12
  s 1(2)..6.4.24
  s 2(1)..6.4.23
  s 3(1)..6.3.3
  s 4...6.5.5
  s 5...6.6.1
  s 11...15.5.5

s 28...2.3.3
s 29...6.5.2
ss 30-31..2.3.3
s 31...6.2.3
s 32...6.2.2
s 33...6.2.3
s 34...6.6.4
s 41(1)..6.6.7
s 42...6.6.4
s 48...2.3.3
s 51...2.3.3
s 58...2.3.3
s 65...6.7.2
s 66...2.3.3
s 68...6.2
s 82...6.2.1

Redundancy Payments Act 1965.......................1.3.5

Road Haulage Wages Act 1938.........................1.3.20

Sex Discrimination Act 1975...........1.3.12, 2.3.3, 2.4.4,
                                        5.1.1, 5.1.16, 5.1.18,
                                         5.3, 6.1, 6.1.1, 6.2,
                                        6.4.1, 6.4.2, 6.4.20,
                                       6.4.22, 6.4.23, 6.4.24,
                                         6.5.5, 6.6.1, 6.6.2,
                                          6.6.4, 6.8.2, 6.8.4,
                                              6.9, 6.9.1
  s 1(1)(a)..6.4.3
  s 1(1)(b)..6.4.12
  s 2(1)..6.3.1
  s 3..6.2
  s 3(1)..6.3.2
  s 4(1)..6.4.23
  s 5(3)..6.5.4
  s 6(1)..6.5.1
  s 6(2)...6.5.3, 6.5.4
  s 6(4)....................................5.2.1, 6.6.5, 6.6.6
  s 6(4)(a)...6.6.5
  s 6(4)(b)...6.6.5
  s 6(4)(c)...6.6.5
  s 7...6.6.1
  s 10...6.2.1
  s 12...15.5.5
  s 17...6.6.5
  s 18...6.6.5
  s 19...6.6.5
  s 37...2.3.3
  s 38...6.5.2
  ss 39-40..2.3.3
  s 41...6.2.2
  s 42...6.2.3
  s 43...6.6.4
  s 49...15.6.2
  s 52...6.6.4
  s 57...2.3.3

s 57(4) 6.8.1
s 60 ....2.3.3
s 66(3) 6.8.1
s 66(4) 6.8.1
s 67 ....2.3.3
s 74 ....6.7.2
s 75 ....2.3.3
s 76 ....6.2.1
s 82(1) 3.3.2

Sex Discrimination Act 1986 ....2.4.3, 6.6.8,
                                          8.3.5
s 1(2) 6.6.2
s 2 ....5.2.1
s 2(1) 6.6.5
s 6 ....6.5.5
s 77 ....6.5.6

'Single European Act':
see European Communities
(Amendment) Act 1986

Social Security and
Housing Benefits Act 1982 ....4.9.12

Trade Disputes Act 1906............................1.3.1

Trade Disputes Act 1965............................1.3.5

Trade Union Act 1913 ....14.10

Trade Union Act 1984
Pt I...1.3.21
s 10 ....1.3.21
s 11 ....1.3.21

Trade Union and Labour
Relations Act 1974
s 18(4) 4.9.38

Trade Union and Labour
Relations (Consolidation)
Act 1992 ....1.3.23, 13.1.3
s 1...................................14.2.1, 14.2.3
s 2(1) 14.5
s 2(4) 14.5.1
s 3 ....14.5
s 4 ....14.5.2
s 4(4) 14.5.2
s 5 ....14.6.1
s 5(b) 14.6.2
s 6(1) 14.5.1, 14.6.4
s 7 ....14.6.4
s 8(1) 14.6.5
s 8(4) 14.6.5
s 9 ....14.6.4
s 9(1) 14.5.2

s 9(4) 2.2.2
s 10(1) 14.3, 14.3.2,
                                          15.3.8
s 10(2) 15.3.8
s 10(3) 14.3
s 11(1) 14.4.1
s 11(2) 14.4
s 12(1) 14.3.1
s 15 ....15.3.4
s 20(1) 16.11.1
s 20(2)-(4) 16.10.1, 16.11.2
s 21 ....16.11.3, 16.11.4
s 22 ....16.12
s 23 ....16.12
s 24 ....15.6.5
s 46 ....15.6.1
s 47 ....15.6.2
s 48 ....15.6.3
s 49 ....15.6.3
s 50 ....15.6.4
s 51 ....15.6.5
s 52 ....15.6.6
s 56(4) 15.6.6
s 57 ....15.6.1
s 58 ....15.6.1
s 62 ....16.10.2
s 63 ....15.3.6
s 64 ....15.5
s 64(2) 15.5.1
s 65 ....15.4.5, 15.4.7,
                                          15.5.2
s 65(2) 15.5
s 66 ....15.5.3
s 67 ....15.5.4
s 67(2) 2.2.2
s 68 ....11.2.20
s 69 ....15.3
s 71(1) 14.10
s 71(1)(b) 14.10.1
s 72(1) 14.10.2
s 72(1)(b) 14.10.2
s 72(4) 14.10.2
s 73(1) 14.10.4
s 73(3) 14.10.4
s 76(1) 14.10.4
s 77(3) 14.10.4
s 77(4) 14.10.4
ss 79-82 ....14.10.5
s 82(1) 4.10.1
s 82(1)(b) 14.10.6
s 82(1)(d) 14.10.1
s 84(2) 14.10.6
s 86 ....11.2.20, 14.10.6
s 109(2) 2.3.5
s 110(2) 2.3.5
s 110(4) 2.3.5

s 111(2) 2.3.5
s 115 ....15.6.8
s 116 ....15.6.8
s 119 ....15.6.1
s 122(1) 14.2.5
s 137 ....15.2.2, 15.2.4,
15.2.5
s 140(1)(b) 15.2.2
s 142(1) 15.2.3
s 142(2) 15.2.3
s 144 ....15.2.4
s 145(1) 15.2.4
s 145(5) 15.2.4
s 146 ....11.2, 11.2.8,
11.2.20
s 146(1) 11.2.7
s 147 ....11.2.9
s 148(1) 11.2.9
s 148(2) 11.2.8
s 148(3) 11.2.8
s 149 ....12.3.44
s 149(2) 11.2.9
s 149(4)-(6) 11.2.9
s 150 ....11.2.9
s 152 ....11.2.3, 11.2.5,
11.2.7, 12.3.18
s 152(1) 11.2, 11.2.5,
11.2.10, 11.3.5
s 152(1)(a) 11.2, 11.2.1,
11.2.5
s 152(1)(b) 11.2, 11.2.1,
11.2.4, 11.2.5
s 152(1)(c) 11.2, 11.2.1
s 153 ....11.2.10, 12.3.18
s 155(2) 11.2.5
s 156(1), (2) 12.3.18
s 158 ....12.3.40
s 158(4) 12.3.42
s 158(6) 12.3.42
s 160 ....11.2.9, 11.4.1,
12.3.43
s 161 ....11.2.5
s 166(1) 11.2.5
ss 168-170 ....11.2.20
s 168(1) 14.9.1
s 168(2) 14.9.1
s 168(3) 14.9.1
s 169(1) 14.9.2
s 169(3) 14.9.2
s 170(1) 14.9.4
s 170(3) 14.9.4
s 172(2) 14.9.3
ss 174-177 ....15.4.1, 15.4.7
s 174 ....15.5.3
s 174(1) 15.4.2
s 174(2) 15.4.3

s 174(3) 15.4.4, 15.4.5
s 176 ....15.5.4
s 176(2) 2.2.2
s 177(2)(a), (b) 15.4.2
s 178(1) 14.8.3
s 178(2) 14.8.3, 14.9.1
s 179 ....16.2
s 180 ....4.9.38
s 180(3) 14.7
s 181(1) 14.8
s 181(2) 14.8.1
s 182(1) 14.8.4
s 182(2)(b) 14.8.4
ss 188-198 ....9.1.1, 9.7.1
s 188 ....9.7.1, 9.7.9
s 188(2) 9.7.6, 9.7.7
s 188(6) 9.7.4
s 188(7) 9.7.5
s 189(3), (4) 9.7.9
s 189(5) 9.7.12
s 191 ....9.7.11
s 192 ....9.7.13
s 193 ....9.7.15
s 193(7) 9.7.15
s 194(1) 9.7.15
s 195 ....9.7.1, 9.7.15,
9.7.16
s 196 ....9.7.3
s 199 ....2.3.1
ss 203-206 ....2.3.1
s 207 ....2.3.1, 16.14.19
ss 209-215 ....2.3.1
s 219 ....16.5.2, 16.13.5,
16.14.8
s 219(1) 16.6.1, 16.6.2
s 219(2) 16.6.1, 16.6.2,
16.6.3
s 220 ....16.14.16, 16.14.17,
16.14.18
s 221 ....16.13.3, 16.13.4,
16.13.5
ss 222-225 ....16.7
s 224(2) 16.8
s 224(3) 16.14.17
s 226(1) 16.9
s 226A 16.9
s 226C 16.4.3
ss 227-232 ....16.9.1
s 227(1) 16.9.2
s 228(1) 16.9.2
s 228(3) 16.9.2
s 229(1) 16.9.3
s 229(1)(A) 16.9.3
s 229(2) 16.9.3
s 229(3) 16.9.3, 16.9.7
s 229(4) 16.9.3

s 230(1) 16.9.4
s 230(2) 16.9.3
s 230(4) 16.9.4
s 231 ....16.9.5
s 233 ....16.9.7
s 234 ....16.9.6, 16.9.7
s 234A 16.9.6
s 235A 16.10.1
s 235B 16.10.1
s 236 ....7.2.23
s 237 ....11.3.2, 11.3.3,
                                          11.3.5, 11.3.9, 16.7
s 237(1) 11.3.8
s 238 ....11.3.1, 11.3.3,
                                          11.3.5, 11.3.9
s 238(1) 11.3.2, 11.3.3
s 238(2) 8.3.9, 11.3.2,
                                          11.3.6, 11.3.7, 11.3.8
s 238(3) 11.3.6
s 238(4) 11.3.7
s 239(2) 8.3.9, 11.3.2
s 240(1) 16.4
s 241(1) 16.14.6, 16.14.8
s 244(1) 14.8.3, 16.6.4,
                                          16.6.9, 16.14.17
s 244(4) 16.6.6
s 244(5) 16.6.4
s 246 ....11.3.3
ss 247-9 ....2.3.1
s 251A 2.3.1
s 254 ....2.3.4
s 256 ....2.2.2
s 290a 2.3.1

Trade Union Reform and
  Employment Rights Act 1993 ....1.3.20, 1.4, 2.1.1,
                                2.2.1, 2.3.1, 2.3.3,4.6.1, 4.6.5,
                                4.11.5, 9.7.1, 9.7.16, 10.2.2,
                                11.1,11.2.22, 11.2.23, 12.3.1,
                                12.3.44, 14.10,15.6.2, 16.9.5
s 1 ....15.6.5
s 2 ....15.6.5
s 7 ....15.6.8
s 13 ....11.2.8
s 14 ....15.4.1, 15.4.7
s 16 ....15.4.7
s 17 ....16.9.3
s 18 ....16.9
s 19 ....16.9.1
s 20 ....16.9.1
s 21 ....16.9.6
s 24(1) 6.5.5, 11.2.17
s 24(2) 11.2.18
s 24(3) 11.2.18
s 24(4) 11.2.19
s 29 ....11.2.20, 12.3.14

s 30(2) 12.3.11
s 32 ....6.5.6
s 33(2) 13.1.3
s 33(4) 13.1.3
s 33(5) 13.2.17
s 33(6) 13.3.3
s 33(7)(a), (b) 13.3.5
s 44 ....2.3.1
Sched 5 ....11.2.23
  para 6 ....12.3.9
Sched 7
  para 1 ....11.2.5
  para 5 ....12.3.15
  para 17 ....16.11.3
Sched 8
  para 8 ....8.5.13
  para 25(a)(i) 8.5.13
  para 47 ....16.10.2
  para 50 ....15.5.3
  paras 79-84 ....16.10.1

Truck Acts 1831-1940 ....1.3.4, 1.3.20,
                                                        4.11.1

Unfair Contract Terms Act 1977 ....4.9.20

Wages Act 1986 ....2.2.1, 4.11.1,
                                                4.11.3, 11.2.20
  s 1 ....4.5
  s 12(3) 1.3.20
  s 14 ....1.3.20
  Sched 1 ....1.3.20

Statutory Instruments

Employment Protection
(Continuity of Employment)
Regulations 1993 (SI 2165)...................12.3.1

Employment Protection
(Part-time Employees)
Regulations 1995 (SI 31)....................4.6.1, 6.1, 8.5.7

Employment Protection
(Recoupment of
Unemployment Benefit
and Supplementary Benefits)
Regulations 1977 (SI 674).....................12.3.36

Equal Pay (Amendment)
Regulations 1983 (SI 1794)....................1.3.17, 5.1.9

Industrial Tribunals
(Constitution and Rules of Procedure)
Regulations 1993 (SI 2688)...................2.2.1

Industrial Tribunals
(Constitution and Rules of Procedure)
(Amendment)
Regulations 1994 (SI 536)...................5.1.11

Industrial Tribunals
(Extension of Jurisdiction)
Order 1994 (SI 1623) 2.2.1

Safety Representatives and
Safety Committees
Regulations 1977 (SI 1500)...................14.9.5

Sex Discrimination Act 1975
(Application to Armed Forces etc)
Regulations 1994 (SI 3276).....................6.2

Sex Discrimination and
Equal Pay (Remedies)
Regulations 1993 (SI 2798)...................6.8.4

Transfer of Undertakings
(Protection of Employment)
Regulations 1981 (SI 1794)....................1.3.17, 7.1.1,
                                              8.5, 8.5.18,
                                              9.7.16, 10.5.8,
                                              13.1.1, 13.1.3,
                                              13.2.3, 13.2.4,
                                              14.7.3
Reg 2(1) 13.2.5
Reg 2(3) 13.3.1
Reg 3...13.2.6
Reg 3(1)...13.2.6, 13.2.11

Reg 4...13.2.8
Reg 5...13.1.13, 13.2.12,
                                              13.2.13, 13.2.15,
                                              13.2.17
Reg 5(1) 13.2.9
Reg 5(2) 13.2.14
Reg 5(2)(a) 13.2.13
Reg 5(4) 13.2.13
Reg 5(4A), (4B)................................13.1.13
Reg 5...13.2.15, 13.2.16
Reg 6...13.3.6
Reg 7(1) 13.2.17
Reg 7(2) 13.2.17
Reg 8(1) 13.2.12, 13.2.15,
                                              13.2.18
Reg 8(2) 13.2.15, 13.2.18,
                                              13.2.21
Reg 9...13.3.7
Reg 10...13.3
Reg 10(1) 13.3.1
Reg 10(3) 13.3.1
Reg 10(5) 13.3.3
Reg 10(7) 13.3.4
Reg 11(1) 13.3.5
Reg 11(7) 13.3.5
Reg 11(8) 13.3.5
Reg 11(11) 13.3.5
Reg 12...13.2.4
Reg 13...13.2.4

Transfer of Undertakings
(Protection of Employment)
Regulations 1987 (SI 442)...................13.2.8

Unfair Dismissal
(Variation of Qualifying Period)
Order 1985 (SI 782) 1.3.20

Chapter 1

Modern Employment Law

Employment law has been one of the most important areas of conflicting ideologies in the UK over the last quarter of a century. Free market economists have sought to destroy the power of trade unions, which are seen as impeding business by acting as a restraint on management and as pushing up prices by gaining larger pay increases for their members than ones given to non-members. A role is reserved for unions: that of acting as a society negotiating benefits such as reduced health insurance premia for members. Linked with this view of unions are the continuing privatisation of former State-run utilities and compulsory competitive tendering for various functions such as the collection of dustbins. Advocates of the market economy have been aided by changes to the UK workforce. There has been a shift from manufacturing and heavy industries such as shipbuilding and mining to the service sector such as tourism and the activities of the City; there has been a move away from full-time to part-time work; and there has been an increase in the number of women as a proportion of workers. Unions have traditionally found difficulty in recruiting in service industries and among part-timers and women. Government policy is to undermine the ability of unions to regulate industrial relations with management through collective bargaining. How much of the undermining of unions since the Conservatives' election victory in 1979 is due to that government's substantial changes in the law and how much is due to other factors such as demography it is impossible to say. The industrial scene has altered radically over the last 15 years. It must, however, be remembered that the most efficient system is not necessarily a free market one (as deregulation of buses outside London demonstrates), and economic efficiency does not take into account other possible bases for unions such as providing training in democracy. Certainly a firm with 6,000 workers cannot effectively bargain with each one individually.

Supporters of unions may turn free market ideas on their head. Management prerogatives should be restrained: why should the law permit a long-serving employee to be sacked at any moment? Membership of a union carries with it various advantages, one of which is that overall members are paid more than non-members. Unions exist to protect their

1.1 Ideological conflict

1.1.1 Pro-unions

members and advance their interests. In 1992 there were some 9.5 million union members, a decline of 3.7 million since 1979. The figure for 1994 was 7.2 million, the decline from 1992 being partly attributable to the legal requirement introduced in 1993 that members must agree to deductions from their pay which form subscriptions to their union, a mechansim know as the check-off. In 1979 over half of the workforce were members: in the mid-1990s only a third are.

1.2   An industrial relations theory

The next part of this chapter briefly considers one of the classic theories of industrial relations. With reference to the model which this analysis provides modern employment law can be discussed. The theory postulates three 'frames of reference': unitary, pluralist and conflictual. By understanding a little about industrial relations the reader may see how the changes in the law over the last 15 years fit together without becoming overwhelmed by the details

1.2.1   The unitary frame of reference

The unitary frame of reference is such that business entrepreneurship is seen as the touchstone by which all activities within the firm are judged. Any development not promoting the business is to be neutered. The outcome for workers is that at the end of the day they will somehow share the profits of their successful enterprise. On this approach unions have no relevance except as bodies involved in the provision of welfare benefits and financial services. Because they are not necessarily in tune with the advancement of the firm, they have no collective bargaining function. Negotiation and compromise as well as employee participation in decision-making are simply not on the agenda, for they potentially hinder the company's objectives. Challenges to managerial prerogatives are viewed as illegitimate. The State can be brought in to control challenges to management. For example, strikes may be made illegal on the grounds that they disrupt commerce. Economic efficiency is the grail. Subordination of workers to management is a staging-post on that trail.

1.2.2   The pluralist frame of reference

The pluralist doctrine notes that the various participants in business undertakings may have different perceptions. What one group wants from the enterprise may conflict with what another section desires. These aspirations are legitimate. Reconciliation of these divided interests is part of the nature of industrial relations. Law may be one of the forces through which interests may be compromised. Unions can be seen as an aid to achieving a balance between the wishes of employers and employees. One employee by herself normally cannot bargain on even terms with employers. The relationship is one of subordination of employees to the employers (see the control test in Chapter 3). Employees by joining together to form unions can negotiate more equally with employers than can one person. The collective interests of employees represented by trade unions, therefore, constitute a good thing. Collective bargaining, being an expression of such an ideology, is to be cherished. Where it does not exist, it is to be encouraged to start, perhaps by the intervention of the State (eg in England through wages councils). Similarly, because collective bargaining is a continuing matter and the parties have to function together when they are not in dispute, reconciliation between their desires can if necessary be provided by the State.

To the pluralist the advent of trade unions is seen as an attempt at equalising the power relationship between employers and employees. For adherents of Marxism in its various forms, pluralism is defective. There is no level playing-field between employees, even when backed by unions, and employers. The whip-hand, to change the metaphor, is held by employers. Lasting compromise is not possible. The interests of one side, capital, or of the other, labour, must prevail. At present capital exploits labour; in a Western-style economy unions may reduce that exploitation but they cannot defeat it. In the long run the means of production will move from the capital-holding group to the labouring classes but for the moment capitalists control workers' terms of employment. Collective bargaining can ameliorate but not destroy the fundamental inequality between the classes.

1.2.3   The conflictual frame of reference

Governments have used the law in several different ways since the Second World War. From the early 1960s, shifts in policies have led to substantial amendments in the law.

1.3   The law and industrial relations

1.3.1   Role of law

The role of the law in industrial relations may be seen as reflecting the first two of the frames of reference stated in the previous section. There has over the last 30 years been an increasing involvement of law in the relationship between employers and workers, but its function has been subject to several significant changes. The law relating to trade unions between 1799 and the 1950s is an oft-told story. The principal statute was the Trade Disputes Act 1906 which withdrew common law liability from unions if they were acting in contemplation or furtherance of a trade dispute. This phrase has come to be known as the 'golden formula', a term coined by Lord Wedderburn, the doyen of UK labour lawyers. This section concentrates on the years after the Second World War.

It is through this framework that the employment law of the 1980s and 1990s can be seen. The rest of this section attempts in a short span to provide that structure.

1.3.2	The start of the modern era

In the 1950s, State intervention was slight. The government, it may be said, broadly supported pluralism. The State, which was itself an employer of many workers, acted as a model employer; that is, since the First World War it strove to encourage its employees to join unions and thereby develop collective bargaining. It had in its other role as legislator since the 19th century enacted laws in favour of health and safety such as those preventing children working as chimney sweeps and women working underground (this type of law is often known as 'protective legislation'). It helped to arrange settlements in industrial disputes through institutions such as the Industrial Court which was established in 1919. In some industries where workers had suffered grave exploitation, since 1909 there had existed wages councils. Such bodies were seen as temporary expedients designed to be abolished when collective bargaining grew strong enough. They were 'props' to collective bargaining, designed to encourage the flourishing of such bargaining and to be abolished once employers and unions were negotiating continuously and successfully. By the late 1950s State intrusions such as contracting in to unions' political funds and wartime compulsory arbitration had been abrogated. Even the courts, not known as the workers' friends, had since the early years of this century adopted a policy of non-intervention in some aspects of trade unionism. For example, the pursuit of a closed shop had been held to be legitimate. Unions were free to conduct industrial campaigns. Industrial conflict and its evolution were concomitant parts of *The System of Industrial Relations in Great Britain*, the title of an influential book published in 1954.

1.3.3	Collective *laissez-faire*

In the book mentioned above, Otto Kahn-Freund, the leading commentator on industrial relations at that time, saw the situation in terms of the law's non-intervention in the collective bargaining process. He did not doubt that the law could and did act as an auxiliary support to the practice of collective bargaining, but he described the scene in terms of 'collective *laissez-faire*', also called voluntarism and abstentionism. By his phrase he meant that by and large the State did not play a part in the procedure and merits of industrial conflict. The parties dealt with the problems by themselves. The joint regulation of industrial matters was seen as the UK's greatest contribution to industrial relations throughout the world. Besides providing a description of the scene, Kahn-Freund gave an analysis which to some degree was a prescription for good industrial relations. Both sides of industry *ought* to be left alone. After all, they were directly involved. Compromises could be reached without State intervention. There was no need for the State to penalise one of the parties to a dispute. Indeed, the governments of the day seem to have decided on a policy of non-intervention. Law merely exacerbated inter-group disputes. It was too blunt an instrument to resolve them satisfactorily, for the parties had to live with each other after the law had moved on. The law was inflexible; collective bargaining was pliable and therefore suitable to a mature industrial relations system. Both sides did not want agreements to commit all parties to exact obligations.

It should, however, be noted that not even in the 1950s did the law play no part in industrial relations. Kahn-Freund thought that the laws then existing were a gloss on collective bargaining. Yet the laws were important. Wages councils, the Fair Wages Resolution (by which the government enforced the level of pay generally existing in the industry among its contractors, an early form of what is now called contract compliance), factories legislation, the Truck Acts (under which, for instance, workers could not be paid in tokens redeemable only in company-owned 'tommy shops') existed. There were also legal interventions in specific industries such as dock-working.

1.3.4	Auxiliary legislation

In 1963 came the harbinger of statutes which gave rights to employees. The Contracts of Employment Act 1963 provided for minimum lengths of notice periods to be given to employees, that length depending on the number of years the relevant employee had worked for the employers, and for a written statement of the terms of employment. The Redundancy Payments Act 1965 continued the process of legal intervention in areas previously the sole domain of collective bargaining. These two statutes now consolidated in the Employment Protection (Consolidation) Act 1978 remain in their essentials unchanged. These statutes constitute the beginning of the 'floor of rights', the minimum rights of employees. The government was also concerned to restrain judicial activism in industrial conflict. It reversed *Rookes v Barnard* (1964) in the Trade Disputes Act 1965.

1.3.5	Beginning of 'floor of rights'

In the 1960s commentators viewed the economic decline of the UK with alarm. One failure singled out for criticism was the increase in 'wild-cat' (ie not union-backed) industrial action. Industry-wide agreements seemed to be in decline, being replaced by plant bargaining. There was apparently less control by union officials over shop stewards than previously. There

1.3.6	Unions and economic decline

was some talk of union corruption, especially Communist infiltration into the electricians' union in the 1950s, and of agitators such as the seamen's dispute of 1966. Some employers said that there were too many unions in the workplace and that multi-unionism led to demarcation disputes.

1.3.7	Donovan	The Donovan Commission (Report of the Royal Commission on Trade Unions and Employers' Associations, Cmnd 3623, 1968) was established to comment on the defects of the UK's industrial relations, including wage drift (local pay rates rose above the level agreed nationally), and to suggest reforms. The Commission considered that more formal procedures than those previously adopted should be followed. Rather than industry-wide bargaining, agreement was to be reached at plant- or company-level. The aims were to improve productivity, resolve grievances quickly, and establish stable pay bargaining.
1.3.8	'In Place of Strife'	The government's proposed solutions, which included penal sanctions for unofficial strikes, were found in a White Paper entitled 'In Place of Strife', 1969. The recommendations were followed by industrial unrest and were lost with the election defeat of 1970.
1.3.9	Industrial Relations Act 1971	The Industrial Relations Act 1971 was largely based on United States' experience. This 'legal transplant' used American terms and concepts such as bargaining agents and bargaining units, these being an attempt to abolish multi-union workplaces. It was a comprehensive and radical Act. Labour law was divorced from prior laws. New torts, called unfair industrial practices, and a new court, the National Industrial Relations Court (NIRC), were created. Unions were given a right to be recognised by employers, and employees obtained for the first time a right to a remedy for unfair dismissal. Collective agreements were legally enforceable, unless a term stating 'This is not a legally enforceable agreement' was included. Such a term was known as a TINA LEA clause. It seems that only one collective agreement did not have such a clause in it. Attempts were made with little success to improve union rule-books. Also unsuccessful was the enactment of a power to order a ballot before a strike. This power was used once. The union won by a six-to-one majority, and the employers granted a substantial pay increase. Exemption from liability for strikes was predicated on unions registering under the Act.
1.3.10	Its failure	Most unions, led by the Trades Union Congress, got round the Act by refusing to register. In this way the Act quickly became a dead letter. Managements did not seek to destroy collective

bargaining. The 1970–1974 government was defeated in a general election after the three-day week.

Two matters deserve comment: first, the increasing use of the law in areas where traditionally there had been collective *laissez-faire*: secondly, the use of the law in non-traditional areas.

1.3.11   Labour Government 1974–1979

The government, having abolished the Industrial Relations Act 1971, returned to the post-1971 structure but re-enacted the unfair dismissal provisions of that statute. Amendments were made to extend employees' and unions' rights against employers. For example, the qualifying period for unfair dismissal was reduced and the legality of the closed shop was widened so that only persons who objected on grounds of conscience to membership of a union had a remedy for being excluded from a job (though in practice the closed shop agreement often had a 'conscience clause' permitting the retention of such workers). Unfair dismissal, which is now seen as the core of employment law, is also central to negotiation outside law. The law was sweeping into areas previously occupied by collective bargaining. Moreover, law was not always as successful as settlements without legal intervention. Outside law re-employment was the principal remedy, whereas under law the remedy most frequently granted is compensation and that often at low levels. Nevertheless, the law was now taking a leading part in industrial relations. The government also intervened between employers and employees and unions and their members in the Sex Discrimination Act 1975 and the Race Relations Act 1976. ACAS was created in 1975.

1.3.12   Pro-employees

The government shied away from using the law to restrain pay deals but did introduce wage restraint. Various training schemes were established. Both work relationships and wages were being regulated by law. The first training legislation was the Industrial Training Act 1964, the first Prices and Incomes Act dates from 1966. Both aspects continued in the 1970s.

1.3.13   Pay and training

The two sides of government policy, industrial training and prices and incomes, were summed up in the term 'social contract'. The unions moderated their pay claims in return for economic and social rights granted by law. These rights included one whereby unions could oblige an employer in a certain industry to increase wages to the general level found there (Schedule 11 of the Employment Protection Act 1975). Other rights included time off for trade union purposes, maternity rights, and the compulsory notification to unions of redundancies. This period is sometimes in political terms seen

1.3.14   Social contract

as an era of corporatism. Unions were joining with the government to tackle the problems of the UK's economic decline in return for the grant of various rights. As some unionists would maintain, rights granted by law can be taken away by law.

1.3.15	European Community Law

In this era the influence of EC law was slight. English law contained or seemed to contain guarantees at least equal to those provided by EC legislation. The Equal Pay Act 1970 was thought to embody the concepts of Article 119 of the Treaty of Rome. The procedure for handling redundancies found in ss 99–107 of the Employment Protection Act 1975 seemed to constitute the UK's equivalent of the Acquired Rights Directive of 1977 (EC 77/187). To modern students the minimal effect of EC law stands out.

1.3.16	'Winter of discontent'

The 1978–1979 'winter of discontent' led to the downfall of the Labour government. It was replaced by a government of a different hue.

1.3.17	Conservatives' approach

It has been a matter of debate whether the anti-union stance of the present government can be seen as a trend underlying all amendments in labour law since 1979 (a thread, the source of which was Mrs Thatcher's espousal of Friedrich von Hayek's theories contained in books such as *The Road to Serfdom*, 1944, and *Law, Legislation and Liberty*, a triple-decker work, the third volume of which appeared conveniently in 1979), or whether the government reacted to circumstances, or whether there was a mixture of the two. Certainly there was no immediate radical overhaul of the law as the Heath government had performed in 1971. An analysis of each provision in each successive statute suggests the last. For example, when parliament enacted a law stipulating that voting members of unions' national executive committees had to be elected at least once every five years, the government seems to have overlooked the fact that at least one influential non-voting member, Mr Scargill, leader of the National Union of Mineworkers, did not have a vote. The government changed the law by means of the so-called 'Scargill clause' to meet its demand that non-voting members should now be elected. The policy of undermining union leaders, who were seen as overmighty subjects, was followed by a measure which was virtually *ad hominem*, directed at one particular union leader. While the Conservative approach to anti-union legislation had often been described as 'step-by-step', it is not that one step has been followed by another according to a pre-existing plan. Rather there has been an Act followed a short while later by a statute on the same topic. Since employment legislation is seen as an arm of economic policy, there appears to be no end in sight. Further measures can be expected at any time.

The general policy of restriction (see below) underlies much of the legislation but there have been other factors at work. One of these factors has been the influence of EC law, which to some Conservatives is seen as permitting socialism to enter by the back-door, it having been thrown out of the front. Unions have reversed their anti-EC stance, seeing the Community as their one hope in a world of anti-unionism. EC-wide norms on matters such as working hours would undermine government policies. Some EC law has been welcomed by the government. An example is the removal of restrictions on women working nights, on heavy work, and underground (s 9 of the Employment Act 1989). This protective legislation was seen by the government as being a barrier to competition. Instead of extending the legislation to men (which would also not have been sexually discriminatory), the government removed it totally. Some EC-based laws were not welcomed. These include the implementation of equal pay for work of equal value in the Equal Pay (Amendment) Regulations (SI 1983/1794) and the partial enactment of the Acquired Rights Directive (EC 77/187) by the Transfer of Undertakings (Protection of Employment) Regulations (SI 1981/1794). Those latter amendments are not in line with government policy. The issue of the European Commission's Social Policy is discussed in the next chapter. Here it can be stated that the government cannot override existing EC legislation, which is, moreover, subject to wide interpretation by the European Court of Justice.

The Conservatives claim success for their approach (which is called deregulation by their supporters and restriction by their detractors): increased productivity, decreased industrial action and improved communication between management and workers. Recently there has been a limit placed on public-sector wage claims, a limit which is inconsistent with the professed policy of leaving industrial relations to employers and employees. Increased automation, world-wide competition, long-lasting recessions, and unemployment have aided these developments, but the increased use of the law has bolstered some of the claimed successes. Nevertheless, the UK's productivity remains stubbornly below that of many competitors, and some pundits argue that the country suffers from a shortage of skills.

1.3.18   Claimed success

The following is a brief description of some of the major changes in industrial relations law made by the government in the 1980s and early 1990s, together with the relevant statute or statutory instrument.

1.3.19   Major legal changes

1.3.20   Reduction of employees' rights

The restrictions on rights of employees against employers are listed below:

- The right to return after pregnancy has been limited and made subject to complex law concerning written notices: Employment Act 1980, ss 11–12.

- After various increases in the qualifying period, the rule now is that only employees with two years' service have a claim for unfair dismissal: Unfair Dismissal (Variation of Qualifying Period) Order 1985 (SI 1985/782). There is, however, still an exception for dismissal on trade union grounds. Protection against unfair dismissal extends from the moment of employment. The burden of proving reasonableness in unfair dismissal no longer lies on the employers, and industrial tribunals must take into consideration the size and administrative resources of the firm: Employment Act 1980, s 6, amending s 57(3) of the Employment Protection (Consolidation) Act 1978. These changes may simply reflect what tribunals were already doing. It is no longer unfair for employers to re-employ former strikers selectively where the workers were engaged in unofficial action: Employment Act 1990, s 3.

- There have been various changes to procedure in industrial tribunals. Deposits of up to £150 may be required from applicants (ie from employees): Employment Act 1989, s 20(1); and there are now pre-hearing reviews by tribunal chairs: Employment Act 1989, s 20(2). Both came into force in 1993.

- The right to reasons for dismissal found in s 53 of the 1978 Act is now available only to persons employed for two years: Employment Act 1989, s 15. The previous qualifying period was six months.

- There is no right to particulars of disciplinary procedures in firms which have fewer than 20 employees: Employment Act 1989, s 13.

- The protection given to young people by wages councils has been abolished: Wages Act 1986, s 12(3). Wages councils could no longer give more than one rate for minimum wages: s 14 of the same Act. The Trade Union Reform and Employment Rights Act 1993 abolished wages councils. Criminal liability for unauthorised deductions from wages has been abrogated: see Schedule 1 of the 1986 statute, which repeals various statutes including the Truck Acts 1831–1940 and the marvellously named Payment of Wages in Public Houses Prohibition Act 1883. By s 19 and

Schedule 2 of the 1980 Employment Act the Road Haulage Wages Act 1938, which provided for the equivalent of a wages council in that industry, was repealed.

- Various legislation in favour of groups of workers has been repealed. The one which caught most media attention was the removal of the law that women could not work underground: Employment Act 1989, s 9. That statute also removed restrictions on women being engaged on heavy and night work, though the latter restraint already had many exemptions. Limits on young persons' hours of work have been removed: s 10 of the same Act.

- Attempts by Labour councils to impose contract compliance have been made illegal: Local Government Act 1988, ss 17–20. No longer is it possible for councils to impose conditions on employers before granting contracts, except in respect of race relations (s 18). This change in the law has prevented councils acting as model employers.

- Time off for trade union duties has been restricted to situations where the union is recognised by the employers on the topic under discussion: Employment Act 1989, s 14.

The government did not rely on empirical evidence which demonstrated that employment protection laws did not affect management decisions. Deregulation was based on untested assumptions.

Restrictions imposed on trade unions are listed below:

1.3.21   Policy of restriction

- Unions have been made liable in tort: Employment Act 1982, s 15. Unlawful acts not repudiated by trade union officials including shop stewards gave rise to vicarious liability to a maximum of £250,000 per action per employer: Employment Act 1982, s 15 and s 6 of the 1990 Employment Act.

- Immunity for trade unions for inducing breach of or interfering with contracts has been limited to secret ballots of all those workers who may be called upon to act: Trade Union Act 1984, ss 10–11, and Employment Act 1988, s 16. Further restrictions were added in 1993. One development, major in terms of theory if insignificant as yet in practice, is the *Citizen's Right of Action* discussed in Chapter 16.

- The golden formula immunity for acts done in contemplation or furtherance of a trade dispute has been limited to disputes between workers and their employers: Employment Act 1980, s 18.

- Picketing is lawful only at the place of work by those engaged in industrial action: Employment Act 1980, s 16.

- Secondary action is now confined to attendance at lawful picket sites: Employment Act 1990, s 4. This limitation began as the 1980 Employment Act, s 17, which produced extremely complicated laws. The government reacted to criticism by the International Labour Organisation's Committee of Experts report of 1989 that the law was in breach of Convention 87 on Freedom of Association and the Right to Organise for not affording sufficient protection to employees by abolishing the immunities for secondary action which remained after the 1980 statute. That was assuredly not the intention of ILO. The exception for secondary picketing is more apparent than real: see Chapter 16.

- Industrial action to enforce a closed shop is illegal: Employment Act 1982, ss 10–14, and Employment Act 1988, s 10.

| 1.3.22 | Union autonomy reduced | The internal regulation of trade unions has been amended as follows: |

- Various rights have been granted to members against their unions eg right to a ballot before industrial action (Trade Union Act 1984, s 10, and Employment Act 1988, s 1), right not to be unreasonably excluded from membership (Employment Act 1980, s 4), and the right not to be disciplined for refusing to participate in industrial action (Employment Act 1988, s 3). These rights were extended in 1993.

- The government has enacted provisions in relation to elections for members of unions' national executive. For example, independent scrutineers must be appointed, and voting must be on the basis of one person, one vote: Trade Union Act 1986 Pt I as amended.

- Unions must not indemnify members who execute unlawful instructions: Employment Act 1988, s 8.

- The Commissioners for the Rights of Trade Union Members and for Protection against Unlawful Industrial Action has been appointed. Refer to Chapter 2.

Unions are now very much more highly regulated than they were before the 1970s. The effect has been to rely more on market forces to regulate industrial relations. In so far as the government had freedom of action (it is somtimes forbidden to act by European Community law), individual employment protection 'rights' have been reduced in order to reduce burdens on businesses.

Provisions dealing with unions are now found in the Trade Union and Labour Relations (Consolidation) Act 1992. Among changes and ones to be mentioned shortly, such as the abolition of the Fair Wages Resolution 1946, the government has reduced the income of strikers' families by deeming that the union is paying them £12 per week even if it is not.

1.3.23   Consolidation of law

The government has withdrawn from its role as a model employer. No longer does it promote trade unionism. It abrogated the Fair Wages Resolution. It abolished the right to belong to a trade union for Government Communications Headquarters workers ostensibly on the grounds of national security. It repealed the right of employees to obtain wages at the general level in the relevant industry (Schedule 11 to the Employment Protection Act 1975) and the right of unions to recognition (s 11 of the same Act). It has abolished several tripartite (ie with representation from unions, employers and independents) bodies such as the Manpower Services Commission.

1.3.24   Model employer role abrogated

The government has been supported by the success of some employers in crippling and defeating unions. The failure of the miners' strike 1984–1985 stands out, but there have been other major victories for employers such as the transfer of part of the London newspaper industry to Wapping and the reorganisation of ferries which led to the P & O dispute. There have occurred many other trials of strength such as the dismissal of 89 women workers at Middlebrook Mushrooms near Selby, North Yorkshire, for going on strike in response to a proposed wage cut. Some employers have demonstrated that they are willing to use the courts to restrain industrial conflict.

1.3.25   Employers' view

There is no doubt that the industrial scene has changed much since 1979. Union membership and density are down. Financially some unions have been hard hit. Mass picketing away from the workplace has virtually disappeared. The closed shop has been undermined both by legal sanctions and employers' withdrawing from schemes, an example being British Rail. How much of the change is due to legislation is at least for the moment impossible to tell, but Conservative laws have affected the power relationship in the workplace. That effect, and the volume of legislation, show no sign of abating.

1.3.26   Decline of unions

Conservative appetite for changes is not decreasing. Several suggestions for amendment of the law have been made but not

1.4   Policies continuing

enacted. One idea is the prohibition of strikes in essential industries. Another is that persons paying the political levy to trade unions should have to opt in to doing so. A third possible change is to make collective agreements legally binding. This long-standing proposal seems to have been rejected because of its reflecting corporatist notions. Moreover, derecognition would be impeded if recognition agreements were contractual. The Green Paper, 'Industrial Relations in the 1990s' (Cm 1602, 1991), considered other proposals, many of which formed part of the Trade Union Reform and Employment Rights Act 1993. There might be a right to restrain unlawful action which affects the provision of public services. Workplace ballots could be made illegal. These ideas are being picked up.

The government continues to support flexible working practices, individual contracts, and the use of the law in industrial disputes. It promised in the White Paper *Competitiveness: Helping Business To Win* (1994) to keep industrial relations law under review. On the other side of industry there has been debate whether unions' immunities against common law liability should be recast as positive rights and whether those rights (or even a modified system of immunity) should be enforced in labour courts separate from the ordinary court structure. Both recommendations reflect trade unionists' concern that ordinary courts with their emphasis on individualism are unlikely to adopt a neutral stance in disputes between employers and employees and have in the past restricted immunities which parliament has granted to unions.

The issue of immunity is dealt with in the last chapter. In conclusion, collectivism has been undermined but not eradicated, while on the individual employment law side deregulation is continuing. A government amendment to the Trade Union Reform and Employment Rights Bill in May 1993, which was enacted, is the epitome of these policies. No longer is it unlawful (as the Court of Appeal has twice said it is though in 1995 the House of Lords overturned that Court's decisions) to offer financial inducements to employees to renounce union membership. Freedom of organisation is being cut back.

Modern Employment Law

Ideological conflict over the role of trade unions has been a feature of UK politics over many years. At present free market economic theory prevails. The labour market has been deregulated and unions have been re-regulated.

Industrial relations experts sometimes model their subject through the use of three 'frames of reference': unitary, pluralist and conflictual. In a unitary firm the workers are seen as part of a team. Their interests are subordinated to the firm. Unions are not legitimate, for they interfere with the company's smooth running by introducing different interests. Pluralism is the thesis by which the power of workers is increased by their banding together to form unions. Only by their so doing is their power made equivalent to that of employers. A conflictual frame of reference is that postulated by Marxists. In the contest between capital and labour there can be no long-lasting equilibrium. Only when workers control the means of production, exchange and distribution.

Frames of reference

Legislation has increasingly intervened in the relationship among employers, employees, and unions. Current government policies are concerned with reducing employees' rights (with the effect that managerial prerogative is increased) and restricting union freedom of manoeuvre. These policies are subject to the laws of the European Community. In recent years the Trades Union Congress has viewed the EC as the sole possible source of salvation for workers. The Conservative opposition to the European Union has stymied the introduction into the UK of employment rights under the Maastricht Treaty and several draft directives are being held up.

Law and industrial relations

The policy of deregulation (or re-regulation) is set to continue. Should the Conservatives lose office, ideas exist to modernise the structure of labour law as it existed from 1906 to the end of the 1970s. There has been for over a decade a debate whether a system of positive rights (eg to strike) and a

The future

structure of labour tribunals outside the present judicial hierarchy would uphold workers' rights in a manner more advantageous to employees than the present system. The advantage of autonomy is to prevent common law such as contract impeding legal developments.

Chapter 2

Institutional Matters

This section deals with bodies created by law to tackle industrial relations issues. The first difficulty is to determine which body deals with the claim at first instance.

The court or tribunal in which an employment case is heard depends on the origin and nature of the claim. In respect of contractual actions such as wrongful dismissal the trial takes place in the county court or High Court in the normal way. Legal aid is available and the limitation period is six years. Appeals lie to the Court of Appeal and then the House of Lords. Statutory claims are heard in industrial tribunals (hereinafter ITs), which are creatures of statute; that is, their jurisdiction is circumscribed by the power entrusted to them by parliament. Exceptionally ITs have been ready to hear cases based on European Community (EC) law even though domestic law does not empower them to do so. There has been some discussion whether ITs can lawfully act in this way but no successful challenge to jurisdiction has been mounted. Some contractual actions in employment law have been transferred to the ITs, subject to an upper monetary limit. The Secretary of State for Employment exercised power to order such a transfer under s 131 of the Employment Protection (Consolidation) Act 1978. Personal injury claims are excluded from transfer. Appeals from ITs go to the Employment Appeal Tribunal (EAT) and thence to the Court of Appeal in the usual way. Diagrammatically the appeal system can be represented thus:

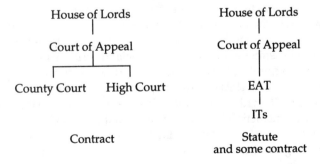

House of Lords	House of Lords
Court of Appeal	Court of Appeal
County Court High Court	EAT
	ITs
Contract	Statute and some contract

2.1 Institutions

2.1.1 County court or industrial tribunal?

Reference to the European Court of Justice (ECJ) may be made by any of these bodies including ITs under Article 177 of the Treaty of Rome. The reference is made in the usual way. The power to refer has been utilised by the various employment law courts and tribunals. For example, the ECJ answered a reference from the House of Lords in the pregnancy discrimination case of *Webb v EMO Air Cargo (UK) Ltd* (1993).

2.2   Tribunals

This section deals with the tribunals particular to labour law. Industrial tribunals were expected to be cheap, speedy and accessible bodies, but there has been an increasing juridification of their functioning. Appeals lie to the Employment Appeal Tribunal.

2.2.1   Industrial tribunals

Industrial tribunals are the judicial bodies in which most statutory employment claims are heard and determined. In 1993/4 71,661 claims were registered and 25,659 cases heard, an increase of some 250% over 1989/90.

- ITs were established by Parliament in 1964. They are composed of a lawyer chair, who must be a solicitor or barrister of seven years' standing, and of two lay members, 'wingmen', one from the employers' side of industry and commerce and one from the employees' side. The government has tried to extend the categories of persons who are appointed wingmen beyond those nominated by organisations such as the CBI and TUC. The lay members can outvote the lawyer chair, surprisingly even on questions of law. The lay persons' function is to use their knowledge and understanding of industrial relations to solve employment disputes in a practical manner. The use of non-lawyers explains the oft-used phrase that ITs are 'industrial juries'.

- The jurisdiction of ITs is extensive. The first main power was over the award of redundancy payments in 1965. Since then jurisdiction has vastly expanded to cover, for instance, unfair dismissal and sexual and racial discrimination in the employment sphere. A substantial proportion of cases (over 16% in 1993/4) involved unlawful deductions from wages. Recent statutes which have given the Tribunals more jurisdiction include the Deregulation and Contracting Out Act 1994 and the Sunday Trading Act 1994. They will also gain jurisdiction when the law on disability discrimination is in force.

- ITs are empowered to disregard the rules of evidence. While not informal (for instance, oaths are sworn), they can be substantially less intimidating to applicants than the county court, though procedure, which is largely governed by the Industrial Tribunals (Constitution and Rules of Procedure) Regulations 1993, SI 2688, varies from tribunal to tribunal. The chair plays the key role in controlling procedure.

- Research has demonstrated that applicants with representation by lawyers are twice as likely to win than those without. Some of the difference may be accounted for by the fact that lawyers may be used only in circumstances where there is some likelihood of success. Experienced lawyers know the ropes and may be familiar faces to the chairpersons. Since legal aid is not available for representation before ITs and since employers normally have more money than employees they have dismissed, there is an imbalance. Part of this imbalance is sometimes rectified by the use of lawyers paid for by unions. Chairs may (but need not) help unrepresented claimants. There have been calls over many years for legal aid to be extended to some tribunals including ITs.

- ITs can act swiftly. Often cases are disposed of within a few weeks of the application's being made.

- The increasing use of lawyers has led to charges of excessive legalism and of increased length of hearings caused by lawyers' prolixity. The European Court of Human Rights held in *Darnell v UK* (1993) that the delays in unfair dismissal cases breached the European Convention on Human Rights, Art 6(1), that 'everyone is entitled to a ... hearing within a reasonable time... ' A public apology was held not to be sufficient reason and the Court ordered the UK to pay damages of £5,000. It must, however, be remembered that some aspects of employment law are in themselves complex and that the loss of a job is an extremely important matter. Income, career, and often personal satisfaction depend on jobs. Loss of a job can be traumatic. The 'day in tribunal' may help to reduce such stress. Legalism is reduced by the presence of lay tribunal members and by the fact that one tribunal is not bound by the decisions of other ITs.

- Normally there is a lawyer in the chair plus two 'wingmen'. If the parties consent, the powers of an IT can be exercised by the chair and just one lay member: s 128 of EP(C)A. The Trade Union Reform and Employment Rights Act 1993 permits the chair to sit alone in various classes of cases, eg where the respondents do not contest the case, the claim is one for interim relief, and the complaint is of an unlawful deduction from wages contrary to the Wages Act 1986.

- Now that some breach of contract claims arising on termination are transferred (by the Industrial Tribunals Extension of Jurisdiction Order 1994, SI 1994/1623, which excludes covenants on restraint of trade, obligations of confidentiality, copyright and other intellectual property rights and the provision of living accommodation, and all claims above £25,000), they are heard by the lawyer chair sitting alone unless he decides differently. Various matters must be taken into account by the chair before deciding to sit alone, including whether the cases disclose an issue of law which it is desirable for a lawyer to resolve and whether other issues between the parties are being dealt with by the full tribunal or just by the chair. The chair may decide to move from sitting alone to sitting with the other members.

- Costs are rarely awarded against former employees. After all, applicants may still be out of work. When costs are awarded, the applicant has been frivolous or vexatious or unreasonable.

The government has published a Green Paper *Resolving Employment Rights Disputes: Options for Reform* (Cm 2707, 1994). The main proposals are to encourage voluntary arbitration as an alternative to the tribunal system, to encourage applicants to use internal procedures (compensation may be reduced if they are not used), to improve information to employers, and to extend the powers of chairs to sit alone. The government also intends to consolidate individual employment law, to remove the requirement that an expert's report must be commissioned in every equal value claim, and to rename Industrial Tribunals as Employment Tribunals. For a devastating critique see P Tsamados (1995) *Legal Action*, March, 6–7.

2.2.2	Employment Appeal Tribunal

Most of the work undertaken by the EAT consists of the hearing of appeals from ITs. Usually only questions of law can be appealed. One exception is that appeals from determinations of the Certification Officer may be on issues of fact (Trade Union and Labour Relations (Consolidation) Act 1992, TULR(C)A, s 256). Similarly, appeals against a refusal by the Certification Officer to list a union (s 9(4)) may involve questions of fact. There were 941 appeals in 1994. Like ITs the EAT is composed of a lawyer chair (a High Court judge) and two or sometimes four lay members, and again the lay persons can outvote the lawyer even on questions of law. If an IT chair is empowered to sit alone, on appeal so may an EAT judge. With consent the case may be heard with one or three lay persons. One judge is nominated President of the EAT. In terms of precedent the EAT binds ITs and is bound by the Court of Appeal and the House of Lords. The EAT has original jurisdiction over exclusion and expulsion claims against unions unless the employee has been admitted to membership (s 67(2) and s 176(2)). Other points of interest are these:

- The EAT could have been called a court. It is indeed a court of record. However, the government which established it did not wish the EAT to be considered in the same way as its precursor, the National Industrial Relations Court, which was instituted by the previous government in the Industrial Relations Act 1971. That Court was inextricably linked to that piece of legislation and on the repeal of the Act the Court was abolished. Many trade union members have, moreover, had a dislike for law, seeing it and its courts as being run by a judiciary opposed to the interests of unions. The name, Employment Appeal Tribunal, was, therefore, chosen to ensure that the body was not tainted by the nature of its predecessors.

- Problems for the EAT have included its workload and its position in the hierarchy. To cut down on the number of appeals it can call disputes questions of fact, which are not appealable. However, to do so can lead to one industrial tribunal directly contradicting another tribunal on exactly the same facts. For example, the issue whether a worker is an employee is a question of fact. If a company dismisses part of its workforce, some workers being in Southampton, some in Sheffield, one tribunal might hold that the workers are employees, another one that they are not. The first set of workers can claim a remedy for being unfairly dismissed, whereas the second cannot. This inconsistency is discreditable to a system of law. One potential escape route was for the EAT to lay down guidelines for ITs. The EAT used guidelines on several occasions, thereby alerting ITs to considerations which they should take into account. The Court of Appeal has, however, rejected the use of guidelines on several occasions. ITs are instructed primarily to consider the words of the statute and to apply them to the facts. There is now little guidance outside of statute and precedent. The result is a wilderness of decisions, and the outcome of ITs' determinations are not always predictable.

Since the mid-1970s governments have created various bodies for the purpose of resolving industrial conflicts and assisting employees both against their employers and their unions. The latest body, the Commissioner for Protection against Unlawful

2.3   Other institutions of English employment law

Industrial Action, was created in 1993 to support citizens in their statutory claims against unions.

2.3.1   The Advisory Conciliation and Arbitration Service (ACAS)

The name of The Advisory Concilation and Arbitration Service (ACAS) reflects to a large extent what it does. Its principal role when it was created at the start of the 1974–1979 Labour government was to assist in the improvement of industrial relations especially through the widening and deepening of collective bargaining. That principle survived until 1993 and was enshrined in s 209 of TULR(C)A 1992. However, it was undermined by the present government's commitment to individual bargaining and to the diminution in power of trade unions and consequent sidelining of trade unions. Since 30 August 1993 ACAS has no longer had a duty to encourage collective bargaining. The Conservative government amended the law in 1993 to emphasise ACAS's functions in aiding settlement of industrial disputes as part of its principal duty of improving industrial relations. The change brings the law into line with the reality of the situation.

- Composition (ss 247–249)

  Like ITs and the EAT, ACAS has a tripartite structure. It is governed by a council of nine. Three members are independent, three represent employers, and three represent unions. The Chair is appointed by the Secretary of State for Employment. Funding is provided by the government. Despite such possible sources of interference, the Service has retained its independence, the separation being confirmed by s 247(3) of the Act. No government minister may direct ACAS as to how to exercise its functions. The original intention was to keep the Service separate from government policies on pay.

- Advice (s 213)

  The service provides a large amount of written and oral advice each year on industrial relations matters. Much advice is given over the phone. There were over half a million enquiries in 1994. Before 1993 ACAS had a wider duty in that it could give advice on employment and not just industrial relations matters. The reference to advice on collective issues was dropped in the revised wording, but there is nothing to stop ACAS giving advice on collective negotiation and it frequently does so. ACAS also publishes various booklets, the most important of which is 'Discipline at Work' (1987). Section 13 gives a lengthy though non-exclusive list of the matters on which ACAS may advise. They include union recognition, joint consultation, discipline, pay systems, and staff turnover. Since 1 April 1994 ACAS has been obliged to charge for its handbooks and advisory booklets.

- Conciliation (s 210)

What may be called 'collective conciliation' is the process by which the service seeks to bring parties in dispute together in an attempt to resolve industrial strife. One party must request the intervention. The aim is not to use an umpire to settle the dispute (or apprehended dispute) but to provide an opportunity for the sides to find a solution away from the heat of battle. ACAS can provide an independent conciliator whose function it is to encourage the parties to reach a settlement. Collective conciliation is important because if it fails, industrial conflict may take place. The Service received 1,207 cases for collective conciliation in 1992, 1,211 in 1993 and 1,313 in 1994. About half the requests involved disputes concerning pay or terms and conditions of employment. The ACAS Report for 1994 stated that in 90% of referrals it had obtained a settlement or had encouraged the parties to make substantial progress towards a settlement.

Individual conciliation (s 211) occurs when an ACAS officer acts to seek a settlement between employees and the party claimed against. When an employee applies to an industrial tribunal, either against her union (eg for being unjustifiably disciplined contrary to s 290(a) of the TULR(C)A) or against her employers (eg for a remedy for breach of her right not to be unfairly dismissed (s 54 of the Employment Protection (Consolidation) Act 1978 but not for a redundancy payment)), the matter is referred to one of these officers, who attempt to find grounds for a settlement before the case reaches the tribunal. Some 70,000 claims are referred each year, the majority of which involve unfair dismissal. ACAS started conciliating in claims for breach of the contract of employment in 1994 and received over 3,000 requests in that year. If a settlement is reached, it must be recorded on form COT 3 to be binding between the parties. The Trade Union Reform and Employment Rights Act 1993 widened the law on compromise agreements with which ACAS is not involved. If individual conciliation fails, the employee can go to the Industrial Tribunals if the matter falls within the jurisdiction of those institutions. About a third of unfair dismissal conciliation cases result in re-employment. The figure for industrial tribunals is under 3%. Perhaps half ACAS's time is on unfair dismissal conciliation.

- Arbitration (s 212)

If both parties agree, a dispute may be referred to ACAS for arbitration. The possibility of settlement by conciliation must first be considered. The arbitrator (there is normally only one but a panel may be appointed) will decide between the competing claims and can reach a compromise (unless the parties agree on 'pendulum arbitration', in which case the arbitrator must accept in full one side's claim). The arbitrator is chosen from a list kept by ACAS or the Central Arbitration Committee. ACAS officers do not themselves undertake arbitration. The arbitrator's decision is not legally binding. ACAS never dealt with more than 260 arbitrations in the 1980s. In 1992 it was 162. The award is not enforceable in a Court. Sometimes the parties use an ACAS arbitrator without the dispute being formally referred.

• Inquiry (s 214)

ACAS may conduct inquiries into any industry (eg newspapers) or undertaking. There is also provision (s 215) for the Secretary of State for Employment to refer industrial disputes to courts of inquiry. An example was the Grunwick dispute (1977).

• Codes of Practice

ACAS may issue, revise and revoke Codes of Practice for the purpose of improving industrial relations (s 199). Breach of a Code does not in itself found liability, but may be taken into account by the Central Arbitration Committee or an industrial tribunal when judging an issue (s 207). The ACAS Codes are:

No 1:   Disciplinary Practice and Procedures in Employment, 1977;

No 2:   Disclosure of Information to Trade Unions for Collective Bargaining Purposes, 1977; and

No 3:   Time Off for Trade Union Duties and Activities, which was revised in 1991.

The Secretary of State for Employment also has the power to issue, revise and revoke Codes of Practice (ss 203–206). These Codes have the same legal effect as ACAS ones except that courts may also take them into account. The power has been exercised in relation to the closed shop, picketing and ballots before industrial action. ACAS did not wish to draw up these codes because it was thought that its reputation for unbiased advice would be blemished. The Secretary of State's Codes have been criticised as extending anti-trade-union measures beyond those approved by parliament. In *Thomas v National Union of Mineworkers (South Wales Area)* (1985) Scott J controversially suggested that the

Code of Practice on picketing's statement that the maximum number of pickets should be six at each entrance also was the law: beyond six there was intimidation. His statement was controversial because the maximum number had not been so stated in a statute or in a judicial decision. This 'back-door' legislation has been attacked as being unconstitutional – law should be laid down by parliament and the courts, not in non-binding Codes of Practice.

By s 251A as inserted by TURERA s 44, ACAS may charge for its services.

The CAC was established in 1975, though its predecessors date back to 1919, to deal with arbitrations in industrial disputes. Since its inception its chair has been Sir John Wood. Arbitration committees are established, composed of an independent neutral chair together with an equal number of representatives of employers and employees. The expectation is that they will reach unanimous decisions but the chair's vote outweighs all other votes. The two remaining functions of the CAC are: first, arbitration over matters referred to it by ACAS, and, secondly, arbitration concerned with the disclosure of information for collective bargaining purposes. The first is voluntary, the second is compulsory. The highest number of voluntary arbitrations was 11 in 1976. There were none in 1992. There is no appeal from determination of the CAC, but there is the possibility of judicial review. The Committee need not give reasons in its first jurisdiction but it has decided to state its 'general considerations' for reaching its conclusions. In the second jurisdiction it must give reasons (TULR(C)A 1992 ss 183–184). In 1992 the CAC received 28 references, all under the second head, which is discussed in Chapter 14. Mostly the information concerns finance, restructuring plans, workforce composition, grading and managing change (eg relocation, privatisation). Formal awards are rare (under 20% of cases go to a full hearing) but twice the CAC has formally stated that employers have not complied with an award. Unlike with the Equal Opportunities Commission and the Commission for Racial Equality the courts have not intervened very much to correct any excesses of jurisdiction by the CAC.

2.3.2 Central Arbitration Committee (CAC)

These institutions were established under the Sex Discrimination Act 1975 (SDA) and the Race Relations Act 1976 respectively. Their composition comprises of between eight and 15 commissioners, who may be part-timers, together with a chairperson. Their functions are similar:

2.3.3 The Equal Opportunities Commission (EOC) and the Commission for Racial Equality (CRE)

- the promotion of equal opportunities;
- the elimination of discrimination;

- the review of the legislation (various documents have been issued but the government has not endorsed them);

- the striking down of discriminatory job advertisements (see Chapter 6);

- the conduct of inquiries ('formal investigations') into discrimination.

The Commissions are empowered to deal with individual claimants if the application is a test case which raises a matter of principle, if it is unreasonable to expect the person to deal with the application unaided, or 'if there is any special consideration' (SDA s 75, RRA s 66). The EOC has adopted a test case strategy. It has attempted to use cases to move English domestic law into line with European Community law when the latter is more favourable to applicants than the former. The CRE granted finance for representation in 112 cases in 1992. The House of Lords held in *R v Secretary of State for Employment ex p EOC* (1994) that the EOC has the power to bring judicial review proceedings to clarify the relationship between UK and EC law as to sex discrimination. The effect was to strike down a long-standing rule as to qualifications for employment protection found in statutes.

The Commissions are empowered to apply to the appropriate county court for an injunction to restrain instructions to discriminate, attempts to procure discrimination, and pressure to discriminate (SDA ss 39–40, RRA ss 30–1). The organisations may also seek injunctions to abrogate discriminatory practices (SDA s 37, RRA s 28).

Formal investigations (SDA s 57, RRA s 48) might be seen as the cutting-edge of the enforcement of non-discriminatory policies. Individual cases improve the lot only of those employees who made the claim. Formal investigations can, however, be targeted at companies with a view to securing their compliance with the legislation. However, such hope has been dashed. Judicial interpretation has restricted the Commissions' potential powers (see *Re Prestige Group Ltd* (1984) where the House of Lords held that the Commissions could not inspect a firm on their own initiative: there had to be a least some grounds for suspecting that the firm was discriminating unlawfully), but there is still scope for a more active use of this tool than has occurred over the past decade. The Commissions have the power (SDA ss 60, 67, RRA ss 51, 58) to issue non-discrimination notices ordering the employers not to discriminate, where there is unlawful discrimination, a discriminatory job advertisement or practice, pressure to discriminate, or an act in breach of an equality clause inserted in an employment contract by virtue of the Equal Pay Act 1970. The notices order the employers to comply with the requirements stated in them. For example, an employment agency in West Yorkshire was told to desist its discriminatory practices and to permit the EOC to monitor the situation for five years. Employers have the opportunity to make representations. Employers must inform the Commission as to the manner in which they have complied with the notice. There is a right of appeal against a notice to an industrial tribunal. The appeal can be on the grounds that a fact relied on by one of the Commissions is open to challenge. The notice is enforceable by a county court injunction if the employers are within five years of the notice likely to discriminate again. However, if the employers did not challenge the legality of the notice when first issued, an Industrial Tribunal must first consider that issue. If the Commission has acted *ultra vires*, judicial review is available. The Commissions have at times been found to have exceeded their powers, principally on the grounds that formal investigations cannot be used unless there is at least suspicion that the employers have been acting discriminatorily. Much has been written on the failure of formal investigations to extirpate unlawful discrimination. The writing is often to the effect that sexual and racial discrimination are based on discrimination against groups, such as women in general, not against individuals within a group, such as a particular woman. Using the law to prevent discrimination against a specific woman does not attack the root of the problem – discrimination against women in general. Formal investigations can however deal with discrimination against groups. The current failure of the formal investigation mode and the lack of fit between the problem of discrimination against groups and the emphasis on individual enforcement has led to the suggestion that there should be instituted 'class actions' such as exist in the USA ie claims on behalf of a group. English law is perhaps moving towards such a concept. Equal pay claims have been made by representatives of groups such as speech therapists ('representative actions'), but there is no possibility in the near future of the government's creating the class action mode of enforcement. It is for consideration whether a more strategic use could be made of representative actions than heretofore.

The Commissions may issue codes of practice in their respective areas. The CRE issued one in 1984 on 'The Elimination of Racial Discrimination and the Promotion of Equality of Opportunity in Employment' and the EOC issued one in 1985 on 'The Elimination of Discrimination on the Grounds of Sex and Marriage and the Promotion of Equality of Opportunity in Employment'. The EOC has issued a draft

Code of Practice on equal pay (1995). It is expected that parliament will endorse it in late 1996. TURERA gives the EOC the power to issue a code of practice on equal pay.

2.3.4   Certification Officer

By s 254 of TULR(C)A, a provision which dates back to 1975, there exists the position of Certification Officer. He fulfils the following duties:

- maintaining the list of trade unions;

- issuing certificates of independence to unions;

- keeping records of annual membership and financial returns from unions;

- keeping various other union records;

- enforcing the law on elections of union officers; and

- enforcing the law on ballots to establish political funds and on political expenditure.

In 1992 six certificates of independence were issued.

2.3.5   Commissioner for the Rights of Trade Union Members (CROTUM)

Since 1988 there has existed the CROTUM. Her functions relate to trade union governance and are:

- to assist trade union members to bring actions against their unions for non-implementation of various statutory rights such as the right of a member not to be unjustifiably disciplined, rights in relation to ballots before industrial action, and rights over the political fund (s 109(1) of TULR(C)A);

- to assist union members in bringing contractual actions against their unions for breach of the rules on eg appointment to union office and the discipline and expulsion of members (s 109(2)).

The former jurisdiction was created in 1988, the latter in 1990. In 1992–1993 the CROTUM received 50 formal applications. In 1993–1994 she received 47 formal applications. An applicant must not be unjustifiably disciplined (see 15.5) for seeking assistance from the CROTUM but she cannot gain assistance from her in respect of the enforcement of this right.

The Commissioner is empowered to give assistance both in the form of advice and legal representation (s 111(2)). There is no means test. Compare the normal industrial tribunal cases where there is no legal aid for actions against employers. Assistance is provided after the Commissioner balances the following factors (s 110(2)): does the claim raise any issues of principle? Is the application so complicated that it would be unreasonable to expect a member to sue without assistance?

And is the matter one of public concern? The answers to these questions are factors which the Commissioner may but need not take into account. In relation to s 109(2) proceedings, there is an additional requirement that the Commissioner believes that the breach of a union rule may affect members of the union other than the applicant or that similar breaches of the rules have been, or may be, committed (s 110(4)). It cannot be said that as yet the Commissioner has had much work to do. Supporters of trade unions say that this lack of work is because there is little to do.

For the new Commissioner for Protection against Unlawful Industrial Action, see Chapter 16, para 16.10. Both posts are currently held by the same person, Gill Rowlands.

2.4 Membership of the European Community

This section may be omitted by anyone who has studied European Community (EC) law. The topic is vast and expanding. Membership of the EC has affected UK law in many different ways. The Chair of the London North Industrial Tribunal issued a heart-felt plea in *Downer v Onyx UK Ltd* (1995):

> 'The tribunals are at present subject to Euroclaim-hysteria to an extent which is likely to bring the tribunals to a standstill with the volume and complexity of the claims ...'

2.4.1 Effect on UK law

By s 2(1) of the European Communities Act 1972 the UK accepted that EC law, created under the Treaty of Rome, as varied from time to time, would be enforced in the UK. Some parts of EC law were indeed 'directly applicable' ie such provisions apply without enactment by the national parliament.

- EC law constitutes a new legal order which is superior to national law: *Costa v ENEL* (1964), a decision of the European Court of Justice (ECJ). Inconsistent domestic law which falls short of EC law is displaced. The national courts are, therefore, under a duty to disapply national law which conflicts with EC law. They must do so without waiting for the domestic legislature to abrogate domestic law. UK courts accepted this principle, which applies even though the domestic legislation was enacted after the relevant EC provision: *Factortame v Secretary of State for Transport* (1989), a decision of the House of Lords. The same Court ruled in *R v Secretary of State for Employment ex p EOC*, above, that Acts of Parliament can be struck down by the judge in judicial review proceedings even though no directly effective right had been given to the body bringing the action.

- EC law applies not just to contracting States but also to individuals: *Van Gend en Loos v Nederlandse Administratie der Belastingen* (1963) . However, for individuals to gain rights under EC legislation, the relevant provisions must be unconditional and sufficiently precise. For example, Article 119 of the Treaty, which deals with equal pay, fulfils those criteria in respect of direct discrimination. Accordingly, individuals can rely on the Article. This method of ensuring that individuals gain rights in EC law is called 'direct effect'. A provision can have direct effect even though like Article 119 it is addressed to Member States.

2.4.2   Several forms of EC law

There are several forms of EC law. The type of direct effect which EC law has depends on the form of the legislation. The Articles in the Treaty and Regulations (which should not be confused with statutory instruments called Regulations adopted under UK statutes) apply both against the Member States and individuals, the latter term encompassing companies: see *Defrenne v SABENA (No 2)* (1976). Accordingly, an employee has a right of action under these forms of legislation against the State and non-State bodies and individuals such as employers. This direct effect is both 'vertical' and 'horizontal'. A claim may be made vertically against the State or horizontally against individual defendants. Therefore, an employee can sue a State organisation which acts as an employer or a private company for equal pay in reliance on Article 119. However, another form of Community legislation, Directives, is only vertically directly effective. That is, those rights can be enforced only against State organisations, not against non-State employers: *Marshall v Southampton & South West Hants Area Health Authority* (1986). The right against the State is based partly on the wording of the Article in the Treaty, Article 189, which defines the nature of the various forms of Community legislation and partly on the theory that a law is presumed to have been enacted to promote some purposes and, therefore, the law should be used to fulfil that purpose (*effet utile*). In the *Marshall* case a female dietician at a hospital had to retire at 60 whereas males could work until 65. UK law permitted this difference. The ECJ held that the relevant Directive, the Equal Treatment Directive 1976, was directly effective but only vertically so. The State was in breach of its duty under the Directive to equalise retirement ages but only in relation to employees working in the State sector. It should be remembered that Directives are not even vertically directive effective unless they are unconditional and sufficiently precise. For example, it has not yet been determined by the ECJ whether the Acquired Rights Directive (77/187) is sufficiently clear, precise and unconditional to be enforceable against the State or an emanation of the State.

The problem of vertical but not horizontal direct effect is particularly acute in EC employment law because most of it is in the form of Directives. Examples include the Equal Treatment Directive (76/107) and the Directive on Acquired Rights (77/187). A more recent one is the Directive on an employer's obligation to inform employees of the conditions applicable to the contract of employment relationship (91/533) which obliged the government to alter English law on written particulars: see Chapter 4. The aim of Directives is to permit Member States some degree of control as to how they are to be fitted into existing national law. Absolute uniformity across the EC is not required. The accent is on the harmonisation of national laws, a useful concept when the labour law and traditions of the national States are as varied as they are. The outcome of *Marshall* is that individuals can use Directives against institutions of the State, that State not having implemented them or having implemented them incorrectly. The theory which the ECJ has accepted which underlies the vertical only effect of Directives is that States should not be able to rely on their own wrong, their failure to enact Directives either at all or insufficiently. Article 5 of the Treaty instructs Member States to take all appropriate measures to ensure the fulfilment of any obligation arising under the Treaty or resulting from the action of Community institutions. The theory is applicable only against States, not otherwise. After all, it is not private employers who are at fault in failing to implement Directives properly. As can be predicted, there is a growing body of law as to what constitutes a State authority (which is called an emanation of the State) and what does not. In *Foster v British Gas plc* (1991) the European Court held that a State employer is:

> '... a body, whatever its legal form, which has been made responsible, pursuant to a measure adopted by the State, for producing a public service under the control of the State and has for that purpose special powers beyond those which result from the normal rules applicable in relations between individuals.'

Applying this definition, the House of Lords held that before privatisation British Gas was an emanation of the State. British Gas paid £800,000 in an out of court settlement to 16 women who had to retire at 60 whereas men could work until 65. In *Marshall* an English Health Authority was held to be a State body, but private employers are not emanations of the State: see *Duke v GEC Reliance* (1988). A privatised water company was held to be an emanation of the State in *Griffin v South West Water Services Ltd* (1995) largely because of the amount of control the government exercised over the

2.4.3   The problem of vertical direct effect

company. It was conceded that the company had special powers and performed a public service. It was immaterial that the service provider was a commercial operator and that its legal form was a company. A company which is 100% owned by the State is not an emanation of the State if it is a commercial undertaking: *Doughty v Rolls Royce plc* (1992), applying the *Foster* criteria. The EAT held that a voluntary aided school was not an emanation of the State because, although education was a public service within *Foster*, it was not a service under the control of the State and the governing body had no special powers (*National Union of Teachers v Governing Body of St Mary's Church of England (Aided) Junior School* (1995)). Blackburne J in *Griffin* said that the issue was whether the service was under State control, not whether the body was.

There is criticism that EC law ought not to be predicated on whether or not a State organisation is the employer. The same rules ought to apply irrespective of the nature of the employers. Employees of private employers ought not to have fewer rights than those employed by State organisations. The answer to this criticism given in *Foster* is that the distinction would not exist if the State had fully implemented the Directive. The UK government has in fact on one occasion equalised rights of employees of State and non-State bodies. The Sex Discrimination Act 1986 changed national law so that retirement ages for men and women were made the same whether they were employed by State or non-State employers.

2.4.4   Indirect effect

One might have thought that the ECJ's ruling that Directives had only vertical direct effect was the end of the story. Recently, however, the ECJ has introduced two doctrines which to some degree get round the distinction between vertical and horizontal direct effects. The first doctrine, sometimes known as 'indirect effect', is that national courts must construe national laws so as to give effect to EC Directives as far as it is possible to do so. In the words of the first case in which the ECJ ruled on this point:

> '... in applying national law and in particular those provisions of national law specially introduced to give effect to a Directive, the national court is bound to interpret its national law in the light of the text and of the aim of the Directive ...'

(other translations are possible): *von Colson v Land Nordrhein-Westfalen* (1984). Mrs von Colson sought compensation in the German courts for being discriminated against when she sought a job with non-State employers. German law provided for only a low level of comparison in such circumstances. Though the relevant source of EC law, the Equal Treatment Directive, was not horizontally directly effective, the ECJ held that in the light of Article 5, national courts are under an obligation to construe national law so as to effectuate the Directive's purpose, at least when national legislation was specifically introduced to implement the relevant legislation. UK courts have accepted that they are under this duty: *Pickstone v Freemans plc* (1989) and *Litster v Forth Dry Dock & Engineering Co Ltd* (1990), both decisions of the Lords. There is no need for the domestic statute to be passed after and in consequence of the Directive. It is usually considered that cases such as *Duke v GEC Reliance*, in which the House of Lords held that the Sex Discrimination Act 1975, being enacted before the Equal Treatment Directive, could not be construed in such a manner as to give effect to it, are incorrect. That *Duke* is wrong seems to have been confirmed by *Marleasing SA v La Comercial Internacional de Alimentacion SA* (1992), in which the ECJ held that national courts must construe national law, so far as possible, to implement the objectives of Directives whether that law pre- or post-dates the relevant Directive. *Marleasing* may also undermine the House of Lords' view in *Webb v EMO Air Cargo (UK) Ltd* (1993) that national courts can construe in conformity with EC obligations only if on the words of the national legislation such an interpretation is possible. The House did accept that an English court 'must construe domestic legislation in any field covered by a Community Directive so as to accord with the interpretation of the Directive as laid down by the European Court, ... whether the domestic legislation came after or, as in this case, preceded the Directive'. On this point *Duke* is a dead duck. The House did, however, cite *Marleasing* for the proposition that domestic legislation must be capable of being construed in accordance with community law, and it applied *Duke* for the proposition that a community interpretation could not be used where it would distort the meaning of English law. For an application of this rule in the area of indirect sex discrimination see *Bhudi v IMI Refiners Ltd* (1994) in Chapter 6. The effect of the obligation laid down in *von Colson* to construe national law so as to effectuate EC law is one method of reducing the State/private distinction which is seen as undermining the effectiveness of Directives. It should, however, be noted that until there is national legislation on the topic at issue there is nothing for the courts to interpret.

English courts have accepted that the duty in *von Colson* is paramount over English 'rules' and canons of statutory interpretation such as the literal rule and the presumption that words and phrases are not to be added to statutes. However, the Lords in *Webb* held that it may be that national courts cannot interpret Directives until their true import has been determined, sometimes by a reference to the ECJ. The House also decided that the national legislation had to be open to construction in accord with Community law, but see *Marleasing* above. Can the process be called 'construction' when national legislation is disregarded when its terms are directly contradictory to EC Directives?

2.4.5	Cause of action against the State

In *Francovich v Italian Republic* (1992) the ECJ held that individuals (including of course employees) have a cause of action against the State for damages in national courts for losses suffered as a result of its failure to implement at all or to implement completely a Directive. The facts of *Francovich* were as follows. Directive 80/987 relates to the harmonisation of national laws on protecting employees on the insolvency of their employers. Article 11 requires Member States to establish institutions which would guarantee wages owing but not paid at the time of insolvency. Italy did not implement the Directive. The Commission brought an action against Italy under Article 169 of the Treaty of Rome (see para 2.4.6 below). This action was successful. Workers were left with unpaid salaries on insolvency. The ECJ held that Article 11 of the Directive was not sufficiently precise and unconditional because it did not specify which institution was to guarantee pay on insolvency. The State was not the institution. Therefore, the State was not liable for not implementing the guarantee of the payment of wages; rather it had failed to designate the responsible non-State body. Accordingly, Article 11 was not directly effective. However, the ECJ held that the Italian State was liable to pay compensation for its failure to implement the Directive. Member States had to implement Directives to protect individuals' rights which derive from EC law. That protection would be diminished if there was no sanction for non-implementation, and in the light of Article 5 of the Treaty national authorities were under a duty to take appropriate measures to secure the fulfilment of EC law. The court stated that damages were available for non-implementation of a Directive where:

- that Directive was intended to confer rights on individuals;

- the width of that right could be identified from the text of the Directive; and

- there was a causal nexus between the State's breach and the loss suffered by the intended beneficiary.

This right to damages was subject to national law provisions governing analogous rights in that legal system, in

England presumably the tort of breach of statutory duty, and was enforceable in national courts. The conditions for enforcement of the right should not be such that enforcement was impossible in practice to achieve or was excessively difficult to obtain. There was no need to wait for the outcome of Article 169 enforcement proceedings.

Perhaps this right to damages against the State exists where there is non-implementation within a national legal system of Articles and Regulations (see *Kirklees MBC v Wickes Building Services* (1992), a dictum of the House of Lords). If damages are available, they could be sought for non-implementation of, say, the whole of Article 119, the equal pay provision. Only in relation to direct discrimination is Article 119 sufficiently precise and unconditional, for only such discrimination can be identified by reference to the criteria of equal work and equal pay. In relation to indirect discrimination, such can be identified only through legal measures implementing Article 119. It was suggested in *R v Secretary of State for Employment ex p Seymour-Smith* (1994) that an action under *Francovich* could be brought in respect of the possible incompatibility between the two-year qualifying period for unfair dismissal and EC equal treatment law. Actions have been brought by unions in England for the failure to implement fully the Acquired Rights Directive in that national law excluded non-commercial undertakings until 1993. There is also an unresolved debate on other aspects of *Francovich*. For example, does it apply to directly effective rights too? Compare the House of Lords' decision in *R v Secretary of State for Employment ex p EOC* (1994), where the Court held that the remedy of an employee for breach of Article 119 lay against her employers, not against the State, because her rights under Article 119 were horizontally directly effective and, therefore, available against her employers. The action could be particularly useful when the employers are insolvent. If *Francovich* is read as giving a general right to damages against the State for failure fully to implement Community obligations, presumably the limitations enumerated above apply in respect of Articles and Regulations.

By virtue of the Treaty of Rome's Article 169 the European Commission may bring 'infringement proceedings' in the ECJ against Member States for their failure to give effect to EC law, as when, for example, Directives are not enacted. The Commission instituted such proceedings against the UK for failure to enact provisions giving the right to equal pay for work of equal value: *EC Commission v UK* (1982). There is also

2.4.6   Infringement proceedings

the possibility under Article 170 of the Treaty of a Member State's bringing an action in the ECJ against another Member State for breach of Community obligations, though politics generally rule out such proceedings. There is no sanction for non-compliance except the weak one of the Commission's bringing another action in the ECJ against the defaulting State. The Commission has often reported that Member States have not complied with Community law. The UK government claims that of the members it is the one which complies best with EC laws.

2.4.7	Present EC and UK social policy

The history of EC social (or employment) policy is normally divided into three stages. The first stage was from the inception of the EC by the Treaty of Rome to the early 1970s. During this period there was little development. Employment law was not a concern of the founding fathers of the EC. They seem to have believed that living conditions would automatically rise through the functioning of the common market and that for that reason there was no need for special provision in the Treaty to give workers rights against their employers. In the Treaty there was Article 119 on equal pay for women and men, a provision inserted at the insistence of the French so that their products would not be undercut in price by other countries which did not have equal pay laws. Little was done to implement Article 119. Article 117 speaks of the progressive raising of living standards of workers, but the Article is not legally enforceable. The preamble to the Treaty of Rome embodies the same concept. Article 118, also not legally enforceable, provides for co-operation among Member States on social matters, including employment law. The second stage was the mid and late 1970s when the EC through its Social Action Programme 1974–1976 enacted several Directives such as the ones mentioned above on equal treatment and acquired rights. The third period has been one of stagnation to a large degree except in relation to health and safety. Advances in workers' rights have been made by the ECJ. The work of the EC Commission and Council, the central organs of the EC, has been stultified by an intransigent UK government, sometimes supported by other States. For this reason the Commission has resorted to 'soft law' in labour affairs such as the recommendation and Code of Practice on sex discrimination. An alternative view to that just stated is that the UK government has been blocking EC measures which would impose financial and administrative burdens on businesses which would undermine British competitiveness in world markets and would reduce job opportunities. UK opposition has so far prevented laws on employee participation (industrial democracy) under the draft European Company Statute and Works Council Directive among other matters, has led to refusal to join in the Charter of Fundamental Social Rights, 1989, which the other 11 Member States have signed, including draft measures under this Social Charter (except health and safety ones), and has resulted in the non-acceptance of the Social Chapter of the Maastricht Treaty. Government policy is that by holding down wage costs employers will be able to compete in the world market. One aim behind non-acceptance of the Social Charter and Chapter is to undercut the developed States' prices for products thereby gaining a competitive advantage over them, and with reduced labour costs and expanding markets employment opportunities will be created. The other Member States have agreed on qualified majority voting for various matters such as equality and informing and consulting workers (the European Council Directive, EC 95/45), which was the first Directive to be passed under the protocol, but unanimity is still needed in respect of others, eg rights of dismissed workers.

While the UK government has generally opposed EC developments in employment law (it has opposed all changes except in relation to health and safety and sexual discrimination), it did ratify the Single European Act 1986 (SEA). The importance of accepting the SEA can be demonstrated thus. When the EC Council of Ministers proposes to enact labour legislation (or any law in any field), it has to find a legal basis for doing so in the Treaty of Rome. In the Treaty as originally drafted, besides Article 119 (equal pay), there were two possible legal bases for labour law. By Article 100 the Council may issue Directives, when the Commission so proposed, which would lead to the harmonisation (approximation) of the laws of Member States in order to secure the successful implementation of the common market. (If the Council thought that the UK would not use its opt-out, it could propose a measure affecting social rights under Article 100.) By Article 235 Directives may be issued to attain a Treaty objective when the Treaty itself did not provide specifically in any other Article for such a power. Both under Articles 100 and 235 have to be unanimous. Accordingly, one State could block draft Directives. The SEA added a new Article, Article 100A, to the Treaty. It provides that 'measures necessary for the establishment and functioning of the internal market' can be adopted by the Council on a 'qualified majority' vote. That last term signifies that the votes of Member States are not equally weighed but weighted

2.4.8 The importance of accepting the SEA

according, approximately, to the State's size. By this method the objection of one State, even a large one such as the UK, could be overridden. In the Europe of 15, 62 votes are needed out of 87. However, Article 100A(2) takes away a large part of what Article 100A has given to the employment sphere by stating that unanimity remains necessary where 'the rights and interests of employed persons' are affected. This stipulation would seem on its face to prevent the adoption of EC employment laws by the qualified majority voting system. There has been much debate about the width of Article 100A(2), especially in the light of Article 118A, which also derives from the SEA. Article 118A provides that Member States should encourage the health and safety of workers, especially in the working environment, and empowers the Council to enact Directives on this matter by qualified majority voting. That power is subject to the stipulation that health and safety measures should not impose administrative, financial, or legal constraints which affect the creation of small and medium business enterprises. One aspect of that debate is whether maternity rights form a part of the law of 'the rights and interests of employed persons' within Article 100A, in which case unanimous voting is required, or whether they constitute part of the law of health and safety in the workplace, in which eventuality Article 118A applies and qualified majority voting is possible. The Action Programme laid down by the Commission in 1989 based on the Social Charter has been successful only in relation to health and safety matters, that is, those measures based on Article 118A. Draft Directives on other matters have not been implemented because of opposition largely by the UK government. The Secretary of State for Employment is opposed to the proposed Directive on posted workers because of the possible effect on jobs on British workers in Germany. To give them the same rights as German workers would result in their being sacked. The Commission is to use the Maastricht Protocol to enact the stalled draft Directives on atypical workers and the burden of proof in sex discrimination. The Social Action Programme for 1995 onwards contains 21 measures, most of which consolidate existing law. The government has blocked draft Directives on paternity leave and part-time workers. There have already been Council Recommendations on social protection and profit-sharing and an Opinion on the equitable wage. In November 1993 the EC Council of Labour and Social Affairs adopted the draft Directive (93/104) on Working Time which states *inter alia* that the average working week shall not exceed 48 hours including working time. The UK government challenges Article 118A as the legal basis. It should be noted that the UK is bound by Directives founded on Articles 100A and 118A despite the refusal to accept the Social Charter and the Social Chapter. For legal scholars this is all very interesting, but there remains no solid legislative under-pinning of EC social policy. After all, much of EC social policy is predicated on implementing the internal market, not on protection for workers pure and simple.

Both with regard to domestic and EC institutions the position has altered substantially over the last quarter of a century. In the late 1960s the UK was not even a member of the EC. The industrial scene was based on informal means of dispute resolution. Even unjustifiable dismissals and industrial conflicts were largely a matter for negotiation between the employers and employees, the latter sometimes supported by trade unions. Many employment law rights such as in the area of sexual discrimination bypass collective bargaining and use industrial tribunals. Custom and practice has partly been replaced by law, but still exists.

2.4.9   Conclusion

Institutional Matters

Institutions; tribunals

English employment law is bedevilled by the jurisdictional problem of knowing in which Court or Tribunal a claim should be brought. Industrial Tribunal (ITs) have concurrent jurisdiction with the ordinary civil courts in most claims involving termination of contracts for sums under £25,000. Applications involving eg redundancy payments and unfair dismissal are determined by ITs with appeal to the Employment Appeal Tribunal. Other English institutions include the well-known ACAS, the Central Arbitration Committee, the two organisations dealing with discrimination, the Certification Officer and the Commissioner for the Rights of Trade Union Members. The text considers their powers and offers some criticism. If a claim is heard in the county courts or the High Court, legal aid is available. The limitation period is a contract action in six years. If the applicant seeks a remedy before an Industrial Tribunal there is no legal aid. The limitation period is dependent on the nature of the claim. For example, in an unfair dismissal case the time limit is, generally speaking, three months from the effective date of termination.

Membership of the European Community

The accession of the UK to the European Community has led to several amendments being made to English labour law. One of the main institutional issues at present is the vertically but not horizontally direct effect of Directives. The European Court of Justice has ruled that national laws must be construed to give effect to Directives and that individuals have a right of action for damages against the State for non-enactment of Directives. Despite such developments by the European Court of Justice, the UK government has opposed recent proposals in the sphere of employment law (social policy) such as the Social Charter of 1989 and the Social Chapter of the Maastricht Treaty. However, acceptance of the Single European Act 1986 has led to attempts to find legal bases in the Treaty of Rome in order to get round the objections of various EC governments, including that of the UK, to giving workers more rights than they have at present. Examples of draft directives to which the government are opposed are those on parental leave (especially for fathers), worker participation and proportional rights for part-time employees. There has been no relenting on opposition to various parts of the Social Charter such as fair wages. The Protocol to the Social Chapter of the Treaty of Maastricht will lead to a two-track social policy in the European Union. There may well be problems with companies which have bases in both the UK and the non-UK Community. Institutions will need to be created to resolve conflicts between UK laws and non-UK laws.

Chapter 3

Formation of the Contract of Employment

A contract of employment, often called a service agreement or a contract *of service*, is a contract. Therefore, general contractual principles covered in contract or common law courses are applicable in the law of employment. For example, material relating to offer and acceptance, consideration, and illegality underlies employment law, and the cases in contract and employment law are to some degree interchangeable. The equivalent to offer and acceptance in contract law is the hiring of the employee; as we shall see the extensive law on dismissal is based on breach of contract. The same problem may arise in both non-employment contract law and employment law: did illness frustrate this contract? Is a minor bound by a contract? Lord Evershed MR in *Laws v London Chronicle (Indicator Newspapers) Ltd* (1959) aptly summarised this idea: 'A contract of service is but an example of contracts in general, so that the general law of contact is applicable.' In legal terms a contract of employment is a binding agreement made voluntarily and the duties are agreed by the parties either personally or through employers' associations and trade unions.

3.1 Employment contracts are contracts

The contract of employment is, however, a specialised form of contract. Just as with other special types of contract such as the sale of goods and agency, different rules have been superimposed on those contractual arrangements classified as employment ones. Parliament has intervened, largely in favour of the individual employee, to rectify what were perceived as abuses. For instance, rights have been given to workers to claim in respect of discrimination on racial and sexual grounds where no such rights existed at common law, and the right to a remedy for unfair dismissal can be seen as an attempt to obtain a 'level playing-field' at the point of termination of employment. Nevertheless, the contract of employment remains the 'cornerstone', as labour lawyers put it, of employment law. It is the foundation for a series of statutory entitlements such as those relating to redundancy payments and unfair dismissal. Moreover, if for some reason an employee is not entitled to a statutory claim, the common law contract remains as a source of rights; on occasion, indeed, contractual rights and statutory ones can be claimed at the same time, and the contractual remedy may be worth more in financial terms than the statutory one. In general the parties

3.1.1 Specialised nature

cannot agree that an employee's statutory entitlements should be diminished, but they may agree to extend them. The statutory notice period to be given to an employee on termination of the contract of employment cannot be reduced by contract between the employers and the employee but a greater length of notice period can contractually be agreed by the parties than that to which the employee is entitled by statute. In the jargon employment law provides a 'floor of rights' which cannot be undercut by agreement, but the parties can agree to build on that floor of rights to provide an employee with greater benefits than those stipulated by parliament. Accordingly, it may be said that the contract of employment is a contract but it is not just a contract; it is also the vehicle through which parliament has given the employee various rights.

3.2   Who is an employee?

Many, but not all, labour law rights are dependent on the applicant's being an employee. In most circumstances there is no problem. Where there is difficulty the courts and tribunals refer to various common law tests. Unfortunately, there is no statutory definition and no one test has been universally approved.

3.2.1   Contract of service or for services?

Once one has determined that there is a contract at all, the problem is to consider whether or not that contract is one of employment. Lawyers distinguish between employees and those people who work for a living but are not employees. Most of those in the latter group are usually called independent contractors or the self-employed. Such persons are said to work under a contract *for services*. It should be recalled that an employee works under a contract of service. In old-fashioned terminology a contract of service constitutes the relationship between masters and servants. The distinction between employees and independent contractors is of fundamental importance to employment law but is not always clear-cut, as we shall see. Besides employees and the self-employed there are other sorts of workers such as apprentices and office holders. Different rules attach to such workers.

3.2.2   Importance of distinction

Smith and Wood, *Industrial Law* (1993) 5th edn, p 9, wrote '... the independent contractor may be in a better monetary position while working, but at a grave disadvantage if he falls off a ladder or is sacked.' It is not beyond the bounds of possibility that a worker may be an employee for one purpose (such as unfair dismissal law) but self-employed for another (eg tax): see, however, 3.8 below.

The significance of the distinction between employees and independent contractors is outlined in the differences listed below:

- Employees owe employers certain obligations which independent contractors do not owe. For example, in every contract of employment there is an implied duty that an employee will serve her employers faithfully, an obligation sometimes known as the duty of fidelity. The nature and extent of such common law implied terms are discussed in the next chapter.

- Similarly, employers may owe employees obligations which they do not owe to independent contractors. Under the Health and Safety at Work Act 1974 employers must adopt a higher standard of care towards their employees than towards independent contractors who work for them.

- By virtue of the doctrine of vicarious liability employers are liable for the torts of their employees committed in the course of employment, but rarely are employers liable for the torts of independent contractors. For example, in *Hillyer v Governors of St Bartholomew's Hospital* (1909) the Court of Appeal held that on the facts a consultant at a hospital was self-employed. Therefore the hospital was not liable to compensate a patient harmed by the consultant's negligent operating technique. Nurses were similarly not employees of the hospital because they took their orders from the surgeon, a fascinating ruling but one logically acceptable under the control test discussed below.

- Sometimes parliament has enacted laws for the benefit of employees. If employers break such laws, sometimes employees can sue their employers for breach of statutory duty, a tort. If employers owe such duties only to employees, they do not owe them to independent contractors, and the self-employed cannot sue for breach. For more on vicarious liability and breach of statutory duty, refer to a standard tort textbook.

- Parliament may give rights to employees only. The principal rights against employers are now found in the Employment Protection (Consolidation) Act 1978. Two illustrations suffice: s 54 provides employees with a right to a remedy for unfair dismissal; s 81 provides for payments on redundancy. These rights form the core of employment law. They are not available to the self-employed. The more persons who are classified as self-employed, the fewer is the number of those entitled to claim statutory employment rights.

- Certain State benefits such as sickness pay apply only to employees.

- The self-employed may be financially better off than employees because of the tax system. They pay tax under Schedule D, whereas employees pay under the PAYE scheme (pay as you earn) under Schedule E. For the advantage see a revenue law text. Independent contractors may be able to recover more of their expenses than can employees. An illustrative case is the decision of an industrial tribunal in *Jennings v Westwood Engineering Ltd* (1975). A worker chose to receive his pay without deduction of tax. On being sacked he claimed a remedy for unfair dismissal. The tribunal determined that he was an employee. (However, he could not obtain redress because his contract was illegal in that it was one designed to defraud the Revenue.)

- Independent contractors may have to register for VAT, value added tax; employees do not.

- Employers may benefit from having independent contractors as workers. They can reduce expenditure on administration because they do not have to establish a system of deducting income tax or national insurance from the self-employed workers' pay. There is no levy for industrial training. And, since unions find grave difficulty in recruiting the self-employed, employers may not have to deal with trade union officials and shop stewards.

- Employees but not independent contractors are preferential creditors on the bankruptcy of their employers.

According to the *Employment Gazette* of July 1993 there are some three million independent contractors, an increase of one million since 1979.

3.3 The tests

Courts and tribunals have adopted several different tests of employment status. The modern approach is to consider all the factors, give weight to each of them and put them into a pan. If the balance of the pan tips towards employment, the worker is an employee; if not, she is an independent contractor.

3.3.1 No statutory definition of employment

For the reasons stated above it is important to distinguish between employees and independent contractors. Often the distinction is easily drawn. The writer of this book is an employee of the University of Sheffield. He is hired (and perhaps fired) by that institution; pay, sick pay and holiday pay come from it; the University deducts income tax under the PAYE scheme. A part-time tutor is likely to be self-employed.

She may work part-time as an assistant solicitor, ie be employed by the partners of her firm of solicitors, but work for three hours a week as a tutor at a university or college. An actor who taught drama part-time at a school was held to be self-employed in *Argent v Minister of Social Security* (1968). The distinction between the two types of workers cannot therefore reside in the nature of the job which they are performing. If a full-time lecturer and a part-time one tutor labour law, they are engaged in the same task. Similarly, the same drains may be unblocked by a plumber employed by the council and one who is self-employed. There is no definition of employment or self-employment provided by parliament. Section 153 of the Employment Protection (Consolidation) Act 1978, the definition section, states merely that an employee is a person who works under a contract of employment. For the purposes of the statute a contract of employment covers both a contract of service and a contract of apprenticeship. Judge-made law does, however, provide a number of tests by which workers may be divided into employees and independent contractors.

It should be noted that the rights given to workers by parliament are not always restricted to employees and apprentices. Each statute must be considered to determine coverage. For example, the Sex Discrimination Act 1975 applies by virtue of s 82(1) to employees, apprentices and those who 'contract personally to execute any work or labour'. This phrase covers a substantial number of the self-employed such as jobbing gardeners.

3.3.2 Variable statutory coverage

The control test was developed by the judiciary in the late 19th century. It is no longer applied by itself but is a part of the modern tests.

3.3.3 Control test

The classic statement of the control test is that of Bramwell LJ in *Yewens v Noakes* (1881): an employee is 'subject to the command of his master as to the manner in which he shall do his work'. If the alleged employers have control over what the worker does and how she does it, she is an employee. A self-employed person is told what to do, but not how to do it. This test is simple to use in relation to some workers such as domestic servants, farm workers, and factory hands. It is, however, impossible to use with regard to many modern jobs. One would not wish the Chair of British Airways to order a pilot how to land at an airport during a sandstorm; yet the pilot may well be an employee. If the control test were applied, the pilot would be self-employed. The test breaks down when dealing with complicated jobs. Persons performing such jobs are employees but they would be categorised as self-employed

3.3.4 Definition and criticism

by this test. The test has for this reason fallen into desuetude.

The defective nature of the control test can clearly be seen from *Collins v Hertfordshire County Council* (1947). Employers are generally speaking liable for the torts of their employees committed in the course of employment but not the torts of independent contractors. In this case a patient was injured through the negligence of both the resident junior house surgeon and the operating surgeon. With regard to the house surgeon there was no problem. She was an employee and the hospital was liable for her tort of negligence. The visiting operating surgeon worked part-time and on a temporary basis at the hospital, although he did have a basic salary and set hours. The court held him not to be an employee. Therefore, the hospital was not responsible for his negligence. The outcome was unfortunate. Whether a plaintiff could successfully sue the alleged employers vicariously depended on whether the person who performed the wrongful act was an employee. If the tortfeasor was an independent contractor, the sole right to sue lay against him and he might be a 'man of straw', unable to pay damages for his wrongdoing.

3.3.5 Continued criticism

Moreover, the fact that there is control is not by itself sufficient to show that there is a contract of employment. In *Gould v Minister of National Insurance* (1951) Mr Gould was a music-hall artiste. The owners of music-halls who engaged him could control what he did to a large degree. They could, for example, tell him at what time he was to appear on stage. Nevertheless, he was an employee. On the other hand, musicians in an orchestra have been held to be self-employed despite the amount of control which the conductor had over their playing: *Addison v London Philharmonic Orchestra* (1981). Control, therefore, is no longer decisive but it remains one of the elements to be taken into account.

3.3.6 Present use

While the control test is no longer decisive, it remains a factor in some of the other tests. In the 'multiple' test, which derives from *Ready Mixed Concrete (South East) Ltd v Minister of Pensions and National Insurance* (1968), the *Ready Mix* case, control was one element in determining whether a driver was an employee or self-employed. There was a large amount of control, but such control was not determinative, for the driver was held to be an independent contractor. The full facts of *Ready Mix* are stated below.

3.3.7 Right to control

For these reasons the courts attempted to update the control test. The right of control was seen in *Short v Henderson Ltd* (1946) as being one of the factors of the 'indicia' test discussed below. Indeed, in one case, *Mersey Docks & Harbour Board v*

Coggins & Griffith (Liverpool) Ltd (1947) the House of Lords treated the right to control as a separate, substantive test. The Court of Appeal had earlier done the same in Walker v Crystal Palace FC (1910). One criticism of the 'right to control' test is that it is circular: when is a worker an employee? When the employers have a right of control. When do employers have a right of control? When the worker is an employee. Another way forward was used by Lord Denning, as he later became, in Cassidy v Minister of Health (1951). He noted that the control test did not adequately deal with skilled workers such as surgeons. He considered that hospitals should be liable for the torts of their surgeons, no matter whether the surgeon was an employee or self-employed. The hospitals after all engaged staff, or they chose them for their ability in performing their job functions; and they could dismiss them. Therefore, they should be vicariously liable for the torts of their surgeons. In Cassidy the plaintiff lost some fingers because of the carelessness of the surgeon. He sued the hospital. The Court of Appeal decided that he was entitled to damages from the hospital because he had entrusted himself to that body. The organisation of the hospital had led to the negligence; therefore, the hospital was responsible.

To remedy the defects of the control test Denning LJ instituted a new test, the organisation test, in Stevenson Jordan & Harrison v MacDonald & Evans (1952). He said that whether a person was an employee or not no longer depended on whether he submitted to orders but:

> '... it depends on whether the person is part and parcel of the organisation. A person under a contract of service does his work as an integral part of the business whereas a person under a contract for service – although he might do his work for the business – is not integrated into it but is only an accessory to it.'

This test would have led to both surgeons being employees in Collins v Hertfordshire County Council, above.

3.3.8   Organisation test

The organisation test may be criticised. First, it sometimes gives the incorrect answer. Homeworkers may be an integral part of the organisation but many are self-employed. There are well over half a million homeworkers and this issue is of importance to them. Similarly, a cleaner in a government office is still an employee even though his job has been privatised. His job remains an integral part of the enterprise of running a government office. It is merely the employers who have changed. A cleaner may, however, be self-employed yet still an integral part of the organisation. If, for example, local government contracts out the cleaning of a building, a former

3.3.9   Criticism

employee tenders for the job, obtains it and does exactly the same job on the cleaning as he did before the contracting out, he is now self-employed. Secondly, the test may be difficult to apply. Is the window-cleaner who cleans windows at a brickworks part and parcel of the organisation (as Denning LJ put it in *Bank voor Handel en Scheepvaart NV v Slatford* (1953))? Some window-cleaners there may be employees, some self-employed, but the test does not enable a judge to differentiate. Thirdly, the organisational test may add nothing to the control test. Determining who was part and parcel of the organisation could only be done by determining whether such workers were under the control of their employers. MacKenna J in *Ready Mix* was strongly of this opinion.

3.3.10 Current use

Despite such criticism the organisation test is sometimes utilised as an additional test to support a conclusion. In *Davis v New England College of Arundel* (1977) the judge stated:

'... whether one applies the test of control, or whether the applicant was part of the organisation of the college, the answer is plainly the same.'

Similarly, in *Whittaker v Minister of Pensions* (1966) the judge held that a trapeze-artiste was an employee because:

'... she had no real independence and had to carry out her contractual duties as an integral part of the business of the company.'

3.3.11 Ordinary person test

The courts realised that the tests already mentioned did not easily fit the fact situations. Novel tests were adopted. One of these tests may be called the 'ordinary person' test. In the words of the judge in *Collins v Hertfordshire County Council*:

'... was his contract a contract of service within the meaning which an ordinary person would give to the words?'

This test was approved by the Court of Appeal in *Cassidy v Minister of Health* and used in *Whittaker v Minister of Pensions*.

3.3.12 Criticism

There are, however, drawbacks. First, who is the ordinary person? If it is the judge this test does not help her. If it is someone else, how does the judge know what the ordinary person thinks? Secondly, surely an ordinary person will never have heard of a contract of service. Thirdly, it may be difficult for legal advisers to say, before a case is heard, whether an individual is an employee or not. Despite such criticisms this test has been used in recent times: see *Withers v Flackwell Heath Football Supporters Club* (1981). If policy issues, however, govern whether a person is to be deemed to be an employee, the 'ordinary person' test does not straightforwardly promote those policies.

A second test from the late 1940s comes from the speech of Lord Thankerton in *Short v Henderson Ltd* (1946). He said that there were four indicators, indicia, of a contract of employment:

- the employers' power to select an employee;

- their payment of wages;

- their right to control the manner in which work was done; and

- their right of suspension or dismissal.

This approach was criticised in *Ready Mix* on the grounds that factors (a), (b) and (d) helped simply to establish whether there was any contract at all, not whether the contract was one of employment. The remaining element, right of control, was the old control test updated to the mid-20th century.

Lord Wright in *Montreal Locomotive Works Ltd v Montreal* (1947), a Privy Council authority, postulated a second four-part test. The court should consider:

- control;

- ownership of the tools;

- the chance of profit; and

- the risk of loss.

He did not think that these four factors were conclusive. Other elements might have to be added. Such an attitude gave rise to the modern approach to distinguishing employees from independent contractors.

One of the well-known staging points on the way towards the current thinking is the *Ready Mix* case. The company sacked its drivers, sold its lorries to them, and re-engaged them under some kind of contract. The written contract stated that the drivers had to wear the company's uniform, use the lorries only on company business, place them at the company's disposal for a set number of hours, and obey the foreman's orders. These factors pointed to the existence of a contract of employment. However, other elements pointed towards the drivers' being self-employed. They had to maintain the lorries and pay running costs. They could own more than one lorry and hire substitute drivers. They had no set hours or meal breaks. They decided on routes and how to drive the lorries. They paid their own tax and national insurance. The judge said that there were three conditions which had to be satisfied before there existed a contract of employment:

- the employee had to agree to provide his own skill in the performance of a service for his employers in return for payment;

- the employers had to have some degree of control; and

- the other terms of the contract must not be inconsistent with the existence of a contract of employment.

3.3.17 Decision in *Ready Mix*	On the facts the drivers were self-employed. Though there was some element of control, they did not have to work personally for the firm. They could provide substitutes. Furthermore, some terms of the contract were not consistent with there being a contract of employment. Yet, as can be seen from the facts, many were, and some factors were indecisive. The drivers were paid according to the work they did. One might think that this element pointed towards their being self-employed, but some employees are paid by results eg piece workers and those on commission.
3.3.18 Modern approach	The multiple test in *Ready Mix* has developed into what is sometimes called the pragmatic test. The judge or tribunal members weighs up all the factors pointing towards the existence of a contract of employment and all the factors pointing towards a contract for services. No one factor is determinative. For instance, the fact that a company pays a person's tax and national insurance does not automatically mean that she is an employee (*O'Kelly v Trusthouse Forte plc* (1984)). Similarly, the fact that a firm does not pay a worker's tax and national insurance does not mean that she is automatically self-employed (*Davis v New England College of Arundel* (1977)). A casual vision mixer was held to be self-employed even though he did not provide the tools of his job (*Hall v Lorimer* (1994)).

It must be questioned whether the first criterion adds anything to the other two. Both the self-employed and employees agree to work in consideration of payment: *Airfix Footwear Ltd v Cope* (1978) and *Thames Television Ltd v Wallis* (1979). In *Market Investigations Ltd v Minister of Social Security* (1969) Cooke J gave some indication of the sort of factors which may be relevant when determining whether there was a contract of employment present. Control was always relevant but other factors might include:

- whether the worker provided his own equipment;

- whether he could hire helpers;

- whether he had some financial risk;

- whether he could profit from the job through what the judge called 'sound management';

- whether he had responsibility for investment and management.

There is however, no checklist of relevant factors. All factors must be weighed in the balance. The Court of Appeal in *Hall v Lorimer*, above, said that the list of factors in *Market Investigations* should not be gone through like a checklist. The court or tribunal should not apply the factors mechanically.

An example of such balancing can be seen in *Hitchcock v Post Office* (1980). A sub-postmaster had to carry out the instructions of the Post Office and he had to tell the head postmaster if he was going to be absent for three days or more. However, he could delegate the performance of his duties and took the risk of profit and loss. The latter factors outweighed the former. Accordingly, the sub-postmaster was self-employed. The case demonstrates that a court or tribunal must weigh the factors, not simply count them. One 'heavyweight' factor can outweigh four 'lightweight' factors. Other factors which may be important include: whether the person works at home or at a workplace, whether she can work for another firm, whether the work is casual.

3.3.19   Example

One factor which has recently come into prominence is whether there exists 'mutuality of obligations' between the parties. A major case is *Nethermere (St Neots) Ltd v Gardiner* (1984). The plaintiffs were outworkers: they made clothes at home. They were paid by the piece. There was no obligation to work at set times to do a certain amount of work. The Court of Appeal held that they were employees, largely because there was a regular arrangement over a period of time whereby the homeworkers would do the work. They had the expectation of being given work. Kerr LJ said:

3.3.20   Mutuality of obligations

> '... the inescapable requirement concerning the alleged employees ... is that they must be subject to an obligation to accept and perform some minimum or at least reasonable amount of work for the alleged employer.'

It must be said, however, that all contracts, even ones of self-employment, have an irreducible minimum.

One difficulty with the mutuality of obligations doctrine is that it may lead to results which are not in accord with the policy of widening the concept of 'employee' so that workers may claim on being dismissed unfairly. Those who work in temporary jobs or part-time or as casual labourers may not be included within the scope of the legislation. Since perhaps one-third of

3.3.21   Criticism of mutuality

the UK workforce is engaged in such jobs, and since more and more workers for the foreseeable future will work in them (the number of full-time jobs occupied by males is decreasing, while the number of part-time jobs held by women is increasing), the effect of this doctrine is not in tune with the legislative objective. Such workers are called 'atypical' workers but they are becoming typical, not atypical. This problem has arisen in an important case. In *O'Kelly v Trusthouse Forte* (1984) the plaintiffs were 'regular casuals'. They came in to help at banquets and similar functions. They often came in at set hours on set days. In industrial relations terms they formed a secondary labour force. The core workers did their jobs full-time and did work daily and regularly. It could be said that there was a tertiary labour force who came in when asked. The 'regular casuals' fitted in between. It might have been thought that these were the very sort of persons whom employment law should protect. The Court of Appeal could have held that the regular casuals were employees. They had no other jobs; they apparently could not provide substitutes; the hotel where they worked gave them uniforms; they did not lay out capital or share in the financial risks. The court decided that the workers were self-employed despite such factors. The court seems to have been impressed by the custom and practice of the business and by the intention of the parties that the waiters were not employees. There was no mutuality of obligations. The employers were under no duty to provide work and the workers were under no obligation to do work, though in practice they would not refuse it for if they did, they would not be offered more work. It should be noted, however, that generally speaking employers have no duty to provide work, and that the effect of the decision is that a large and growing class of workers is not protected by the employment legislation. Moreover, not even the Court of Appeal has applied the mutuality of obligations principle (*McLeod v Hellyer Bros* (1987)) though compare the decision in *Scarah v Fish Container Services Ltd* (1995) where the Court of Appeal held that there was no mutuality of obligation between those who unloaded crates of fish and the defendant company so that there was a global contract covering the period off work because they were not obliged to turn up to work. And once the 'regular casual' workers have begun to work, there is mutuality of obligation. The fact that they need not accept work is irrelevant if they have done so. *O'Kelly* has been criticised on other grounds. If one enquires in the terms of the next test whether the waiters were in business on their own account, it is impossible to say that they ran the risk of profit or loss. They were not entrepreneurs but were under the control of the hotel managers. Furthermore, employers should not be able to deprive workers of the protection of employment legislation.

A test formulated by Cooke J in *Market Investigations Ltd v Minister of Social Security* (1969) was:

> '... is the person who has engaged himself to perform those services performing them in business on his own account?'

3.3.22   Independence test

If a person invests money in her job, she is likely to be self-employed. If a plumber works when she wishes, buys her own tools, and can send someone else in her place, she is likely to be employed. If, however, the worker is provided with tools and materials, she is likely to be an employee: *Airfix Footwear Ltd v Cope* (1978). This test has been used several times eg *Young & Woods Ltd v West*, a decision which is described below, and the Privy Council in *Lee v Chung* (1990), where a casual construction worker in Hong Kong was held to be an employee because he ran no risk of profit or loss while working, approved Cooke J's approach. This definition of an independent contractor has been criticised as in reality being the outcome of the other tests and not a test in its own right, but it has certainly been used by the courts and tribunals independently of the other tests. Moreover, casual workers may not be in business on their own account but they are not necessarily employees: *Wickens v Champion Employment* (1984), in which temporary workers were held not to be employees of an employment agency. The EAT held that the agency had no duty to secure work for them and they had no obligation to accept any work secured for them by the agency.

This section discusses the situation where in the contract there is an express term that the worker is an independent contractor. This issue is sometimes known as 'labels'. Despite the doctrine of freedom of contract the courts and tribunals have cut through the label to reveal the true situation.

3.4   'Labels'

A problem which sometimes arises is when all or most of the elements point in one direction but there is a clause in the contract between the worker and her company which states that she is self-employed. Is she an employee or an independent contractor? Take, for example, a building worker who works on what is called 'the lump'. The labourer takes a job on the basis that he is to be treated as a 'self-employed labour only sub-contractor'. Most other factors eg wages, times of work, personal service, point towards his being an employee. While in work the labourer enjoys the advantages

3.4.1   The problem

associated with being self-employed (though there are special revenue rules which apply to working on the lump), but what happens if he is injured or wishes to claim statutory rights? He can do so only if he is an employee. A recent illustration is *Catamaran Cruisers v Williams* (1994) (EAT). The worker in order to avoid PAYE established a company which sold his services to a firm which provided a riverbus facility on the Thames. He paid tax on the money he received from the company (which was given to it by the riverbus firm) and the company paid corporation tax. It was held that he was an employee for the purposes of his claiming employment law rights. The fact that there was a company between him and his employers did not affect the substance of the transaction.

3.4.2   *Ferguson's* case

One of the main authorities is *Ferguson v John Dawson & Partners (Contractors) Ltd* (1976). Mr Ferguson was a worker on the lump. He fell through the roof of a building and was injured. He contended that the company was liable for the tort of breach of statutory duty for failing to provide a guard rail. By a majority the Court of Appeal held that he was an employee. Therefore, he was awarded damages. The majority held that the 'label' of self-employment was simply a smokescreen which hid the true relationship. That smokescreen could be pierced by the courts and the true relationship discovered. Later cases have followed the majority in *Ferguson: Davis v New England College of Arundel* (1977), *Tyne & Clyde Warehouses Ltd v Hamerton* (1978) and *Thames Television Ltd v Wallis* (1979).

3.4.3   The dissent

The dissenting judge, Lawton LJ, would have given the worker no compensation. He stated that there was no reason why a person could not be self-employed if he chose, and it was against public policy for a person to be an employee for the purpose of torts law but self-employed in relation to tax. 'The prime object of the bargain', he said, was that the plaintiff had the status of self-employment.

3.4.4   *Massey's* case

The case with which to compare *Ferguson* is *Massey v Crown Life Insurance Co* (1978). The applicant was a branch manager for the defendants. There was no doubt that he was at that stage an employee. Later the parties agreed that he should become self-employed. After taking independent professional advice he accepted his new status. He was taxed as self-employed and he paid national insurance as a self-employed person. He was dismissed. He claimed compensation for unfair dismissal. He could succeed only if he was an employee. The Court of Appeal held that he was self-employed. The Court stated that the parties could not alter the true relationship by putting a label on it falsifying the real situation. However, if the relationship was not clear, the label was strong evidence of what the relationship was. In *Massey* there was no attempt to defraud the Revenue, unlike in *Ferguson*: it was an agreement to treat the former employee as self-employed. By choice the worker had, during the running of his contract, agreed to change his relationship.

The judgment in *Massey* was unanimous. The Court was influenced by the fact that the manager had altered his status for tax purposes. The judges did not want him to be self-employed for the purposes of taxation but an employee for unfair dismissal purposes. Lawton LJ, the dissentient in *Ferguson*, said in *Massey* that:

3.4.5   Decision in *Massey*

'*Ferguson* clearly established that the parties cannot change a status merely by putting a new label on it. But, if in all the circumstances of the case, including the terms of the agreement, it is manifest that there was an intention to change status ... there is no reason why the parties should not be allowed to make that change.'

The principal authority is now *Young & Woods Ltd v West* (1980). The applicant was a sheet metal-worker. He was engaged as a self-employed person and the Inland Revenue treated him as such. He was dismissed and claimed compensation for unfair dismissal. The Court of Appeal did not accept the words of Lawton LJ quoted above. The Court held that the label was one factor which a court or tribunal had to take into account. It was decisive only when, all other factors having been weighed, there was still doubt as to the nature of the contract. The Court thought that more weight should be attached to a label if there had been a deliberate change in the relationship than otherwise, the situation which had occurred in *Massey*, or if the type of job was unusual. In *Massey* the post was unusual. In the present case there was nothing unusual about the job. The Court did not consider, however, that an intent to change the status should automatically take effect; rather the label was a factor in the equation. On the facts of the case the label was not decisive because the other elements pointed towards employment: they were not evenly balanced. The applicant worked alongside employees doing the same work as he did. There was no doubt as to the relationship, disregarding the label. Therefore, the label was not decisive. Accordingly, the applicant was an employee.

3.4.6   *Young & Woods v West*

The Court did, however, say that courts or tribunals which characterised a relationship as one of employment which had

3.4.7   Tax consequence

been thought to be one of self-employment should inform the Revenue to recoup back tax on an employment basis (PAYE). The result might be that the employee would lose more on tax than gain on compensation for unfair dismissal.

3.4.8   Avoidance provision

It should be noted that s 140 of the Employment Protection (Consolidation) Act 1978 prevents the parties from contracting out of the rights provided in that statute. To permit 'labels' would defeat this non-contracting-out rule. This policy has been effected to some extent by the courts in their decisions on labelling.

3.4.9   Critique

One criticism of the 'label' cases is that they are not easily squared with the doctrine of freedom of contract. By that principle contractual parties should be free, subject to some limitations based on public policy, to determine their relationship. If they have chosen to state whether orally or in writing that a worker is an independent contractor, why should the courts intervene to change the nature of the relationship? The fact that the worker does not realise all the consequences of being self-employed is not to the point. After all, the parties are bound by the contract in general whether or not they understood the terms. Moreover, the worker has taken the financial benefits of being self-employed. Should she now not take the disadvantages? The opposing view is that employment legislation is to protect workers and therefore coverage should be broad.

3.5   Special types of workers

The law has found difficulty in dealing with several classes of workers. Separate treatment is made of these categories. The principle is that tribunals and courts apply the above-stated tests to determine status.

3.5.1   Office holders

Where a person holds an office (defined as a permanent post which exists independently of the person who holds it), she is neither employed nor self-employed (though there is also authority which holds that an office holder may also be an employee). She falls into a separate category then office holders. Police constables comprise the principal illustration of this class. They do have some of the rights held by employees such as written terms, minimum notice period, and redundancy payments, but they are subject to specialised terms and conditions in the performance of their duties. There are other office holders such as JPs, judges, trade union officials, trustees and Salvation Army officers.

3.5.2   Clergy

The courts have said that other clergy are neither office holders nor employees because there is no intent to enter into legal binding relations: eg *Davies v Presbyterian Church of Wales* (1986).

However, in *Coker v Diocese of Southwark* (1995) Professor Rideout, Chair of the London South Industrial Tribunal, said that an Anglican assistant curate was an employee. He criticised an earlier case which had held that the relations between the Methodist Church and a minister were purely spiritual: the spiritual nature of the work did not preclude a contract. The Church of England exercised a high degree of control. In sum the curate was under a contractual duty to adhere to Church rules. Because he was an employee, he could bring a claim for unfair dismissal:

Persons in training who do not have contracts of apprenticeship may also fall into a special class called appointees for training by Lord Denning MR in *Wiltshire Police Authority v Wynn* (1980). The Court of Appeal determined that despite wages and hours of work a police cadet was not an employee. A university research student seems to be in a similar position: *Hugh-Jones v St John's College* (1979). *A fortiori*, undergraduates are not employees. However, an articled clerk is an employee: *Oliver v J P Malnick & Co* (1983).	3.5.3 Trainees
The above two classes of workers form exceptions to the usual division into employees and independent contractors. The next two categories constitute types of workers where rules have been developed to deal with the nature of the worker.	3.5.4 Difficult jobs
A worker in a co-operative venture registered as a limited company was held to be an employee in *Drym Fabricators Ltd v Johnson* (1981). Facts may, however, lead to another conclusion as in *Addison* above.	3.5.5 Workers' co-operatives
Perhaps surprisingly a director may be an employee and may be so despite the fact that she runs the company. Cohen J made the point in *Trussed Steel Concrete Co Ltd v Green* (1946):	3.5.6 Directors

> 'When I find a man who is bound to devote his whole time to the affairs of the company, to do all in his power to develop and extend the business of the company, not to engage in any other business and who is engaged on the terms that his employment may be determined by notice in writing, I find it impossible to say that he is not employed by the company.'

A company has a legal personality separate from the natural persons who own and manage it. For example, like a natural person, a company can employ people whether as factory floor workers or as directors.

The main authority is *Lee v Lee's Air Farming Ltd* (1961), a decision of the Privy Council on appeal from New Zealand. The deceased owned all the shares except one in a company.	3.5.7 *Lee's* case

He was killed in a flying accident. His widow claimed compensation. By the law of New Zealand as it then was, she could succeed only if the deceased was an employee of the company. The Judicial Committee held that he was an employee even though the company was a 'one-man company', he being the one man.

3.5.8	*Parsons's* case

A director is not, however, always an employee. A contrasting case is *Parsons & Sons Ltd v Parsons* (1979). The applicant sought compensation for unfair dismissal when he was removed by his brothers from his directorship. The Court of Appeal noted that he was regarded as self-employed for the purposes of national insurance; he did not receive a salary but directors' fees; and the firm's accountant regarded him as self-employed. He was held to be an independent contractor. One indication that he was not an employee was that he had no written contract of employment (or written memorandum) as required by what is now s 318 of the Companies Act 1985.

3.5.9	Partners

A partner is self-employed. She is the employer. Care must be taken to distinguish true partners from salaried partners, the later being employees, whereas the former share the profits, often in proportion to the amount of capital each has invested.

3.5.10	Agency workers

Agency workers are those workers who are sent by employment agencies to work in firms. Whether such workers are employees or self-employed depends on the general law. Indeed, where a worker agrees with one firm to work exclusively for another, it is thought that there is neither a contract of service nor one for services but a contract *sui generis* (*Construction Industry Training Board v Labour Force Ltd* (1970)). If, however, the terms of the contract indicate that the worker is an employee, he is so (*McMeechan v Secretary of State for Employment* (1995)). A locum doctor was held not to be an employee of the agency which sent him to jobs because he could choose whether to work or not and the sole control the agency exercised over him was a monitoring one (*Sreekanta v Medical Relief Agency (Stoke-on-Trent) Ltd* (1995)). A fitter/machinist was held to be an independent contractor in *Pertemps Group plc v Nixon* (1994) because all the terms of the contract so indicated. Three situations may be distinguished:

- if employers take on a person and she is under an obligation to do the work herself, she is likely to be an employee;

- if the firm contacts the agency for a worker but there is no duty on the agency to provide a specific person, the worker may well not be an employee of the firm;

- if the company pays the agency for the worker and the agency pays the worker, there is no contract between the company and the worker. The agency may be the worker's employer. This determination will be supported by the agency acting as if it were the employer eg by deducting tax and national insurance. An agency, however, may have no duty to find work for the persons on its books.

Crown employees may work under a contract eg *Reilly v R* (1934). However, the Crown is not bound by an Act of Parliament unless the statute says so. For some purposes, such as unfair dismissal (see Employment Protection (Consolidation) Act 1978, s 138(7)), civil servants are treated as employees, but for some other employment law purposes they are not. Central government employees cannot claim statutory redundancy payments (s 138(1)). Members of the armed forces cannot claim under unfair dismissal legislation (s 138(3)), and employees of the NHS cannot claim redundancy payments (s 99(1)(c)). There are other exemptions and exceptions which are well discussed by Fredman and Morris in *The State as Employer* (1989).

3.5.11   Crown employees

In the light of the difficulties which courts and tribunals have come across when determining whether a contract is one of employment or for services, it has been said that the issue is one of fact for the fact-finding tribunal. The strongest authority to that effect is the Privy Council decision in *Lee v Chung* (1990). Only where the difficulty relates solely to the construction of a written document is the question one of law: see *Davies v Presbyterian Church of Wales* (1986). The legal effect is that in general questions of fact cannot be appealed to the Employment Appeal Tribunal and thence to the Court of Appeal and House of Lords. The practical effect is that the Employment Appeal Tribunal cannot intervene (except where the industrial tribunal has misdirected itself as to law or where the result is 'perverse') in order to correct inconsistent decisions by industrial tribunals: on the same facts one worker may be an employee (and therefore able to make a claim for unfair dismissal, for example) and another worker an independent contractor. Such an approach does not reflect creditably on a legal system. The determination that the issue is a question of fact is often said to be the result of the higher tribunals' striving to reduce their workload. It is an unfortunate side-effect of their doing so that some workers may be deprived of their rights to which they would otherwise be entitled. Should administrative convenience be permitted to defeat rights?

3.6   Law or fact?

3.7   Who are the employers?

It may be certain that a worker is an employee but not who employs her. A person may have two employers: for example, a person may work for one employer in the morning and another in the afternoon. The problem really comes when one firm sends an employee to another firm for a certain time or to complete a set task. The basic rule is that the first firm remains the employer unless the employee has consented to the move. In *Mersey Docks & Harbour Board v Coggins & Griffith (Liverpool) Ltd* (1947) the Board had loaned a crane and its driver to a firm. He was careless and an accident happened. The Board was held by the House of Lords to be still the worker's employer and so liable vicariously for the employee's negligence.

3.7.1   Exception

At times, however, the second firm is the employee's employer. In *Garrard v A E Southey & Co* (1952) the plaintiff was loaned by the first defendant to the second defendant. The latter's foreman controlled what the worker did and how he did it. The worker was injured. He sued both defendants for negligence. The Court held that the second defendant was his employer and was liable. The Court said that if the employee's labour was alone loaned, it will often be that the hirers are his employers but if he is loaned with a complex piece of machinery it may well be that the first firm remains the employer.

3.8   General criticism

In law there is a doctrine that one cannot blow hot and cold. Differently put one cannot, for example, be two inconsistent things at the same time. In the present context one cannot in English law, it would seem, be an employee for one purpose but self-employed for another. If one is an employee for the purposes of the employment legislation, one is also an employee for tax purposes (*Calder v H Kitson Vickers Ltd* (1988)). That is why the industrial tribunal, having re-characterised a worker as an employee from being an independent contractor, informs the revenue authorities of the change. Nevertheless, first, there is no bright line between employees and independent contractors; secondly, the answer to the question whether a worker was an employee or self-employed may be 'result-pulled'; that is, a Court or tribunal may hold a worker to be an employee if such is in tune with some policy. This attitude may be seen especially in cases involving vicarious liability. To gain damages from someone the plaintiff has to prove that the person who injured him was an employee. The Court in order to be able to award damages to a person who has been injured must hold that the worker was an employee and accordingly does so. For this reason cases on vicarious liability should be treated carefully when applying them into the area of employment protection.

Similarly, in order to have jurisdiction to hear a case on unfair dismissal the industrial tribunal must hold a worker to be an employee. Therefore, it does so determine. In tax matters the courts may be striving to prevent evasion.

Certainly there is no one factor which marks out a contract of employment. A factor which is important in one case may be insignificant or not present in the next. The judge or tribunal has to weigh up the factors in the context of each particular case. Since the policy behind the various rulings about employment status vary so markedly, it is not surprising that the judiciary have failed to come up with a simply stated and easily applied test. While the multiple test is the one which is most often used, there is nothing in the cases to prevent the courts or tribunals from running together the tests, giving priority to one test rather than the multiple test or inventing new tests. The sole test which stands rejected is the first, the control test.

Government policy is in favour of the switch from employees to independent contractors. The effect, it is hoped, is to unleash the hidden hand of the market with consequential reductions in permanency of employment and the level of pay. One result in employment law is that proportionately fewer workers are able to claim their statutory protection rights than in 1979.

Formation of the Contract of Employment

A contract of employment or of service is an example of contracts in general, but it has specialised features due to statutory intervention in favour of individual employees. Despite parliamentary inroads, contract remains the cornerstone of employment law: *Laws v London Chronicle* (1959).

Employment contracts are contracts

Many rights are granted to employees but not to other workers, in particular the self-employed. The distinction is therefore important: *Hillyer v St Bartholomew's* (1909).

Who is an employee?

Parliament has not defined an 'employee'. The Courts and tribunals have used a variety of tests to distinguish employees from the self-employed: control, right to control, organisation, ordinary person, 'indicia', multiple, the modern or pragmatic approach, and independence:

The tests

- Control: *Yewens v Noakes* (1881)

- *Stevenson Jordan & Harrison* (1952)

- Ordinary person: *Collins v Herts CC* (1947)

- 'Indicia': *Short v Henderson* (1946)

- Multiple: *Ready Mix* (1968)

- Modern Approach: *Market Investigations* (1969); mutuality of obligations: *Nethermere v Gardiner* (1984)

- Independence: *Market Investigations* (1969).

If the parties agree on the status of the worker, effect will be given to such oral or written statement, provided that the 'label' does not hide the true relationship:

'Labels'

Ferguson v John Dawson (1976)

Massey v Crown Life (1978)

Young & Woods v West (1980).

Some persons form specific classes of workers. An example is office holders. Other types of workers require particular treatment, Crown employees being an illustration: *Wiltshire PA v Wynn* (1980); *Lee v Lee's Air Farming* (1961).

Special types of worker

Law or fact?

Surprisingly the determination of whether a worker is an employee or an independent contractor is a question of fact, except where the matter is one of the construction of a written document: *Lee v Chung* (1990).

Who are the employers?

The question whether an employee is employed by the employer who loaned her out or by the employer who hired her is resolved by considering the factual matrix of the case: *MD & HB v Coggins & Griffith* (1947).

General criticism

The outcome in the cases may be 'result-pulled' because of policy. There is no list to be ticked off in deciding whether a contract is one of employment. Factors have to be weighed. The Courts and tribunals are at liberty to apply more or less any of the tests used since the Second World War.

Chapter 4

The Common Law of Contract

In the last chapter it was noted that the contract of employment was a contract. Therefore, general contractual principles such as the doctrines of consideration and privity apply to service agreements. This chapter opens by examining three matters of contract law as they apply to employment contracts: minority, illegality, and form. Linked with form is the statutory provision of written terms of employment. Also considered are express and implied terms, the latter supplementing the former. While contracts of employment are becoming more formal than previously, offer and acceptance can be simple: 'Will you start on Monday at 8 am?' 'Yes.' The terms of the contract may derive from various documents such as the company handbook. In the event of a dispute it may be very difficult to discover what the parties are to be taken to have agreed.

4.1 Common law contract

As with other contracts, offer, acceptance, consideration and intention to create legal relations, the last requirement being presumed unless the contrary is demonstrated, must be present. An offer need not be in any set format. It could be a notice pinned on a board, though the notice is likely to be an invitation to treat. An advertisement may or may not be an offer, as every first-year law student knows from *Carlill v Carbolic Smoke Ball Co* (1893). Offers may be made subject to conditions such as a medical examination. It is thought that an offer of employment subject to satisfactory references is to be tested subjectively: Did these employers consider the reference to be satisfactory? (*Wishart v NACAB* (1990)). Acceptance may be a simple nod or handshake. Terms tend to be dictated by employers, though there may be chaffering over some terms, especially pay, and sometimes terms may be laid down in a collective agreement.

4.2 Offer and acceptance

The law relating to minors' contracts applies to employment contracts (and indeed contracts for services). An infant (ie a person under 18) is bound by an employment contract if overall it is for her benefit. For example, a boy of 16 can agree to serve at low wages as a trainee chef in the expectation that he will be able to use his training and experience in later life. In *Chaplin v Leslie Frewin (Publishers) Ltd* (1966) a contract with Charlie Chaplin's son, Michael, to write a book was binding

4.3 Infancy

because he received an adequate amount of money in return for his work. In comparison the agreement was void in *De Francesco v Barnum* (1890). There were onerous obligations on a 14-year-old but little obligation on her employers. It is possible for a term which is not for the infant's benefit such as a covenant in restraint of trade to be severed.

4.4   Illegality

The law of illegal contracts applies to contracts of employment. Contracts tainted with illegality or immorality cannot be enforced by courts or tribunals. Such agreements may be contrary to public policy at common law or expressly or impliedly prohibited by parliament. A contract which is illegal *ab initio* is not enforceable by either party. The fact that the plaintiff or applicant does not know of the illegality is irrelevant. This law is laid down in the well-known contract case of *St John Shipping Corp v Joseph Rank Ltd* (1957). An employment case is *Corby v Morrison* (1980). An agreement to pay £5 without deducting tax made the agreement illegal at and from its commencement. If the contract is illegal, an employee cannot rely on any contractual or statutory rights to which she would otherwise be entitled, such as the rights to be awarded damages at law for wrongful dismissal and to be granted a remedy for unfair dismissal under statute. In *Cole v Stacey* (1974) an employee received additional tax-free pay. The contract was void for illegality and the right to a redundancy payment was lost. If there is a period of illegality, continuity of employment for eg the purpose of determining the qualifying period for unfair dismissal is broken: *Hyland v J H Barker (Northwest) Ltd* (1985). If the illegality occurs during a contract and is then stopped, one cannot add together the two lawful periods to create one period of at least two years' duration for the purpose of claiming statutory employment rights such as redundancy payments, unfair dismissal, and written reasons for dismissal: *Attridge v Jaydees Newsagents Ltd*, an unreported decision of the Employment Appeal Tribunal (EAT 603/79 11 March 1980). This case and the previous one illustrate the proposition that a contract once illegal can become lawful again. In the opinion of the writer, it is the height of absurdity that the doctrine of illegality applies even in the area of sexual and racial discrimination. If an employee is sacked on racial grounds, she has no claim if she has been employed under an illegal contract. An employee will be deprived of employment rights even though, for example, the amount of untaxed pay was small in comparison with the gross wages and even if the scheme to defraud the Revenue was instituted by the employers: *Newland v Simons & Willer (Hairdressers) Ltd* (1981). The EAT held that the parliamentary policy of widening the rights of employees did not prevail against the common law policy of safeguarding the Revenue. See, however, para 4.4.5, below.

Accordingly, even though it is the contract which is void, statutory rights are not enforceable. If only employees may claim various rights, 'employee' is defined in terms of working under a contract of employment or apprenticeship. If there is no contract, there is no contract of employment. Statutory rights are dependent on there being such a contract. (This argument reinforces the view that contract remains the 'cornerstone' of employment law.)

4.4.1   Statutory rights negated

To the rule about illegality there are exceptions.

4.4.2   In performance

• Mode of performance

If the unlawfulness was not present at the inception of the contract but came about as a result of the method in which it was performed, the agreement is not automatically unenforceable. In *Coral Leisure Group Ltd v Barnett* (1981) the hiring of prostitutes for clients was held not to be part of an employee's terms of employment but merely a way in which his job was performed. It is not always certain whether a contract is illegal from its inception or only during performance. *Corby v Morrison*, above, could have been treated as one in which only the performance was unlawful: the illegal payment occurred during the running of the contract. It seems that contracts in which there is a payment of wages without deduction of tax or national insurance will be void automatically.

The last sentence is, however, contradicted by a number of other cases. In relation to contracts illegal in performance an employee will lose her rights only if she knew of the illegality. This principle has been used in tax evasion cases: *Tomlinson v Dick Evans 'U' Drive Ltd* (1978) (*obiter*), *Davidson v Pillay* (1979) and *McConnell v Bolik* (1979). In the latter two cases the employee did not know of or participate in the illegal transaction. In the first case the employee did know of the illegality. He was paid a £15 per week bonus out of petty cash and did not pay tax on it. The EAT held that both parties 'were in it up to the neck'. In *Salvesen v Simons* (1994) the employee, an estate manager, was paid largely free of tax. The Scottish EAT held that it was immaterial that he did not know that what he was doing was unlawful. What he knew was the fact of the arrangement and that knowledge was sufficient. Therefore, he could not claim a remedy for unfair dismissal. If, however, the payment is a bonus given, for example, when a greyhound won a race, the trainer's contract is not

4.4.3   Knowledge

unenforceable even though he knew that the payment was free of tax (*Annandale Engineering v Samson* (1994)). The test for knowledge is a subjective one: did the employee know of the illicit activity? It is not material that the employee ought to have known of the illegality: *Newland v Simons & Willer (Hairdressers) Ltd*, above. Therefore, as the EAT said, 'stupidity or misunderstanding or inexperience' can provide the employee with a defence. When the employee does come to know of the illegality, she must do all she reasonably can to stop it (*Davidson v Pillay*). Compare *Begacem v Turkish Delight Kebab House* (1988), an unreported EAT decision. The employee was paid in cash. No national insurance contributions or tax were deducted. He asked his employers why this was so, but he was always assured that all was fine. The Tribunal held that the employee could not have a remedy for being unfairly dismissed. He should have told the Revenue of the illegality so that his true situation could be investigated.

4.4.4   Gravity: the role of public policy

Not every illegality is sufficiently heinous to avoid the contract. Illegality will take effect, at least if it is a statutorily based one, if Parliament must have intended to make the agreement void. (Similar thinking pervades the previous point. The fact that while performing the contract an employee has done something illegal does not make a service agreement void eg a lorry driver's contract will remain in existence even though she has broken the speed limit.) Because of this principle, it is uncertain whether cases such as *Tomlinson v Dick Evans 'U' Drive*, above, survive in their entirety. In that case the EAT noted that the employee may be less blameworthy than the employers but decided that 'even in such cases the evil lies in the dishonesty in which the employee knowingly participated'. There were, therefore, no degrees of blame. However, the courts have recently established that public policy is not dictated by the sort of considerations which applied in *Tomlinson*. In *Hewcastle Catering Ltd v Ahmed* (1991) the Court of Appeal held that two employees could complain of unfair dismissal when their employers had instructed them to participate in a scheme to evade VAT. Kerr LJ said that the relative moral culpability of the parties may be relevant in ascertaining whether employment law rights would be unenforceable because the underlying contract was tainted by fraud. On the facts the Court of Appeal held that public policy did not operate to render illegal the employees' contracts. There was nothing in the contracts of employment which stated that the workers had to participate in the fraud. They did not benefit from it. It was the employers' duty to make

VAT returns. The fraud would presumably have continued without the employees' participation. And if the employees lose their right to claim, others would be deterred from disclosing illegality, a significant point which is applicable to cases dealing with fraud on the Revenue instigated by employers. Therefore, in this situation employees may claim even though they know of and participate in the scheme. It may be suggested that in order to save employees being deprived of their employment protection rights, Parliament should change the law to make the doctrine of illegality inapplicable to such claims.

The doctrine of severance of illegality can apply to employment contracts (*Kearney v Whitehaven Colliery Co* (1893)). It is thought that severance of frauds on the Revenue is not permissible.

4.4.5   Severance

One last point on illegality is that a contract is unlawful if there are 'servile incidents' attached to it. Perhaps an example might be a contract of employment under which an employee agreed not to move house at all without the employers' permission.

4.4.6   Servile incidents

Because the contract of employment is a contract, there must be consideration (or a deed). There is no set form, and in general writing is not required. There are, however, some exceptions.

4.5   Form: in writing

- There are various complex rules on the right to return to work after maternity. An employee must inform her employers in writing at least 21 days before her absence because of pregnancy that she intends to return: s 33(3)(d) of the Employment Protection (Consolidation) Act 1978, hereinafter EP(C)A. If requested by her employers, she must give written confirmation seven weeks after birth that she intends to return. If the employers do so request they must include in writing a statement that she will lose her right to return unless she replies within two weeks of receipt or as soon as possible thereafter: s 33(3A) and (3B) of EP(C)A.

- An employee on a fixed term contract can agree in writing to exclude her right to a remedy for being unfairly dismissed. Similarly an employee working under a fixed term contract of two years or more can waive her rights to a redundancy in writing: EP(C)A s 142.

- Contracts of apprenticeship must be in writing and signed. The common law so states.

- A merchant seaman's contract must be in writing signed by him and on behalf of the employers: Merchant Shipping Act 1970 s 1(1). This provision applies only to seamen on UK registered ships.

- Some deductions from pay must be in writing or evidenced in writing: s 1 of the Wages Act 1986. This stipulation does not apply to deductions for industrial action. Deductions from wages for income tax, it will not surprise the reader, do not need to be in writing.

4.6   Written statement

Once an offer of employment has been accepted, there is a contract of employment in existence. Since the contract may be made orally or partly orally, partly in writing, there may be disputes over terms. The topic of implied terms is treated later. This section considers one way in which disputes over contractual issues may be avoided.

4.6.1   Basic consideration

Employers must provide to persons to whom the Act applies a written statement of the main terms and conditions of employment within two months of the employee's starting work: s 1 of EP(C)A. as amended by the Trade Union Reform and Employment Rights Act 1993. The 1993 Act substitutes new ss 1-6 into the 1978 statute. This part of the 1993 Act enacts the Written Particulars Directive (EC91/533). (This Directive has other names eg 'terms and conditions'.) Employees already in work on 30 November 1993 are not entitled to the new-style statement unless they request one. The employers have two months in which to reply. This document is also called the s 1 statement and written particulars. One can see that the statement is not the contract of employment. The contract is made at the start of employment, but the statement need not be given until two months have elapsed. Therefore, by the time the statement is given, the worker is already doing her job under a contract of employment. There are various categories of workers to whom this statement need not be given. These include merchant seamen, Crown servants, those working wholly or mainly outside Great Britain and share fishermen (ie those paid by a share of the catch). The previous exception of part-time employees was abolished by the Employment Protection (Part-time Employees) Regulations 1995, SI 31, which came into force on 6 February 1995.

4.6.2   Contents

The matters which must be included in the written statement are:

Principal statement

- the identity of the parties;

- the date of commencement;

- job title or a brief description of the work;

- whether employment with a previous employer is to be

counted towards continuity of employment (this is important because only continuous service counts towards the two-year qualification period for employees and because the amount of compensation depends on the length of continuous employment);

- the amount of pay;
- when remuneration is paid;
- any bonus or commission;
- the hours of work;
- holidays and holiday pay; public holidays;
- title of the job (employers should include wide ones, eg secretary, not typist, in order to obtain flexibility from their workforce);
- the place of work, and important matter in relation to redundancy and picketing.

The Principal Statement must be one document but particulars may be given in instalments provided that the two month deadline is not exceeded and the Principal Statement remains one document.

In addition to the Principal Statement the particulars must include:

- any terms as to sickness or injury including sick pay;
- length of notice;
- pensions, including whether there is a contracting out certificate;
- if the work is temporary, its duration;
- any collective agreements which affect the employee's terms and conditions; if the employers were not a party to the agreement, the identity of the person who made it is to be stated;
- where the employee is to work outside the UK, the period of work abroad, currency of pay, any additional benefits, and any term relating to return to the UK;
- disciplinary and grievances procedures (see the next paragraph).

These matters need not be in the same document as the Principal Statement. If not, they must be in a document (or collective agreement) which the employee has a reasonable opportunity to read in the course of employment or which is otherwise reasonably accessible. A company handbook is the sort of document which may contain these particulars.

If no particulars on any points apply, that fact must be stated (eg there may be no pension). The statement as to the length of notice may be left to the general law or to a collective agreement.

| 4.6.3 | Disciplinary procedures |

There need be no statement about discipline and grievance in relation to health and safety. Disciplinary rules need not be given in firms employing fewer than 20 employees: s 13 of the Employment Act 1989, inserting s 2A into EP(C)A. Section 2A is interesting. It was apparently introduced as a result of the government's efforts to reduce administrative burdens on small employers. One might nevertheless justifiably say that parties to a dispute should know where they stand: small employers are not exceptional. Moreover, while disciplinary and grievance procedures need not be as formal in small workplaces as in large unionised workplaces, one would expect the State to encourage the settlement of disputes without recourse to courts and tribunals. It should be noted that the ACAS Code of Practice, Disciplinary Practice and Procedures in Employment (1977), applies to all workplaces irrespective of size. Even if the employers have fewer than 20 employees, they must give details of the person to whom an individual can take grievances.

| 4.6.4 | Changes |

Any changes to the statement must be notified to the employee *individually* at the earliest opportunity not later than a month after the change (s 4). Changes in respect of matters other than found in the Principal Statement need not be given to each employee. It is sufficient that she has reasonable access to them as in a company journal. It should be remembered that the contract of employment, being a contract, cannot be changed without agreement. New particulars need not be given if the employee is re-employed within six months of leaving employment and the terms of the job are unchanged. If there has only been a change of employers, the new ones need just inform the employees of the change, but notice of the change must include the date of the start of continuous employment.

| 4.6.5 | Enforcement |

If the employers do not provide a statement or there are omissions in it and there is a dispute over the statement, they or the employee may refer the matter to an industrial tribunal under s 11 of EP(C)A as amended. There is no power to award compensation even when the applicant has suffered loss through the employers' failure to include one of the written particulars in the statement. The tribunal may confirm, amend or substitute particulars. Since the tribunal has the power to write in terms, it is better for employers to state a term at the start of the employment relationship.

Where the employers must include a matter (eg the name of the parties), the tribunal must insert a term. If the dispute relates to an item which is not mandatory (such as sick pay), the tribunal will insert a term if the parties expressly or impliedly had agreed to it. If there is no agreement, the tribunal should so state. In *Mears v Safecar Security Ltd* (1983) the Court of Appeal decided that a tribunal had jurisdiction to amend inaccurate particulars, a point which had been unclear. There is a time limit of three months from the termination of employment, or within a reasonable time thereof if it was not reasonably practicable for the employee to claim within three months. It has happened that employees who made a claim under s 11 have been dismissed for doing so. Section 60A of the Act, inserted by the Trade Union Reform and Employment Rights Act 1993, deems a dismissal for bringing such a claim an inadmissible reason for the purposes of unfair dismissal: see Chapter 11.

An industrial tribunal can declare what the parties meant to include. It cannot go further and interpret the terms. For instance, in *Cuthbertson v AML Distributors* (1975) a tribunal was able to state that an employee should not be dismissed without reasonable notice, but it could not say how long that notice was. It was for the civil courts to determine that issue. The EAT took a similar view in *Construction Industry Training v Leighton* (1978). A tribunal could declare that an employee was owed so much a year, but it could not rule whether or not that amount included a bonus. The Court of Appeal approved this stance in *Mears*.	4.6.6 Jurisdiction
The remedy is weak, and there is a possibility that if the employee did apply to a tribunal for amended particulars, she might be dismissed. From the viewpoint of employers the 1993 amendments are onerous. The response is that the statement contains the fundamental rights of the parties and may lead to the prevention of disputes.	4.6.7 Criticism
The written statement is not the contract of employment. It is only evidence of the contractual terms. If the statement is the sole evidence of the terms, it is treated as strong evidence: *System Floors (UK) Ltd v Daniel* (1982). It is not conclusive: *Turiff Construction Ltd v Bryant* (1967). It may be the law there is a heavy burden of proof on employers to show that the written statement does not accord with the contract, whereas employees have only a burden of persuasion to show the same: the *Daniel* case.	4.6.8 Legal status

4.6.9	Transmutation	There is one situation where the statement is treated (miraculously) as being the contract of employment, and that is where the employee signs it as being the contract. It is insufficient to sign it simply in acknowledgement that it has been received. This was held in the Court of Appeal case of *Gascol Conversions Ltd v Mercer* (1974). There was a dispute over the number of hours the employee had to work. The Court held that the statement which was entitled 'Non-staff employees' contract of employment' was conclusive because the employee agreed it as being the new contract. This effect was said to derive from the parol evidence rule. This case shows the importance of getting the correct term into the written statement. And since one has to get the right term into the statement, one ought to get the right term into the contract, even when the statement is merely evidence of the contract.
4.6.10	Not contract	The view is that the written statement is not a contract, subject to *Gascol*. The contrast may be seen from another Court of Appeal decision, *Robertson v British Gas Corp* (1983), which like *System Floors Ltd v Daniel* approved *Gascol*. The employee was due a bonus under his contract. The employers withdrew the bonus and said so in the written statement. The Court held that the employee was still legally entitled to the bonus under the contract. Since the statement was not the contract, it did not apply. (Indeed, the statement was not given until the employee had worked for seven years.) For the employers to win, they would have to negotiate the contract to get rid of the bonus, or use the *Gascol* approach. The fact remains that the change of such a term in the contract cannot be foisted on the employee. If there is no other evidence of the contract, saying that the written contract is not the contract of employment wears a little thin.
4.7	**Express terms**	Subject to general principles of law such as illegality and restraint of trade, the parties can agree on anything eg I can agree to serve you as a shoe-shine boy for 1p a year. Fortunately for me the courts have set their face against the specific performance of contracts of personal service. The principal remedy for breach of an express or implied term is damages. Such claims are heard in the ordinary civil courts, the county court and the High Court (normally the Queen's Bench Division). Some contracts especially of managers and specialists are formal; many are not. Express terms override particulars in the written statement. In *Hawker Siddeley Power Engineering Ltd v Rump* (1979) an oral promise that he would not be asked to work outside the South of England made when

he was being engaged overrode references in the statement to a collective agreement which provided for employees to be moved anywhere across the country.

Express terms are those which the employer and employee have agreed, whether orally or in writing. For example, if the employer says 'I offer you the post of Sales Manager at £20,000 per annum plus a car commensurate with your status' and the employee says 'I accept', there is a contract of employment with several express terms:

- the job of Sales Manager;

- the pay;

- the car.

4.7.1   Definition

To find out, for example, what the post of Sales Manager entails, or what type of car he or she will get, we have to look elsewhere, perhaps to the company handbook. Conditions set out in the handbook may be incorporated by reference into the contract of employment. Those conditions, ones which are not expressly stated by the parties, are called implied terms (see later).

It should be noted from the above that not all terms in a contract need to be express ones – indeed, it is still rare to find a contract where all the terms are expressed – but implied terms are just as binding as express ones. So, if the job description for the Sales Manager does not expressly state that part of the work involves telephone sales, but the job implicitly does, then that implied term applies just as if it were an express one. A second point to remember is that if there is a conflict between an express term and an implied one, the express term prevails, eg if a person is employed as a Sales Manager, he or she is not subject to an implied term that he or she helps out in the production process as and when required. An express term would be needed in this case. See also para 4.9.3 below.

Advantages of express terms over implied ones are as follows:

4.7.2   Advantages

- There is little or no room for dispute. Take, for example, a clause which provides 'You are employed at any of the company's factories.' A worker has made widgets all her life at the firm's Leeds works. Because of a lack of orders, the company decides to close down the Leeds works and concentrate production in Halifax. Since the employee is employed at any of the factories, there can be no dispute that the company is entitled to close down the Leeds branch and transfer the employee to the same job at

Halifax. Obviously, there will be a saving in time and money if disputes over the meaning of employment terms can be avoided. Grievance procedures and litigation are thereby avoided.

- This advantage is also perceived in legal terms. If a claim is made by the employee on the facts above, it will fail. The closure of the Leeds factory will not amount to a dismissal; therefore, there is no liability for wrongful dismissal, unfair dismissal, or redundancy payments, because each of these claims is based on the requirement of a dismissal. Even if there is a dismissal, there is no redundancy if, on the above facts, all of the firm's works have not closed. (A term which permits transfer between offices, branches, etc is generally known as a 'mobility clause'.) Another example similar to the one involving a transfer from one place to another is a term which states the employee's task in wide terms. (This type of term is sometimes called a 'flexibility clause'.) If an employee works as a press operator at a hot water bottle factory, and there is a clause stating that he is employed not just on presses but also on sweeping and cleaning duties, he is legally obliged to do those duties as well as be a press operator.

4.7.3   Disadvantage

The drawback with an express term is the converse of the advantage. If it is stipulated that an employee works in 'Leeds or Halifax', what happens if both of those works are closed down in order to create a super-factory in Bradford? Legally, the employee is not obliged to accept the transfer, and this is so despite the fact that Bradford is near Leeds and within commuting distance. If, however, there had been no express clause, a term might have been implied that, although the employee normally worked in Leeds, she could be transferred to any place within reasonable commuting distance, and the courts have been prepared to imply such a term (see later for how this is done). The tip is: draft express terms widely. Rather than say that the worker is employed in 'Leeds or Halifax' say 'anywhere in the UK' or 'any of the company's workplaces'.

4.7.4   *Nelson v BBC*

An example which, however, worked against the employers, is *Nelson v BBC* (1977). One might expect that employers would wish to argue against redundancy, because if they lose, they will have to make the statutory redundancy payment. However, if there is a redundancy, they will have to make only a payment for that, and they may be able to avoid compensation for unfair dismissal. Since the amount for unfair dismissal substantially exceeds the amount for redundancy usually, employers may for this reason argue redundancy. In *Nelson*, there was an express term that the employee would work when and where the BBC demanded. The BBC closed down its Caribbean service where he worked. The court held that, since only one of the services had been cut back, he was not redundant.

Since certain terms have to be in the written statement and since the statement can refer to other documents such as a written contract of employment, it is administratively convenient for employers to provide employees with one document. This document should be provided at the start of employment so that any disputes are nipped in the bud.

4.7.5   Advice to employers

Restraint of trade clauses are express terms which seek to restrain an employee either alone or for another firm competing with the employer during or after employment. A clause may read: 'the employee agrees that he will not solicit persons who have been clients of the company within two years preceding termination for six months after such termination'; or 'the employee covenants that she will not disclose or use any confidential information belonging to the company'; or 'the employee stipulates that he will not work in any business competing with that of the employer within a radius of five miles from Sheffield Town Hall for two years from the termination of employment'.

4.8   Restraint of trade

While the rules are easy to state, they are hard to apply, and this aspect of the contract of employment is predominantly one for the lawyers, both as to drafting and as to enforcement. The basic principle is that the courts do not like covenants in restraint of trade.

4.8.1   General

The rules were laid down at the turn of the century in a series of cases culminating in *Herbert Morris Ltd v Saxelby* (1916).

4.8.2   Basic rules

- Employers may protect only legitimate proprietary interests. While the list of those interests is not closed, in employment law there are only two such interests: trade secrets and customer connection (a no-poaching agreement seems also to fall within the doctrine). An employer cannot gain protection from competition *per se*.

- A restraint is valid only if it is reasonable both between the parties and in the interests of the public. (As stated above, there is a debate whether express terms are subject to an implied duty on employers not to exercise them unreasonably but in respect of restraint clauses there is an in-built requirement of reasonableness.)

The burden of proof is on the employers, except in relation to the public interest where it is on the party asserting that the covenant is unenforceable for this reason.

4.8.3 Secrets and connection

Trade secrets do not include:

- the employee's skill and knowledge;
- information which is publicly available;
- knowledge of general methods of running businesses.

The epitome of confidential information is a well-guarded secret formula. For customer connection to be protected, there must be recurring and influential contact. So there is a relevant connection between estate agent, a doctor, and a milkman with the client or customer, but probably not with a second-hand car salesperson.

4.8.4 Reasonable between parties

'Reasonable between the parties' means that the clause must not give the employer more protection than is necessary. If six months is sufficient to protect a hairdressing establishment, two years will be too broad, and the clause will fail. Similarly, if an area 250 yards round a salon would protect a hairdresser's in a suburb, a covenant covering the whole town is too expansive.

4.8.5 Public interest

The clause must also be reasonable in the interests of the public. Covenants concerning employees are unlikely to be struck down on this basis at present. The exceptional cases were covenants attached to pension schemes, though they can perhaps be explained on the basis that they were unreasonable between the parties: see *Wyatt v Kreglinger & Fernau* (1933).

4.8.6 Examples

There are many cases of which the following are illustrative.

- *Commercial Plastics Ltd v Vincent* (1965)

  A covenant for one year after employment was held invalid where (a) there was no limit on area, and (b) the clause covered the whole of the PVC field and not just the nearest area in which the employee was a research worker.

- *Fitch v Dewes* (1921) in the House of Lords

  A restraint on a Solicitor's Clerk that he would never work as a Solicitor's Clerk within seven miles of Tamworth Town Hall was held to be valid because the restricted area was so small.

  The rule is that the duration and area are inversely proportional to each other: the wider the area, the shorter the duration, and the smaller the area, the longer the duration.

4.8.7 Practical help

Since each case in this area is judged on its own facts, guidance is hard to give. One hint is: think of the area and time which would protect the business and then halve it. Even then employers may lose. In relation to trade secrets there need be no limit on the area or duration of the covenant.

Employers have two more bullets in their gun with regard to express restraint covenants: construction and severance.

4.8.8   Construction and severance

- The clause may be read in such a way that it is valid, provided that the parties meant it to be read in that fashion. A good illustration is *Home Counties Dairies Ltd v Skilton* (1970). A milkman covenanted that he would not 'serve or sell milk or dairy products'. One might have thought that the clause was invalid because it went beyond protecting the employee's business: it would have stopped the employee from serving in a grocer's shop. The Court, however, construed the clause to restrain only employment as a milkman, since that was the intention of the parties. 'Dairy products' was therefore construed restrictively, and the covenant was valid.

- If a clause can be construed as two promises and grammatically one of those clauses can be struck out, the remainder will be upheld if valid by itself. So, if a salesman promises not to compete for six months after termination 'in Leeds or elsewhere in the UK', the phrase 'or elsewhere in the UK' can be cancelled out, leaving a grammatically correct phrase of a covenant not to compete 'in Leeds'. If that clause passes the tests for restraint of trade, it is enforceable. If, however, the clause contains only one promise, it cannot be severed, eg in *Attwood v Lamont* (1920) the Court of Appeal held that a covenant that an employee would not serve as 'a tailor, dressmaker, general draper, milliner, hatter, haberdasher' could not be severed so as to restrain the employee from serving only as a tailor. There was only one promise. Severance in England is often called severance by the 'blue pencil' test, and will be more readily applied if there are separate clauses containing covenants rather than one 'catch-all' clause.

The clause must cover the breach. One preventing a person from carrying on a competing business does not stop him from being an employee of that business: *WAC Ltd v Whillock* (1990) a Scottish case.

4.8.9   Breach

If an employer dismisses wrongfully, ie without giving the correct length of notice and there is no justification for so doing, he cannot rely on a restraint covenant. So held the House of Lords in *General Billposting Co Ltd v Atkinson* (1909). English courts continue to affirm this rule eg *Rex Stewart Jeffries Parker Ginsberg Ltd v Parker* (1988). In that case the covenant

4.8.10   Effect of wrongful dismissal

continued to apply because the contract openly provided for termination to be with notice or for wages to be paid in lieu of notice. A summary dismissal (with wages in lieu) was therefore not a wrongful dismissal since the contract itself allowed the employers not to give notice provided that they paid wages in lieu. There is some debate whether that rule can be got round by inserting words into the clause to the effect that it will apply despite a wrongful dismissal, eg a phrase such as the covenant applies after a termination 'however caused'. There is, however, no trace of such a rule in *Atkinson*. In *Owen & Briggs v Oates* (1990) Scott J thought that employers could not evade the rule in this way. Moreover, since the policy of English law is against such promises, there is no necessity for striving to uphold them by means of such a device.

| 4.8.11 | Effect of repudiation | No doubt the principle in *Atkinson* applies where the employee is forced to leave because of the employer's repudiation of the contract, eg by not paying salary. The breach of a fundamental term has obliged the employee to quit, a situation which is known as 'constructive dismissal' in the context of statutory employment claims. |

| 4.8.12 | Fall-back position | Where the covenant is unenforceable, the employers may still be able to rely on the implied duty of confidentiality considered below at para 4.9.25. |

| 4.8.13 | Final remedies | If the covenant is enforceable, employers can claim at full trial both damages to compensate for past loss (eg the solicitation of clients) and an injunction to stop future activities in contravention of the clause. The injunction will not last longer than the period stipulated in the contract. While courts will not force an employee to work for an employer, they generally will stop him or her working for someone else, provided that there is a clause in the covenant which is both enforceable and expressed in negative terms (this is known as the rule in *Lumley v Wagner* (1852)). Accordingly, an employer can stop the employee's violating the covenant, which is a clause expressed negatively: 'Thou shalt not disclose or use trade secrets.' |

| 4.8.14 | Interlocutory injunction | The principal remedy is, however, a so-called 'interlocutory' injunction. That is one which is granted pre-trial to uphold the *status quo* before the alleged breach until trial. Since most cases do not proceed to trial, and since it is fairly easy to obtain such an injunction, employers normally have little to fear at this stage. Basically courts dealing with interlocutory proceedings are instructed not to investigate the merits in |

order to avoid a 'mini-trial'. The law on this point was laid down by the Lords in *American Cyanamid Co v Ethicon Ltd* (1975). The application of *American Cyanamid* to restraint clauses was confirmed by the Court of Appeal in *Lawrence David Ltd v Ashton* (1989). There is the possibility of an order for speedy trial. Despite the application of *American Cyanamid* to covenants, the Court of Appeal said in *Lansing Linde Ltd v Kerr* (1991) that first instance courts could investigate the enforceability of the clause at the interlocutory stage.

Both the interlocutory and final injunctions are subject to equitable principles. One effect is that an injunction will not be granted to enforce a covenant applying during employment when the issue of one would be tantamount to ordering the employee back to work for the employers. See also 7.2.24. The old employers can gain an interlocutory injunction to prevent the company which the former employee has set up from fulfilling contracts they have gained (*PSM International Plc v Whitehouse* (1992)).

In relation both to express and implied terms it is wise to remember that employees are likely to be 'men of straw' unable financially to pay damages, and that legal claims by either party to the employment contract may well exacerbate industrial relations. For these reasons actions by employers against employees are rare. For an exceptional case, see *NCB v Galley* (1958) discussed under collective agreements, below.

4.8.15   Damages not often helpful

If there is no express term, an implied one *may* take its place. If, for instance, there is no express mobility clause, the courts may imply one.

4.9   Implied terms

An illustration is *Stevenson v Teesside Bridge and Engineering Ltd* (1971), a decision of the Divisional Court. The employee, a steel erector, refused to transfer to another site from one which was near his home. There was no express mobility clause. The Court held that, since it was part of the nature of his job, and since the contract mentioned travelling and subsistence allowances, there was an implied term of mobility. In *Courtaulds Northern Spinning Ltd v Sibson* (1988) (CA) an employee was held to be under an implied duty to move to another site because he had worked there previously. His disobedience to an order to work there was a breach of this implied mobility clause and this was a breach of contract. Therefore, he was not constructively dismissed. The Court said that on the facts some term as to mobility had to be incorporated. Slade LJ stated that the term was 'one which the

4.9.1   Illustration

parties would probably have agreed if they were being reasonable, not one which the parties, if asked, would have agreed to before entering the contract'. The width of the term was determined by the parties' practice – reasonable commuting distance. The second depot was within that range.

A contrasting case is *O'Brien v Associated Fire Alarms Ltd* (1969). An electrician, who had worked exclusively in Liverpool, was asked to transfer to Barrow when orders in Liverpool dropped. There was no express agreement about mobility, and the Court held that, though there was to be an implied one, that one stretched only so far as the area of daily travel. Since Barrow was beyond that limit, the employee won. How much easier it would have been for the employers to have an express term! In *Stevenson*, there would have been no dispute: in *O'Brien* had any dispute arisen, the employers would have won it.

4.9.2	Practical guidance

The fact remains, however, that many employers do not think about the terms of employment, and accordingly the conditions under which an employee works are relegated to implied terms. The implied term which arises may not be one which the employer wanted. It is therefore worthwhile thinking seriously about either expressly agreeing on the terms orally or, better still, in writing. That way both sides know the nature of the obligations. For example, if employers do not wish to pay sick pay, it is worthwhile expressly saying so; otherwise the courts may say that the employers implicitly promised to pay sick pay.

4.9.3	How implied

There are several ways of incorporating terms, many of which apply to all contracts. It is insufficient to imply a term on the grounds that it is reasonable, the principal authority being *Reigate v Union Manufacturing Co (Ramsbottom) Ltd* (1918). In *Sibson*, above, Slade LJ said that where a contract had to have a term (eg as to place of work), 'the implied term is one which the parties would probably have agreed if they were being reasonable.' Express terms override the sort of implied terms considered in this section but not terms which are implied (or better put) imposed by statute. An implied term cannot overturn an express one. There is an on-going debate whether an express term, such as a mobility clause, can be qualified by an implied term that the express term will not be exercised unreasonably. In *Sibson*, above 4.9.1, there was a limit placed on an implied mobility term but none on the exercise of managerial discretion to move the worker between depots. *United Bank v Akhtar* (1989) supports the view that an express term can be qualified by an implied one. An express term that the employers could transfer the employee was held to be subject to an implied term that they would not do so unreasonably. An employee was not contractually obliged to uproot himself over the weekend despite the width of the express term. Similarly, in *Prestwick Circuits Ltd v McAndrew* (1991) the Court of Session held that employers must give employees reasonable notice of a change in the workplace and that on the facts a move to a factory 15 miles away needed more than a week's notice. Failure to give reasonable notice was a constructive dismissal. This case and *Sibson* look irreconcilable. In *McLory v Post Office* (1992) a contractual power to suspend was held not to be exerciseable unreasonably. In *Johnstone v Bloomsbury Health Authority* (1991), the case in which junior doctors sought to restrict their hours of duty, a majority of the Court of Appeal seemed to say that if employers asked for 168 hours per week they could do so under the contract, subject to a vaguely formulated duty not to break the health and safety legislation. *Johnstone* is not a clear authority. *United Bank* is irreconcilable with cases such as *Rank Xerox Ltd v Churchill* (1988), where the EAT held that where a term was unambiguous, the literal phrasing could not be modified by an implied term that the employers would not exercise their powers unreasonably. The effect is that employers could send an employee anywhere covered in the mobility clause, say from London to Carlisle, at any time and without a second's notice. The latest EAT case, *White v Reflecting Roadstuds Ltd* (1991), attempts to cut through this impasse by arguing that *United Bank* really decided that the employers could not enforce an express term in such a way that the employee could not perform her part of the contract. Where there do not exist reasonable grounds for moving the employee, an attempt to transfer her is a breach of a fundamental term of the contract entitling the employee to resign and claim unfair dismissal. (On the facts a contractually permitted transfer to other work was not a breach of a contractually implied condition that the power was to be exercised only in a reasonable way: an express term was not subject to any such implied term. If the move was capricious, then there would be a breach of the implied term.) This argument seems to go contrary to the Court of Appeal in *Western Excavating (ECC) Ltd v Sharp* (1978), which held that reasonableness was irrelevant to the presence of a breach of contract. Again, the debate can be side-tracked by the insertion of an express term.

Business efficacy is perhaps better put as 'business commonsense'. The term is so basic that it is needed to make the contract function. This is known as the rule in *The Moorcock*

4.9.4   Business efficacy

(1889). For instance, it may be necessary to imply a term like the place of work on this basis. It should be noted, however, that business efficacy may well work in the employers' favour. If one asks whether an employee really would have agreed to a term whereby her employers could transfer her anywhere at any time, one is likely to get a dusty answer. An example of a term implied through the business efficacy mode is *Star Newspapers Ltd v Jordan* (1994) where the EAT held that the company breached an implied term by not reconsidering the applicant's amount of commission when it reduced her area.

4.9.5	Officious bystander	If an officious bystander put it to the parties that a certain term ought to be in the contract, and the parties would say 'Oh, of course!', then that clause is implied. The case always cited for this proposition is *Shirlaw v Southern Foundries (1926) Ltd* (1939).
4.9.6	Status	The relationship of the parties may necessitate the implication of a term. Where it is essential that some term has to be included in the contract, eg whether there is sick pay, the Court of Appeal was once willing to invent a term of reasonable width: *Mears v Safecar Security Ltd* (1983) but the Court of Appeal has ruled that it is no longer open to industrial tribunals to 'invent' terms as a last resort in pursuance of their duty to determine the content of the written statement: *Eagland v British Telecommunications plc* (1992). Teachers, for example, are under a professional obligation to do marking. In *Sim v Rotherham MBC* (1986) Scott J held that a teacher was under a duty to cover for absent colleagues. He said that a professional was subject to the expectation of the public. As Keith Ewing commented in his book *The Right to Strike*, 1991, it was 'a truly remarkable development' that 'the legal obligations of employees can be set by the social expectations of third parties.'
4.9.7	Custom	A custom in a certain trade is implied into the contract, provided that it is certain, general (also called notorious) and reasonable. Some work practices fit this rule. An illustration is *Sagar v Ridehalgh* (1931). The Court accepted that it was part of the custom and practice of the Lancashire cotton industry that employers could deduct money from weavers' pay for bad workmanship. Compare *Hardwick v Leeds Area Health Authority* (1975): it was an unreasonable custom to dismiss after expiry of sick pay. 'Unreasonable' here means 'unfair'. It is thought that an employee is subject to custom even though she does not know of it (never mind accept it), but the legal position remains unclear. For example, an industrial tribunal in *Samways v Swan Hunter Shipbuilders Ltd* (1975) noted that employers knew of the practice of changing back from

chargehands to labourers (with a consequent loss of pay) but their knowledge was insufficient to convert what had happened before into a custom. The mere fact that they acquiesced in the arrangement did not signify that they had agreed to it, for a better explanation of their behaviour was that if they did not acquiesce, they would be dismissed.

Some rules in company handbooks may be held to have contractual force, but not all will. A 'work-to-rule', ie in accordance with the handbook, does not necessarily mean that the work-to-rule is valid, contractually speaking. The question is whether the parties wanted the rules to be contractually binding, eg a notice on a noticeboard about sick pay was held in one case to be binding, but a string of highly detailed rules about how to carry on the business of running a railway was held not to be binding. For a case, see below under the 'Duty of cooperation' *Secretary of State for Employment v ASLEF (No 2) (1972).*

4.9.8   Works rules

These terms are those which derive from the relationship being one of employment. Some terms are so fundamental that they are implied into every contract of employment. Terms imposed on employers can be seen as the courts' striving to restrain the freedom of managers to do as they please. Although the law is not settled, it is possible that some of these implied terms may override express terms. They are characteristic of a contract of employment, which the parties are deemed to accept. Paragraphs 4.9.10 to 4.9.20 deal with duties of employers. Paragraphs 4.9.21 to 4.9.32 deal with duties of employees. The list of implied terms is not closed. For example, on appeal from Northern Ireland the House of Lords in *Scally v Southern Health & Social Services Board* (1992) held that employers who failed to bring the right to purchase additional years of pension entitlements to the attention of doctors were in breach of an implied term to take reasonable steps to bring the terms to their notice.

4.9.9   Implied in law

While there may be highly exceptional cases where the employer is under no duty to pay wages, normally he or she is. If the amount is not fixed by the parties, the courts imply a term that the employee is to receive a reasonable amount (*quantum meruit*). In *Way v Latilla* (1937) the defendant promised to look after the employee's interests if he secured for him a gold-mining concession. The Lords held that he was entitled to £5,000 on this *quantum meruit* basis. Sometimes the contract may give the employee only the chance to earn wages. Where pay is fixed by contract, there exists a duty to continue to pay it. A non-contractual change in the method of assessing

4.9.10   Pay

pay is a breach of contract. In *RF Hill Ltd v Mooney* (1981) a change from a commission on all sales to the payment of commission only when the employee exceeded the target was a breach of contract. This term is subject to express terms. For example, a clause may permit the employer to suspend the employee without pay as a sanction for ill-discipline and indeed suspension without pay may be an implied term in some factories and trades.

| 4.9.11 | Industrial action |

While the point is not entirely free from doubt, it seems that an employee who is performing part but not the whole of the contract is entitled to payment for what is done, provided that the employers accept the work which is being done. In *Royle v Trafford BC* (1984) a teacher, who was taking part in industrial action, refused to have more than 31 pupils in his class, though he had been allocated 36. It was held that he was entitled to 31/36ths of his pay. If, however, the employers do not accept the reduced work, the employee is entitled to nothing (*Miles v Wakefield Metropolitan DC* (1987)). Equitable set-off for non-performance of duties is a possibility: see *Sim v Rotherham MBC*, above.

| 4.9.12 | Sick pay |

There is apparently a slight presumption that wages are payable during sickness but the court must look at all the facts (eg at practice) to determine whether there is a term: *Mears v Safear Security Ltd* (above). In that case, the employers had never awarded sick pay and the employee had never asked for it. Therefore, on the facts there was no sick pay. (Note also statutory sick pay under the Social Security and Housing Benefits Act 1982 as amended.) In fact some 80% of employees are covered by a company scheme.

| 4.9.13 | Short-time working |

Wages during short-time or lay-off. As with sick pay the express or implied terms govern eg there may be a custom. Without such suspension withholding pay amounts to a repudiation of the contract. Basically speaking, pieceworkers have a right to earn remuneration, as do commission workers. Therefore, without the employees' consent an employer *cannot* close down his works because of a lack of orders where employees are paid by the piece (*Devonald v Rosser* (1906)). However, the position is different where the closure is outside the control of the employer: *Browning v Crumlin Valley Collieries Ltd* (1926) – closure of pit for repairs (though it must be said that the repairs were foreseeable) – or if in the industry there is a custom that lay-offs without pay are permissible. If an employee's contract contains an express clause that he will not be paid when there is no work, then he is not entitled to pay if he is laid off during industrial action by colleagues. The express term overrides the implied one. Note also guarantee payments under the Employment Protection (Consolidation) Act 1978.

Employers must provide work for those who need publicity in their jobs, eg actors, and for those paid on commission or by piece rates. Indeed, there may be an express term to such effect.

4.9.14	Work

It may be that highly skilled employees such as computer programmers must be given work. This exception may in time swallow the rule, and it has been said judicially that more employees than previously are owed a duty to provide work. This consideration has been treated as important in a case dealing with the lawfulness of 'garden leaves' ie lengthy notice periods which the employers do not require employees to work out, the workers spending the time in the garden. The preservation of a financial director's skill was a relevant factor in holding that he could move to a competing firm before the end of his garden leave (*Provident Financial Group plc v Hayward* (1989)). Otherwise, there is no duty to provide work. In the famous words of Asquith J in *Collier v Sunday Referee Publishing Co Ltd* (1940): 'Provided I pay my cook her wages regularly, she cannot complain if I choose to take any or all of my meals out.' Perhaps nowadays, however, chefs are such publicity-seekers that we have to put them with other artistes such as actors. Failure to give work may amount to redundancy and may activate guarantee payments (both in EP(C)A). In a series of cases Lord Denning MR stated that there was a duty to provide work but these rulings such as *Langston v AUEW* (1974) seem to be part of his campaign against unions. They have not been followed since he retired.

4.9.15	No duty to provide

In *Wilsons & Clyde Coal Co Ltd v English* (1938) the House of Lords laid down a threefold duty on employers. They must take reasonable care to provide safe equipment, a safe workplace, and safe fellow employees. So the employer can sack dangerous practical jokers. There is, however, no implied term that employers will provide or give advice on insurance for workers they send abroad (*Reid v Rush & Tompkins Group Plc* (1989)). The case of *Johnstone*, above at 4.9.3, has dicta from Stuart-Smith LJ that employers could not order employees to harm their health and safety, no matter what the express term said. If he is correct, this implied duty overrides express contract clauses contrary to the classic concept of contract law. In *Walker v Northumberland CC* (1995) the High Court held that employers were under a duty not to cause psychiatric harm to an employee by overloading him with work.

4.9.16	Safety

| 4.9.17 | Property | The employer is, however, under no duty to take care of the employee's goods: *Deyong v Shenburn* (1946). Note also the Health and Safety at Work Act 1974 and the Employers' Liability (Defective Equipment) Act 1969. |

| 4.9.18 | Indemnity | An employer is under a duty to indemnify the employee for expenses necessarily incurred in the course of employment. This will cover eg defending legal proceedings for breaches committed by the employee. |

| 4.9.19 | Mutual trust | While the width of the duty of mutual trust and confidence (or respect) varies from job to job and some criticism by management must be expected in all jobs, since the 1970s there has developed a duty on employers to treat their employees with respect. They must protect employees against sexual harassment (*Bracebridge Engineering Ltd v Darby* (1990)). They must not attempt unilaterally to reduce an employee's status of pay (*Arden v Bradley* (1994)). They must not criticise employees in front of their peers (the case best remembered by students is *Isle of Wight Tourist Board v Coombes* (1976), where the EAT held that a director's statement to an employee that his personal secretary was 'an intolerable bitch on a Monday morning' was conduct which breached the duty of trust and confidence, entitling her to resign) and they should not swear at a domestic gardener (*Wilson v Racher* (1974)). The term was summarised by the EAT in *Woods v WM Car Services (Peterborough) Ltd* (1981): employers must 'not without reasonable and proper cause, conduct themselves in a manner calculated or likely to destroy or seriously damage the relationship of confidence or trust ... '. There is no need to show that the employers intended to get rid of the employee. |

| 4.9.20 | Death/injury | One point to bear in mind is that employers cannot contract out of or restrict liability to employees for death or serious injury: Unfair Contract Terms Act 1977. |

| 4.9.21 | Obedience | Employees are also subject to implied terms. An employee must obey lawful orders. The duty to obey a lawful and reasonable order has been said to be 'a condition essential to the contract of service' (*Laws v London Chronicle (Indicator Newspapers) Ltd* (1959) CA). What is lawful depends on the contract. Recall *O'Brien v Associated Fire Alarms Ltd*. The employer could not transfer the employee from Liverpool to Barrow. Therefore, the order was not lawful, and the employee need not obey it. |

| 4.9.22 | Illegality | Moreover, the employer must not order something illegal eg falsify accounts (*Morrish v Henlys (Folkestone) Ltd* (1973)), and must not command an employee to go into immediate danger |

eg *Ottoman Bank v Chakarian* (1930). It was unlawful to order the employee to go to Turkey where he was under sentence of death. However, a disagreement over policy or the implementation of policy does not justify a refusal to obey an order.

An example of a successful order is *Cresswell v Board of Inland Revenue* (1984): an order to work computers in PAYE administration was upheld because it was within the scope of the employee's duties that he would use new methods of doing his job. New methods of work after training fit under this head.

4.9.23   Duty to adapt

Like employers, employees are under a duty to use reasonable care eg not to drive so carelessly that one knocks someone down. The principal authority is the well-known House of Lords one of *Lister v Romford Ice and Cold Storage Co Ltd* (1957). And an employee is under an implied duty to be reasonably competent in the job.

4.9.24   Care

The duty of fidelity or faithful service takes several forms:

4.9.25   Fidelity

* not to take bribes;
* not to put one's hand in the till;
* not to use one's position to make a secret profit;
* not to keep secret the misconduct of colleagues;
* not to harm the employer's business by working in one's spare time for a competing business;
* not to solicit customers before employment ends;
* not to use or disclose trade secrets eg formulae, blueprints.

An employee must not copy out a list of customers if the list is secret. She can, however, make preparations to enter into competition during employment to take effect after employment. What is acceptable and what is not is difficult to state in advance.

It is this last aspect which causes most difficulty. The law is now laid down in the wonderfully named case of *Faccenda Chicken Ltd v Fowler* (1987). This important case held that after employment ended the employer was entitled to protect only such legitimate interests as may be safeguarded by a covenant in restraint of trade: trade secrets (and highly confidential information) and customer connections. It did not cover the employee's skill and knowledge such as information concerning the amount of discount his former employers gave customers: for protection against these there had to be an

4.9.26   *Faccenda Chicken*

express covenant. The duty of confidentiality after employment does not extend to the recall (as opposed to the memorisation) of information.

| 4.9.27 | Memory rule | The duty will apply not only where eg the employee has taken a written list of customers but also where he or she has memorised a list. |

| 4.9.28 | Just cause or excuse | The duty, however, is subject to an exception, that of public interest or just cause or excuse. An interesting case is *Initial Services Ltd v Putterill* (1968). Employers had established a cartel to keep up prices. They blamed a new government tax for keeping prices high. It was held that an employee was justified in revealing the companies' misdeeds to the press. The information must be disclosed to the appropriate body. In this case the press was appropriate. In other cases it may be appropriate to disclose it only to the police. |

| 4.9.29 | Remedy | If an employee has misappropriated a trade secret and disclosed it to a competitor, the employer has a whole battery of remedies available eg damages against the employee and an injunction to stop further revelations, an injunction against the competitor, perhaps damages or perhaps account of profits, and delivery up for destruction of goods made with the confidential information. |

| 4.9.30 | Patent and copyright | For patents, see Patents Act 1977, ss 39–40. Copyright normally belongs to the employer. The Patents Act overrides any contrary agreement, whereas the provision on copyright may be overridden by agreement. |

4.9.31   Cooperation

'I have no hesitation in implying a term into the contract of service that each employee will not, in obeying his lawful instructions, seek to obey them in a wholly unreasonable way which has the effect of disrupting the system, the efficient running of which he is employed to secure.'

So said Roskill LJ (now Lord Roskill) in *Secretary of State for Employment v ASLEF (No 2)* (1972). On the facts a work-to-rule was in breach of contract because it impeded the running of the employer's business. A more recent case is *Ticehurst v British Telecommunications plc* (1992) CA, where a withdrawal of goodwill by a manager (who was also a union officer) was held to be in breach of her duty as manager to advance the interests of her employers. It may be that *Ticehurst* represents a withdrawal by the judiciary. The court emphasised the position of the employee in the hierarchy, whereas in *ASLEF (No 2)* the Court of Appeal said that every contract of employment included a duty to cooperate. The duty of cooperation permits free range to managerial discretion.

Under the Health & Safety at Work Act 1974 there is a duty on employees to cooperate in the execution of duties under that statute (s 7).

An illustration of how the courts imply a term. In *Cole v Midland Display Ltd* (1973) Mr Cole was a manager hired on a 'staff' basis. He refused to do overtime without pay and was dismissed. It was held that:

4.9.32   Example

- being a member of staff meant that he was paid whether there was work to do or not;

- he was required to work reasonable overtime without pay.

    My own employers seem to rely on reasonable overtime without pay a lot!

Cf *Lawton v BOC Transhield* (1987): no implied duty to supply a reference. Employers who supply references should be careful in so doing for otherwise they may now be liable in tort for negligent misstatement (*Spring v Guardian Assurance plc* (1994) HL).

4.9.33   Reference

Express and implied terms may be conditions, warranties or innominate terms depending on their importance. For example, in *Laws* case (see 4.9.21) Lord Evershed MR said that the duty to obey was a fundamental aspect of the employment relationship.

4.9.34   Contractual effect

These are arrangements between managements and trade unions. Normally they are not legally binding ie they are not contracts between those parties: the common law authority is *Ford Motor Co Ltd v AUEFW* (1969). Nevertheless they may be incorporated into the contract of employment and so be binding between employers and employees. Even if the agreement says that it is binding in honour only it may still be contractually binding between employers and employees.

4.9.35   Collective agreements

There are several ways of incorporating terms. One is by express reference. A good illustration is *NCB v Galley* (1958). The defendant employee refused to work on Sundays. However, a term was incorporated from the collective agreement that he was to work 'as may reasonably be required', a phrase which covered Sundays. This contract referred to the collective agreement, which had become binding on him. The employee need not know of the collective agreement.

4.9.36   Ways of incorporation

Not all terms are appropriate for incorporation into an individual's contract. A quite recent case is *NCB v NUM* (1986): an agreement between these two parties to establish negotiation and conciliation procedures was not intended to take effect

4.9.37   Suitability

between the employer and the individual employees. In general, matters of policy will not be incorporated. In *Griffiths v Buckinghamshire CC* (1994) the High Court held that redundancy procedures including discussions with unions were not apt for incorporation. In *British Leyland UK Ltd v McQuilken* (1978), a collective agreement on retraining was not apt for incorporation. The distinction between those clauses apt for incorporation and others is not always clear-cut, but the principle is that purely collective matters such as recognition of the union are not suitable matters for incorporating into an individual's contract.

| 4.9.38 | 'No-strike' clauses |

There is a special process for incorporating 'no-strike' agreements formerly found in s 18(4) of the Trade Union and Labour Relations Act 1974, now the Trade Union and Labour Relations (Consolidation) Act 1992, s 180:

- it must state that there is a no-strike clause;

- it must be reasonably accessible to each employee during working hours at each workplace;

- the union must be independent;

- the contract must impliedly or expressly incorporate the no-strike clause.

In fact breach of a no-strike clause has little legal effect. Industrial action is, it seems, always a breach of contract anyway. The superadded breach of the clause does not increase damages for breach of contract. Moreover, statute forbids the courts to order strikers to return to work. The existence of a no-strike clause does not affect this prohibition.

| 4.9.39 | As implied term |

A collective agreement may also be impliedly binding on the grounds mentioned above, eg under the officious bystander test: 'Are you employed on union rates?' 'Oh, of course!' It may possibly be in small workplaces that the employee is bound by the doctrine of agency, but normally the device of agency will be inapplicable: staff turnover means that the principals are not identifiable at the time of the agency. It was said in *Joel v Cammell Laird* (1969) that a member is bound only when he knows of the agreement and accepts it and there is evidence of incorporation.

| 4.9.40 | National/local level |

If a national collective agreement conflicts with a local one, it will be a question of fact as to which prevails and is incorporated. A case mentioned already, *Gascol Conversions v Mercer*, illustrates the proposition. The national agreement stated that the employee worked a 40-hour week; the local one said he worked 54 hours. The employers gave him a written statement saying that he was bound by the national agreement and he signed it as being his new contract. As we have seen, the Court of Appeal held that he was bound by the national agreement because he had expressly agreed to it. No doubt normally, however, it will be the local agreement which will be binding because that agreement will be one which adds to the national one to adapt it to local conditions. It is worthwhile saying which agreement is the governing one.

If the clause in the collective agreement is incorporated, it will remain binding between the employer and the employee even though it has been terminated between employer and union. In *Robertson v British Gas Corporation* (1983), mentioned above, the employers repudiated the agreement with the union. It continued, however, to be binding on them and their employees. Therefore, they were in breach of contract for failing to pay incentive bonuses. That term had become incorporated into the individual contracts of each employee. There is House of Lords authority to similar effect (*Rigby v Ferodo Ltd* (1988)). The outcome is the same if it is the union which withdraws from the agreement. The same applies the other way. Once bound by the contract as incorporated from the collective agreement, an employee cannot unilaterally withdraw and say that he or she is no longer bound. Of course, the contract of employment can be terminated by lawful notice. Employees may have to 'agree' to a change or face the sack.

4.9.41   Binding nature

The position with regard to non-unionists is not settled. If the contract refers expressly to the collective agreement, the non-union member is bound, but it seems that he or she is not bound where there is no express incorporation. So if employers negotiate a change in the shift-system with the union, that will not bind the non-member (*Singh v British Steel Corporation* (1974)). The employers will have to reach a separate agreement with that person. The same principle applies where the employee is a member of a union but not of the union which negotiated the change in working practice (such as a reduction in the hours worked) (*Miller v Hamworthy Engineering Ltd* (1986) CA). The court may, however, say that among the terms incorporated into the individual contract is one whereby the parties agree to be bound to the collective agreement as varied from time to time. So the non-union member must also take the rough with the smooth. Similarly employers who were part of a federation which negotiated an agreement remain bound until renegotiation, if they knew of the collective agreement.

4.9.42   Non-union members

4.9.43	Statute	Parliament's method of making women's pay equal to that of men is through the so-called 'equality clause', if her work is so like that of the man that there are no practical differences or her work has been rated as equivalent to that of the man or the work of the woman and the man are of equal value to the employer. The women and men must be in the same employment.
4.9.44	Equality clause	The woman's contract is deemed to include an equality clause to the effect that any clause in her contract which is less favourable than a similar one in the man's agreement is treated as being no less favourable than the man's term, or if she does not have a term which the man has, her contract is deemed to include it. This law is stated in the Equal Pay Act 1970, which is the subject of the next chapter.
4.9.45	'Imposed' terms	It might be better to call terms implied by statute 'terms imposed by law'. Even had the parties thought about the matter, they may not wish to have an equality clause; such a provision is not really an implied term. Moreover, even if the parties put expressly into the contract a clause which is contrary to the statutorily imposed one, that clause is overridden by the statute. This overriding is contrary to the usual rule, that express terms prevail over implied ones. For instance, if the employer seeks to avoid the employee's rights under the Employment Protection (Consolidation) Act 1978, such a term is of no effect. In the jargon of employment lawyers, there is a 'floor of rights' for employees which the parties cannot contract out of. (As always with law there are exceptions eg an employee can contract out of a claim for unfair dismissal, provided that he or she does so in writing, the contract is for a fixed term of one year or more, and the contract is terminated by expiry of that fixed term.)
4.9.46	Length of notice	Another way in which statute has intervened in the area of express/implied terms to protect an employee is in the length of notice he or she must be given. The rules are, basically, if there is a period stated in the contract that will apply unless it is less than the statutory period. If there is no express notice period, there will be implied a period of reasonable length: what is reasonable depends on the facts of the case; if the reasonable length is less than the statute stipulates, the statutory period will take effect. The statutory period is one week for each year of service over two years up to a maximum of 12 years. It should be noted that the statutory minimum period for employees to give to employers is only one week, but this may be increased by agreement. An employee may waive the notice requirement and accept pay in lieu.

The subject of implied terms is sometimes presented in contract textbooks as being static. In fact, the topic is dynamic. The mechanism of implying terms is one of the ways in which courts and tribunals can affect the content of the employment relationship. They may use it to favour employers. In *Secretary of State for Employment v ASLEF (No 2)*, above, the Court of Appeal held that employees were under a contractual duty not to disrupt their employers' business, even though what they were doing was fully in accord with the instructions of management. However, in a series of cases in the late 1970s and early 1980s the EAT held that employers were under an obligation to treat their workers with respect. If they did not do so they were in breach of a fundamental implied term. That breach constituted a constructive dismissal; therefore, for the purposes of statutory employment rights, the employees had been dismissed. Therefore, they had a claim. With the growth of standard implied terms as an incident of the employment relationship and of terms statutorily imposed, the contract of employment is looking less like a contract and more like a status.

4.9.47   Dynamism

Employers are not permitted to alter contractual terms unilaterally, unless the clause allows such a change. A mobility clause, which was noted above at para 4.7.2, is an example of such a clause. This section discusses how employers can vary contracts where there is no flexibility under the contract at issue.

4.10   Variation

The contractual nature of the service agreement is further illustrated by the need for a bilateral alteration of the terms for the parties to vary the contract. An important case is *Rigby v Ferodo Ltd* (1988). Employers sought to impose a wage cut unilaterally. The pay was contained in a collective agreement which was incorporated into the employee's contract. The House of Lords held that the employee was entitled to the difference between the pay he received after the cut and that to which he was due under his contract. Similarly, in one of the dinner-ladies's cases, *Burdett-Coutts v Hertfordshire CC* (1984), the employers reduced pay in a one-sided (as Mrs Thatcher would say) way. The Divisional Court held that the employees were entitled to the pay agreed by the parties. A proposal to vary unilaterally an employee's hours of work coupled with a proposal to give her notice that her contract would be terminated unless she consented was held to be an anticipatory breach in *Greenway Harrison Ltd v Wiles* (1994). In *Miller v Hamworthy Engineering Ltd* (1986) the Court of Appeal awarded an employee his full wages when he was unilaterally put on to short-time working by his employers. One way for

4.10.1   Contractual nature

employers to side-step the rule as to acceptance is to insert a wide express term into the contract of employment, permitting them to do anything with regard to the employee's wages, place of work, job specification, and so on.

| 4.10.2 | Protest |

If an employee works under the unilaterally imposed conditions, after a time she will be deemed to have accepted them. Periodical protest is needed to preserve the pre-imposition terms. A case which at first sight is difficult to reconcile with this rule is *Jones v Associated Tunnelling Co Ltd* (1981). An employee was given a revised written statement. A clause purported to give his employers the power to move him from his place of work. He did not protest. They, four years later, tried to move him. He refused. The EAT held that he was entitled to refuse. His lack of protest was put down to the fact that the new clause did not affect him at the time when it was imposed. The position would have been different had the change had immediate effect, as a reduction in pay would have done. It has been held that a claim for unfair dismissal is not lost when the employee works under a new contract but objects to the change and says that he is working under the new contract without prejudice (*Hogg v Dover College* (1990)).

| 4.10.3 | Dismiss |

One contractual way for employers to obtain a variation is to dismiss employees lawfully (by applying the relevant notice period) and then re-employ them on new, revised contracts. There may be liability for statutory unfair dismissal, but none for contractual wrongful dismissal for the contract has been lawfully terminated. It seems that the words of dismissal, whether verbal or in writing, must be unequivocal; otherwise what looks like a lawful termination with an offer to re-employ will be read as an unlawful unilateral variation.

4.11   Payment of wages

Normally wages are agreed by the employers and employees often in a collective agreement. One area where the law intervenes is in relation to equal pay for men and women, which is discussed in the next chapter. This section deals with two issues in the law relating to wages: the legality of deductions and the former support for wages in various industries in the form of wages councils.

| 4.11.1 | Wages Act |

The Wages Act 1986, which replaced the Truck Acts, deals with among other matters the unlawful deductions from wages. All workers are covered except merchant seamen and those ordinarily working outside Great Britain. There are no longer restrictions on the ways in which wages may be paid. This rule is designed to facilitate cashless pay, such as by cheque or by transfer into a bank account.

The exceptions are:

- deductions authorised by statute such as tax and national insurance;

- deductions agreed in writing eg trade union dues and payments to charity;

- deductions authorised by contract.

With regard to the third exception, which largely covers deductions ('fines') for loss of stock and breakages, the Act lays down complex rules. No deduction may exceed 10% of the gross wages on any one pay day in relation to retail workers. Employers must therefore wait to recover the whole loss. In respect of stock losses, deductions must be made within 12 months of the date when the loss was uncovered or ought reasonably to have been discovered. The employer must tell the worker in writing of her total debt and must make a demand in writing for payment on or before the date of the first deduction. If the worker leaves employment, the restriction to 10% is abrogated.

Exceptions to the Wages Act are these: overpayment of wages or expenses; deductions in respect of a strike or other industrial action; and payment of a court or tribunal order requiring an employee to pay something to her employers. In these instances deductions are lawful even if they would otherwise break the Act. (It may be, however, that the deductions are unlawful on other grounds.)

Enforcement lies in the hands of the wages inspectorate, but a worker may bring a claim before an industrial tribunal for compensation or repayment. Payment in lieu of wages (except when the employers lawfully terminate the contract but do not require the employee to work out the notice period) constitutes 'wages'. Therefore, non-payment can be dealt with by the tribunal: *Delaney v Staples* (1992).

A point to bear in mind is that the Act applies only to the amount of money to be deducted. It does not affect the grounds on which money is to be deducted. Employers may deduct money for reasons which to many are not fair. For instance, it is not unlawful to have a term in the contract of employment that an employee will make up losses at a petrol station even if such a deficit is not the fault of the employee, as when a customer has acted fraudulently by passing a dud cheque.

From 1909 to August 1993 there existed wages councils which established minimum rates of pay in various low-paid industries such as hairdressing. The government considered

4.11.2   Deductions

4.11.3   Exceptions

4.11.4   Enforcement

4.11.5   Wages councils

that they interfered with the free market and finally abolished them in the Trade Union and Employment Rights Act 1993. At that time the minimum ranged between £2.66 and £3.20 per hour. The Trades Union Congress has complained to the Social Affairs Directorate of the Commission that the government has infringed Article 119 of the Treaty of Rome in that one of the 'effective means' of achieving equal pay has been abrogated. The Yorkshire Low Pay Unit reported in 1994 that pay in former wages councils' trades was being cut and there was no corresponding increase in jobs. The Agricultural Wages Board continues in existence. A study by the London School of Economics found that the effect of this Board was to increase, not destroy, jobs. The government is consulting to see whether it should be abolished. The UK is the sole EC State without provision for minimum wages.

An order of a Wages Council which took effect before abolition takes effect as a contractual term. Therefore, it cannot be varied except contractually. Employers wishing to force down wages will in law have to negotiate changes in the ways stated in para 4.10 above.

The Common Law of Contract

This chapter considers the content of common law contract of employment and the connected issue of statutory written particulars.

Common law contract

There is no set form for offer and acceptance.

Offer and acceptance

A contract of employment is binding on a minor if overall it is to her advantage: *Leslie Frewin v Chaplin* (1966).

Infancy

Contracts of employment illegal at the inception are void, but ones illegal in performance are not. There is a growing jurisprudence on the courts' and tribunals' taking into account the seriousness of the illegality:

Illegality

Newland v Simons & Willer (Hairdressers) (1981)

Coral Leisure v Barnett (1981)

Hewcastle Catering v Ahmed (1991).

Most contracts of employment need not be in writing.

Form

Parliament obliges employers to give written particulars to an employee within eight weeks of her commencing employment. This statement, which is not the contract, need not be supplied if there are in existence documents constituting the contract. Changes must be notified within four weeks. A tribunal cannot interpret the statement:

Written statement

Mears v Safecar Security (1983).

Clauses expressly agreed take precedence over ones judicially implied:

Express terms

Nelson v BBC (1977).

Negative covenants are valid only if they protect a legitimate proprietary interest, are reasonable between the parties, and are in the public interest. Covenants may be construed in order to validate them and can be severed. In the event of wrongful dismissal, the clause falls. The remedy sought is in interlocutory injunction:

Restraint of trade

Herbert Morris v Saxelby (1916)

Home Counties v Skilton (1970)

General Billposting v Atkinson (1909)

Lawrence David v Ashton (1989).

Implied terms

Terms may be implied by the judges:

business efficacy: *The Moorcock* (1889)

officious bystander: *Shirlaw v Southern Foundries* (1939)

status: *Sim v Rotherham MBC* (1987)

custom: *Sagar v Ridehalgh* (1931)

works rules: *SSE v ASLEF (No 2)* (1972).

Terms may be implied as a result of the contract's being one of employment. The following duties are imposed on employers:

pay: *Way v Latilla* (1939)

(sometimes) work: *Devonald v Rosser* (1906)

safety: *Wilsons & Clyde Coal v English* (1938)

indemnity: employers must repay employees' expenses necessarily incurred in performing the contract, such as travel costs for sales representatives.

mutual trust and confidence: *Wilson v Racher* (1974).

Employees are also subject to implied duties:

obedience: *Cresswell v Inland Revenue* (1984)

care: *Lister v Romford Ice* (1957)

fidelity: *Faccenda Chicken v Fowler* (1987)

cooperation: *ASLEF* (above).

Collective agreements can become part of an employee's contract either expressly or impliedly. Non-union members may be bound. Not all collective terms are appropriate for industrial enforcement. There is a special procedure for 'no-strike' clauses:

NCB v Galley (1958)

NCB v NUM (1986).

Terms may be implied by statute, the example being the 'equality clause' in the Equal Pay Act 1970.

Variation

Varying the terms is possible only bilaterally:

Burdett-Coutts v Herts CC (1984).

Payment of wages

The Wages Act deals with deductions from wages. Wages councils formerly provided minimum wages in some low-paid Industries.

Chapter 5

Equal Pay

The Equal Pay Act 1970 was intended to increase women's hourly earnings to the same level as those of men. Initially the Act, which came into force in 1975, had some impact on female wages but the position has for some years been stabilised. Women continue to earn less than men overall. The present figure is that women's hourly pay is about 75% of that of men. It is thought that much of the difference is explained by women's traditional responsibility for child care. They often leave employment to have and look after children and then return to work at a lower post than the one they left. Male earnings in manual jobs are often boosted by overtime pay, which means that gross pay difference is more substantial than the 75% figure would suggest. The weekly earnings of female manual workers are only 60% of that of men. If women have to look after children, they cannot do overtime. Some women may form part of the 'secondary labour force'; that is, unlike 'core' male workers they are brought in to work only when the going is good for the firm; they are also the first to be sacked during a recession. Many women work in 'occupationally segregated' jobs ie ones in which there are few or no male employees. These jobs, such as industrial cleaners, canteen assistants, and typists, tend to be low-paid, perhaps because there are so few men working in them. There is some suggestion that women face a 'glass ceiling'. They rise so far in corporate hierarchies but discrimination by men keeps them out of the top jobs. Women often work in jobs which are poorly unionised, and they suffer poorer wages as a result. Moreover, women often work in jobs which fit in with their child-care responsibilities. Many part-timers do not have access to all the perks which full-time employees have. As with the law on sexual and racial discrimination the Equal Pay Act is aimed at undermining stereotypical images, in this instance of women being worth less to employers than men.

The 1970 Act applies only to terms of employment. It does not apply pre-employment, for example at interviews. Where this statute does not apply, the Sex Discrimination Act 1975 may apply. The courts have said that the two Acts fit together like a jigsaw puzzle to form one code. In general the Equal Pay Act applies to contractual benefits, the Sex Discrimination Act to non-contractual ones such as promotion. 'Pay' is not restricted to money but extends to equivalents such as concessionary

5.1 Equal pay: introduction

5.1.1 Application

coal. The Equal Pay Act is not restricted to employees but applies also to independent contractors who personally do the work (s 1(6)(a)). While the principal beneficiaries have been and were intended to be women, the Act also applies to men who are not treated as favourably as women. There are exceptions to the Act: terms affected by protective legislation (s 6(1)(a)); terms connected with pregnancy or childbirth (s 6(1)(b)); and terms related to or connected with retirement and death (s 6(1A)(b)).

| 5.1.2 | Equality clause |

The main thrust of the Act can shortly be stated. By s 1(1) a woman's contract is deemed to include an equality clause, which states:

- if any term of her contract is less favourable than a similar clause in a man's contract, her term is deemed to be no less favourable; and

- if her contract does not include a beneficial term which is in a man's contract, her contract is deemed to include that term. If the applicant wins she may be awarded damages (s 2(1)) or arrears of pay, but the claim for both is limited to the previous two years: s 2(5).

This limit may be inconsistent with *Marshall v Southampton and South-West Hampshire Area Health Authority (No 2)* (1993). Claims are made to industrial tribunals. There is no age limit, qualifying period, or minimum hours of work. The burden of proof is on the applicant. According to *British Railways Board v Paul* (1988) there is no time limit for an applicant to bring an equal pay claim but this case has been judicially criticised (and it can be confidently asserted, is wrong: *Etherson v Strathclyde RC* (1992), a Scottish case). It should be noted that the woman cannot obtain a proportional amount of the man's wage. If, for example, she earns at present 60% of a man's pay, but should earn 75%, she cannot get the 75%, for that amount is not equal pay. If, however, she is at present earning less than the man, but should be earning more, she can be awarded equal pay, at least when EC law applies (*Murphy v Bord Telecom Eireann* (1988)). The point is moot in English law (in *Waddington v Leicester Council for Voluntary Services* (1977) it was held that a female employee who worked more than a man was paid less could not obtain equal pay!) but it is suggested that it is the same as EC law. Accordingly, if a woman earns now 60% of the man's pay, but she should earn 115%, the tribunal inserts an equality clause to give her the man's pay (ie she obtains 100%, but not 115%).

| 5.1.3 | Male comparator |

For there to be an equality clause the woman must be able to compare herself with a man in the same employment (the male comparator) and both must be employed on 'like work', 'work rated as equivalent', or 'work of equal value'. The woman can choose which man she wishes to have as her male comparator (*Ainsworth v Glass Tubes Ltd* (1977)). She may choose more than one comparator. The Court of Appeal in *British Coal Corporation v Smith* (1994) held that the chosen man had to be a representative of the class of male employees from which he was selected. If he is not, the employees have a material factor defence (see 5.1.14). In that case all the applicants had chosen more than one comparator and most had selected men from different establishments. There is difficulty in finding male comparators in occupationally segregated industries. The applicant need not compare herself with a worker doing a similar task eg an administrative worker can compare herself with a male executive (see below for equal value). It should be noted that separate claims must be brought by each woman, even though several or even thousands of women are claiming, using the same male comparator. While representative actions are possible, there is no 'class action' in the UK.

The restriction to 'same employment' means that the woman cannot compare her pay with that of men in other firms or industries. However, being in the same employment covers men working for companies associated with her employers: s 1(6). By that sub-section 'same employment' is defined as the same establishment or at different establishments where common terms and conditions of employment apply. A nursery nurse and a member of the clerical staff had each common terms when a collective agreement applied to both (*Leverton v Clwyd CC* (1989)). In *British Coal Corporation v Smith*, above, the CA held that female canteen workers and cleaners were not in the same employment as male clerks and surface workers. The fact that they worked at different establishments and there were incentive bonuses and concessionary coal for the surface workers undermined the conclusion that all worked under common terms and conditions, namely the national agreement. In other words 'common terms and conditions' means 'same terms and conditions', and having one term the same does not mean that there are 'common terms and conditions'. EC law may be to different effect. Section 1(6) is being undermined by the move from collective bargaining to individual agreements: fewer workers will have common terms and conditions. Though the Act was not so worded, as a result of EC law a woman can compare her pay with that of a male predecessor in her job: *Macarthys Ltd v Smith* (1980), a decision of the European Court of Justice. It is thought that a woman can compare her pay with that of a male successor in her job. It would be helpful to have the Act amended to take account of these developments.

5.1.4   Same employment
          (s 1(6))

5.1.5 **Like work** (s 1(2)(a))	One of the three ways in which a woman can compare her wages with those of a man is if they are engaged on 'like work' for the same or associated employers. This term is defined in s 1(4) as being work 'of the same or broadly similar nature'. Any difference not 'of practical importance' is to be disregarded. The tribunal should take a broad-brush approach to whether the jobs are similar. In one case the fact that the woman prepared 10 or 20 meals for doctors at lunch-time, whereas the male comparators provided more meals at different times of the day, did not by itself signify that they were not doing broadly similar work (*Capper Pass Ltd v Lawton* (1977)). Tribunals must investigate the work which the woman and the man actually do. The employment of a man to deter trouble-makers at a betting shop does not justify a difference in pay if he has not been trained for the job or there never has been any trouble (*Shields v E Coomes (Holdings) Ltd* (1978)). It is irrelevant that the men were contractually obliged to undertake additional work if they did not in practice do so. For example, in *Electrolux Ltd v Hutchinson* (1977) the EAT disregarded the fact that the men had to transfer to other jobs (if there was a demand) and to work overtime (if there was a demand) because in practice they rarely performed these functions.
5.1.6 **Practical difference**	The time at which women and men work is irrelevant if the duties are in practice the same or broadly similar. Accordingly, the fact that women work on day-shifts, the men at night, does not matter. There may, however, be a bonus for anti-social hours working, provided that the bonus is based on the anti-social nature of the time of work and not on any difference of sex (*Dugdale v Kraft Foods Ltd* (1976)). Extra responsibility through working at night is the sort of factor which means that the two jobs are not broadly similar. Working alone at night was held to be a practical difference from working in a group during the day in *Thomas v NCB* (1987). A man's responsibility for items of greater value than those for which a woman was responsible defeated her claim in *Eaton Ltd v Nuttall* (1977). A mistake by him would be more serious than one by her.
5.1.7 **Work rated as equivalent** (s 1(2)(b))	The second way in which a woman can obtain equal pay with a man working in the same employment is if their jobs have been equally ranked by a job evaluation scheme. The survey is binding even though the employers have not put it into effect (*O'Brien v Sim-Chem Ltd* (1980)). It must, however, have been accepted as valid by the parties (normally employers and the union) who agreed to carry it out (*Arnold v Beecham Group Ltd* (1982)). The employers cannot be forced to carry out job ranking.

The Court of Appeal in *Bromley v H & J Quick Ltd* (1988) held that the evaluation had to be done analytically. That is, it is not sufficient that the study was performed subjectively. The survey has to look at each element in both jobs and compare them; it is illegitimate to undertake what is called 'whole-job' comparison. The study must not itself be so sexually biased that the discrimination appears on the face of the record or is fundamental (*Eaton Ltd v Nuttall*, above).

5.1.8   Analytical nature

When the Equal Pay Act was originally passed, only the first two methods of acquiring equal pay were available. By acceding to the European Communities the UK accepted the Treaty of Rome. Article 119 of that Treaty, inserted as a result of French insistence, states that 'men and women should receive equal pay for equal work'. The UK government contended that the two methods of claiming equal pay, 'like work' and 'work rated as equivalent', matched up to EC norms ie Article 119 was restricted to these methods. This view was successfully challenged by the EC Commission. As a result of the ruling of the ECJ in *EC Commission v UK* (1982) the government enacted a third mode of acquiring equal pay, 'work of equal value' by inserting a new paragraph into the 1970 Act by means of the Equal Pay (Amendment) Regulations 1983 (SI 1983/1794). The ECJ held that the law before the amendment did not conform with EC law in Article 119 because workers could not ask a judicial body to do, or order to be done, a job evaluation study. The government reacted with bad grace and instituted a long-winded procedure for resolving equal value claims.

5.1.9   Equal value
(s 1(2)(c))

The amended Act states that a woman is entitled to equal pay if her work:

> '... is, in terms of the demands made on her (for instance under such headings as effort, skill and decision) of equal value to that of a man in the same employment.'

5.1.10   Definition

For instance, in *Hayward v Cammell Laird Shipbuilders Ltd* (1988), a woman's claim that her work as a cook was of equal value to that of men working as painters, joiners and thermal insulation engineers was upheld. The Lords emphasised that the woman's application was successful if one of her terms of employment fell short of one of the terms in the men's contract. It was immaterial that her 'job package' ie the overall pay elements in her job were equivalent to or better than the job package of the men. Concern has been expressed that there could be 'leapfrogging' pay claims. If her pay was, for example, increased to the men's level, the effect might be that her supervisor's pay might be less than the woman's revised pay.

The supervisor might, therefore, put in a claim for increased pay to preserve her differential. The effect might be to destroy (to 'dynamite' is the term used) long-established pay structures. Moreover, since the comparison is between individual terms in the contract, not between the female and the male job package, it could be that some terms in the men's contract are less favourable than terms in the woman's contract. The effect of the *Hayward* case is to give men the opportunity to claim that an equality clause should be inserted into their contracts to equalise upwards all their unfavourable terms and conditions. In fact perhaps because of the lengthy procedure of equal value claims, leapfrogging does not seem to have occurred. The European Court of Justice in *Barber* (1990) also said that each individual term has to be compared. The 'package' approach therefore cannot now be adopted by domestic courts or by Parliament. The *Hayward* case also illustrates how long-winded the process can be. The case took four years to conclude.

5.1.11   Procedure

As stated, the procedure is complex. The equal value process was strongly criticised by Wood P in *Rankin v British Coal Corporation* (1993). The claimant starts the application in the tribunal. If there are no reasonable grounds for determining that the work is of equal value (including the material factor defence), the claim is dismissed. Since 1994 a material factor defence cannot be considered at a later stage if it was considered at this stage except in exceptional circumstances: Industrial Tribunals (Constitution and Rules of Procedure) (Amendment) Regulations 1994 (SI 536). If there are reasonable grounds, the case gets farmed out to an independent expert on industrial claims, that person being on a panel nominated by ACAS. The expert drafts her report, taking into account representations made by the parties. She has no power of access to the employers' premises. She is under the legislation expected to produce her report within 42 days. Since December 1993 she has been under a duty within 14 days of the commission to tell the IT when she expects to submit the report and must inform the tribunal of any delay. In fact the report can take up to two years. The delay has been a source of constant criticism. Similarly, the expert has no power to order a person to give evidence. The report is not binding on the tribunal (*Tennants Textile Colours Ltd v Todd* (1989)). Throughout the expert is striving to see whether the women's and men's work are of equal value. The tribunal is under a duty to consider whether the result the expert has reached is one which could reasonably be reached. She must comply with the procedural requirements laid down by Parliament, and the report can be excluded if it is defective for some material reason or is perverse as to its conclusions. Challenges to the report must be made at this stage. If the report is not accepted, the tribunal instructs another expert. On acceptance the tribunal holds a hearing. The expert can be cross-examined. The parties are allowed to call one of their own experts to challenge the tribunal's expert's conclusions. Usually the tribunal will accept the expert's decision, at least when it is unchallenged. If the report is rejected, the IT may commission a new report.

An equal value claim cannot be heard if there has been a job evaluation study which has ranked the comparison job unequally, provided that the study is not vitiated by sexual bias (s 2A(2)). Surprisingly, the claim is blocked if the survey is completed at any time before the final hearing: *Dibro Ltd v Hore* (1990). The study will be vitiated if, for example, it ranks characteristics which have traditionally been recognised as feminine (eg manual dexterity) less than traditionally male traits (such as strength to lift heavy objects). The burden of proving that there has been an unbiased survey is on the employers.

5.1.12   Defence

The House of Lords held in *Pickstone v Freemans plc* (1988) that an equal value claim cannot be stopped even if there are men other than the comparator who are doing 'like work' to the woman or whose jobs have been rated as equal by a job evaluation study. Accordingly, if a woman chooses a mode not in these categories, her claim can proceed. This ruling was given in spite of the wording in s 1(2)(c), for the Lords considered that EC law gave women a right to claim that their jobs were of equal value to those held by men. The right is free-standing, not dependent on whether the woman could rely on 'like work' or 'work rated as equivalent'. If, however, she chose as her male comparator a man working on 'like work' or 'work rated as equivalent', then and only then did she not have a right to make an equal value claim.

5.1.13   No token male

By s 1(3) a woman loses her claim if her employers prove that the variation 'is genuinely due to a material factor which is not the difference of sex'. 'Due to' connotes causation. The employers' intention is irrelevant just as it is in discrimination cases (*British Coal Corporation v Smith*, above at *Ratcliffe v North Yorkshire County Council* (1995)).

5.1.14   Genuine material difference: defences to equal pay claims (s 1(3))

It used to be common to divide the defences of employers into two 'material difference', which applies to 'like work' and 'work rated as equivalent', and 'material factor', which applies to the equal value claim. In relation to 'like work' and 'work rated as equivalent', the defence is one of a material factor which *must* be a difference between the man's and the women's case. In relation to 'equal value' the material factor *may* be a difference between the woman's and the man's case.

This division, however, has been largely rendered otiose by the House of Lords' decision in *Rainey v Greater Glasgow Health Board* (1987). Nevertheless, it remains convenient to retain the distinction.

The following have been held to be material differences:

- grading scheme: *National Vulcan Engineering Insurance Group v Wade* (1978);

- having acquired a training role and being involved in teaching others: *Baker v Rochdale Health Authority* (1994);

- long service, superior qualifications, higher output, different location: *NAAFI v Varley* (1977): paying 'London weighting' to a male but not paying a supplement to a female employee of the same firm in Sheffield can be justified on this basis;

- economic necessity which leads to a later female employee being paid less than an earlier male one: *Albion Shipping Agency v Arnold* (1982);

- newcomer's wages protected when he joined an NHS department from private practice as a prosthetist: *Rainey* (above);

- full-time employment when part-timers were not as economically productive as full-timers: *Jenkins v Kingsgate Ltd* (1981);

- a mistake by the employers in placing the comparator higher on the pay scale than the applicant: *Yorkshire Blood Transfusion Service v Plaskitt* (1994). The error must be one that was genuine and the employers must try to end the anomaly: *Young v University of Edinburgh* (1995);

- 'red-circling' ie preserving wages of an employee's previous job when he works on a less well-paid job, provided the red-circling is not the result of sex discrimination: *Snoxell v Vauxhall Motors Ltd* (1977). The red-circle must be phased out within a reasonable time: *Outlook Supplies Ltd v Parry* (1978). If the reason for the difference disappears, so should the red-circle: *Benveniste v University of Southampton* (1989). Accordingly, a female lecturer appointed at a low point on the wage scale because of economic necessity should have her pay raised once that necessity has disappeared.

In *North Yorkshire CC v Ratcliffe* (1994), which was heard with the case of *British Coal Corporation v Smith*, the court held that variation in pay caused by compulsory competitive tendering was a material factor.

The Court of Appeal held in *Calder v Rowntree Mackintosh Confectionery Ltd* (1993) that where the employers relied on two or more genuine material differences, they do not have to prove which proportion each element contributes to the whole. A bonus for working on rotating day shifts was justified by the disturbance caused to men working on it. The same Court held in *British Coal v Smith*, above, that there cannot be a material factor defence to an equal value claim where there is direct sex discrimination, for if there is, the employers have treated the applicant less favourably than a man 'on the grounds of her sex'. For example, if women's rates were depressed in order to win a tender, there would be discrimination (*North Yorkshire* (*obiter*)).

In *Reed Packaging Ltd v Boozer* (1988) the EAT held that lower female pay was justified when it resulted from two different collective bargaining systems. The use of two systems was administratively justified within *Rainey*. The Scottish EAT in *Barber v NCR Manufacturing Ltd* (1993) ruled that collective bargaining explained but did not justify differences in pay; whereas in *British Coal Corporation v Smith*, above, the Court of Appeal considered that separate pay structures for men and women were justified because they were not tainted with sex discrimination. The European Court's decision in *Enderby v Frenchay Health Authority* (1993) which requires the difference to be objectively justified and not due to sex supports the Scottish EAT's approach. Employers cannot justify having separate collective bargaining agreements even if those arrangements are not discriminatory in themselves: separate pay bargaining is not by itself an objective justification, though if it is not tainted by discrimination, it may be an element in determining whether there was such justification according to the Court in *British Coal*. *Enderby* also demonstrates the effect of the lack of a 'class action'. 1,395 female speech therapists brought a claim and the industrial tribunals had difficulty coping. In the *British Coal* case there were 1,286 applicants, mainly canteen workers, working in 258 establishments.

5.1.15   Separate pay systems

The burden of proof is on the employers. The standard of proof is on the balance of probabilities. It is not sufficient for the employers to show that they did not intend to discriminate on grounds of sex. What they have to show is that they have objectively justified grounds for the difference: *Rainey*, applying the European Court of Justice's authority of *Bilka-Kaufhaus GmbH v von Hartz* (1986). It is for the national Court to determine whether there was justification. The Court of Justice held that differential pay could be justified only when the factors distinguishing the men's and women's

5.1.16   Burden of proof

remuneration:

> '... correspond to a real need on the part of the undertaking, are appropriate with a view to delivering the objectives pursued and are necessary to that end.'

The ECJ clarified the issue of proof in *Enderby v Frenchay Health Authority* by placing it on the employers once the employee has shown that statistics disclose a significant difference in pay between two jobs, one largely undertaken by men. The burden of proof, it was said in *British Coal Corporation v Smith*, above, is not necessarily discharged by showing that there was no direct sex discrimination within the 1975 Act of that name. Market forces can be taken into account.

5.1.17   Economic forces

The 'material factor' defence was intended by the government to be wider than the material difference defence in that it would also cover economic realities and market forces. In fact *Rainey* has extended the 'material difference' defence to include these matters. Any distinction is now nebulous. The Lords in *Rainey* who considered that administrative efficiency (which need not be based on economic forces) would provide the employers with a defence if their firm was not concerned with trade or business, but the main effect of *Rainey* is to give employers a defence to all three modes of claiming equal pay when economic factors dictate that the woman gets less pay than the man. This ruling is inconsistent with earlier cases which said that differences in pay were justified only where there was a difference in the 'personal equation' between the woman's and man's case, such as when he had undergone training courses but she had not. Nowadays extrinsic factors such as market forces are relevant. The principal criticism of this development is that the reasons why women are paid less than men include market forces. To allow free rein to the defence negates the whole point of the equal pay legislation. The Court of Appeal said in response to this point that the market forces must be ones which are untainted by sexual discrimination (*British Coal Corporation v Smith*, above).

One unresolved matter is whether under s 1(3) each individual term has to be compared or whether the whole job package is the point of comparison. As we have seen, the Lords in *Hayward v Cammell Laird Ltd* held that in relation to s 1(2)(c), the equal value claim, each term in the woman's contract must be compared against each term in the male contractor's contract. In *Hayward*, Lord Goff thought that the employers could have a s 1(3) defence if the female employee had better sick pay and pension but the men had higher pay, ie if overall the jobs were such that there was no genuine material difference (see also *Leverton*, above). On the facts of

Hayward the woman's and the man's pay package were determined through different pay structures. Lord Goff considered that the material difference defence failed however, where sexual discrimination was part of the pay structures. It may be that Lord Goff's approach has been undermined by the decision of the European Court of Justice in *Barber v Guardian Royal Exchange Assurance Group* (1990), which is dealt with in the next section. *Barber* held that each part of the pay package has to be compared. Therefore, looking at the package in the round was not·acceptable. *Barber* was, however, concerned with the situation when the males and females were governed by one pay structure and is not necessarily applicable to cases such as *Hayward* where there are two structures, neither of which is discriminatory. The Court of Justice resolved this issue when it considered the claim of (female) speech therapists to be doing work of equal value with (male) pharmacists in *Enderby* (above). The employers unsuccessfully argued that any unintentional indirect pay discrimination was the result of separate bargaining procedures, neither of which was in itself discriminatory. *Reed Packaging Ltd v Boozer*, above, is overruled. The ECJ held that whether economic forces justify the difference is a matter for national courts, which should take into account the general principle of proportionality found in EC law.

The width of this exception undermines the thrust of the equal pay law.

The differences of the Equal Pay Act from the Sex Discrimination Act should be noted.

5.1.18   Differences from SDA 1975

- The Equal Pay Act does not apply to unequal pay on the basis of marriage, whereas the Sex Discrimination Act prohibits discrimination against married people.

- For the Equal Pay Act to apply there must be an actual male comparator; for the other Act to apply it is sufficient to compare the woman with a hypothetical male. The EOC proposes to abolish this requirement in the Equal Pay Act in order to improve the pay of women in occupationally segregated industries.

- The Equal Pay Act does not expressly deal with indirect discrimination, whereas the Sex Discrimination Act does. However, the Employment Appeal Tribunal held in *Jenkins v Kingsgate Ltd* that the 1970 Act does apply to indirect discrimination. The basis for this decision was that the 1975 Act prohibits indirect discrimination; the two Acts form part of one code; therefore, the Equal Pay Act must also prohibit indirect discrimination which affects terms of employment.

There is debate whether the same test for indirect discrimination applies to both of the Acts. *Staffordshire CC v Black* (1995) states that the English law on indirect discrimination applies to equal pay claims brought under Article 119: there must be a requirement or condition with which considerably fewer women than men can comply and the emplyers cannot justify the difference. It is suggested that this case is inconsistent with the ECJ decision in *Enderby* above, which disapproved of applying the rules on indirect discrimination to equal pay claims.

• The Equal Pay Act does not require a 'requirement or condition' when dealing with indirect discrimination in 'pay', whereas the Sex Discrimination Act does.

5.2   Effect of EC law

As stated previously in this chapter, in some respects Article 119 is more generous to women than English domestic law. See the case of *Macarthys Ltd v Smith*, mentioned above. In such circumstances applicants can rely on EC law and can do so in an industrial tribunal. There is some doubt noted in Chapter 2 whether a tribunal does not have jurisdiction in such circumstances but this point seems now to have been settled in favour of jurisdiction. The early EAT case of *Amies v ILEA* (1977) which denied jurisdiction has not been followed: see eg *Albion Shipping* (above) and *Griffin v London Pension Funds Authority* (1993). The same point could have been at issue in the cases in English courts where domestic law fell short of EC norms but the assumption has been that industrial tribunals have jurisdiction. There is jurisdiction to hear claims falling under the Treaty of Rome and EC directives. It has been held that where English domestic law gives a remedy equivalent to that of EC law, the tribunal should not consider EC law (*Blaik v Post Office* (1994)). Only where English standards fall short of EC law should EC law be investigated.

5.2.1   Direct effect

Article 119 is directly effective insofar as the discrimination is direct. The ECJ at first restricted this point to discrimination which was 'direct and overt' (ie obvious on its face) (*Defrenne v SABENA* (1976)) but has since widened the right by dropping the need for overtness. However, where the discrimination is indirect, the ECJ held in *Jenkins v Kingsgate Ltd* (1981) that Article 119 was not directly effective. Accordingly, on this point English law which prohibits indirect discrimination in pay (*Jenkins v Kingsgate Ltd* when the case came back to the EAT) is wider than EC law. For example, in *British Coal Corporation v Smith*, above, the Court of Appeal ruled that giving concessionary coal to (male) mineworkers but not to (female) canteen workers was indirectly discriminatory and the difference had not been justified. The ECJ has now, however, moved to holding that indirect discrimination is covered by EC law. By Article 119, the 'equal pay for equal work' principle, as clarified by the Equal Treatment Directive (below), is not restricted by a narrow view of what constitutes pay. It includes:

- concessionary fares for retired workers: *Garland v British Rail Engineering Ltd* (1982);

- sick pay: *Rinner-Kühn v FWW Spezial Gebäudereingung GmbH* (1989);

- paid leave for taking part in training courses: *Arbeiterwohlfahrt der Stadt Berlin v Bötel* (1992);

- pension scheme supplemental to the State provision: *Bilka-Kaufkaus* (above). This is so even though the occupational pension simply substitutes for the State pension: see *Moroni v Firma Collo GmbH* (1994); access to occupational pension schemes must be given to to married women (*Fisscher*, 1994, and *Vroege* 1994) and to part-timers (*Vroege*); pension schemes must not discriminate against men; the right to join these schemes is not affected by *Barber*;

- occupational pension schemes linked to the State retirement age: *Barber v Guardian Royal Exchange Assurance Group* (1990); survivor's pensions are included: *Coloroll Pension Trustees Ltd v Russell* (1994) ECJ; however, pensions paid by statutory authority are excluded: *Griffin v London Pensions Fund Authority*, above, a case seemingly wrong after the ECJ decisions on pensions; the *Barber* case is limited to benefits in respect of periods of employment after the date when the case was decided: eg *Neath v Hugh Steeper Ltd* (1994); (*Neath* and similar cases are in accord with the Maastricht Protocol mentioned in 5.2.2); *Neath* and *Coloroll* furthermore affirm that sex-based actuarial factors are permitted in determining the amount of pensions;

- *ex gratia* payments and contractual and statutory redundancy payments: see *Barber*. *Barber* may also qualify the principle stated in the next but one paragraph. *Barber*, moreover, held that the English method of comparing each term (the *Hayward* case) was correct.

- retirement ages: *Marshall v Southampton & South West Hants Area Health Authority*, a decision which led to equalisation in the Sex Discrimination Act 1986, s 2, which amends s 6(4) of the Sex Discrimination Act 1975, rendering illegal discrimination in relation to retirement, promotion, demotion, training, transfer, and dismissal. The decision also led to the amendment of s 64(1)(b) of the Employment Protection (Consolidation) Act 1978 in respect of the exclusion from unfair dismissal law of persons above the 'normal retiring age'.

5.2.2   Extent of *Barber*

As a result of *Barber* some employers have been equalising retirement ages at 65. Pension rights must be equalised upwards after the date of Barber, but inequality is permissible before then in respect of pension benefits based on service before *Barber (Smith v Avdel Systems Ltd* (1994) ECJ). Trustees may raise the pension age to 65 to equalise benefits but if they do so, men's benefits will have to be raised to the women's level from the date of *Barber* to the date of equalisation (*Coloroll Pension Trustees Ltd v Russell* (1994) ECJ). The changes to pension rights made by the ECJ are to be put into a statute. It should be noted that *Barber* does not apply to single sex pension schemes (*Coloroll).* There are vast financial implications in the outcome of these cases. The Maastricht Treaty has a Protocol under which *Barber* is restricted to prospective application. The Protocol applies to benefit to pension schemes. It does not affect the right to join schemes. This right applies from 1976, the date when the ECJ ruled that Article 119 was directly effective. The temporal limitation in *Barber* does not affect the right to join. A worker can therefore join a pension scheme retrospectively but must pay the missing contributions. National limitation periods apply. The ECJ has ruled that *Barber* is prospective unless the claim was lodged before 17 May 1990, the date of *Barber*, in *Ten Oever v Stichtung Bedrijfspensioenfonds* (1993) ECJ among others. The effect is to undermine the fundamental nature of the right to equality, a right which indeed the ECJ reaffirmed in its reasoning in some of the 1994 cases involving pensions; full equality will take 40 years.

5.2.3   Article 119's limits

The ECJ has held that Article 119 does not cover deductions from gross pay which are paid into a company pension scheme even though such deductions were not made from female workers' pay (*Newstead v Department of Transport* (1988)). The Court held that such deductions did not constitute a difference in pay, which Article 119 requires. Moreover, social security schemes which are laid down by the State do not fall within the concept of 'pay' (*Defrenne v Belgium* (1971)). Payments to employees who retire early ('bridging pensions') to tide them over until the State pension age is not discriminatory (*Birds Eye Walls Ltd v Roberts* (1994) ECJ). The payments on redundancy found in the Employment Protection (Consolidation) Act 1978 were held, however, 'pay' within Article 119 by the House of Lords in *R v Secretary of State for Employment ex p EOC* (1994). 'Pay' covers within Article 119:

'... any other consideration, whether in cash or in kind,

which the worker receives, directly or indirectly, in respect of his employment from his employers.'

The fact that 'pay' does *not* arise out of the contract of employment is immaterial; it can arise out of the State's action in legislating on the subject of 'pay'. For example, the EAT ruled in *Mediguard Services Ltd v Thame* (1994) that compensation for unfair dismissal was 'pay' within Article 119, thereby clarifying the effect of the *EOC* case: the ECJ has not ruled on this matter but there is little doubt that the EAT is correct. By comparison there is no definition of 'pay' in the 1970 Act.

On its face Article 119 is restricted to 'equal pay for equal work'. That idea has been read as covering what in UK terms is equal pay for work of equal value.

5.2.4   Equal value covered

The EC enacted the Equal Pay Directive (EC 75/117) in order to explain the width of the principle of equal pay for equal work in Article 119. It states that that principle:

5.2.5   Equal Pay Directive

'... means, for the same work or for work to which equal value has been contributed, the elimination of all discrimination on grounds of sex with regard to aspects and conditions of remuneration.'

As stated in Chapter 2, directives are enforceable only against emanations of the State: see *Marshall v Southampton & South West Hants Area Health Authority*, above. Accordingly, the Equal Pay Directive is effective only against State organs. Since, however, the Directive clarifies the extent of Article 119 rather than is a separate source of law, this restriction has not had much effect. Similarly, the wider the ambit of Article 119, the less need there is to rely on the Equal Treatment Directive 1976 (EC 76/207), which of course is directly effective only against emanations of the State. Article 119, when it is directly effective, is so against both State and private employers. As the European Court held in *Barber*, above, benefits paid by employers which are connected to an employee's compulsory redundancy fall within Article 119 as being 'pay' and, therefore, an employee can rely on the horizontally direct effect of Article 119, even though the benefits also fall within the Equal Treatment Directive, which is, however, only vertically directly effective. Similarly, in *Mediguard*, above, the decision that compensation for unfair dismissal falls within Article 119 means that the dismissed employee has a claim against private employers as well as against employers who are emanations of the State.

In *Handels-Og Kontorfunktionaerernes Forbund i Danmark v Dansk Arbejdsgiverforening* (1989), the 'Danfoss' case, the European

5.2.6   *Danfoss* case

Court of Justice held that under the Directive pay differentials between men and women such as those found in incremental pay schemes had to be justified without reference to sex in order that they could still be lawful. Adaptability could be a lawful criterion if the criterion was important for the performance of the job. It could not be justified if it was not so related but simply had the effect of leading to the underpayment of women. The Court said that increments linked to seniority did not in general require justification, the argument being that experience is linked to performance. However, in criticism it may be said that the connection is not a necessary one. In some jobs such as assembling electrical components experience does not lead to increased productivity. It was also stated that the concept of transparency does not require employers to demonstrate exactly how they determined that the premium pay for a certain additional criterion was to be such and such an amount. The European Court seems to have resiled from its position in *Danfoss* when it said in *Nimz v Freie und Hansestadt Hamburg* (1991) that increments based on length of service require justification. What the Court of Justice is seeking is 'transparency'. That is, a woman must be able to work out why she has been placed at a certain pay point. If it is not transparent as to why she has been placed where she has been, the burden of proof is on the employers to demonstrate that their pay structure is not discriminatory. For example, merit pay must be justifiable.

5.2.7   Exclusions

The Directive in Article 7(1)(a) excludes provisions in relation to death and retirement 'and the possible consequences thereof for ... benefits'. Nowadays this exemption is read narrowly: see *Marshall* and *Barber*.

5.2.8   Objective justification

The European Court of Justice has allowed employers to have a defence to a claim of indirect sexual discrimination in pay when the difference is objectively justified. In *Rummler v Dato-Druck GmbH* (1987) the Court upheld a job evaluation study in a collective agreement by which points were awarded for muscular effort. The applicant argued that this criterion benefited men more than women. The Court did not accept her contention. It said that such a factor was permissible, provided that it was objectively justified. However, this criterion had to be balanced by factors which traditionally favoured women (presumably matters such as manual dexterity). Once the factors had been set out, the evaluation of them, eg by awarding so much weighting to each factor, must not disadvantage employees of one sex: if it did, there was the possibility of indirect discrimination. There is some debate at present whether direct justification can ever be justified in EC law. Certainly it cannot be in UK national law.

One way of viewing the effects of EC law on the Equal Pay Act is that the former impliedly amends the latter. If, however, UK law is more favourable than Article 119 as restated in the Equal Pay Directive, UK claimants can rely on domestic law. If EC law is wider than UK law, UK claimants can use EC law as a 'free-standing' right enforceable by industrial tribunals. One difference between the two sets of laws arises from *Stadt Lengerich v Helmig* (1995) ECJ. The Court held that a rule giving part-timers overtime pay only when they had worked the same number of hours full-timers worked before getting overtime payments was not discriminatory because part-timers and full-timers were treated alike. In domestic law there was a requirement or condition: part-timers must work full-time hours before receiving extra pay: could considerably more men than women comply? Was the rule justified? Just as the law on trade unions has been consolidated, it would be helpful for students for the domestic and EC law of equal pay to be put into one statute for reference purposes, though students should recall (see Chapter 2) that Articles of the Treaty of Rome may be directly applicable. Integration is necessary, for the law can be bewildering.

5.2.9   General

Some criticisms have already been mentioned such as the 'volleying' of equal pay claims – from UK law to EC law back to UK law – the interrelationship between the Sex Discrimination and Equal Pay Acts, and the issue whether either UK or EC law covers indirect discrimination. On the last point the matter is crucial for UK women in relation to their employment law rights. Unlike the Sex Discrimination Act there is no express reference to the concept of indirect discrimination in the Equal Pay Act. However, as we have seen, the English courts have read such a concept into the 1970 Act. The European Court of Justice has also used the disparate impact argument in cases such as *Kowalska*, above. In that case the Court held that a redundancy scheme which excluded part-time workers was discriminatory. The effect of the scheme was that substantially more women than men were excluded from the benefits. The Court determined that part-timers should receive the money on a pro rata basis. This reasoning is important to UK women, for some 90% of part-timers in the UK are women, one of the highest proportions in the Community.

The EOC has strongly criticised the detailed workings of the equal value claim. In *Equal Pay for Men and Women –*

5.3   Critique

Strengthening the Acts, 1990, it proposed among other matters that some experts should work full-time, that experts should be trained and they should be able to inspect the workplace. Time limits were also recommended in order to quicken the long-winded procedure. The report is worth studying by students in order to understand both the law and criticism of it. For instance, in relation to procedure the Commission proposes that employers should be obliged to give equal pay to all women in the same employment who do 'like work' with a woman who has succeeded in her claim. This statutory duty would be a method of getting round the lack of a 'class action'.

Equal Pay

The Equal Pay Act 1970 is aimed at the upwards equalisation of women's pay with that of men. It operates by inserting a contractual 'equality clause', if the woman is engaged on 'like work', 'work rated as equivalent', or 'work of equal value'. Like work is defined as the same work or work which is so similar that there is no practical difference between the man's and the woman's job. Work rated as equivalent is where a job evaluation study has ranked the jobs equally. Work of equal value occurs where the jobs are of the same worth to the employers as determined by an independent expert. Employers have a defence of genuine material difference; examples are red-circling, London weighting and incremental payments for long service:

Shields v Coomes (1978)

Bromley v Quick (1988)

Hayward v Cammell Laird (1988)

Rainey v Greater Glasgow Health Board (1987).

Effect of EC law

EC law based on Article 119 of the Treaty of Rome has extended English law, but at present important issues await resolution by the ECJ:

Barber v Guardian Royal Exchange (1990).

Smith v Avdel Systems Ltd (1994).

Pay is widely defined under EC law and covers, for example, occupational pension schemes and payments on redundancy: *Barber*, above.

The width of Article 119 is clarified by the Equal Pay Directive 1975. The European Court of Justice is seeking 'transparency' in payment systems and distinctions in pay are permitted only when they are necessary and appropriate. It is thought that separate collective agreements for men and women which in themselves are not discriminatory has not survived scrutiny by the ECJ where female and male earnings are unequal.

Criticisms

The law and procedure are complex, not found in one place, and in places they are uncertain:

R v SSE ex p EOC (1993).

The equal value process has been severely criticised because of its long-windedness, the lack of expertise of the independent 'experts' and the time it takes to draft the report. To understand the law, knowledge of UK and EC law is needed, and several points remain unclear. In the future pressure will build up for the repeal of laws which exclude part-timers from benefits on the ground that such workers are more likely to be women than men. A recent attempt, supported by the Equal Opportunities Commission, failed. The government believes itself under a duty not to increase burdens on business.

Chapter 6

Discrimination on the Grounds of Sex or Race

The law on sexual bias in employment was laid down in the Sex Discrimination Act 1975 (SDA), that on racial discrimination in the Race Relations Act 1976 (RRA). The two statutes are similarly phrased. For example, both Acts prohibit indirect discrimination. To avoid duplication this chapter will refer to sex discrimination except where racial discrimination law exhibits differences. One difference is immediately evident: the SDA prohibits discrimination on the grounds of sex, whereas the RRA forbids discrimination on the grounds of race. (There are difficulties with persons who have been discriminated against on both grounds ie black women: they may be more than doubly disadvantaged.) One other difference needs noting. The list of exceptions to sexual discrimination is longer than that to racial discrimination. One may wish on the grounds of decency to prevent men from using women's lavatories, but there would be an outcry if black men were prohibited from entering (white) men's lavatories. This topic is dealt with under the exceptions to the SDA and RRA, below. The enforcement methods of the Equal Opportunities Commission and the Commission for Racial Equality are considered in Chapter 2. They have issued Codes of Practice on discrimination (SI 1985/387 and SI 1983/1081 respectively). As with equal pay there is a Directive on sexual discrimination (76/207). Being a directive it is only vertically directly effective (see Chapter 2). The House of Lords ruled in *R v Secretary of State for Employment* (1994) that the provisions (now repealed) in the Employment Protection (Consolidation) Act 1978 which prevented part-time employees from claiming a remedy for unfair dismissal contravened this Directive. The government swiftly introduced legislation to give effect to this ruling in the Employment Protection (Part-time Employees) Regulations 1995 (SI 1995/31).

6.1 Introduction: basic approach

The aim of the Acts is to provide equality of opportunity. There is little attempt to provide equality of outcome. What is sometimes called positive action, the specific encouragement of, say, Asian women to apply for places on training courses where they are underrepresented is permitted but in general 'reverse discrimination' is not eg a firm cannot decide just to employ Afro-Caribbean men in the workforce because they are not represented at all, for that would be discrimination against white people. While the Acts are directed at discrimination

6.1.1 Aim

against women and blacks, they also apply to discrimination against men and white persons. It is moot how far the Acts have eradicated discrimination. The Conservative government may see the acts as burdens on business but no attempt has been made to repeal them.

6.2   Coverage: effect and width

Until quite recently the law *per* Lord Davey in the House of Lords in *Allen v Flood* (1898) was that:

> 'an employer may ... refuse to employ [a person] from the most mistaken, capricious, malicious or morally reprehensible motives that can be conceived but the workman has no right of action against him.'

In general this statement remains true today. The rules of natural justice do not apply to prospective employees. Employers can turn down people whom they consider too old, too experienced, and so on. A trade union can refuse to employ a full-time official because no money is available. The SDA changed the position in relation to sex. The Act prohibits discrimination on the grounds of sex against women and men before, during, and after employment. Accordingly, it applies even when no contract is in existence such as at the interview stage pre-employment. The Act also forbids discrimination on the grounds of married status (s 3) but not on the grounds that the applicant is single and victimisation on sexual grounds. The Race Relations Act 1976 also changed the law laid down by Lord Davey. The Acts extend beyond employees and apprentices to cover those working under a contract to do work personally (eg a self-employed plumber who does the job herself). An example of coverage is an articled clerk (*Oliver v J P Malnick & Co* (1983)). An insurance agent working on a commission-only basis was held to be working under a contract to perform the work personally (*Hill Samuel Investment Services Group Ltd v Nwauzu* (1994)). The definition excludes some jobs eg a postmaster for he or she does not have to do the work personally, just supervise it (*Tanna v Post Office* (1981)). Members of the armed forces used to be exempt from the requirements of the Sex Discrimination Act but they no longer are except where the discrimination is done to ensure effectiveness in combat: Sex Discrimination Act 1975 (Application to Armed Forces etc) Regulations 1994 (SI 3276) with effect from 1 February 1995. In relation to employment matters the forum is the industrial tribunal. There is no qualifying period or minimum number of hours. The claim must be made within three months of the prohibited act or omission unless the IT considers it just and equitable to extend the limit: SDA, s 76, RRA, s 68. The ECJ held in relation to the SDA that that statute did not fully implement EC law (*Marshall v Southampton and West Hampshire Area Health Authority (No 2) (1993)*). Time limits where English law falls short of EC norms do not run until the date of the full transposition of EC law into English law (that is, not from the date of the ECJ judgment); otherwise individual rights under EC law would not be protected. In that eventuality the limit must not be less favourable than domestic limits, or perhaps it must be a reasonable one (*Rankin v British Coal Corporation (1993)*). Someone who has lost under English law but then discovers that EC law is wider can bring a claim in an IT in reliance on EC law provided that she does so within a reasonable time of the clarification of EC law.

The Acts apply to employment at an establishment in Great Britain only: SDA, s 10; RRA, s 82. Therefore, a cashier on a cross-channel ferry is not covered (*Haughton v Olau Lines (UK) Ltd (1986)*).	6.2.1 Territorial ambit
Employers are responsible for the acts of their employees who discriminate unless they show that they took reasonably practicable steps to stop discrimination (s 41 of the SDA, s 32 of the RRA). The employers' lack of knowledge and lack of approval are irrelevant. An equal opportunities policy or a policy of investigating every complaint of discrimination is evidence that the employers are taking such steps to prevent discrimination, but the section does require them to take 'such steps as [are] reasonably practicable to prevent the employee from doing that act', which can be read as '*all* such steps' for only then will discrimination be averted.	6.2.2 Vicarious liability
It is unlawful for employers to give instructions to discriminate. Aiding or pressuring another into discrimination is illegal (SDA, s 42, RRA, s 33). Inducement to racial discrimination is also unlawful: RRA, s 31.	6.2.3 Instructing discrimination
Discrimination on the grounds of sex, marital status and race are discussed below.	**6.3 Grounds**
The SDA applies to discrimination against women and men (s 2(1)). Within the Act 'women' means 'biological woman'. A woman who dresses as a man and for many years has been treated as a man remains a woman for the purposes of the SDA. For the present English position in relation to pregnancy, see Discrimination in dismissal, below.	6.3.1 Sex
The SDA, s 3(1), prohibits discrimination against married people. It does not, however, forbid discrimination against single people. This distinction looks inelegant and appears to	6.3.2 Marital status

fall short of the Equal Treatment Directive (EC 76/107), which prohibits discrimination 'in particular by reference to marital or family status'. Marital status assuredly includes the status of not being in a marital situation ie being unmarried. An early case exemplifies the effect of s 3(1) and the near-absurdity it can give rise to. In *Bick v Royal West of England School for the Deaf* (1976) an employee was dismissed one day because she was going to get married on the next. She had no claim since at the time of dismissal she was not married.

6.3.3   Race

The RRA is not restricted to 'race' in any narrow sense but extends to 'colour, race, nationality or ethnic or national origins' (s 3(1)). None of these terms is defined in the Act. The landmark authority is *Mandla v Dowell Lee* (1983). Lord Fraser, relying on New Zealand authority, said that:

> '... a group is identifiable in terms of its ethnic origins if it is a segment of the population distinguished from others by a combination of shared customs, beliefs, traditions and characteristics derived from a common or presumed common past, even if not drawn from what in biological terms is a common racial stock.'

The last phrase extends coverage of the RRA to converts to religions included within the term 'ethnic origins'. In *Mandla v Dowell Lee* Sikhs were covered. In view of that decision and the policy behind the Act Jews are covered, and the EAT did not doubt in *Seide v Gillette Industries Ltd* (1980) that the conclusion was correct. However, adherents of other religions and sects such as Catholics, Moslems, and Rastafarians (*Crown Suppliers (PSA) v Dawkins* (1993)) are not included because they do not fall within Lord Fraser's definition. (In fact there are conflicting tribunal decisions on Moslems. In one tribunal case *Hansard* was used to demonstrate that 'Asian Muslims' fell within a protected class. I thank my former student, Mohammed Dosanjh, for this information.) In England, Wales and Scotland there are no laws expressly forbidding religious discrimination. From the viewpoint of religion present law appears absurd eg Jews are protected but Moslems are not by the law of racial discrimination, but the outcome is consistent with Lord Fraser's definition. After all, Parliament could easily have added 'religion' to s 3(1) but it did not.

6.4   Definition

Sexual and racial discrimination are prohibited when they fall within the relevant statute. The several types of discrimination are discussed below.

6.4.1   Disparate treatment/impact

Both the SDA and RRA prohibit two forms of discrimination. There forms are generally called 'direct' and 'indirect'. The US terminology is 'disparate treatment' and 'disparate impact', those terms perhaps reflecting more closely what is prohibited than the English terms do. Indirect discrimination was included by the then Home Secretary, Roy (now Lord) Jenkins, as a result of a visit to the USA. He was convinced that the law should root out practices which disfavoured women as well as straightforward discriminatory treatment (eg 'no women need apply'). Indirect discrimination is the tool for testing hidden or institutional discrimination.

Both Acts require a comparison to be made between the man (or white) and the woman (or black). The necessity for comparison has caused problems in relation to pregnancy. The issue is noted at 6.5.4. The next sections deal with the modes of discrimination forbidden by the Acts.

6.4.2   Comparing

This form occurs where a man treats a woman less favourably than he treats or would treat a man. Unlike in the Equal Pay Act 1970 there is no need for an actual male comparison. A 'hypothetical male' is used – would these employers treat a (hypothetical) man more favourably than they treated this woman? An example occurred when the army gave a smaller amount of non-statutory redundancy payments to members of the Women's Royal Army Corps than to similarly placed male soldiers. The Southampton IT held in 1995 that the women were entitled to compensation of £6–7,000 after the Ministry of Defence admitted liability. Since an aim of the law is to avoid employers' using stereotypes about women, discrimination is prohibited only if it was done on the grounds of sex. Accordingly, if the employers rejected a puny woman because the job required a strong person to do it, she has not been discriminated against because the unfavourable treatment, the rejection of her job application, is not on the grounds of her sex but because she cannot do the job. (See below for indirect discrimination.) If, however, all women were rejected because the employers considered that all women were weak, then the applicants would have been rejected on the grounds of their sex, for not all women are weak. Pregnancy discrimination is direct discrimination. For discussion see below at 6.5.4. It has been held that it is not discrimination to apply a dress code to both sides but to have different constituents in the code for each sex (*Burrett v West Birmingham HA* (1994)). The fact that a female nurse thought it demeaning to wear a cap when men did not was not 'less favourable treatment'. It was a matter for the tribunal to decide on the issue. The difference in uniform was not less favourable treatment to the woman.

6.4.3   Direct (s 1(1)(a))

Contrary to early authority, the law is that the employers' motives are irrelevant. (See also para 6.4.8 below.) If they

6.4.4   Motive irrelevant

think that it is not in the woman's best interests to promote her, there is discrimination. An important case is *Ministry of Defence v Jeremiah* (1979). The defendants refused to allow women to work in part of their plants. They did so because the job was dirty. However, there was more money in doing that job than in the work which the women actually did. The Court of Appeal rejected the idea that the employers' chivalry provided them with a defence. Their motive was irrelevant. (In fact it was the men who were claiming: why should they alone do the dirty jobs?) Similarly, a refusal to employ a black person will be discriminatory even if opposition to his appointment among the workforce would lead to industrial strife.

| 6.4.5 | Example |

Hurley v Mustoe (1981) illustrates direct discrimination. A woman was sacked because the employer had a policy of not employing married women. He considered that because of their child-care responsibilities these women would be more likely to take time off to the detriment of his restaurant business than unmarried women without children. It was held that the rule was discriminatory against women and it contravened the prohibition of discrimination on grounds of marital status. This case shows the law's attack on stereotypes. (See also below.)

| 6.4.6 | *De minimis* |

There is a possibility that discrimination will not be unlawful if it is *de minimis*. Lord Denning MR was of this view in *Jeremiah*, above. The contrary view is that all sexual and racial discrimination should be expunged and, therefore, the *de minimis* exception should not apply. Eveleigh LJ said so in the non-employment case of *Gill v El Vino Co Ltd* (1983). Another issue resolved in *Jeremiah* was that men were discriminated against by being given dirty jobs, which were not given to the women, even though the employers compensated them for the dirt. Differently put, employers cannot buy the right to discriminate on sexual or racial grounds.

| 6.4.7 | Activating cause |

One limitation on direct discrimination should be noted. The discrimination must be the 'activating cause' of what the employers did: *Seide v Gillette Industries Ltd*. It is not sufficient that discrimination existed as a background factor. The fact that Mr Seide was Jewish was not the activating cause, just a factor explaining why the employers acted as they did in response to complaints about him. There is, therefore, no liability for racial or sexual discrimination if the treatment was caused by non-racial or non-sexual grounds. Presentation of the issues at the tribunal can affect the outcome.

| 6.4.8 | Objective cause |

There has been extensive discussion in the cases whether or not the employers' intent or motive is relevant in discrimination cases. The principal authority is *James v Eastleigh Borough Council* (1990). The Council gave free admission to their swimming-pool to women over 60 and men over 65. Those ages were the State pension ages. Men aged 60–64 had to pay, whereas women of the same age did not. The Lords held that the charging of fees to men aged 60–64 was discriminatory. Using the 'but-for' test, men would have been treated as favourably as women but for their sex. The Council's motive (to benefit the poor) or intention was irrelevant. The sole intent which is relevant is the intent to do the act/omission which is alleged to be discriminatory. The Lords' decision was only by a 3:2 majority (though it had earlier reached the same decision in a case involving the allocation of grammar school places) and has been criticised, but to the present author it seems correct both on the wording of the statutes and in terms of policy. One criticism which has been made is that, since damages are not awardable for unintentional indirect discrimination, but are awardable for intentional indirect discrimination (see Remedies, below), damages are available both for intentional and unintentional direct discrimination. This argument, however, fails to prove that the sole type of direct discrimination is one where the employers intend to discriminate. Perhaps intent is relevant at the stage of assessing compensation; it is not relevant at the earlier stage of inquiring whether or not there has been direct discrimination.

Two cases have been selected to demonstrate how the law has been used to attack stereotyping by employers. In *Horsey v Dyfed County Council* (1982) the Council refused to send the applicant on a training course in the London area. Her husband was employed there. They assumed that she would stay in London on completion of the course and not return to her job with the Council. The EAT said that the Council would not have treated a married male employee in the same way if his wife lived near London. Accordingly, there was discrimination. In *Coleman v Skyrail Oceanic Ltd* (1981) a female booking clerk was dismissed when she married a man working for a rival firm. The Court of Appeal held that her sacking was discriminatory: the employers had assumed that the husband would be the breadwinner. The width of such cases should be noted. If this female employee was dismissed for giving up her job to join her husband or for divulging confidential information to her partner, she would not have been dismissed on the grounds of her sex (though she might have been dismissed unfairly).

6.4.9   Stereotypes

One aspect of disparate treatment is sexual harassment. In *Porcelli v Strathclyde Regional Council* (1985) the (Scottish) Court

6.4.10   Sexual harassment

of Session held that sexual harassment such as a male's putting his hand up a woman's skirt did constitute discrimination for the man would not have acted in like manner towards another man. Calling out 'Hiya, big tits' to a woman is directly discriminatory. The remark is sex-related and would not have been said to a man (*Insitu Cleaning Co Ltd v Heads* (1995)). 'Harassment' is an ill-chosen word (and not one which appears in the statute) insofar as it connotes a sequence or series of acts. There is no doubt that one act is sufficient (*Bracebridge Engineering Ltd v Darby* (1990)). In *Insitu* the EAT said that whether one act was sufficient to found a complaint was a matter of fact and degree for the IT. Conduct of a sexual nature which may be welcome from one colleague may not be welcome when performed by another; in the latter event there can be sexual harassment. It seems to be the law that there will not be discrimination if the affected employee was sensitive to the alleged harassment but a reasonable employee would not have been. There have been decisions which can be seen as anti-women. In *Wileman v Minilec Engineering Ltd* (1988) the EAT gave only a small amount of compensation because the applicant wore 'provocative' clothes and was in the habit of 'flaunting herself'. In *Snowball v Gardner Merchant Ltd* (1987) the EAT permitted cross-examination concerning a woman's consensual sex life to see whether she had suffered a detriment in relation to unwanted advances and in *Stewart v Cleveland Guest (Engineering) Ltd* (1994) displaying nude pin-ups of women did not amount to treating the applicant less favourably than men. All these decisions are controversial.

6.4.11   EC on harassment

The EC has become increasingly interested in sexual harassment. It commissioned a study (*The Dignity of Women at Work* by M Rubenstein, 1987), has issued a Code of Practice (1992), and has made a Commission Recommendation (1991) that Member States adopt the Code. The Code speaks of 'unwanted conduct' but that does not mean 'that a single act can [n]ever amount to harassment because until done and rejected it cannot be said that conduct is "unwanted". We regard this argument as specious. It it were correct it would mean that a man is always entitled to argue that every act of harassment was different from the first and that he was testing to see if it was unwanted: in other words it would amount to a licence for harassment ... the word "unwanted" is essentially the same as "unwelcome" or "uninvited".' The definition of sexual harassment in the Recommendation is:

> '... conduct of a sexual nature, or other conduct based on sex affecting the dignity of men and women at work, including conduct of superiors and colleagues.'

Pressure is building up for a directive on sexual harassment. The EAT in *Wadman v Carpenter Farrer Partnership* (1993) advised ITs to have regard to the Recommendation.

Indirect discrimination (s 1(1)(b)) is defined as occurring where the employer applies to a woman a requirement or condition which he applies or would apply to a man but:

6.4.12   Indirect discrimination

- which is such that the proportion of women who can comply with it is considerably smaller than the proportion of men who can comply with it; and

- which he cannot show to be justifiable irrespective of the sex of the person to whom it is applied; and

- which is to her detriment because she cannot comply with it.

An example is *Price v Civil Service Commission* (1978). The Civil Service had age limits of 17 to 28 for the job for which the applicant wished to apply. She was over 28. The Employment Appeal Tribunal held that the rule's effect was to discriminate against women because in practice fewer women than men could apply for the job when they were aged between those age limits because they were away from the labour force having and rearing children. Although women were not physically prevented from applying for the job, in practice the condition of being aged between 17 and 28 affected women considerably worse than men. It was to their detriment because a woman over 28 (such as the applicant who was 35) could not get the job, and the employers could not demonstrate that the rule was justified. In *Meade-Hill v The British Council* (1995) the Court of Appeal held that a mobility clause was indirectly discriminatory because fewer married women than men could comply in practice with the requirement that they transferred to any part of the UK as the defendant required – at that stage it was for the employers to justify the inclusion of the clause. Similar is *Clarke v Eley (IMI) Kynoch Ltd* (1982). The firm was faced with selecting workers for redundancy. Part-timers were chosen to be sacked first. The EAT held that the company's selection, the condition or requirement, amounted to indirect discrimination. The part-timers were women. They could not comply in practice with the requirement that they work full-time in order to avoid redundancy. It was to their detriment for they were dismissed. And the requirement could not be justified. It was said in *Brook v London Borough of Haringey* (1992) that a policy of 'last in, first out' was justifiable because it was accepted industrial relations practice, even though women would be more likely to be

6.4.13   Examples

dismissed than men because of their absence from the labour market through rearing children. In *Home Office v Holmes* (1984) the employers refused to allow a woman with children to do part-time work. They did not attempt to justify the requirement of full-time work. The requirement was discriminatory. However, full-time work may be part of the nature of the job. In *Clymo v Wandsworth LBC* (1989) the EAT instanced the post of managing director. In other words in that instance the necessity to work full-time would not be a 'requirement or condition' within the statute. However, an obligation on a cleaner to work full-time would be a requirement or condition. Northern Ireland prefers *Holmes* to *Clymo*. Full-time working can become part of the nature of the job and a requirement or condition (*Briggs v North Eastern Education and Library Board* (1990)). English tribunals may follow this lead.

If a woman moves from full-time to part-time work, say when coming back after child-birth, she cannot choose to work only those hours which suit her (*Greater Glasgow Health Board v Carey* (1987)).

6.4.14   'Must'

In *Perera v Civil Service Commission* (No 2) (1983) the CA held that the phrase 'requirement or condition' was a 'must'. That is, absolute qualifications for a job, in this case that the applicant be a barrister or solicitor, constituted a requirement or condition but factors influencing the decision to employ, such as whether the job applicant could communicate well in English, were not. With regard to three cases just noted, in *Price* there was a requirement or condition that the women be aged 17–28. In *Clarke* there was a requirement or condition that part-timers be dismissed first. In *Home Office* there was a requirement or condition that employees worked full-time. The 'requirement or condition' bar has been criticised on the basis that it may not match up to EC norms, which require only a discriminatory 'practice'. That term can cover criteria which are not absolute bars. Obviously at present employers can evade the law by making absolute bars into discretionary factors. *Perera* was followed by the Court of Appeal in *Meer v LB of Tower Hamlets* (1988) but Balcombe LJ thought that the case may be inconsistent with the purposes of the legislation. Both the CRE and the EOC have called for the repeal of the necessity for an absolute bar and its replacement by the phrase 'practice or policy'. The ECJ ruled in the equal pay case of *Enderby v Frenchay HA* (1994) that no 'requirement or condition' rule applies in relation to discriminatory pay but the EAT held in *Bhudi v IMI Refiners Ltd* (1994) that the rule continues to apply to sex discrimination law outside the field of pay.

Considering the words 'considerably smaller proportion' one might expect that if no woman could comply, indirect discrimination would not apply, for 0% is not a considerably smaller proportion but no proportion at all. This argument was rejected, however, in *Greencroft Social Club and Institute v Mullen* (1985). In *Wetstein v Misprestige Management Services Ltd* (1993) the EAT held that the question whether one group was considerably smaller than another was a question of fact for the tribunal. Therefore, it could not interfere with an IT decision that the number of Jews who could comply with a requirement that they work on Friday evenings in winter (90–95%) was not considerably smaller than non-Jews who could comply (100%). 'Considerably' means 'much' or 'a good deal'. It does not mean 'worthy of consideration' (*McCausland v Dungannon DC* (1993)), a decision of the Northern Ireland Court of Appeal on the Province's fair employment legislation which is worded similarly to the English sex and race statutes. The Court said that whether one pool was considerably smaller than another was a matter for the IT members in their role as an industrial jury. The difficulty is that employers cannot say whether the pools are discriminatory without an IT decision.

The Court of Appeal in *Jones v University of Manchester* (1993) approved guidance in a social security case as to how the pool should be chosen: '(1) Identify the criterion for selection. (2) Identify the relevant population, comprising all those who satisfy all other criteria for selection ... (3) Divide the relevant population into groups representing those who satisfy the criterion and those who do not. (4) Predict statistically what proportion of each group should consist of women. (5) Ascertain what are the actual male/female balances in the two groups. (6) Compare the actual with the predicted balances. (7) If women are found to be under-represented in the first group and over-represented in the second, it is proved that the criterion is discriminatory.' In the USA the Courts apply the 'four-fifths rule', ie if women do not, for example, form 80% of the male workforce, there is a disparity which must be explained. There is no such rule in the UK – it was rejected in *McCausland* – and surprisingly the EAT held in *Greater Manchester Police Authority v Lea* (1990) that it was unable to interfere with the 'factual' holding of an IT that 95.3% was a considerably smaller proportion than over 99%. In *Staffordshire CC v Black* (1995) 89.5% was held not to be a considerably smaller proportion than 97%. The most criticised case in this area is *Kidd v DRG (UK) Ltd* (1985). An IT determined it was not necessarily true that a greater proportion of married women looked after children than unmarried ones. The EAT held that it could not interfere for the selection of the groups for comparison was a question of fact. The comparison pools must be appropriately selected. In *Pearse v Bradford Metropolitan Council* (1988) EAT it was held that the pool was those qualified to apply for a full-time job as senior lecturer in the department of applied and community services and not just those men (47%) and women (22%) who worked full-time: in other words 'like' must be compared with 'like'.

6.4.17   'Can comply'

As *Price v Civil Service Commission* (above) demonstrates, 'can comply' does not mean 'can physically comply'. Women can comply with a requirement that they are aged between 17 and 28 when they are aged between 17 and 28. However, for various reasons they might not be able in practice to comply with that requirement. The landmark authority is *Mandla v Dowell Lee* above. A headmaster refused to let a Sikh boy wearing a turban into his Christian-ethic school. The boy could physically comply with a requirement that boys remove their headgear at school. However, in accordance with Sikh customs he could not do so. The Lords held that 'can comply' means 'can consistently with the customs and cultural conditions of the racial group' comply. Since he was forbidden by the customs of his racial group from removing his turban, he could not comply with the school's requirement.

6.4.18   Time of test

Two further points require mention.

- The time of assessing whether an applicant can comply is the time of the non-satisfaction of the requirement or condition. In *CRE v Dutton* (1989) a pub banned travellers. Some gypsies were barred. The defendant unsuccessfully argued that gypsies could in the past have stopped being travellers; therefore, they could have complied with the 'no travellers' sign.

- In *Enderby v Frenchay Health Authority* (1992), the speech therapists' equal pay case considered in the previous chapter, the EAT held that the rule that the requirement or condition was indirectly discriminatory when a considerably smaller proportion of one sex could comply with it only applied where that requirement or condition caused the unfavourable treatment. It was not sufficient that there was a substantial difference in numbers. The Court of Appeal referred the case to the ECJ which did not rule on this matter. As a matter of English law, however, it must be said that the words of the statute do not support the EAT's judgment.

Detriment means simply 'putting someone under a disadvantage': *Jeremiah*, above. There is no need for hostility towards women. The burden of proof is on the claimant. Whether something is a detriment depends on whether a reasonable worker would consider that she was disadvantaged (*De Souza v Automobile Association* (1986)). May LJ said: 'Racially to insult a coloured employee is not enough by itself, even if that insult caused him or her distress ...'. Oral racial abuse is therefore not *per se* a detriment. It should be added that *De Souza* is out of line with modern mores and has not always been followed by industrial tribunals. Examples of 'detriment' include:

- transfer to a less interesting job: *Kirby v MSC* (1980);

- searching all black workers: *BL Cars Ltd v Brown* (1983); and

- a condition of continued employment that a woman worked full-time: *Home Office v Holmes* (above).

Surprisingly, a manager's saying: 'Get the typing done by the wog' (*De Souza*, above) was held not to be a detriment for the typist was not disadvantaged in the way in which she was to do the work. Compare *Bracebridge*, above, where the harassment was by a supervisor and so done to her in relation to her employment.

There has been much debate over the width of the term justification. In the USA it approximates to 'business necessity'. UK law has fluctuated. From the viewpoint of women the nadir was *Ojutiku v Manpower Services Commission* (1982). The Court of Appeal defined the term as 'acceptable to right-thinking people as sound and tolerable reasons'. Since then on the spectrum between 'convenient' and 'necessary' the law has shifted. The latest decisions hold that the requirement or condition must be objectively justified, a definition borrowed from EC law: see the equal pay case of *Rainey v Greater Glasgow Health Board* (1987) and the non-employment case of *Hampson v Department of Education & Science* (1989), a decision which was reversed by the Lords but not on this point. For EC law see *Bilka-Kaufhaus GmbH v Weber von Hartz* (1986). The effect, said Lord Keith in *Rainey*, is to bring the law on discrimination into line with that on equal pay law's defence of material defence (s 1(3) of the Equal Pay Act 1970). *Bilka-Kaufhaus* requires:

- a real need on the part of the employers;

- their practice must be appropriate in their determination to attain their objective; and

- the practice must be necessary to attain it: if other means could be used, presumably there is no necessity and the practice is discriminatory.

These rules are much more stringent than the *Ojutiku* test.

It is not yet clear whether UK law in *Hampson* measures up to EC law. The Court of Appeal spoke of balancing the discrimination contained in the requirement or condition against the reasonable needs of the employers. The EAT spoke to similar effect in *Clymo*, above, which is an employment authority. Proportionality is the key concept, not that there is no way of achieving the object of the business. The House of Lords approved this test in *Webb v Emo Air Cargo (UK) Ltd* (1993). That test appears easier to satisfy than the *Bilka-Kaufhaus* one of real need and appropriate and necessary measures. (A reasonable need is less of a need than a real need and a balancing test seems easier to satisfy than a proportionality test.) The House of Lords in the Equal Access to employment rights case of *R v Secretary of State for Employment v EOC* (1994) accepted the *Bilka-Kaufhaus* test. Lord Keith said that the promotion of job opportunities for part-timers was a possible justification but the government had on the facts failed to justify the exclusion of part-timers from the main employment rights. Balcombe LJ in the Divisional Court in *R v Secretary of State ex p Seymour-Smith* (1994) rephrased the test as: (1) Does the measure pursue a legitimate object of social policy? (2) Is it a suitable measure for attaining that aim? (3) Is it requisite for achieving that aim? If so, the Equal Treatment Directive is vertically directly effective and the UK statute, the SDA, should be construed in conformity with it so far as possible: there is nothing in the statute to prevent such an interpretation. Be that as it may, the application of the *Hampson* test can be seen in *Greater Manchester Police Authority v Lea*, above. The employers imposed a condition that they would not accept applications from those, *inter alia*, in receipt of an occupational pension. The EAT held that this requirement was not justifiable. The condition did not reflect a need by the authority. This good motive, the desire to help unemployed persons, was irrelevant. In *R v Secretary of State for Employment ex p EOC*, above, the House of Lords held that attempts to justify the exclusion of part-time workers from a remedy for unfair dismissal failed because there was no factual objective justification of the hours thresholds for making claims. The government had argued that the abolition of the thresholds would add to the cost of employing workers and reduce job opportunities, but Lord Keith commented that there was no 'factual evidence' in support. In *Board of Governors of St*

Matthias Church of England School v Crizzle (1993) the EAT held
that the requirement of a 'committed communicant Christian'
was justifiable on the basis of the governors' legitimate and
reasonable objective of preserving the school's Anglo-Catholic
ethos. It was not out of proportion with its discriminatory
effect on the complainant, who was of Asian origin. The EAT
held that the IT was wrong to hold that the sole objective was
efficient education: if it was, the applicant was the most
suitable applicant. The EAT may have applied the *Hampson*
test incorrectly. The needs of the school eg for serving mass
could be done by other members of staff. The *Bilka-Kaufhaus*
proportionality test would overturn some English decisions. In
Kidd v DRG (UK) Ltd, above, the selection of all part-timers
before any full-time employees seems not to be justified by the
slight advantage the firm gained: the gain was not
proportional to the decision to dismiss part-timers first. It
remains to be added that justification is a question of fact:
Clarke v Eley (IMI) Kynoch Ltd above, and the House of Lords in
Mandla v Dowell Lee, above. Moreover, the application of the
test is one for the tribunals. It is possible for one tribunal to
decide one way, another to decide differently, and the EAT is
powerless to intervene, unless the outcome is perverse or a
tribunal misdirected itself as to law. An example of
justification in the race discrimination area is the banning of
beards in a chocolate factory on health grounds: *Singh v
Rowntree Mackintosh Ltd* (1979). It has been held justifiable on
non-racial grounds that the employers have a requirement for
all workers including Jews to work on the Jewish Sabbath.
However, what is justifiable in one case in relation to certain
employers may not be so with regard to all others. Payment of
a bonus with the aim of making employees continue in
employment until relocation was justifiable, even though
women who were working part-time as a result of a career
break lost out, because the bonus was directed at persuading
employees to stay on, not at rewarding past service (*Barclays
Bank plc v Young* (1994)).

'Third party discrimination', unlawful discrimination,
sometimes called 'transferred discrimination', has arisen
through judicial interpretation. In s 1(1)(a) of the RRA it is
unlawful to discriminate 'on racial grounds'. If employers did
dismiss an employee for serving a black customer, it can be
said that she has been discriminated against on racial grounds.
The principal decision is *Showboat Entertainment Centre Ltd v
Owens* (1984). The employers instructed the applicant, the
(white) manager of one of their slot-machine arcades, not to
admit young blacks. He disobeyed the order and was

6.4.21   Third party

dismissed. The Tribunal held that he had been treated less favourably on racial grounds than a person who would have excluded blacks ie there was direct discrimination. It did not matter that the racial grounds were those of customers, not of the person sacked. The EAT was strongly of the opinion that employees should not be placed in a position where they had to choose between obeying the law and disobeying an order (and so losing their job).

| 6.4.22 | Problem in SDA |

It is uncertain whether the ratio of *Showboat* can apply to the SDA. That statute prohibits unfavourable treatment of a woman 'on the ground of *her* sex' (emphasis supplied). If a woman is dismissed for serving a man when her employers have instructed her not to do so, it is difficult to say that she has been treated less favourably on account of her sex; rather, she has been treated less favourably on the ground of her potential customer's male sex. Perhaps the drafter of the SDA did not see this issue; presumably there was no intent to distinguish between the SDA and RRA on this point; there is, however, a demonstrable parliamentary intent to have the two statutes read together, and so the situation ought to be unlawful. Alternatively, perhaps the draftsman thought that the facts were too rare to contemplate arising.

| 6.4.23 | Victimisation |

Both the SDA (s 4(1)) and the RRA (s 2(1)) prohibit the less favourable treatment of applicants who bring proceedings, give evidence or information, allege a breach of the SDA, RRA, or Equal Pay Act 1970 or act under those Acts, or intend to do any of these. Halting internal investigations into a complaint of racial discrimination when the employee has commenced a claim before an IT constitutes victimisation (*Northamptonshire CC v Dattani* (1994)). Similarly failing to organise an internal appeal constitutes victimisation (*Allen v Cannon Hygiene Ltd* (1995)). The treatment must be less favourable than the treatment accorded to one who does not perform these actions. A causal link must, therefore, be demonstrated. If the applicant was dismissed because he secretly taped discussions for use in a racial discrimination claim, it was held that since a person who secretly taped matters for any other reason would have been expelled from the association, he was not victimised (*Aziz v Trinity Taxis Ltd* (1989)). There are, however, other statements by the Court of Appeal which are inconsistent with modern law: the motive of the alleged discriminator is now irrelevant in a direct discrimination case. A refusal to re-employ because of the applicant's attitude towards management in his previous job cannot be victimisation because the wording of the relevant sections is directed at discriminatory treatment during present employment (*Nagarajan v Agnew* (1994)); a controversial decision.

In the RRA (s 1(2)), but not in the SDA, there is provision that it is unlawful to provide separate facilities for persons of different races, even though the facilities are of equal quality. This stipulation prevents the development of apartheid as in South Africa and the 'separate but equal' doctrine which existed in the US law until the 1950s. The main case is *Pel Ltd v Modgill* (1980). The employers had mainly white workers on one shift in their factory: Asian employees worked on another. There was, therefore, *de facto* segregation. It was held that the employers were under no duty to integrate the workforce by putting Asians into the mainly white shift. Therefore, s 1(2) prevents segregation where the employers have adopted a policy of segregation but does not oblige employers to destroy it once it has arisen eg by employee preference.

6.4.24 Segregation

The scope for cases of discrimination in selection, job adverts, employment and dismissal are discussed below.

6.5 Scope

It is unlawful for employers to discriminate in the selection of workers and in the terms on which they offer employment and in refusing to offer work to a woman (s 6(1)). The principal cases are *Saunders v Richmond LBC* (1978) and *Brennan v J H Dewhurst Ltd* (1984). In the former case questions which were asked of a woman applicant wishing to be a golf professional but not of men were not discriminatory (but may be now). In the latter case the manager of a butcher's by his conduct implied that he did not want a female employee. The EAT held that his behaviour was unlawful, for the arrangements for selection were discriminatory, even though no one was in fact appointed to the job. Controversially the EAT held that a discriminatory advertisement was not discrimination by the employers who inserted the advertisement because they did not discriminate in fact but they (only) intended to discriminate (*Cardiff Women's Aid v Hartup* (1994)). The remedy lay in the hands of the EOC or CRE as noted in the next paragraph.

6.5.1 Discrimination in selection (s 6(1))

Section 38 of the SDA bans discriminatory jobs advertisements. Only the Equal Opportunities Commission can bring proceedings under s 38. The best illustration of s 38 is *EOC v Robertson* (1980). The employer advertised for 'a good bloke or blokess to satisfy the fool legislators'. The advertisement was held to be discriminatory. No one was fooled. It should be noted that although only the EOC can bring an action under s 38, the same fact may constitute an arrangement for selection and fall within s 6(1). The equivalent provision of s 38 SDA in the RRA is s 29. Such actions are brought in the ITs, but if the advertisement may be repeated, a county court can grant an injunction.

6.5.2 Discrimination in job adverts

6.5.3	Discrimination in employment (s 6(2))	Employers are prohibited from discriminating against a woman in the way they afford or refuse to afford her an opportunity for promotion, transfer, or training or for any other benefit, facility or service, or if they subject her to any detriment. For instance, the award of postal rounds on the basis of seniority works against women who have not achieved the requisite number of years in service because of their absence from the job due to child-rearing. For the meaning of detriment, see above. For the meaning of detriment, see para 6.4.19. Sexual harassment falls under the 'detriment' part of s 6(2).
6.5.4	Discrimination in dismissal (s 6(2))	Employers who dismiss women or Asian employees and not men or white workers discriminate unlawfully. However, an employee who is dismissed has no claim where his or her appeal is dealt with in an otherwise discriminatory fashion because he or she is no longer an employee (or a person engaged personally to execute a contract) but an ex-employee (*Nagarajan v Agnew* (1994)). An example of dismissal is when employers dismiss a man for having long hair when they would not have dismissed a woman in similar circumstances (*Smith v Safeway Plc* (1995)). The lay members of the EAT said that such conduct was discriminatory in the light of current social conditions, and they referred to the fact that the employers' 'short hair' rule affected non-working life. The employers had no rule banning long hair of women. The dissentient, Pill J, said that employers were entitled to have a dress code which applied to both sexes but which have different requirements for men and women depending on 'current perceptions' of convention.

Sacking a woman who is pregnant is the epitome of this type of discrimination in dismissal (*Hayes v Malleable WMC* (1985)). English law used to compare the situation of a woman who is dismissed for pregnancy against a man who is suffering from a long-term illness. If he would not have been dismissed but she was, there was discrimination. The previous law was that since men cannot get pregnant, there was no even hypothetical male comparator; therefore, a woman sacked for pregnancy (etc) was not discriminated against on the grounds of her sex. The law was criticised for comparing pregnancy, which is not an illness, against illness (though some illnesses such as prostate trouble affect only men); and both English and EC law provide that special treatment for women in relation to childbirth is not discriminatory against men. The House of Lords in *Webb v EMO Air Cargo (UK) Ltd* (1993) referred the issue to the ECJ, which ruled that discrimination on the grounds of pregnancy was direct discrimination, at least where the contract was not a fixed term one. There was no need to compare a pregnant woman with a male absent on health grounds. One problem with this response in English domestic law is s 5(3) of the SDA: 'A comparison of the cases of persons of different sex or marital status under s 1(1) or 3(1) must be such that the relevant circumstances in the one case are the same, or not materially different, in the other.' It may be that s 5(3) will as a result of EC law have to be ignored when pregnancy is the cause of the discrimination. The ECJ has previously ruled that it is unlawful to refuse to employ a woman on the ground that she was pregnant, despite the fact that the employer would suffer serious financial hardship (*Dekker v Stichting v Armingscentrum voor Junge Volwassenen-Plus* (1991)). See also *Hertz v Aldi Marked K/S* (1991). Refusal to continue to allow a pregnant woman to work at nights where her contract was of indefinite duration is discriminatory: *Habermann-Beltermann Varbeiterwohlfahrt* (1994) ECJ, again at least where the contract is not for a fixed term. Where, however, a woman becomes ill after the end of her maternity leave through a pregnancy-related illness, the ECJ has ruled that then the tribunal must compare her with a sick male (*Handels-og* (1991)). The Court of Session (Inner House) applied this case to dismissal for a pregnancy-related illness after maternity leave in *Brown v Rentokil Ltd* (1995) but the case being inconsistent with *Webb* is wrong.

It should be noted that the same facts which give rise to an SDA or RRA claim can also give rise to an unfair dismissal claim. However, generally there is a two-year qualifying period for unfair dismissal remedies. There is none under the SDA and RRA. Similar provisions to paras 6.5.1 to 6.5.4 above are found in s 4 of the RRA. In relation to pregnancy and childbirth it is automatically unfair to dismiss a woman for pregnancy: see s 60 of the Employment Protection (Consolidation) Act 1978 as substituted by s 24(1) of the Trade Union Reform and Employment Rights Act 1993. This provision means that the ECJ ruling in *Webb* is less important than it would otherwise have been. It should be noted that the amended s 60 still applies only to dismissal. Action short of dismissal continues to be dealt with solely under discrimination laws.

6.5.5   Overlap with unfair dismissal

The Sex Discrimination Act 1986, ss 6 and 77, render void discrimination in collective agreements and the rules of organisations, professions and occupations, even though they are not legally binding. Strange as it may seem, the government did not give jurisdiction to any tribunal or court to rule non-contractual agreements and rules invalid until the Trade Union Reform and Employment Rights Act 1993, s 32, inserted a new

6.5.6   Unions etc

ss (4A-C) into the 1986 Act, allowing an employee or a potential one to complain to an industrial tribunal about the rule's effect on her. The IT issues a declaration that the rule is void. It cannot rewrite the rule. The EOC or a union has no *locus standi*. The change may still not measure up to EC norms.

6.6   Exceptions

If the employers fall within one of the exceptions, they may treat a member of one sex or race less favourably than they would treat a member of the other sex or another race. The principal exceptions constitute 'genuine occupational qualifications' but there are others.

6.6.1   Genuine occupational qualifications (SDA, s 7; RRA, s 5)

A worker may be excluded from a job if the work falls within one of the genuine occupational qualifications. If, however, the applicant is offered the job, the SDA and RRA apply with full vigour. Even if there is a genuine occupational qualification (often abbreviated to goq) the employers must still consider whether or not it would be reasonable to use current employees in the relevant job (with the result that the potential worker can have a job to which the goq does not apply). This proviso applies to both sex and race goqs.

6.6.2   In SDA

With regard to goqs and sex discrimination the following constitute goqs:

- The nature of the job is such that a man is needed because of physiology. The usual example is modelling.

- The job is such that authenticity is needed. An example might be that only male actors need apply for the role of King Lear.

- Decency or privacy form the third goq. An example might be a female nurse whose job it is to change women's incontinence pads. This goq failed in the early case of *Wylie v Dee & Co (Menswear) Ltd* (1978). A refusal to employ a woman in a menswear shop was held to be discriminatory. Measurement of men's inside leg could be done by male shop assistants.

- The job involves a single-sex establishment where the inmates require special supervision or care eg in prison.

- The job involves personal services in the provision of welfare or education and can be done more effectively by members of one sex than another. An example might be the job of social worker with children who have been sexually abused by their fathers.

- The job consists of work abroad which under that country's laws can be done only by men. An example is that in Saudi Arabia women are not permitted to drive cars. Accordingly, a job agency can advertise for men only to act as chauffeurs.

- The job is one of two which can be held only by a married couple. The usual illustration is that of a club steward.

- It is impractical for the worker to live other than on the premises supplied by the employers; the only premises are available for men; and it is not reasonable for the employers to build separate premises for women. The usual example is a light-house.

- The post is likely to involve the worker's performing the job or living in a private house and must be held by a man because of the degree of social or physical contact with the person living in the home. An example is the provision of a female companion to an elderly woman. The exemption also extends to knowledge of the intimate details of the private householder's affairs. It was added by the 1986 Sex Discrimination Act, s 1(2), as a result of infringement proceedings brought by the EC Commission against the United Kingdom in the Court of Justice.

- The final exemption is now detailed in the Employment Act 1989, s 4. By it employers may offer employment only to men to comply with a statutory requirement existing before the enactment of the SDA which is for the protection of women in relation to pregnancy or maternity or other risks which are specially associated with women, to comply with the Health and Safety at Work Act 1974, or to comply with the laws mentioned in Schedule 1 to the 1989 Act.

The RRA provides a much shorter list of goqs than does the SDA. The second, third, fourth and fifth exceptions (see points in para 6.6.2) apply. There is also an exception for waiters in ethnic restaurants eg Chinese – ethnic waiters in Chinese restaurants. The personal services exception was utilised in *Tottenham Green Under Fives' Centre v Marshall* (1991). Looking after children in a nursery constituted a personal service. 84% of the children were of Afro-Caribbean origin. Someone was needed to talk and read to the children in West Indian patois. Selecting someone of Afro-Caribbean or African origin for work in the nursery was a genuine occupational qualification. The contrasting case is *Lambeth London Borough v Commission for Racial Equality* (1990). The personal services goq did not apply where the posts of group manager and assistant head of housing benefits did not have much contact with the public.

6.6.3   In RRA

Therefore, the post-holders did not need to have experience of the special problems faced by blacks and, accordingly, the employers were wrong to restrict job applicants to those of Asian or Afro-Caribbean origin.

- Acts done to safeguard national security: SDA, s 52; RRA, s 42.

6.6.4   Other exemptions

- (a) For the private household exemption in the SDA see para 6.6.2 above. The RRA retains the private household exception. It is not subject to the limits set out above in the amended SDA. Normally the RRA is brought into line with the SDA when it is changed to bring it into line with EC law. It is suggested that the government's respect for privacy among individuals should yield to the anti-discrimination principle.

  (b) In relation to the RRA there is a wider private household exemption than in the SDA. There is no restriction as to physical or social contact or intimate knowledge.

- Charitable trusts: SDA, s 43, RRA s 34. A case is *Hugh-Jones v St John's College* (1979). The College was a charitable trust. A woman was refused access to the Senior Common Room. The EAT held that the College was not liable for sexual discrimination because it was a charitable trust.

6.6.5   Other exemptions in SDA

The SDA further exempts:

- sports and sporting facilities (s 17);

- police and police cadets in relation to height, uniform, equipment, pregnancy and pensions; prison officers in relation to height (s 18);

- ministers of religion, if the credo so provides (s 19) (compare the present position of the Church of England);

- special protection for women during pregnancy and childbirth;

- provisions in respect of death or retirement (s 6(4)).

To this exception Parliament in the Sex Discrimination Act 1986, s 2(1), engrafted exceptions ie where now the SDA does apply. Section 6(4)(a) states that s 6(4) does not apply to the ways in which and terms on which promotion, transfer, and training are made; nor does it apply to demotion, dismissal, or any other detriment involving demotion or dismissal. Section 6(4)(b) provides that benefits, facilities or services under an occupational pension scheme are not affected by the restriction found in s 6(4); s 6(4)(c) refers to dismissal.

The same exception in respect of death or retirement applies in the Equal Pay Act 1970. The European Court of Justice ruled in *Barber v Guardian Royal Exchange Assurance Group Ltd* (1991) that payments under occupational pension schemes constitute 'pay' for the purposes of Article 119. Since Article 119 is horizontally directly effective, s 6(4) is implicitly overruled by *Barber* where 'pay' in the EC sense is concerned.

6.6.6   Death/retirement

The RRA further exempts:

6.6.7   Others exceptions in RRA

- rules in relation to immigration;

- rules concerning qualifications for employment in the civil service (there are special rules in relation to the Ministry of Defence, the Diplomatic Service, and the Cabinet Office);

- employment abroad on a ship (eg British workers can be sacked in favour of cheaper Filipino or Lascar crew);

- qualifications (nationality, place of birth, duration of residence) for national and local sides (eg the English football team);

- acts done under any statute or statutory instrument (s 41(1)).

There used to be an exemption in favour of small employers but the ECJ ruled that it contravened the Equal Treatment Directive (EC 76/207) and the exception was repealed by the Sex Discrimination Act 1986. It is possible that some of the exceptions which remain are inconsistent with the Directive.

6.6.8   Small employers

Some procedural matters require elucidation and are discussed below. Claims must be brought within three months of the last act of discrimination. An act which continues over a period is deemed to have been performed at the end of that period (*Barclays Bank Plc v Kapur* (1994) (HL)), a race case which also applies to sex. A line is drawn between a continuing act and an act which has continuing consequences. The latter is not a continuing act. Accordingly, the appointment of a nurse at a certain grade was not a continuing act. The three months ran from the date of appointment (*Sougrin v Haringey HA* (1993) (CA)). An example of a continuing discrimination is the refusal to grant a subsidised mortgage to a woman. The IT may extend the limitation period if it considers it just and equitable to do so.

6.7   **Procedure**

There is conflict as to where the onus of proof lies once the applicant has pointed to a *prima facie* case. The Court of Appeal in *Noone v North West Thames Regional Health Authority* (1988) and *Baker v Cornwall County Council* (1990) said that the legal burden switches to the employers once the applicant has

6.7.1   Burden of proof

established a *prima facie* case. Even after those cases, however, the EAT has continued to hold that the burden is on the applicant throughout: *British Gas plc v Sharma* (1991) and *King v Great Britain-China Centre* (1991). The Court of Appeal in *King* held the law was that a tribunal may draw inferences from the facts including discrimination; if so, it is then for the employer to provide an explanation. In *Qureshi v London Borough of Newham* (1991) (CA) it was held that an inference of discrimination from the facts is a matter for the tribunal. On the facts failures to apply a policy against discrimination, to follow the employers' procedural rules and to supply the CRE with statistics in response to a questionnaire (see next paragraph) did not automatically mean that the employers had discriminated. The burden of proof of 'justification' is on the employers. The UK government has vetoed a draft Directive on the burden of proof in discrimination. Under it the applicant would have to prove less favourable treatment; then the employers would have to show that the less favourable treatment was not on the grounds of sex.

| 6.7.2 | Questionnaire | An employee may submit a questionnaire to her employers to gain information on discrimination. If they fail to reply or do reply but do so evasively, the IT may draw on inference of discrimination. See SDA, s 74; RRA, s 65. |

| 6.7.3 | Statistics | Statistical evidence may be of value in establishing discrimination. For example, the use of statistics may demonstrate a pattern of not employing blacks. There is no duty on employers to undertake studies of patterns of employment in their firm, but if there is such a study, the tribunal may draw adverse inferences from its non-disclosure. See *Carrington v Helix Lighting Ltd* (1990). While the tribunals have said that elaborate statistics are not required, their use is increasing, and such evidence entitles the tribunal to draw an inference of discrimination when the employers do not adduce evidence to the contrary. |

| 6.7.4 | Discovery | The legal process of discovery is available in discrimination cases. For disclosure the material in the hands of the employers must be relevant, necessary for the fair disposal of the case, and not oppressive to them (eg the documents can be obtained cheaply) (*West Midlands PTE v Singh* (1988)). |

6.8 Remedies

The Acts empower tribunals to award several remedies. Two points should be emphasised. Tribunals have no power to award damages for unintentional, indirect discrimination and exemplary damages. The success rate if the case should reach the tribunal is not high.

The Industrial Tribunal can do any or all of the following:

- make declaration that the employee's rights have been infringed;

- order compensation (which was calculated up to a maximum of £11,000 until the ECJ's ruling in *Marshall (No 2)*, mentioned in 6.8.4 below). Compensation covers both special damages such as for loss of salary and general damages such as for injury to feelings. Tort law principles govern the assessment of compensation (*Ministry of Defence v Cannock* (1995));

- make recommendations that the employers remove the discrimination.

The tribunal can award damages for injured feelings (s 66(4) and s 57(4)). The injury to feelings must be proved and the sum awarded is not to be used as a deterrent (*Cannock*). Injured feelings includes the emotion felt at losing a congenial job. While compensation for injured feelings is not automatically awarded, it is rare for it not to be granted (*Ministry of Defence v Sullivan* (1994)). In general a sum of £500 is the minimum tribunals award on this ground (*Sharifi v Strathclyde Regional Council* (1992)). The median award in sex cases was £1,416 in 1992–3 (the median nearly doubled to £2,999 in 1993–4), in race cases £3,333. Now that the financial limit has been removed, the median award will increase. Damages running into £100,000s have been awarded by industrial tribunals for dismissal from the armed forces for becoming pregnant. A Leeds IT has awarded £10,000 in a sex case and a London IT has awarded £10,000 in a race case for injury to feelings. A Leicester IT awarded £3,500 to a black woman training to be a solicitor who was dismissed for failing her exams when two white trainees who had failed were retained. All these occurred in 1994/5. In *Noone v North West Thames Regional Health Authority*, above, the Court of Appeal awarded £3,000. The principles guiding the assessment of compensation for the dismissal of service women who became pregnant were laid down in the *Cannock* case but they apply generally to direct discrimination claims. The tribunal has to estimate the chances of the woman returning to work, had she been allowed to take maternity leave; whether she would have been promoted; and whether she would have had more children. Morison J criticised high awards (such as one for £300,000). Child-care costs are deducted from the sum. There is no separate head of compensation for loss of career prospects. The employee must mitigate her loss. There should be no 'uplift' for compensation because the employers form part of the State. Compensation may not be awarded for indirect discrimination if the employers did not intend to discriminate on the grounds of sex (s 66(3)). This provision has been criticised for failing to eradicate sexual discrimination. Employers would act strongly if they had to pay compensation for unintentional indirect discrimination. In August 1994 a tribunal ruled that a part-time teacher who was female was indirectly discriminated against when her employers decided that a job should be done by one full-time teacher rather than two part-time ones, and it awarded compensation for unintentional indirect discrimination in reliance on the Directive (*Tickle v Governors of Riverview CF School* (1994) unreported).

6.8.2 Exemplary damages

The principal recent debate has been concerned with whether or not tribunals may award exemplary damages for discrimination. In a reserved judgment the Employment Appeal Tribunal in *Deane v London Borough of Ealing* (1993) ruled in reliance on a non-employment Court of Appeal authority that the Court of Appeal had been incorrect in *City of Bradford Metropolitan Council v Arora* (1991) to award exemplary damages under the RRA. Such an award was available only in relation to torts which existed before the famous House of Lords' decision in *Rookes v Barnard* (1964). Since neither the SDA nor RRA existed in 1964, exemplary damages could not be granted for breach of those statutes. Some of the sting in *Deane* may be reduced by tribunals awarding aggravated damages for injured feelings. The Law Commission in a Consultation Paper in 1993 recommended exemplary damages in discrimination cases.

6.8.3 Recommendation

The recommendation is just that, a recommendation, not an order. For example, an IT cannot order the employers to provide showers: *Ministry of Defence v Jeremiah*, above. More recently, the EAT held that an IT was wrong to recommend that the applicant should be appointed to the next available job, because that was unlawful discrimination (*British Gas plc v Sharma*, above). These cases may be incorrect in the light of EC law, which requires effective remedies. A recommendation is also limited to 'a specified period'. For this reason a recommendation that the applicant should be promoted when a vacancy arose was held to be invalid in *Irvine v Prestgold Ltd* (1981). In that case it was also held that it was not possible to include in a recommendation as an alternative to promotion that the applicant should receive the difference in pay between her present job and the post to which she was to be promoted. Monetary matters should fall within the award of compensation. If the employers do not carry out the recommendation, compensation may be awarded, but only if it could have been awarded in the first instance.

Interest on ITs' compensation awards was not allowed: *Marshall v Southampton & South West Hants Area Health Authority (No 2)* (1990), a criticised authority. The Court held that the word 'damages' in the English statute could not be construed as including interest on damages. The ECJ in 1993 ruled that national measures implementing EC law on sexual discrimination should be sufficiently powerful to achieve the objective of that law and be capable of effective enforcement in national courts. The objective was stated to be real equality of opportunity. Loss sustained by dismissal must be fully recompensed. An upper limit on the amount of compensation and the inability to award interest were inconsistent with achievement of the objective. Interest will now be awarded from the date of discrimination, not the date of the hearing. It may be that English courts can construe 'damages' to include injury to feelings. If so, there would not be a difference between State and non-State employees (this is the *Marleasing* approach discussed in Chapter 2). If such a construction is not possible, non-State employees will be able to rely on *Francovich*, also discussed in Chapter 2, to obtain damages against the failure properly to implement the Equal Treatment Directive. Accordingly, the English law limiting the maximum amount which could be awarded in a SDA claim and the English law under which no provision was made for the award of interest in SDA claims were abrogated by the Sex Discrimination and Equal Pay (Remedies) Regulations 1993 (SI 1993/2798) in November 1993. The law on maximum compensation in racial discrimination cases was changed by the Race Relations (Remedies) Act 1994, which abolished the financial limit on race cases. It may be that the ECJ's decision implicitly overrules the limit to two years' back pay in the Equal Pay Act 1970 for that maximum may not fully recompense the applicant. The £11,000 limit also was not consistent with EC law because it does not provide a remedy which deters employers from unlawful acts (*von Colson v Land Nordrhein-Westfalen* (1984)). The ECJ in *Marshall (No 2)* ruled that this limit was to be disregarded because otherwise the principle of no discrimination on the grounds of sex would not be 'fully effective'. One effect of the ruling will be to increase the amount for injury to feelings, that amount formerly being restricted by the overall limit on compensation. It is suggested that the UK non-provision of compensation for unintentional indirect discrimination falls short of EC norms. See 6.8.1, above. The Equal Treatment

6.8.4   EC law

Directive 1976, Article 6, obliges all Member States to adopt 'all the measures necessary to ensure that the Directive is fully effective'. In *Marshall (No 2)* the Court of Appeal had held that Article 6 is not unconditional and precise enough to be directly effective, but it was wrong; but the Directive's Article 6 is only vertically directly effective. Certainly the ECJ had no doubt that it did apply to emanations of the State. A claim for damages against the State by employees of private employers for improper implementation of the Directive is possible.

6.9   Differences from equal pay

- The Equal Pay Act 1970 applies only if there is a male comparator; under the SDA it is sufficient that there is an hypothetical male whom the employers would have treated better than the claimant.

- The SDA covers discrimination on the grounds of marital status, which the 1970 Act does not.

- A claim for equal pay is limited to two years' back pay. There is no such limit in sex discrimination law.

- There was a limit of £11,000 (1993 figures) for compensation under the SDA but see para 6.8.4, above. The 1970 statute has no such limit.

- The hurdle of 'requirement or condition' applies to the 1976 statute but not to equal pay claims where the applicant is claiming that the employers have indirectly discriminated against her. The EAT in *Bhudi v IMI Refiners Ltd*, above, held that English law could not be construed in conformity with EC law in this point without distorting its meaning. It is suggested that the English statute could be construed to give effect to EC law by reading 'requirement or condition' as 'practice or policy'. Moreover, the same rules apply at the EC level to equal pay and equal treatment. The defence of material difference in the English equal pay law and the defence of justification in sex discrimination law are read in the same way despite the fact that they are drafted differently in the statutes. For both of these reasons it is thought that *Bhudi* will not survive scrutiny in a higher court.

6.9.1   'Pay'

It should be remembered that the Equal Pay Act is not restricted to 'pay' but applies to all terms and conditions during employment. Once the worker has accepted the job the 1970 Act applies, not the SDA. This is not a problem with the RRA which covers contractual terms and conditions too.

The effect of EC law must be understood. It is dealt with in general in Chapter 2 and in the particular context of equal treatment in the previous chapter. While the use of directives in the area of sex discrimination leaves the domestic government with a choice as to specific measures, 'the objective is to arrive at real equality of opportunity' and national 'measures must be such as to guarantee real and effective judicial protection and have a real deterrent effect on the employer', as the ECJ put it in *Marshall (No 2)*.

6.9.2   Effect of EC law

Discrimination on the grounds of Sex or Race

The Sex Discrimination Act 1975 and Race Relations Act 1976 prohibit discrimination on the grounds of sex and race respectively.	**Introduction**

The Acts cover employees and independent contractors doing work personally. Employers are vicariously liable. **Coverage**

The Acts cover discrimination on the grounds of sex, married (but not single) status, and race, which include ethnic origins: **Grounds**

Mandla v Dowell Lee (1983).

The Acts covers direct (unfavourable treatment) and indirect (requirement or condition, considerably smaller proportion, can comply, detriment, not justifiable) discrimination as well as third party discrimination, victimisation and, in the case of the RRA, segregation: **Meaning**

direct: *Ministry of Defence v Jeremiah* (1979)

motive irrelevant: *James v Eastleigh BC* (1990)

harassment: *Porcelli v Strathclyde RC* (1985)

indirect: *Price v CSC* (1978)

requirement: *Perera v CSC* (1983)

proportion: *Kidd v DRG (UK)* (1985)

'can comply': *Mandla v Dowell Lee* (1983)

detriment: *Ministry of Defence v Jeremiah*

justification: *Hampson v DES* (1989)

third party: *Showboat Entertainment v Owens* (1984)

victimisation: *Aziz v Trinity Taxis* (1988)

segregation: *Pel v Modgill* (1980).

The Acts cover discrimination before, during, and after employment. Pregnancy dismissals constitute direct discrimination. **Scope**

Exceptions	Exemptions called 'genuine occupational qualifications' and other exceptions are available:
	Tottenham Green Under Fives' Centre v Marshall (1991).
Procedure	To aid applicants there are special rules on burden of proof, questionnaires, statistical evidence, and discovery:
	King v Great Britain-China Centre (1991).
Remedies	ITs can award a declaration, compensation and recommendation. Exemplary damages are no longer awardable:
	Marshall (No 2) (1993)
	Deane v London Borough of Ealing (1993).
Differences from equal pay	The Equal Pay Act 1970 applies to contractual terms.

Chapter 7

Termination of the Contract of Employment at Common Law

When the contract of employment is terminated without the employee's being dismissed, she has no common law claim for wrongful dismissal and no statutory claim for a redundancy payment or unfair dismissal.

The contract of employment is a personal relationship. If the employee dies, the contract cannot be enforced against her. If the employer is a natural person and she dies, the contract also terminates. If, however, the business is carried on by the employer's personal representatives the contract is deemed to continue for the purposes of redundancy payments. If they do not carry on the business, the employee may claim a redundancy payment from them: Employment Protection (Consolidation) Act 1978, Schedule 12 (hereafter EP(C)A). If the employer is a company and the court winds it up, the employee is taken to be dismissed; if, however, the winding up is voluntary the contract terminates only if the business is not carried on. Similarly, if the court appoints a receiver, the contract ends, but usually it continues if the debenture holders appoint the receiver. Dissolution of a partnership operates as termination of the contract of employment with the partners, but employment under a new partnership with some of the old partners constitutes a waiver of the right to sue in respect of the termination. For continuity of employment and the effect of the Transfer of Undertakings (Protection of Employment) Regulations (SI 1981/1794) see the relevant sections of this book.

The contract of employment is automatically terminated if without fault of either party its performance becomes illegal, completion of the contract becomes impossible, or if performance of the contract would produce a situation radically different from that agreed. Subject to the possible exception of the imprisonment cases discussed below, the law is the same as that in general contract law. Accordingly, authorities such as the Coronation cases, *Davis Contractors Ltd v Fareham UDC* (1956) and *The Hannah Blumenthal* (1983) remain relevant.

An example is *Morgan v Manser* (1948), the case involving Charlie Chester, now a Radio 2 disc jockey. He was called up

7.1 Termination without dismissal

7.1.1 Death and winding up

7.1.2 Frustration

7.1.3 Definition

for the army. His contract of employment was frustrated. The judgment of Streatfeild J sums up the law in one sentence:

> 'If there is an event or change of circumstances which is so fundamental as to be regarded by the law as striking at the root of the contract as a whole, and going beyond what was contemplated by the parties and such that to hold the parties to the contract would be to bind them to terms which they would not have made, had they contemplated that event or those circumstances, then the contract is frustrated by that event immediately and irrespective of the volition or the intention of the parties, or their knowledge as to that particular event, and this is even though they have continued for a time to treat the contract as still subsisting.'

7.1.4   Effects

The effects of frustration are these:

- The contract is terminated by operation of law. Neither party need do anything.

- Wages due up to the date of frustration may be recovered: Law Reform (Frustrated Contracts) Act 1943. Wages due after that date are not recoverable, unless it is just and equitable to award a sum representing the wages.

- Because the contract is determined by law, not by the act or will of either party, there is no dismissal. The principal employment claims, wrongful dismissal, redundancy payments, and unfair dismissal are all predicated on dismissal. If the employers have not dismissed the employee, no claim can arise. To this rule there is an exception. By s 93 of EP(C)A, if the frustrating event is the dissolution of corporate employers or the death of natural ones, the termination by frustration is deemed to be a dismissal for the purposes of redundancy payments. This rule applies even when Parliament has made the employment illegal.

7.1.5   Problems

Two particular frustrating events have caused problems to labour lawyers: sickness and imprisonment, though other events such as mobilisation and suspension on medical grounds do lead to frustration.

7.1.6   Sickness

A worker's contract may be frustrated by illness, as the classic case of *Poussard v Spiers* (1876) illustrates. An opera singer fell sick. She missed rehearsals and four performances. The contract was frustrated. Similarly, in *Condor v Barron Knights* (1966) a pop group's drummer fell ill and could not perform his agreement to drum seven nights a week. Again the contract was frustrated. Both cases involved short-term engagements. What of indefinite employment? Guidelines were laid down by Donaldson P, as he then was, in *Marshall v Harland & Wolff Ltd* (1972). A court or tribunal has to consider:

- the terms of the contract, including any term as to sick pay;
- how long the employment was likely to last in the absence of illness: a short-term hiring was more likely to be frustrated than a long-term one;
- the nature of the employment: for example, was the employee the holder of a key post?
- the nature of the illness and the prospect of recovery;
- the duration of past employment: the longer the length, the less the possibility of frustration.

The EAT in *Egg Stores (Stamford Hill) Ltd v Leibovici* (1977) added:

- the risk to the employers of being liable for a redundancy payment and unfair dismissal to an employee who is the replacement for the sick person;
- whether wages have continued;
- the acts and statements of the employers; and
- whether it was reasonable to expect the employers to wait any longer before dismissing.

An illustration is *Maxwell v Walter Howard Designs Ltd* (1975). An employee was off work ill for almost two years. However, there was no need for a permanent replacement. The contract was not frustrated.

7.1.7   Notcutt

The principal modern case is *Notcutt v Universal Equipment Co (London) Ltd* (1986). The worker had been employed since 1957. He had a heart attack in 1983. His contract of employment stated that the employers could dismiss him with one week's notice. There was no sick pay. After a while it became clear that he would never work again. The court held that the contract was frustrated and that the doctrine of frustration did apply to a contract which was terminable by one week's notice. The fact that the employee would never return constituted a fundamental change in the contract. The court emphasised that the doctrine of frustration did apply to a contract determinable with one week's notice and that attempts by employers to plead frustration should be closely scrutinised to ensure that employees were not deprived of their employment protection.

7.1.8	If no frustration	If the contract is not frustrated by sickness, but the employers have dismissed the employee for being ill, there exists a dismissal for common law and statutory purposes. Where there is illness, that is a potentially fair reason for dismissing someone. See the chapter on unfair dismissal.

7.1.9   Imprisonment

In contract law the doctrine of frustration does not apply where the frustrating event was self-induced. Nevertheless, the courts have held in several cases that imprisonment can frustrate a contract of employment. In *Hare v Murphy Bros Ltd* (1974) the imprisonment for 12 months frustrated the contract. Lord Denning MR said that the relevant event was the sentence of the court, a matter outside the control of the parties. Therefore, imprisonment was not self-induced. This argument looks thin.

7.1.10   *Jerrom*

The most important modern case is *FC Shepherd & Co Ltd v Jerrom* (1986). The Court of Appeal said that a sentence of imprisonment was potentially a frustrating event but was not so if the parties had foreseen the eventuality, as occurred on the facts, for neither party could rely on his own misconduct. In the worker's contract of apprenticeship there was a clause that his employers could dismiss him for misconduct. His misbehaviour was therefore a foreseen event, and no frustration occurred. Since it was the employers who were seeking to rely on the employee's misbehaviour, there was no frustration. There would have been frustration, had the employee been seeking to rely on his own misconduct. The result is not necessarily in line with general contract laws and is different from the view of Lord Denning MR mentioned in the previous paragraph. The time of frustration is when it was commercially necessary for the employer to decide whether to get a replacement or not (*Chakki v United Yeast Co Ltd* (1982)). On the facts of that case the employee served only one day in prison when he was released pending his appeal. The EAT remitted the case for the tribunal to determine when a reasonable employer would have decided to replace the employee.

7.1.11   Expiry of a fixed-term contract

Where the parties agree that a contract of employment shall last for a precise duration, when the agreement terminates there is at common law no dismissal. For example, a post which is accepted on the basis that it will terminate when external funding runs out ceases without dismissal on the occurrence of that event. There are, however, two important statutory consequences of the expiry of a fixed-term contract:

- If such a contract is not renewed, non-renewal is deemed to be a dismissal for the purposes of redundancy payments and unfair dismissal: EP(C)A, ss 83(2)(b) and 55(2)(b) respectively.

- An employee under a fixed-term contract can agree in writing to surrender her rights to redundancy pay if the contract is for two years or more, and to a remedy for unfair dismissal if the contract is for one year or more: s 142 of EP(C)A. The one-year period remains even though the qualifying time for unfair dismissal is two years. Waiver comes into effect only on expiry; if the employers breach the contract during the fixed term, s 142 is not applicable.

The definition of a 'fixed-term' contract has caused some problems. It is one which expires on a particular date. It is not one which terminates on the completion of a certain job (such as completion of the Channel Tunnel) or the occurrence of a certain event (such as the non-renewal of funding). A contract which contains a clause concerning notice is still one for a fixed term, if it otherwise fits the definition (*Dixon v BBC* (1979)). The waiver rule applies even though the fixed term has been extended, for example, because funding has been granted for an extra period (*Mulrine v University of Ulster* (1993)), a decision of the Northern Ireland Court of Appeal. Where, however, there are in truth two or more separate contracts, one looks at the final contract to check whether it was one for a fixed term (*Open University v Triesman* (1978)).This definition applies both in respect of the statutory consequences noted above. Therefore, employers may insert a break clause in a fixed-term contract of one year or two years or more and still be able to exclude a remedy for unfair dismissal and redundancy payments respectively. If waiver of these claims is not fair to employees, this effect of the definition of fixed-term contracts is doubly unfair.

7.1.12   Definition

As with any other contract a contract of employment is terminated by agreement. An interesting case is *S W Strange Ltd v Mann* (1965). The defendant was the plaintiffs' betting-shop manager. In his contract there was a clause stating that he would not compete with his employers after the termination of his contract. After arguments he stopped being manager and took over the running of one department only. On his leaving the plaintiffs sought to enforce the covenant in restraint of trade. The Court of Appeal held that the first contract had been terminated by mutual consent. When he started his job running the one department, his new

7.1.13   Mutual consent

contract did not contain the clause; therefore it could not be enforced.

7.1.14   Cases

Termination by mutual consent worked in favour of the employee in this case. Normally, however, it will be the employee who suffers for if there is termination of agreement there is no dismissal, and therefore no claim for wrongful or unfair dismissal or redundancy payments is possible. An important illustration is *Birch v University of Liverpool* (1985). Two members of the employers' staff opted for early retirement under a scheme agreed between the University and the union. The scheme gave the employees more money than the statute did and the agreement expressly included money in lieu of statutory redundancy payments. The court held that the contracts had terminated by agreement and therefore the employers had no statutory rights. Employees should be aware of the effect of such early retirement schemes. Termination by consent can even occur when the employee is under notice of redundancy. If an employee accepts the money she will have no claim to a redundancy payment (though the scheme may well provide her with more money than the statutory payment, which is on the low side). For this reason courts and tribunals have investigated whether there truly was consent or whether the facts really constituted dismissal. An offer to resign in an appeal hearing in disciplinary proceedings may in truth be a dismissal. The question which must be asked is: 'Who really terminated the contract of employment?' In *McAlwane v Broughton Estate Ltd* (1973) the employee was given notice of dismissal. He was set to leave on 19 April. The employers agreed to his request to leave on 12 April. The employee contended that the employers should pay him a redundancy payment and compensate him for unfair dismissal. The employers argued that he had left by consent. The National Industrial Relations Court held that what occurred was merely an arrangement to alter the date of his departure, not an agreement that he should leave voluntarily. Therefore, he was dismissed and his claims could proceed. The Court of Appeal approved this decision by a majority in *Lees v Arthur Greaves (Lees) Ltd* (1974). A more recent case is *Caledonian Mining Co Ltd v Bassett* (1987) EAT. The employers intimated that they would have to make some employees redundant. The men found work with the National Coal Board. The employers contended that the employees had resigned and so could not claim redundancy payments. The EAT held that the employers had by their actions (which included asking the men if they were interested in other employment) obliged the employees to resign. Therefore, the employees had been constructively dismissed and the contract had not been terminated by consent.

The most important case is *Igbo v Johnson Matthey Chemicals Ltd* (1986). The employee requested extended leave to visit her husband and children in Nigeria. The employers granted it on condition that she signed a letter stating that: 'You have agreed to return to work on 28.9.86. If you fail to do this your contract of employment will automatically terminate on that date.' She signed. She did not return on the due date because she was ill. The Court of Appeal held that the contract had not been terminated by agreement, but by dismissal. The letter the employee had signed was a means of avoiding giving her employment rights. Such a device was void under s 140(1) of EP(C)A. The court thought that if the contract had been terminated by consent, all employers could insert similar clauses into the contracts, thereby depriving employees of their rights.

7.1.15   *Igbo v Johnson Matthey Chemicals Ltd* (1986)

Other instances of termination by mutual consent include: resignation to avoid disciplinary proceedings (*Martin v MBS Fastenings (Glynwed) Distribution Ltd* (1983)); resignation in order to obtain compensation after falling out with the company's owner (*Sheffield v Oxford Controls Co* (1979)); and a resignation to obtain a lump sum under a pension scheme, the alternative being a (lesser) redundancy payment (*Scott v Coalite Fuels and Chemicals Ltd* (1988)). The courts and tribunals look at whether the employee had a (fairly) free choice, but it must be said that they have only rarely taken into account s 140(1) of EP(C)A. The Court of Appeal in *Martin* said that the question to be asked was: 'Who really terminated the contract of employment?'

7.1.16   Further illustrations

One point about mutual termination requires emphasis. If an employee is under notice and she give her employers notice that she wants to leave before the expiry of her employers' notice, she is deemed to have been dismissed for statutory purposes. Notice must be given by her in the period of notice provided by statute and not within such extra period stipulated in the contract. If these conditions are satisfied, she will retain her entitlement. The requirement of writing for one claim but not the other seems to act merely as a trap for the unwary and deserves to be abolished. The notice need not be in writing for unfair dismissal (EP(C)A, s 55(3)), but must be in redundancy payments (s 85(2)). Employers may give a further notice which requires the employee to work until the

7.1.17   Counter-notice

termination of her contract. If she then leaves before termination, the tribunal may reduce the redundancy payment and may do so even to nothing.

| 7.1.18 | Performance |

Like other contracts a contract of employment is terminable by performance of all the obligations arising under it. In such circumstances the employee is not 'dismissed' for the purposes of statutory rights: eg *Ironmonger v Movefield Ltd* (1988).

7.2 Termination by dismissal

This section considers situations where an employee is dismissed. The common law action of wrongful dismissal occurs where the employers dismiss the employee with short notice or with no notice at all and there is no justification.

7.2.1 Notice

Contracts of employment usually have a term that they may be terminated by either party's giving notice. There may be a clause which restricts the reasons which may be given for dismissal. If there is no express term, the courts imply a term in the usual ways (eg the officious bystander test). This term is of a reasonable length. What is reasonable on one set of facts may not be so on another. In one case it was held that an editor required 12 months' notice; in another, only six. The higher in the corporate hierarchy the longer the length of notice. The duration of the period of reasonable notice may be longer than the statutory minimum period. Since the period of notice must be noted in the written statement there is now less scope than previously for the implication of a term of reasonable notice. Since notice is a common law concept, the determination of implied terms and reasonable periods is for the ordinary courts.

7.2.2 Rules

Notice must be given to each employee individually. The dismissal notice must be such and not merely a warning of dismissal: *Morton Sundour Fabrics Ltd v Shaw* (1967) and *Haseltine Lake & Co v Dowler* (1981). Once notice is given it cannot be withdrawn unilaterally. Both parties must agree to revocation: *Harris & Russell Ltd v Slingsby* (1977). Dismissal takes effect when notice runs out.

7.2.3 Statutory period

The common law of notice could be used by employers to wreak injustice on employees. If the contract contained a clause that a worker could be dismissed with one hour's notice, then one hour was legally sufficient notice to terminate the contract lawfully. The employee had no remedy, despite perhaps working for the firm for 30 years. Parliament has intervened in favour of the employee. Statute overrides contractual provisions unless those are longer than the statutory notice period. Under EP(C)A Pt IV the length of the statutory period depends on how long the employee has worked for the employers. Section 49 stipulates the following:

- where the employee has worked continuously for the employers for under two years – one week;

- where she has worked for more than two years – one week for each year of service to a maximum of 12 weeks.

Therefore an employee with five years' continuous service is entitled to five weeks' notice; one with 30 years is entitled to 12 weeks. The right to a minimum of one week's notice does not apply if a casual worker is employed to do a particular task for under three months: s 49(4A), inserted by Schedule 2, para 3(3), to the Employment Act 1982. The law provides that an employee must give one week's notice if she has been employed for four or more weeks (s 49(2)).

Section 49 provides, moreover, that the minimum statutory periods do not apply where either party is entitled to terminate the contract because of the other's conduct (see para 7.2.5 below); either party may waive the right under s 49; and either party may accept payment in lieu of notice (s 49(3)). The right to pay in lieu of notice is lost if the employee waives notice (*Trotter v Forth Ports Authority* (1991)), a decision of the Court of Session which was applied by the High Court in *Baldwin v British Coal Corporation* (1995). Where the employee does waive notice or accept pay in lieu, employment ends on that date, not when the notice would otherwise have run out. Thus rule is important in relation to the amount of continuous employment the employee must have before claiming a statutory employment right. Employers can decide not to enforce the contractual requirement that an employee work out her period of notice. In this way she cannot cause harm to the business, say by poaching customers for her employers-to-be.

7.2.4   Application

Employers may dismiss without giving notice if they have good reason to do so. This occurrence is known as 'summary dismissal'. For example, where the employee has repudiated the contract by breaking a condition of the agreement eg by going on strike, the employee breached a fundamental term of the contract, the duty to work (*Simmons v Hoover Ltd* (1977)). Other examples include where the employee has disobeyed a lawful order or has misbehaved grossly such as by stabbing a colleague. If the employee deals with money, theft of a small amount may be a good cause for dismissal (*Sinclair v Neighbour* (1967)).

7.2.5   Cause

7.2.6	Examples	Employers may be entitled to dismiss for one 'offence' (*Taylor v Alidair Ltd* (1978)). One bumpy landing by a pilot amounted to gross negligence. A series of incidents eg of drunkenness will be evidence of gross misconduct (*Clouston v Corry* (1906)). Two gardening cases illustrate the law. In *Pepper v Webb* (1969) a gardener refused to do some work and swore. The Court of Appeal held that his refusal and swearing were the last straw and the dismissal was lawful. In *Wilson v Racher* (1974), however, the gardener was ordered to use electric hedge-cutters in the rain. He was sacked for refusing. His dismissal was unlawful. One difference between those cases is that in the latter the event was isolated, whereas in the former it was part of a series. Employers should bear in mind that dismissal is a severe punishment and should only be the response to a serious situation.
7.2.7	Various issues	Several points arise:

- the statutory period of notice in s 49 of EP(C)A does not apply where the employee is dismissed for cause: s 49(5);

- a dismissal for cause remains valid if the employers dismissed for one reason which turned out to be not justified, but after dismissal they discovered a valid reason: *Boston Deep Sea Fishing & Ice Co v Ansell* (1888). (The position is different in unfair dismissal: employers must have a fair reason for dismissal at the time of dismissal – an after-discovered reason will not make fair a previously unfair reason: *W Devis & Sons Ltd v Atkins* (1977));

- employers need not give any reason for dismissal at law. However, by EP(C)A s 53 as amended, they must provide written reasons to dismissed employees who have worked two years continuously for them.

7.2.8	Wrongful dismissal	Where employers dismiss an employee without notice or with insufficient notice, they are said to have wrongfully dismissed her unless they have a good cause to dismiss with no or insufficient notice.
7.2.9	Definition	Wrongful dismissal covers situations both where the employers sack the employee expressly (eg 'I sack you', 'get your cards', 'f... off and don't return') and where they act in such a manner that the employee is contractually entitled to leave and does so. The former situation has no title except dismissal though the terms 'express dismissal', 'actual dismissal' and 'direct dismissal' are increasingly accepted. The second situation, breach of a fundamental term (such as

non-payment of wages), is called 'repudiation'. In the event of an employee claiming a redundancy payment or unfair dismissal, the second situation is usually known as 'constructive dismissal'. Repudiation and constructive dismissal denote the same concepts, and the courts and tribunals use the terms more or less interchangeably.

It must be emphasised that if the employers do comply with the notice requirement, there is no wrongful dismissal. There is no need for them to provide any reason at all why they dismissed the worker. If they do give a reason, there is no need for the reason to be a good or valid one. An employee at common law could not challenge being dismissed, for example, for having red hair, no matter how long she had worked for the firm.

7.2.10 No reason needed

The primary and normally the sole remedy is damages. The rule is that the employee can obtain damages only for the notice period because at the end of that period the employers could have dismissed lawfully. If the notice period, whether contractual or the minimum statutory one is four weeks, that duration will be the basic quantum. To be added are sums for the loss of contractual benefits, such as bonuses and company car. The employee cannot instead of suing for damages sue in debt for her wages which should have been paid under the contract.

7.2.11 Damages for notice period

To the rule that damages are only for the notice period there are three exceptions, if they can be called exceptions:

7.2.12 Exceptions

- damages may be claimed for loss of employment rights which the employee would have acquired, had she not been dismissed before the qualifying period (*Stapp v Shaftesbury Society* (1982));

- if the contract is for something other than just wages, the employee may obtain damages for the further loss. For example, an apprentice who is sacked during the running of the apprenticeship can obtain damages for loss of training and of job prospects (*Dunk v George Waller & Son Ltd* (1970)). A public entertainer is partly rewarded through publicity: loss of publicity can increase damages;

- if the contract is for a fixed term and there is no provision for termination by notice (in the jargon there is no 'break clause') damages are awardable for the period the employee would have worked under the contract, had the agreement been performed. For example, assume that E serves under a 10-year fixed-term contract commencing in

1990; she is dismissed wrongfully in 1994. Her basic quantum is for salary for the remainder of the term, six years, which could be a substantial sum. The position would have been different if there had been a clause stating that her employers could dismiss by giving three months' notice. If they dismissed wrongfully, basic damages would only amount to the three months required contractually. Negotiation and drafting reveal their importance. Even in this situation the employee must mitigate (see below).

Beyond these exceptional cases the rule requires that in contract actions the aim is to put the aggrieved party in the position she would have been in, had the contract been lawfully performed. A contract with a three months' notice period can be terminated legally by giving notice of that length. Accordingly, damages are only for that period.

7.2.13 Uncompensatable losses

No damages are awarded for loss of reputation or the manner in which the employee was dismissed (*Addis v Gramophone Co* (1909)). This rule cannot be evaded by arguing that the employees were dismissed in breach of the implied term of trust and confidence, in that the employers had been acting fraudulently with the effect that the employees had suffered such a stigma that they could not obtain jobs (*Malik v Bank of Credit and Commerce International SA* (1995) CA). Damages will not be awarded to compensate for an illness brought on by the dismissal (*Bliss v South East Thames Regional Health Authority* (1987)).

7.2.14 Contractual benefits

Employees may obtain damages only to cover losses of benefits to which they were legally entitled. If bonuses were at the discretion of employers, no compensation is payable for their loss. *Laverack v Woods of Colchester Ltd* (1967) demonstrates that no damages are granted to cover increases in remuneration during the period in which the contract should have continued. Other examples of contractual benefits which will be compensated by the award of damages include membership of a private health-care scheme and of an occupational pension scheme.

7.2.15 Mitigation

As with other types of contract, employment law tells the aggrieved party to mitigate her loss. For example, the employee must find a new job if possible. An employee need not take any job that is offered: if the employers sack her and then offer her a job at a lower status than before the employee need not take that offer into account: *Yetton v Eastwoods Froy Ltd* (1966). An employee is not expected to take a job in which her skills are not used or her status is reduced.

Damages up to £30,000 are awarded net of tax under the rule in *British Transport Commission v Gourley* (1956), as amended by statute. Over £30,000 the amount is given gross, but the Inland Revenue taxes it.

7.2.16   Tax

Unemployment benefit is deducted (*Parsons v BNM Laboratories Ltd* (1964)). So is income support (formerly supplementary benefit). Redundancy payments are not deducted: *Wilson v NCB* (1980). Compensation for unfair dismissal is deducted, subject to the following limitation in *O'Laoire v Jackel International Ltd* (1991). If the employee's loss exceeds the amount awarded in the unfair dismissal claim there is no deduction because the court cannot say that the amount falls within one or other of the heads of damages awarded in a wrongful dismissal action. Payment for occupational pension schemes on termination of employment are not deducted because they comprise deferred pay to which the employee is entitled and are analogous to insurance (*Hopkins v Norcros plc* (1994) CA).

7.2.17   Deductions

A wrongful dismissal action is one for breach of contract. It is, therefore, heard in the normal courts. Legal aid may be available. The limitation period is six years. Proceedings are the same as any other civil litigation.

7.2.18   Process

17.2.19   Table

Tabular representation of differences between wrongful and unfair dismissal:

	Wrongful dismissal	*Unfair dismissal*
Basis	common law	statute (EP(C)A)
Coverage	all employees	some exceptions
Qualifying period	none	2 years (normally)
Dismissal	express & repudiation	express & constructive & non-renewal of fixed-term contract
Basis	no / insufficient notice	dismissal & unfair
After-discovered reason	yes (*Boston*)	no (*Devis*)
Remedy	damages	reinstatement of re-engagement or compensation
Limit to damages	no	yes
Where	High Court / County Court	IT
Time limit	6 years	3 months
Legal Aid	yes	IT - no; EAT - yes
Compensation for mode of dismissal	no	yes

Wrongful dismissal looks to the form of the sacking. Employers may lawfully dismiss for any or no reasons provided that they give the correct period of notice. Unfair dismissal concentrates both on procedure and substance. Both claims may be brought at the same time. Most contractual actions concerning dismissal can now be heard in industrial tribunals. Where they are heard in different fora, normally the wrongful dismissal action will be stayed so that the unfair dismissal claim can be heard separately and quickly.

7.2.20   Comparison with unfair dismissal

Though unfair dismissal has largely displaced wrongful dismissal it has not totally done so. An employee may be unable to claim a remedy for unfair dismissal, eg because she does not have the two years' continuous employment qualifying period. They are instances, mainly involving lengthy fixed-term contracts without a notice clause, where an employee can obtain more in damages than she can in an unfair dismissal application. The latter has a statutory 'cap' to the amount of compensation. Sometimes unfair dismissal may prove a better deal to employees. An illustration is that an IT may order the employers to reinstate the employee. Such a remedy is not possible in a wrongful dismissal action. Indeed, it was the deficiencies existing in wrongful dismissal which was one of the motivating factors which led to the institution of a remedy for unfair dismissal in 1971. The drawbacks of unfair dismissal have in turn led to renewed interest in wrongful dismissal and a search for fresh remedies.

7.2.21   Survival of wrongful dismissal

To determine a case of wrongful dismissal one should note the following:

7.2.22   Summary of wrongful dismissal

- Has there been a dismissal? Dismissal may be either 'express' or repudiation of the contract by breach of a fundamental term.

- Was the dismissal wrongful ie with short or no notice?

- Can the employers justify their otherwise wrongful dismissal?

- If the first and second criteria are fulfilled, and the third is not demonstrated, how much can the worker obtain?

The general rule is that neither employee nor employers can obtain specific performance of the contract or injunction restraining one party from doing something in breach of contract. A service agreement is a contract of personal service. Once the relationship is destroyed, the courts cannot

7.2.23   Other remedies

force one party to work with another. By s 236 of the Trade Union and Labour Relations (Consolidation) Act 1992:

'... no court shall, whether by way of

(a) an order for specific performance ... of a contract of employment, or

(b) an injunction ... restraining a breach or threatened breach of such of a contract,

compel an employee to do any work or attend at any place for the doing of any work.'

Specific enforcement of a contract of employment is thought to be equivalent to forcing a husband and wife to live together after their marriage has irretrievably broken down. Courts will not grant orders which require supervision, and usually damages are an adequate remedy in the view of the judiciary. One effect of the doctrine of no specific performance is that an employee at common law has no right to regain her old job. Even if an injunction is granted, the effect may be only to hold off dismissal. Provided the employers act properly, they may still dismiss. Nevertheless, one effect of the issue of an injunction is that there is now a method whereby management decisions can be challenged and reversed (if only for a short while). The remedy of damages cannot attain this end. There are exceptional situations listed in paras 7.2.24–27.

7.2.24   Negative covenants

Negative restraints in contracts (such as a covenant in restraint of trade) can be enforced by injunction even though enforcement will indirectly persuade the employee to perform the contract. In *Lumley v Wagner* (1852) the court enforced an agreement not to perform for any other theatre owner during the contract. A negative clause will not be enforced if enforcement would lead to an employee working for the employer or starving (*Rely-a-Bell Burglar & Fire Alarm Co v Eisler* (1926)). The courts also investigate whether the clause is a true negative one rather than a positive one expressed in negative language, though the line between the line is narrow if it exists at all. The courts will not enforce a provision that the employee will not work for others after the contract has terminated but will enforce valid restrictive covenants (see 4.8, above). In such cases damages will normally not be an adequate remedy.

7.2.25   Statute

Courts will grant an injunction to restrain dismissal where the contract of employment has 'statutory underpinnings': see *R v East Berkshire HA ex p Walsh* (1985) *per* Donaldson MR. A teacher in a grant-maintained school is in such an employment. In *R v Crown Prosecution Service ex p Hogg* (1995) the Court of Appeal held that a prosecutor's job with the CPS was not underpinned by statute but was an ordinary employment relationship. Therefore, his dismissal could not be challenged on public law grounds by judicial review. The Court thought that judicial review was perhaps available if he was dismissed for a reason which impugned his independence as a prosecutor. This topic is normally dealt with in administrative law texts. The basic rule is that ordinary master and servant cases do not give rise to remedies other than damages (*Ridge v Baldwin* (1964) *obiter*) but public employment may. Public employment covers jobs where there is some kind of public office which is fortified by statute. Judicial review is available for public employment matters, provided that the employee is not seeking to enforce private law rights. For example, in *R v Secretary of State for Employment ex p EOC* (1994) the House of Lords held that an 'ordinary' employee could not challenge the former qualification for unfair dismissal and redundancy payments that she had to have worked for five years at 16 or more hours per week by means of judicial review. She could, however, rely on her private law right to bring her claim before an industrial tribunal against her former employers. Declarations have been granted in relation to public employment and office holders eg in relation to a trade union officer in *Stevenson v URTU* (1977). In such instances *ultra vires* and natural justice comes into play as does judicial review under Ord 53. The Court of Appeal went further in *Gunton v Richmond-upon-Thames LBC* (1980) when it granted a declaration that the plaintiff's contract of employment continued in existence until the period of notice which would have been due, had his employers followed the disciplinary procedure laid down in his contract. The effect was that the amount of damages he obtained was small. It has been suggested that the applicant must show not solely a breach of natural justice but also that she has been materially prejudiced.

Where there remains mutual trust and confidence between the parties and damages are inadequate recompense, the employee may obtain an injunction to restrain dismissal where the dismissal is in breach of contract (*Irani v Southampton and South West Hampshire Health Authority* (1985)). This head of jurisdiction stems from *Hill v CA Parsons & Co* (1972). There are a growing number of authorities in this area. There is a view that mutual trust is not required where the employee is not seeking to get her job back.	7.2.26 Mutual trust
Where there is an elaborate system eg of appeals before dismissal, an injunction may be granted to restrain the employers' acting beyond their contractual powers by dismissing in breach of the terms: see for example *R v BBC ex p*	7.2.27 Workability

Lavelle (1983) and *Robb v London Borough of Hammersmith and Fulham* (1991). Employees are not restricted to the common law remedy of damages. In *Jones v Gwent CC* (1992) Chadwick J granted a declaration that a letter of dismissal was invalid because it did not comply with the contract and an injunction to restrain the defendants from treating him as being dismissed, despite the fact that there was no mutual trust and confidence. In this situation the order sought must be 'workable', though this condition has not always been required.

| 7.2.28 | Automatic termination |

One sometimes academic point is the following. If dismissal led to the contract of employment's being terminated automatically, ie without any need for acceptance of the breach of a fundamental term by the employee, there would be nothing to perform specifically or to enjoin. General contract law is to the effect that the doctrine of what might be called 'elective termination' applies – the aggrieved party may elect whether to bring the contract to a close or to continue with it (and claim only a monetary remedy). The elective theory was summed up pithily in *Howard v Pickford Tool Co Ltd* (1951): 'an unaccepted repudiation is a thing writ in water and no value to anybody'. Acceptance of the breach can be demonstrated by applying for a remedy for unfair dismissal. Employment law has shifted between the two theories. The present law is that the contract of employment's termination must be accepted by the employee as a matter of law, but in practice the contract is terminated by the employers' repudiation: *Gunton v Richmond-upon-Thames LBC*, above, which is binding on the Court of Appeal and below, and *Rigby v Ferodo Ltd* (1988). In the *Ferodo* case the House of Lords accepted that the quote from *Howard* represented both contract law and employment law, though Lord Oliver did state that this was so except in 'the extreme case of outright dismissal or walk-out'. Because elective termination is now adopted, there is the possibility of the issuance of an injunction to restrain the employers from acting in breach of contract. The question whether termination is automatic or elective is also important when deciding the date of termination: that decision may affect whether an employee has a statutory employment right. If the elective theory is accepted, the employee who does not accept the repudiation is entitled to sue in debt for wages and does not sue for damages for breach of contract (*Morgan v West Glamorgan County Council* (1995)).

| 7.2.29 | Effect of remedy |

Before an injunction is granted, the courts act as they do in non-employment cases. An injunction is an equitable remedy awarded at the court's discretion following the maxims of equity such as inquiring whether the employee came with clean hands. No relief will be granted if damages constitute an adequate remedy.

Termination of the Contract of Employment at Common Law

Like other contracts, service agreements may be terminated by death, frustration, elapse of a fixed term, mutual consent and performance:

Notcutt v Universal Equipment (1986)

Shepherd v Jerrom (1986)

Birch v University of Liverpool (1985)

Igbo v Johnson Matthey (1986).

The principal issues which arise are the application of the contractual doctrine of frustration to short-term contracts of employment, the possibility of losing one's employment protection rights by leaving early, and the effect of the anti-evasion provision in s 140(1) of EP(C)A.

Where the contract of employment ends by operation of law or agreement, there is generally no dismissal and accordingly no statutory or contractual claim.

Termination other than by dismissal

Contractual notice periods may be extended by statute. The notice period may be expressly stipulated in the contract; if there is none, it must arise impliedly and be of a duration reasonable in the circumstances. Statute (s 49 of EP(C)A) builds on the contractual period. It is calculated by the formula of:

Termination by dismissal

- one week for up to two years; or

- one week for each year between two and 12 years; or

- 12 weeks for over 12 years.

The statutory minimum cannot be reduced by contract. An employee employed for whatever length of time must give her employers at least one week's notice.

Summary dismissal occurs when employers dismiss without giving the correct length of notice.

Employers may dismiss lawfully for cause: *Taylor v Alidair* (1978).

Wrongful dismissal means summary dismissal without cause which is not justified. Justifications include disobedience, theft, swearing and clocking-in on behalf of a colleague, but each case depends on its own facts. Usually one act of carelessness will not be sufficient to justify a dismissal.

The principal remedy is damages. Normal contract rules governing calculation and deductions including mitigation apply. In the normal run of cases the amount of damages will be small because the sum is determined by the length of the notice period. At times wrongful dismissal remains a better remedy for employees than unfair dismissal such as when she is not qualified for the latter. Compensation for unfair dismissal is limited to a maximum amount. The limitation period for wrongful dismissal is six years, whereas it is, in the general run of unfair dismissal cases, three months. Legal aid may be available for wrongful dismissal. It is not available for unfair dismissal at the industrial tribunal.

There is a growing jurisprudence on injunctions to restrain dismissals: *Irani v Soton & SW Hants* (1985). The law is not settled but the cases have largely turned on the existence of statutory underpinning, the continued presence of mutual trust between the parties and the 'workability' of the remedy on the facts.

Elective not automatic is the preferred theory of dismissal: *Gunton v Richmond LBC* (1981). The elective theory is that as with other contracts a contract of employment is not terminated by the employers until the employee accepts the repudiation. She may wish to affirm the contract. The automatic thesis is that the contract is determined by the employers and the employee plays no part in the termination. In practical terms the difference may be none. If the employers refuse to pay the employee, she cannot normally work for nothing and the doors may be closed against her.

Chapter 8

Common Issues in Redundancy Payments and Unfair Dismissal

Statutory redundancy payments and unfair dismissal claims share common features. This chapter deals with qualifications for the two claims, noting any differences. It begins with flowcharts (algorithms) detailing the stages in these claims where the case is a straightforward one. Chapter 11 treats unfair dismissal applications which do not fit within the general scheme.

Redundancy flowchart:

8.1   Statutory claims

8.1.1   Redundancy

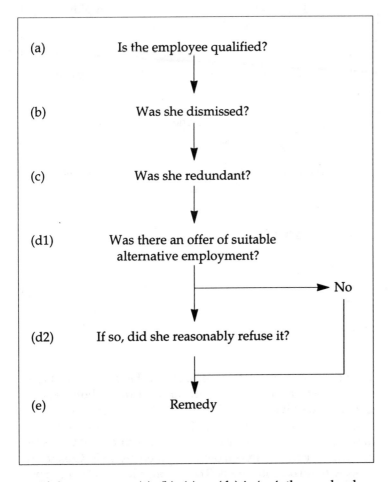

If the answer to (a), (b), (c) or (d2) is 'no', the worker has no remedy.

8.1.2   Unfair dismissal

Unfair dismissal flowchart. The sequence may be remembered as QDR^3.

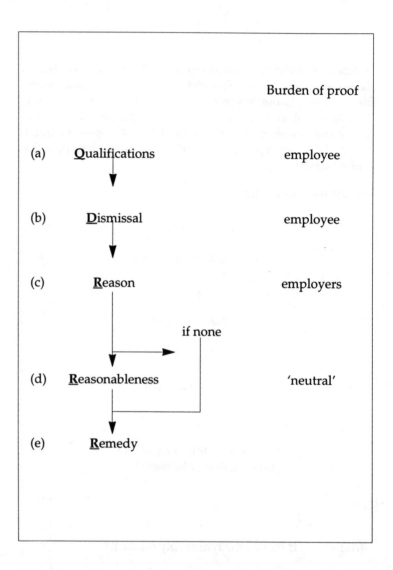

8.1.3   Layout of chapters

The next five chapters consider parts of the above flowcharts. This chapter is concerned with (a) and (b) of both charts. Chapter 9 considers (c), (d1) and (d2) of the redundancy chart. Chapter 10 deals with (c) and (d) of the unfair dismissal flowchart. Chapter 11 considers issues which do not fit within that chart such as dismissal on trade union grounds. Chapter 12 deals with (e) on both charts. The law may look unmanageable, and certainly the case-load has become unwieldy, but with the above frameworks in mind the reader should not go astray.

Both redundancy payment and unfair dismissal claims are made to industrial tribunals (not the courts). Legal aid is not available for either at that stage: Green Form advice is available. Both claims are made under the Employment Protection (Consolidation) Act 1978 (EP(C)A).

8.1.4   Procedure

There has been much discussion of the policies underlying the law on redundancy payments and unfair dismissal. It has been argued that although these policies favour employees their effect has been to legitimise managerial prerogatives. In relation to redundancy the aims are thought to be these:

8.2   Policy

- recompense to employees who are dismissed through no fault of their own, the remedy being compensation for long service;

- money is given to employees to buy-off attempts to disrupt the restructuring of industry.

In the light of these industrial relations aims one might expect that a wide interpretation would be given to the concept of redundancy but as will be seen the judiciary has taken a narrow view. The aims of the unfair dismissal legislation are thought to be:

- to promote the improvement of employers' treatment of employees;

- linked with the improvement of treatment of employees is the improvement desired for companies' personnel records;

- to prevent strikes concerned with dismissals. The law was drafted so as to provide more protection for employees than does the common law of wrongful dismissal (see the previous chapter).

The second aim has been achieved, though the true influence of the legislation is unknown. The third one apparently has not been achieved. It should be noted that most claims are brought by applicants who are not members of unions, and that most claims are brought against small employers: perhaps unions keep employers up to the mark, and small employers continue to act like tsars.

The following qualifications apply to both redundancy payments and unfair dismissal. The burden of proving that she is qualified rests on the employee.

8.3   Qualifications

The applicant must be an employee or an apprentice (see s 153(1)). This matter is considered in Chapter 3. The self-employed have no claim. The more independent contractors there are, the less relevant is unfair dismissal.

8.3.1   Employee

8.3.2	Continuous employment	The employee must have two years' continuous employment. An attempt to overturn the two-year qualifying period in *R v Secretary of State for Employment ex p Seymour-Smith* (1994) on the basis that the requirement was indirectly discriminatory against women failed in the Divisional Court. The application for judicial review should have been brought within three months of the Statutory Instrument which increased the general qualified period from one year to two years; and it had not been demonstrated that a considerably smaller proportion of women than men could comply with the rules: the percentage of women who qualified was 89.1% of the percentage of qualifying men. The previous exclusion of part-time employees was repealed by the Employment Protection (Part-time Employees) Regulations 1995 (SI 31) as a result of *R v Secretary of State for Employment ex p Equal Opportunities Commission* (1994) (HL). The issue of continuity is dealt with separately in the next section. While there are varying definitions of part-time work, there is no doubt that the proportion of part-time to full-time employment has increased over the last 20 years, just as the proportion of independent contractors has increased in relation to employees. The coverage of the law is decreasing. The two-year limit was chosen in 1985 in order to reduce the burdens on businesses. However, in *ex p Seymour-Smith* the Court held that there was no evidence that the two-year qualifying period increased the availability of jobs than did the previous one-year period. (There is no qualifying period for those dismissed for trade union membership or activities or for any other inadmissible reason.)
8.3.3	Excluded classes	The employee must not be a member of an excluded class such as share fishermen (ie those paid by a share of the catch) (s 144(2)). There are various other excluded classes of employees. For example, central government employers cannot claim a redundancy payment (they have better contractual arrangements). Section 138(4) allows a Minister of the Crown to exclude employees from their statutory rights on the grounds of national security. This power was famously used in relation to workers at the Government Communications Headquarters.
8.3.4	Outside Great Britain	She must, for a remedy for unfair dismissal, not ordinarily work outside Great Britain (ie England, Wales and Scotland): s 141. There are slightly more complex rules dealing with redundancy payments. If it is not clear whether the employee works within Great Britain, the tribunal should investigate where the employee's base is (*Todd v British Midland Airways Ltd* (1978)). It must be stressed that it is the wording of the

section which matters and the tribunal should not become too wrapped up in deciding where the employee's base was. It does not matter that the employee spent more time away from base than at it, ie one looks at the base in the contract, not at the base in practice (*Wilson v Maynard Shipbuilding Consultants AB* (1978)). Unfortunately *Todd* says one does investigate where the base was in practice, and Lord Denning MR said that contractual terms were often of little help in determining the base. A further ruling is needed to clarify the law. The most recent authority, *Geest Line v Wright* (1995), stresses that the contract must first be construed to determine whether the employee worked ordinarily outside Great Britain; only if there was no clear answer should the tribunal investigate the base. A worker sent abroad on a posting is likely to remain based in the Great Britain.

The employee must for the purposes of unfair dismissal not be over the normal retirement age for workers of her category in her firm. If there is no such age, the limit is 65 years for both sexes. The law is laid down by s 64(1)(b) as amended by the Sex Discrimination Act 1986. For the purposes of redundancy payments the maximum age is 65 or if less the normal retirement age: Employment Act 1989, s 16 amending s 82(1) of EP(C)A (ie the test is different). In unfair dismissal in the leading authority the House of Lords held in *Nothman v Barnet LBC* (1979) that if there is a normal retirement age, only that age is considered. The age of 65 is only a fall-back provision. Accordingly, if there is no normal retirement age, the maximum age one can claim at is 65. The normal retirement age need not be the one stated in the contract but can be the date at which employees in the position of the applicant retire in practice (*Waite v GCHQ* (1983)). However, there is a rebuttable presumption that the contractual age is the normal retiring age. In *Brooks v British Telecommunications plc* (1990) CA the contractual age was 60. Some employees in the same position as the applicant had been allowed to work beyond that age, but the reasonable expectation was that employees would retire at 60 and accordingly 60 was the normal age of retirement. The practice of permitting some employees to work beyond that age did not affect the reasonable expectation. The reasonable expectation can be altered by the employers informing the employees of a change (*Hughes v DHSS* (1985) HL). For a summary of the law see *O'Brien v Barclays Bank plc* (1995) CA.

   The age limit does not apply to unfair dismissal claims concerned with sackings for membership of an independent trade union, taking part in its activities, or for refusing to join or to remain a member of any union.

8.3.5   Normal retiring age

8.3.6	Exempted industry	The employee must not be employed in an industry which has been exempted from coverage of the legislation by the Secretary of State for Employment: s 65. The sole industry so treated is the electrical contracting industry. The Secretary of State may designate an agreement between employers and independent trade unions under s 65 only if the collective agreement provides better protection for employees than does the law of unfair dismissal. Section 65 was inserted to preserve collective bargaining over dismissals. The fact that it has been little used may be surprising to those imbued with the spirit of collective *laissez-faire*.
8.3.7	National security	With regard to dismissal for the purposes of safeguarding national security, Schedule 9 para 2 provides that the employee has no claim. There must be a ministerial certificate to this effect. This can be issued quickly.
8.3.8	Waiver	She must not have waived her right in writing. She must be employed on a fixed-term contract lasting two years or more for redundancy payments purposes or one year or more for unfair dismissal purposes. The definition of fixed term was given in Chapter 7. No consideration need be given for the waiver. The exemption applies only when the contract terminates at the end of the fixed term. It does not apply if the employers breach a fundamental term during the running of the contract. In that eventuality the employee may make a claim. The law is laid down in s 142(1) as amended.
8.3.9	Claim in time	In the case of unfair dismissal the employee must apply within three months of the 'effective date of termination' (s 67). The rule is to find the effective date, take the preceding day, and then add three months (*University of Cambridge v Murray* (1993)). In the case of redundancy payments the limitation period is six months from the 'relevant date'. In both claims there is an exception. In redundancy payments the limitation period can be extended by a further six months if the tribunal thinks it 'just and equitable' to do so. For unfair dismissal purposes the claim may be heard if presented 'within such further period as the tribunal considers reasonable in a case where it is satisfied that it was not reasonably practicable for the complaint to be presented before the end of the period of three months'. In relation to unfair dismissal proceedings concerned with sackings during a lock-out or industrial action when the employers have selectively re-engaged those directly interested in the lock-out or on strike (see s 238(2)-(3) of the Trade Union and Labour Relations (Consolidation) Act 1992) the limitation period is six months: s 239(2) of that Act. There is the usual extension to a period the tribunal deems reasonable

if it was not reasonably practicable to present the claim within the six months.

Ignorance of the right not to be unfairly dismissed is not sufficient to bring an employee within the 'reasonably practicable' exception. A desire not to antagonise the employers is no excuse (*Birmingham Optical plc v Johnson* (1995)). Similarly, the fact that the employee has been going through the company's internal appeals procedure will not excuse (*Palmer v Southend-on-Sea BC* (1984)). It is unfortunate that the Court of Appeal was unwilling to extend the deadline and thereby aid the voluntary settlement of disputes. Illness is one of the excuses for not complying with the time limit. In *James W Cook & Co (Wivenhoe) Ltd v Tipper* (1990) the Court of Appeal decided that it was not reasonably practicable to present applications for redundancy payments when employees thought that the amount of work would shortly increase. Excuses given by the Court of Appeal in *Wall's Meat Co Ltd v Khan* (1979) were a physical impediment, a postal strike, an absence overseas. Discovering that the dismissal was given for a bogus reason more than three months after dismissal was treated as a valid excuse in *Churchill v Yeates & Son* (1983). If a solicitor does not present the claim in time, the remedy is an action in negligence against her for failing to meet the deadline.

The effective date of termination (often called EDoT or EDT) is the date from where the time limit for unfair dismissal claims runs. It is also the date up to which the two-year qualification period runs. The same rules apply in redundancy payments law, except that the date is called the 'relevant date'. The law is laid down in ss 55 and 90 of EP(C)A.

The rules are these:

- If either the employee or employers terminate the contract by giving notice, the EDoT is the date on which notice expires. This rule applies even if the notice was not of the relevant length. Where notice is given orally, the period begins on the next day. The law on notice was considered in the previous chapter (paras 7.2.1–4).

- If there is a lawful dismissal or resignation with no notice, the EDoT is when the termination takes effect. This rule applies even when the effect is to deprive the employee of the qualifying period for employment protection (*Stapp v Shaftesbury Society* (1982)). The rule applies even though the employee is dismissed summarily when under notice of dismissal already.

8.3.10 'Reasonably practicable'

8.4 The effective date of termination

8.4.1 Rules

- If a fixed-term contract expires, the EDoT is the date of expiry.

- If an employee under notice gives a counter notice to end employment earlier, the EDoT is the date of expiry of the counter notice: *Thompson v GEC Avionics Ltd* (1991).

- If wages are given in lieu of notice, the EDoT is when the employee leaves, according to *Robert Cort & Son Ltd v Charman* (1981). This rule applies whether or not the dismissal was lawful. It should be noted that there is another line of cases which hold that if dismissal is by notice but the employee is informed that she need not work out that period, the effective date is when the notice expires, not when she left.

- Neither s 55 nor s 90 deals with the EDoT where there is a constructive dismissal. The EAT held in *BMK Ltd v Logue* (1993) that, aplying s 55(4), the EDoT was the date when termination took effect. A constructive dismissal was treated as a dismissal without notice. Termination need not be on the date when the employee accepted the repudiation as terminating the contract. On the facts, removal of the applicant's directorship terminated the contract. The fact that he did not understand the true legal position was irrelevant.

8.4.2 Difference

While the effective date of termination is generally the same for both continuity of employment and limitation period purposes, there is one difference. For continuity purposes only, where the employers have dismissed with less notice than is provided by statute, that extra period (but not any contractual period) beyond the notice actually given is added on (s 55(5)). The effect may be to push the employee over the two years' qualifying period for statutory claims. Apparently s 55(5) applies even though the dismissal is for gross misconduct (*Lanton Leisure Ltd v White* (1987)).

8.5 Continuity

Separate treatment is awarded to this topic because of its complexity. The effect of the Transfer of Undertakings (Protection of Employment) Regulations 1981 (TUPE) is considered in Chapter 13. References below are to various paragraphs of Schedule 13 to EP(C)A.

The basic ideas behind the concept of continuity of employment are these.

8.5.1 Breach of continuity

If continuity is broken, the employee must start again to build up length of service for the purposes both of qualifying to claim and of calculating the amount due. For example, if the employee has overall worked for the employers for five years but seven months ago she took an unauthorised holiday for a month but was then re-employed, subject to the rules below she has only six months' continuous employment. Therefore, if she is now dismissed, she does not have the requisite two years' qualifying period for a normal unfair dismissal claim. The requirement of two years' continuous employment works harshly against temporary employees such as seasonal workers and members of the peripheral labour force: see the case of *O'Kelly v Trusthouse Forte plc* (1984) discussed in Chapter 3.

Sometimes continuity is preserved but the week does not count. The principal provision is para 15. If the employee has been on strike, the period of the strike does not count towards the qualifying period; however, the time before and after the strike do count. Therefore, the employee does not lose the years and months which she had accumulated before the strike. That period is added to the time after the strike. The whole of a week in which the employee was on strike does not count, even though the strike lasted for only a minute. It does not matter that a striker was dismissed and then taken back by the employers. By para 14(3) weeks spent abroad do not count for the purposes of redundancy payments (but continuity is preserved).

8.5.2   Counting

It does not matter if the employee has had different jobs with the employers (or with the employers to whom the employee's contract has been transferred). Continuity runs from the commencement of employment, not eg from promotion or the change to a different department (*Wood v York City Council* (1978)). As that case demonstrates, it does not matter that the employee resigned from one council post to obtain another. The continuity provisions apply even though the previous employment with the relevant employers has come to an end through frustration (*Tipper v Roofdec Ltd* (1979)).

8.5.3   Different jobs

There is a presumption of continuity: para 1(3). (This presumption does not apply in relation to the transfer of a business: see para 17(2) discussed at para 8.5.15 below.) If the employee shows that a week counts, the burden is on the employers to prove that other weeks do not count (*Nicoll v Nocorrode Ltd* (1981)).

8.5.4   Presumption

Employment with an 'associated' employer counts.

8.5.5   Associated employments

'Any two employers are to be treated as associated employers if one is a company of which the other (directly or indirectly) has control or if both are companies of which a third person (directly or indirectly) has control ...' (s 153(4)).

Though the issue is not settled, the Court of Appeal held in *South West Launderettes Ltd v Laidler* (1986) that voting control was needed. A group of persons can be the controlling body (*Zarb v British & Brazilian Produce Co (Sales) Ltd* (1978)).

8.5.6 Re-employment

Where the employee is successful in an unfair dismissal claim and is reinstated or re-engaged by the employers, their successors or by associated employers, continuity is preserved and the weeks between dismissal and re-employment count. The same applies to re-employment as a result of the intervention of a conciliation officer or a result of a voluntary agreement. See Chapter 12 below.

8.5.7 Which weeks count?

By paragraph 4 as amended by the Employment Protection (Part-time Employees) Regulations 1995 (SI 31) 'Any week during the whole or part of which the employee's relations with the employer are governed by a contract of employment shall count in computing a period of employment.' The previous rules which excluded part-time employees have been abolished. These provisions found in paragraphs 3, 5–8, were abrogated by the Secretary of State for Employment as being sexually discriminatory. Part-time employment no longer affects continuity.

8.5.8 No contract

The main difficulty surrounds para 9, which applies in four situations to preserve continuity.

- If the employee is incapable of work through sickness, para 9(1)(a) preserves continuity for 26 weeks. If a person is absent through illness then stays off for pension reasons, the latter absence breaks continuity: *Pearson v Kent CC* (1992).

- If she is absent because of a 'temporary cessation of work', continuity is preserved for the duration: para 9(1)(b). It is possible that continuity is preserved where the employee lost his first job and later was re-employed by the same employers on a different job (*Cannell v Council of the City of Newcastle-upon-Tyne* (1994), *obiter*). It is the employee's work which must have ceased. Whether the cessation was temporary is looked at with hindsight ie at the end of the cessation, can one say that it was temporary (*Fitzgerald v Hall, Russell & Co Ltd* (1970)? This provision will cover a phased return to work after industrial action. In *Ford v Warwickshire CC* (1983) the Lords held that a teacher with eight September–July contracts could include the weeks in between, for the time off between contracts was temporary. To break continuity the time between the contracts had to be assessed as longer than of short duration. Two years can be temporary (*Bentley Engineering Co Ltd v Crown* (1976)). However, the EAT held in *Berwick Salmon Fisheries Co Ltd v Rutherford* (1991) that a cessation was not temporary when the employee was laid off through lack of work for more time than he spent at work as a salmon-netter.

- If she is absent by arrangement or custom, sub-para (1)(c) operates to preserve continuity. The sub-paragraph covers a situation where the employee has been granted time off for personal reasons and where she is placed on a holding list pending return to work after lengthy absence. The law as to determining whether absence is temporary remains uncertain. A case is *Lloyds Bank Ltd v Secretary of State for Employment* (1979). A bank clerk worked one week on, one week off. There was no contract in the weeks off. The EAT held that para 9(1)(c) applied. This case has come in for criticism. In *Ford v Warwickshire CC*, above, the Lords emphasised that the side-note to para 9 read: 'records in which there is no contract of employment'. In *Lloyds*, however, there was a contract throuhout the whole period. If para 9 is restricted to non-contractual periods, *Lloyds* is wrong. (It should be noted that the normal rule is that side-notes are irrelevant to the process of interpretation.)

- If the employee is absent from work wholly or partly because of pregnancy or childbirth, para 9(1)(d) preserves continuity for 26 weeks. However, if the employee exercises her right to return in accordance with EP(C)A, by para 10 all weeks count (ie 11 weeks before childbirth, 29 weeks afterwards), but that provision applies only to women who, by already having two years' continuous employment, qualify for the right to return. The term 'childbirth' was substituted for confinement by the Trade Union Reform and Employment Rights Act 1993, Schedule 8, para 8. It is defined in s 153(1) of EP(C)A as inserted by para 25(a)(i) of Schedule 8 to the 1993 Act as 'the birth of a living child or the birth of a child whether living or dead after 24 weeks of pregnancy'.

It should be noted that there is no need to consider para 9 if there is a continuing contract of employment. In that situation the rule discussed in para 8.5.7 applies to preserve continuity (eg the contract usually continues when an employee is sick).

8.5.9   Subsisting contract

In the event of a change of employers the basic principle is that continuity of employment is broken. There are, however, six situations in which continuity is preserved by Schedule 13:

8.5.10   Transfer of employers

- where the trade, business or undertaking of the old employers is transferred: para 17(2). A person's continuous employment is preserved where he is retained by the old employers after sale of their business and then employed by the new ones, provided that the machinery of the transfer was taking place throughout that period. Moreover, a short gap in employment even one for which the applicant claimed unemployment benefit can be bridged by para 17(2). The test is whether there has been a transfer of the business as a going concern. Usually there must be a transfer of goodwill. It is not enough that the employee has the same working environment. The principal authority for these propositions remains *Woodhouse v Peter Brotherhood Ltd* (1972). Accordingly, para 17(2) will not apply if there has been merely a transfer of assets (*Melon v Hector Powe Ltd* (1981)). For example, in *Crompton v Truly Fair (International) Ltd* (1975) there was no transfer when the old employers made children's clothes, the new ones men's trousers. The distinction between transfer as a going concern and transfer of assets applies to TUPE. The burden of proving a transfer is on the employee (*Secretary of State for Employment v Cohen* (1987)) despite the presumption that the employee did have continuity of employment;

- where Parliament causes one company to replace another: para 17(3);

- where an employer who is a natural person dies and the personal representatives take over: para 17(4);

- where the employers are a partnership, personal representatives or trustees, and the composition of that body changes: para 17(5). A transfer from a partnership of four doctors to one is caught by para 17(2): *Jeetle v Elster* (1985);

- where the employee is employed by an associated company: para 18. See 8.5.5. above for the definition of associated employers;

- where the employee is employed by the governors of a school maintained by a local education authority (LEA) or by the LEA itself, and she is transferred to governors of another school or to another LEA: para 18A.

| 8.5.11 | Employee's role |

It does not matter that the employee did not work for the transferees as long as the business was transferred: *Lord Advocate v de Rosa* (1974).

| 8.5.12 | Moment of transfer |

For para 17(2) to apply the employee must be employed 'at the time of the transfer'. In *Teesside Times Ltd v Drury* (1980) the

Court of Appeal controversially said that that phrase meant 'at the moment of transfer'. If she was not, continuity was not preserved. This decision is not in accord with the purpose of the legislation, which is to preserve continuity on a transfer (*Macer v Abafast Ltd* (1990) EAT).

Superimposed on Schedule 13, paras 17 and 18 are TUPE. TUPE partly but not totally replaces para 17(2), which is not repealed. Where TUPE applies, continuity is preserved. See Chapter 13 below for TUPE. It should be noted that the enactment of TUPE does not affect the construction of para 17(2), which is read in the light of purely domestic authorities (*Green-Wheeler v Onyx (UK) Ltd* (1993)).

8.5.13   Transfer regulations

For both redundancy payments and unfair dismissal purposes there are three types of dismissal: ss 55(2) and 83(2). The burden of proof is on the employee.

8.6   Dismissal

'Express', 'actual' or 'direct' dismissal occurs where the employers terminate the contract with or without notice. Such a dismissal occurs where the employers say, eg, 'You're fired', 'Get your cards'. There have been cases where tribunals have had to consider whether the words used did consitute dismissal eg 'Fuck off' may not amount to dismissal (*Futty v D & D Brekkes* (1974)). The tribunals have also held that words of dismissal spoken in anger can be withdrawn and that words indicating a dismissal were not to be taken as such when they occur in the heat of the moment (*Tanner v Kean* (1978) EAT).

8.6.1   'Express'

The expiry of a fixed-term contract without renewal (for definition see Chapter 7). It is thought that this type of termination of a contract was deemed by Parliament to be a dismissal in order to prevent employers' putting workers on to such contracts to avoid the employment protection legislation. The ending of a contract of apprenticeship is the expiry of a fixed-term contract and by definition it cannot be extended. It should be noted that in any case there is an anti-avoidance provision in EP(C)A, s 140 (see *Igbo v Johnson Matthey Chemicals Ltd* (1986) in the previous chapter).

8.6.2   Non-renewal of fixed-term contract

There has been debate about the meaning of the handy phrase constructive dismissal. The Court of Appeal in *Western Excavating (ECC) Ltd v Sharp* (1978) held that constructive dismissal is the same as the common law concept of repudiatory breach. The employee must be contractually entitled to leave because of the employers' breach of a fundamental term or because they have evinced an intention no longer to be bound by the contract (ie anticipatory breach). An

8.6.3   Constructive

example of anticipatory breach is *Greenaway Harrison Ltd v Wiles* (1994). The employers proposed to vary the applicant's hours of work unilaterally unless she agreed and they said that they would dismiss her in accordance with her contract otherwise. It did not matter that the threat to terminate the contract was lawful. The EAT said that if they were not correct, employers could avoid constructive dismissal simply by threatening to give notice of dismissal. (It may be enquired which condition in the contract the employers were proposing to breach, for after all Western Excavating requires such a breach.) The reasonableness of the employers' conduct is irrelevant. For example, in *Courtaulds Northern Spinning Ltd v Sibson* (1988) the Court of Appeal held that an order to move to a nearby site was permitted impliedly by the contract. Whether the order was unreasonable was immaterial. There must be no waiver of the breach. Express and constructive dismissal were dealt with in the previous chapter. Both can give rise to a common law action for wrongful dismissal. Except for the non-renewal of a fixed-term contract, what does not amount to a dismissal at common law does not amount to a dismissal under EP(C)A. For example, an employee has no claim for unfair dismissal if her contract of service is terminated by frustration. In all three instances of dismissal the touchstone is the termination of the employment contract. It is immaterial that the employment relationship continues, as it does if an employee is sacked and then taken back on. In this situation there is a dismissal because the employers have sacked the employee (*Hogg v Dover College* (1990)).

8.6.4   Examples

The following cases are a few of the multitude dealing with constructive dismissal:

- giving an employee an unjustified warning: *Walker v Josiah Wedgwood & Sons Ltd* (1978);

- using extremely foul language: *Palmanor Ltd v Cedron* (1978);

- failing to provide a safe system of work: *British Aircraft Corp v Austin* (1978);

- failing to pay wages: *R F Hill Ltd v Mooney* (1981);

- imposing a penalty disproportionate to the offence: *BBC v Beckett* (1983);

- being unfairly critical on several occasions: *Lewis v Motorworld Garages Ltd* (1985). This case is an illustration of a 'last straw' dismissal. It does not matter that the last breach was not repudiatory as long as cumulatively the breaches destroyed the trust underlying the contract;

- dressing down an employee in front of colleagues: *Hilton International (UK) Ltd v Protopapa* (1990);

- appointing another person to do the employee's job even though the employers believed on reasonable grounds that he would not be returning: *Brown v JBD Engineering Ltd* (1993). The fact that there has been a mistake is relevant to whether there has been a repudiation but does not decide it.

A case where there was no contructive dismissal is *Dryden v Greater Glasgow Health Board* (1992). The employers introduced a no-smoking policy but without breaking contract. Since there was no breach of contract there could be no constructive dismissal. Many instances of constructive dismissal stem nowadays from breach of the implied term of trust and confidence, which includes the duty not to treat employees arbitrarily or capriciously.

Whether the conduct of the employers is sufficiently serious to entitle the employee to leave immediately is a question of fact for the tribunal: *Woods v WM Car Services (Peterborough) Ltd* (1982). Accordingly, one tribunal may find that conduct is repudiatory in one case but not in the next and the Employment Appeal Tribunal cannot intervene in the interests of consistency. Moreover, should a tribunal wish to give itself jurisdiction to hear the merits of the case it will hold that there has been a constructive dismissal, for without a dismissal the claim cannot proceed. Since constructive dismissal is largely dependent on there being a breach of a fundamental term and the term may be an implied one, tribunals may invent or discover novel implied terms such as the duty to treat employees with respect (see Chapter 4), thereby giving themselves jurisdiction. It is interesting to note the number of reported cases from the late 1970s, after the Court had ruled in *Western Excavating* that constructive dismissal required breach of a fundamental contractual term, in which tribunals sought to get round the need to find breach of such a term.

8.6.5   Problems

One sophisticated point is this: where the employers break the contract and the employee leaves as a result, is this a dismissal by the employers or a constructive dismissal? The answer would seem to be both. Which it is matters when discovering the effective date of termination (see above).

8.6.6   Who terminates?

Common Issues in Redundancy Payments and Unfair Dismissal

Redundancy payments and unfair dismissal are employment protection laws created by Parliament.

Statutory claims

Parliament's aims include recompensing employees for loss of their jobs and improving personnel management.

Policy

Employees must be qualified to apply for these remedies. Basically they must have two years' continuous employment, not be members of excluded classes, not ordinarily work outside GB, not be over the retirement age, not have waived their rights, and claim in time:

Qualifications

Nothman v Barnet LBC (1979)

Palmer v Southend-on-Sea BC (1984).

The effective date of termination is the date to which continuous employment runs and from which the limitation period runs. Where the employers dismiss with notice, the effective date is when the notice expires.

Effective date

Employment must be continuous for statutory claims, and weeks count towards the qualifying period (and the quantum of compensation). The rules are complex. Continuity is preserved in the absence of contract by para 9 of Schedule 13 to EP(C)A and on transfer by para 17(2):

Continuity

Fitzgerald v Hall, Russell (1970)

Ford v Warwickshire CC (1983)

Woodhouse v Peter Brotherhood (1972).

During a strike, continuity is not broken but the weeks do not count. There is a presumption of continuity: the burden of disproof lies on the employers. The effects of the Transfer of Undertakings (Protection of Employment) Regulations 1981 are considered in Chapter 13.

For statutory purposes 'dismissal' covers dismissal by employers, non-renewal of fixed-term contracts, and constructive dismissal. The last is defined in contractual terms and covers eg 'last straw' cases:

Dismissal

Western Excavating v Sharp (1978)

Lewis v Motorworld (1985).

There are hundreds of cases on what amounts to constructive dismissal ie to conduct entitling the employee to leave without notice. Since constructive dismissal is defined in contractual terms, industrial tribunals have to consider whether or not a fundamental term, whether express or implied, has been breached. Tribunals may 'invent' an implied term in order to give themselves jurisdiction to hear the merits of the case, which they cannot do if they conclude that there has been no dismissal.

Chapter 9

Redundancy Payments

The statutory scheme for redundancy payments is found in ss 81–120 of the Employment Protection (Consolidation) Act 1978 (EP(C)A). Private schemes may be more advantageous to employees than the State scheme, which provides only a minimum (a 'floor of rights') supplementable by contractual or ex gratia payments. The maximum State payment is £6,150 but private schemes eg in coalmining and shipbuilding provide substantially more. When redundancy payments were first introduced in 1965, they were intended to ease demanning in traditional heavy industries. Their purpose now would seem to be to facilitate dismissals without friction.	**9.1 Introduction**

A flowchart on redundancy was provided at the start of Chapter 8, which also deals with the first two stages of the claim: was the employee qualified and was she dismissed? This chapter considers the next two stages: was the employee redundant and did the employers make a suitable offer of alternative employment, and, if so, did the employee reasonably refuse it? Also considered is the procedure for handling redundancies now found in ss 188–198 of the Trade Union and Labour Relations (Consolidation) Act 1992 (TULR(C)A). The amount of compensation is detailed in Chapter 12.

    9.1.1   Coverage of chapter

The misconduct exclusion is such that an employee will not be awarded a redundancy payment if she is dismissed for misconduct (s 82(2)).

9.2   Misconduct

The contract of employment must be terminated without notice or with insufficient notice. If full notice is given, the employers may give notice in writing that they are contractually entitled to dismiss summarily ('special notice'). In *Simmons v Hoover Ltd* (1977) the EAT held that a strike was misconduct. Section 82(2) applies where the employers could have dismissed for gross misconduct but in fact dismissed for redundancy. This ruling explains why s 82(2) exists, for a person who is dismissed for misconduct is not dismissed 'by reason of redundancy'; in other words s 82(2) seems to state the obvious unless this interpretation is used.

    9.2.1   Effect

9.2.2	Deduction	If dismissal for misconduct occurs during the period of notice of redundancy, an industrial tribunal is empowered to pay all or part of the redundancy payment depending on the justice and equity of the case (s 92(3)). If the dismissal is for a strike during the statutory notice period, the employee retains the right to the payment (s 92(1)). The aim of s 92(1) is to preserve the right when industrial action is undertaken as a reaction to management's decision to declare redundancies. Since s 82(2) refers to misconduct and s 92(3) does so too, it might look uncertain what the relationship between the two sub-sections is. Under s 82(2) the right is lost totally; under s 92(3) the right survives but the quantum is reduced. The law seemingly provides inconsistent norms. The difference lies in s 92's applying only during the redundancy notice period.
9.2.3	Extension notice	If s 92(1) applies, employers may serve a 'notice of extension' on the employees. This notice obliges the workers to make up the days lost through their action. If the employees do not do so, they lose their right to redundancy payments.

9.3 Definition of redundancy

Parliament has defined redundancy in a special way. If the definition is not satisfied, there can be no claim for a redundancy payment, no matter how 'redundant' the employee looks in ordinary language.

9.3.1	'By reason of redundancy'	For a claim to succeed the dismissal must be 'by reason of redundancy'. If the dismissal was for another reason, it will not be 'by reason of redundancy'. In *Sanders v Ernest A Neale Ltd* (1974) a strike caused the closure of a factory. The National Industrial Relations Court held that the employees were not dismissed 'by reason of redundancy'.
9.3.2	Presumption	If an employee is dismissed, there is a statutory presumption in favour of redundancy: s 91(2). Therefore, the burden of disproof is on the employers. It should be noted that this presumption does not apply to unfair dismissal where one of the potentially fair reasons is that the employee was redundant. What sometimes surprises readers is that employers often argue in favour of redundancy. They do so because the definition of redundancy is the same for the purposes of unfair dismissal and redundancy payments; compensation for the former is at a higher rate than for the latter; therefore, the employers try to prove redundancy as a potentially fair reason to dismiss. Redundancy payments were instituted in 1965, unfair dismissal in 1971. The efforts by employers to prove redundancy were not foreseen by Parliament in 1965. It may be that the employee is seeking to demonstrate that she is not redundant with the effect that the

employers have to show that the reason why they did dismiss was a *prima facie* fair reason for dismissal within the unfair dismissal legislation, unfair dismissal leading to greater compensation than redundancy payments ie it is to the employee's benefit not to be redundant. Previously employers used to get a rebate from the State for part of the costs of redundancy payments. This rebate has been abolished. Employers ought to be more ready to contest redundancy claims than was the case before.

Redundancy is defined in s 81(2) of EP(C)A. The dismissal must be wholly or mainly attributable to:

9.3.3   Section 81(2) of EP(C)A

- the employers' ceasing to carry on the business for the purposes of which the employee was employed or they intend to do so; or the employers' ceasing to carry on the business in the place where the employee was employed, or they intend to do so; or

- '... the requirements of that business for employees to carry out work of a particular kind or for employees to carry out work of a particular kind in the place where he was employed, have ceased or diminished, or are expected to cease or diminish.'

In the discussion below, 'work of a particular kind' is abbreviated as WOPK. It has been held that WOPK is defined as 'work which is distinguished from other work of the same general kind by requiring special aptitudes, special skills or knowledge' (*Amos v Max-Arc Ltd* (1973)).

Only the statutory definition is used in determining whether or not an employee is redundant. The fact that an employee is 'redundant' in ordinary language is immaterial. The case of *Vaux Breweries Ltd v Ward* (1968) strongly emphasises this point. The applicant was dismissed as not fitting the requirements of her employers. They thought her too old to fit the image they were trying to present. Your parents might say that she was redundant but because as we shall see the requirements of the business for WOPK had not ceased, she was not statutorily redundant. Similarly, local authorities' contracting out of services does not seem to lead to statutory redundancy for the WOPK, collecting dustbins, remains to be done.

9.3.4   Statute prevails

If the definition applies, it does not matter what the reason for the redundancy was. Perhaps management bungled, or as in *Moon v Homeworthy Furniture (Northern) Ltd* (1977) the employer dismissed the employees because their factory had

9.3.5   Reason for redundancy

a bad industrial relations record. No investigation is undertaken by the tribunal of the true ground behind the redundancy when s 81(2) applies. Kilner Brown J stated that legislation 'has taken away all powers of the courts to investigate the rights and wrongs of industrial disputes ...'. A façade of political neutrality is preserved.

9.3.6   Closure of place of work

An example of the closure of the business for which the employee was employed is *Nelson v BBC* (1977) discussed in Chapter 4. The employee was employed under a contract under which he was required to work when and where the employers chose. He worked on the Caribbean service, which the employers closed down. The employers contended that he was redundant. The Court held that he was not, for he could by contract be moved to other services provided by the employers. Therefore, he was not redundant. The case illustrates the importance of express terms. The flexibility clause was so wide that the employers were caught on Morton's fork. If it had been narrowly drafted, they could not have lawfully transferred him to another service; on the facts it was widely drafted and accordingly the employee was not redundant. *Nelson* is a classic case of employers eating their cake and wanting to have it. They obtained the benefits of the term during employment but did not want to suffer the disadvantage to them at the termination of employment. *Rank Xerox Ltd v Churchill* (1988) involved a mobility clause, stating: 'The Company may require you to transfer to another location.' Employees were told to move from the company's London headquarters. The EAT held that the employees were employed as per the express term (which was not to be cut back by an implied term that the employers would not move them beyond reasonable commuting distance). A redundancy claim was not possible. Accordingly, if the worker is employed under a contract to the effect that she is to do two tasks, and the first task disappears, she is not redundant, for the second remains (*O'Neill v Merseyside Plumbing Co Ltd* (1973)). If, however, she is contractually employed on only one job, and that disappears, she is redundant (*Haden Ltd v Cowen* (1985)). It should be recalled that mobility and flexibility clauses may be express or implied. Since 1993 the written statement must contain particulars of any mobility clause. The effect should be that the difficulty in stating where the employee was employed will be reduced.

While these cases investigate the contractual width of the clauses, the EAT held in *Bass Leisure Ltd v Thomas* (1994) that the tribunal should look at where the employee did work, not at where he could be obliged contractually to work. A mobility clause in the employee's contract was irrelevant if it was phrased that her domestic situation would be taken into account or that the new place of work would be suitable or both and neither condition applied.

WOPK is a difficult concept. Following is a list of five Court of Appeal cases in chronological order in which work had not ceased or diminished.

9.3.7   Work of a particular kind

- *Vaux Breweries Ltd v Ward* (1968)

  A barmaid was sacked when the employers decided to modernise a pub to attract a younger, more free-spending, clientele than previously. She was replaced by 'bunny girls'. Her WOPK had not ceased or diminished. There was still work to be done serving customers.

- *Hindle v Percival Boats Ltd* (1969)

  A boatbuilder was used to working with wood. He was dismissed for being 'too good and too slow' when the yard changed from wood to fibreglass. He was not redundant. The particular kind of work had not changed.

- *Chapman v Goonvean and Rostowrack China Clay Co Ltd* (1973)

  The employers withdrew the bus service they provided to take seven employees to work. The service had become uneconomic, and the employers wished to save money. There was no redundancy. Indeed, the seven men were replaced.

- *Johnson v Nottinghamshire Combined Police Authority* (1974)

  Women workers' five-day week was reorganised into a six-day shift system. Because the amount of work remained the same, they were not redundant. The Court did say, however, that the tribunal can investigate whenever the reorganisation was a smokescreen hiding redundancy.

- *Lesney Products & Co v Nolan* (1977)

  The employers changed from day and night shifts to double day shifts, one result being that the employees lost overtime pay. There were no redundancies: the work remained the same.

  Therefore, a change in contractual terms may mean that there has been a constructive dismissal, but does not *per se* mean that a redundancy payment is due. The law of redundancy payments does not act as much of a restraint on managerial prerogative. As these cases demonstrate, replacing employees by cheaper workers does not mean that the employees are redundant.

9.3.8   Efficiency reorganisations

As can be seen from these five Court of Appeal cases, if the employers reorganise the work in the interests of efficiency (eg to stop losses, to increase profits) and they dismiss employers actually or constructively, the workers have not been dismissed by reason of redundancy. Therefore, they did not succeed in their claims for redundancy payments – despite their jobs being reorganised away. They got nothing; yet the employers saved or gained money through dismissing them. Lord Denning MR was a strong upholder of employers' rights to reorganise their business 'in the interests of efficiency', as he put it in *Chapman*, above, with consequential changes to contractual terms but without redundancy. If a remedy for unfair dismissal is claimed, a reorganisation in the interests of efficiency is treated as 'some other substantial reason', which is one of the five potentially fair reasons. Provided the employers have acted reasonably, the employees will have no remedy. The concomitant effect of the narrowness of the definition of redundancy is that it is difficult for employers to demonstrate that a dismissal was for redundancy in an unfair dismissal case.

9.3.9   Narrowness of definition

As a result of these cases one can say that WOPK ceases when the employee's job function has been superseded, for example when her job is done by someone else (*Sutton v Revlon Overseas Corp* (1973)). In *European Chefs (Catering) Ltd v Currell* (1971) the employee's job as one type of chef disappeared. His WOPK had ceased, despite there being a demand from his employers for another type of chef. This case amply illustrates the precision with which WOPK is defined. Since whether the work is WOPK is a question of fact, one tribunal's decision may be inconsistent with another's and the EAT cannot intervene. For example, if the WOPK was serving mild and bitter to old fogies in *Vaux Breweries Ltd v Ward*, the employee's WOPK would have ceased when the business requirements were for serving Pernod to young trendies. There may be a redundancy even though the employee knew that the job was only temporary (*Nottingham CC v Lee* (1980)). It should be noted that consistently with the period in which the redundancy payments scheme was established, the era of the 'white heat of the technological revolution', the definition of WOPK is phrased so as to cover the requirements of the business for an employee to do WOPK have ceased or diminished. It does not matter that the work done by the employers has in fact increased. Accordingly, an employer who is replaced by a machine is redundant and is so even though the employers automated production in order to step up output because demand had increased. *A fortiori* the employee is redundant when the work is the same but the number of employees to do it is reduced (*McCrea v Cullen & Davison Ltd* (1988)), a decision of the Northern Ireland Court of Appeal. The test is whether the reorganisation:

'... results in the employee's work being encompassed in other posts and whether the employer's business is such that it no longer has a requirement for a separate and additional employee to carry out the work.' (*Sutton v Revlon*, above)

Therefore, the dismissal of staff taken on in the expectation of a large order which did not materialise is by reason of redundancy because the words of the statute are fulfilled (*O'Hare v Rotaprint Ltd* (1980)). The main point remains the difficulty in determining what is WOPK. If a plumber who dealt with the heating is dismissed when the employers replace him with a heating technician, have the employers' requirement for WOPK ceased or diminished? The Court of Appeal thought so in *Murphy v Epsom College* (1985); but the answer is not obvious.

One particular kind of redundancy dismissal should be noted. If as a result of a downturn in demand in one department there is a need for redundancy, and the employers transfer a person from that department into a second department and sack an employee in the second department, that employee is dismissed for redundancy (eg *W Gimber & Sons Ltd v Spurrett* (1967)). The industrial relations term for this situation is 'bumping'.

9.3.10   'Bumping'

If the employers, successors, or associated employers (or the new employers on a transfer of the business) offer the employee a renewal of the contract or offer to her suitable alternative work before the end of the contract, there is no redundancy if she unreasonably refuses the offer: s 82. The offer must contain details of the job. The renewal or re-engagement must take effect immediately on termination of the previous contract or within four weeks thereof. Continuity is preserved.

9.4   Suitable employment unreasonably refused

What is suitable depends on an objective test. The best-known case is *Taylor v Kent CC* (1969). A former headmaster was offered a place in a 'floating pool' of teachers, ie he was to do supply work as and when required. The Divisional Court held that because of the loss in status the offer was not of suitable employment (even though his pay remained the same). It was

9.4.1   Suitability

as if a company director had been offered the job of navvy. Similarly in *Sheppard v NCB* (1966) the loss of fringe benefits made the job offer unsuitable. Tribunals should not investigate the financial situation of the employers to determine whether an offer of a job with substantially reduced terms was suitable for the employee (*Sennitt v Fysons Conveyors Ltd* (1994)). In *Carron Co v Robertson* (1967) Lord Parker CJ said:

> '... in deciding as to the suitability of employment in relation to an employee, one must consider not only the nature of the work, hours and pay, the employee's strength, training, experience and ability, but such matters as status.'

The burden of proof is on the employers to demonstrate suitability. In *Anglia Regional Co-operative Society v O'Donnell* (1994) the employers failed to show that a transfer fell within the term of a mobility clause and that the employee had accepted new terms and conditions which would have permitted them to move her but they did demonstrate that the offer to move her was suitable alternative employment which she had unreasonably refused.

9.4.2 Reasonableness

Even if the offer is suitable, the employee will retain the right to a redundancy payment if her refusal of it is reasonable. What is reasonable is judged subjectively: was it reasonable for this employee to refuse the offer of alternative employment? Reasonable reasons include family commitments, lack of good schools for the employee's children, loss of friends and travel problems. In an important decision, *Thomas Wragg & Sons v Wood* (1976), it was held that fear of future redundancy in the new job coupled with the employee's being near retirement age made the refusal reasonable. It has, however, been said that a personal fad is not a good reason. *Fuller v Stephanie Bowman Ltd* (1977) illustrates this proposition. A female employee was asked to move from Mayfair, a salubrious part of London, to an office above a sex shop in Soho. The Court, surprisingly to the author, held that she unreasonably refused the offer. The job was the same; therefore, it was suitable. The offer was refused unreasonably as a consequence of a 'personal fad'. The fact that work will not last for long does not *per se* mean that refusal was reasonable.

9.4.3 Separate stages

Though the tribunals and courts have treated the (un)reasonable refusal of suitable alternative employment as separate, factors relevant to one may be relevant to the other too (*Spencer v Gloucestershire CC* (1985)).

9.5 Trial periods

If the employee wishes to try out the job, there is a trial period of four calendar weeks: s 84(3) and (4). If she does not like the new job, she retains her right to a redundancy payment. The four week trial period may be extended by the parties for a period which must be expressly stated provided they do so in writing and do so for the purposes of retraining: s 84(5). Perhaps the EAT held in *Kentish Bus and Coach Co Ltd v Quarry* (1994) EAT 287/92 that the trial period was preceded by a common law 'thinking time' of a reasonable duration during which the employee could consider whether to access the new terms.

If the employee is constructively dismissed on the grounds of redundancy, it has several times been held that the employee is entitled to both a common law trial period (of reasonable duration) followed by the s 84(3) trial period (eg *Air Canada v Lee* (1978)). The employers moved the employee to another office. Under her contract they were not permitted to do so. She agreed to the change on a trial basis. After two months she left. There was no doubt that she had been constructively dismissed, but she had left after the statutory four-week period. The EAT held that she had left within the common law trial period. The statutory period had not even begun to run. What is a reasonable length depends on the facts. Twelve months were held to be of a reasonable duration in *McKindley v William Hill (Scotland) Ltd* (1985). What is reasonable is dependent on the common law concerned with acceptance of a breach of a fundamental term or affirmation of the contract.

9.5.1   Effect of repudiation

If the employers dismiss the employee during the trial period for whatever reason (eg incompetence), she is treated as having been dismissed for redundancy, ie her claim springs up again. If she resigns during the period because she has sampled the job and does not like it, she is deemed to have been dismissed, but whether the job was suitable and whether the ground for leaving was reasonable are matters for the tribunal.

9.5.2   Deemed redundancy

An employee who is given notice of dismissal by reason of redundancy is entitled to a reasonable amount of time off work to seek employment or retraining: s 31 of EP(C)A. Only employees who have worked for two years continuously at 16 or more hours a week or five years at eight or more hours per week may claim. The application is made to an industrial tribunal if the employers unreasonably refuse time off. The maximum award the tribunal may give is two-fifths of a week's pay, but the award may be less for it is otherwise based on the pay which the employee would have received, had she been allowed time off. If the employee does obtain a new job during the time off, the liability of the employers to make a redundancy payment is unaffected. (The same indeed applies generally: a payment is still due even if an employee steps into a new job the moment after dismissal.)

9.6   Time off

9.7 **Redundancy procedure**	The Employment Protection Act 1975 introduced a special procedure for handling redundancies. The then government considered that that law fulfilled, and was indeed broader, than EC law. The present government, however, found that the English provisions fell short of EC norms and drastically amended the law in 1993 to embody the relevant EC directive. Current law still does not satisfy EC law in that it is restricted to consultation where there is a recognised independent trade union. See 9.7.16.
9.7.1 Consultation with unions	Section 188 of TULR(C)A imposes a duty on employers to consult with 'authorised representatives' of recognised independent trade unions on redundancy (as defined in s 195 as inserted by the Trade Union Reform and Employment Rights Act 1993 as dismissal not being for a reason – such as misconduct – connected with the individual employee ie 'redundancy' is wider in ss 188–198 than in the previous sections of this book and in the next three chapters: the pre-1993 definition was held by the ECJ in *Commission of the European Communities v United Kingdom* (1994) to fall short of EC standards) 'at the earliest opportunity'. In the event of non-compliance an industrial tribunal may award a 'protective award' unless there are 'special circumstances' excusing non-compliance. Consultation may reduce the number of employees to be dismissed or other work may be found. There is a presumption of redundancy found in s 195.
9.7.2 Recognition	Recognition is discussed in Chapter 14. Since recognition is not obtained through law, employers can refuse recognition or derecognise without legal sanction. The non-implementation of EC law in these circumstances was strongly condemned in the *Commission* case, above. Consultation must occur even though there is only one employee to be made redundant in the category of workers for which the union is recognised, and even though that employee is not a member of the union. The latter proposition was upheld in *Governing Body of the Northern Ireland Hotel and Catering College v National Association of Teachers in Further and Higher Education* (1995).
9.7.3 Authorised representatives	Section 196 of TULR(C)A defines authorised representatives as officials or other persons authorised to carry on collective bargaining with the relevant employers. An example is a shop steward: *GMWU v Wailes Dove Bitumastic Ltd* (1977). On the facts of that case there was no duty on the employers to consult with a full-time union officer because he had never taken part in collective bargaining with the employers. Bargaining had been with the shop steward.

The term consultation is not fully defined in the statute. Certainly full-blooded negotiation is not required. In a case on a similar statute, *R v British Coal Corporation ex p Price* (1994) Glidwell LJ defined the term 'fair consultation' as '(a) consultation when the proposals are still at a formative stage; (b) adequate information on which to respond; (c) adequate time in which to respond; (d) conscientious consideration by an authority of the response to consultation.' The employers must disclose in writing the number of jobs to go, the reason for the redundancies, the total number of employees, the method of selection for redundancy, the length of notice and the amount, if any, they will give above the statutory redundancy payment and the method of calculating the sum payable on redundancy. Providing the union with the number of those to be made redundant analysed into manual, clerical and technical/management grades is insufficient to comply with the duty to disclose 'the numbers and descriptions of employees whom it is proposed to dismiss as redundant'. Therefore, merely telling the representatives that there will be redundancies is not enough: *Electrical & Engineering Association v Ashwell-Scott Ltd* (1976). Since 1993 consultation must be concerned with ways of avoiding dismissals, reducing the number of employees to be dismissed, and mitigating the effects of the dismissals: s 188(6) as revised. While consultation does not mean negotiation, it goes beyond simply telling the representatives that dismissals will occur shortly. In *TGWU v Ledbury Preserves (1928) Ltd* (1985) the employers informed the union of the dismissal half an hour before giving the workforce their notice of dismissal. This was not consultation, but a sham. The consultation must since 1993 be with a view to reaching agreement. This change reinforces the view in this case that the consultation must be meaningful. The amendment makes consultation more like negotiation than previously.

9.7.4   Consultation defined

Parliament has given a defence to the employers if they are afflicted with special circumstances (s 188(7)). (There is no such defence in the Directive relevant to the area: see 9.7.16.) If the defence applies, subsection (7) nevertheless imposes a duty on them to

9.7.5   Special circumstances

'... take all steps towards compliance ... as are reasonably practicable in those circumstances.'

'Reasonably practicable' steps could mean that the duty may be satisfied by the employers' doing nothing.

The burden of proving special circumstances and reasonably practicable compliance is on the employers: s 189(6). The sort of situation envisaged by the special circumstances defence occurred in *USDAW v Leancut Bacon Ltd* (1981). The employers were heading for insolvency. Their directors undertook talks with a third party to buy shares, but the talks broke down. Employees were dismissed for redundancy. It was held that special circumstances existed. The employers thought that there would be a rescue operation but virtually at the last moment their hopes evaporated. The EAT considered in *Association of Patternmakers & Allied Craftsmen v Kirvin Ltd* (1978) that a line was to be drawn between a reasonable hope that the company would be saved (as in *Leancut Bacon*) and a foreseeable insolvency, the latter not amounting to a special circumstance. (The hope, in the former instance, must not be one based on no evidence: the employers have no defence if they are wilfully blind, ie they shut their eyes to the obvious.) A well-known instance of a foreseeable redundancy was *Clarks of Hove Ltd v Bakers' Union* (1978). The employers found that they had insufficient money to carry on. They realised what was happening but did not tell their workforce until two hours before they closed down. On the facts the employers should have consulted with the union well before the closure for they knew that the shutdown was inevitable. The Court said that for employers to have this defence the circumstances must be uncommon or out of the ordinary, such as occur when the factory burns down, or the main suppliers suddenly stop delivery, or as in *Hamish Armour v ASTMS* (1979) the failure to obtain a loan from the government leads to dismissals for redundancy. An administration order does not make it impracticable to comply. Since 1993 employers do not have a special circumstances defence where failure to consult is due to a controlling persons did not give them the information: s 188(7). The effect is that an English company has no defence if its parent company based abroad does not provide it with the requisite information. If the defence applies no protective award (see para 9.7.9 below) is awarded.

9.7.6   Earliest opportunity

Section 188(2) provides:

'(t)he consultation must begin at the earliest opportunity, and in any event –

(a) where the employer is proposing to dismiss as redundant 100 or more employees at one establishment within a period of 90 days or less, at least 90 days before the first of those dismissals takes effect;

(b) where the employer is proposing to dismiss at least 10 but less than 100 employees at one establishment within a period of 30 days or less, at least 30 days before the first of those dismissals takes effect.'

It must be stressed that the earliest opportunity occurs before the specified number of days in s 188(7)(a) and (b), the latter being only a fall-back position if consultation cannot take place before then at the earliest opportunity. The consultation period can begin before the information for consultation is provided. 'Proposing' to dismiss covers where there is a settled intention to do so but not where the employers think that there is only a remote possibility of dismissal for redundancy (*NUPE v General Cleaning Contractors* (1976)). Similarly, thinking about a problem the solution to which may be dismissals is not proposing to dismiss (*Hough v Leyland DAF Ltd* (1991)). The duty on the employers to consult exists even though consultation would have made no difference (*Sovereign Distribution Services Ltd v TGWU* (1989)). The relevant EC Directive applies at an earlier stage, when employers were contemplating redundancies: see *R v British Coal Corportion ex p Vardy* (1993), the case on the government's proposal to close most collieries. Indirect effect would be given by interpreting 'proposing' to mean 'contemplating'. The numbers who count within s 188(2) need not be union members, nor indeed do they have to be employees who are qualified to bring redundancy payments claims (eg they need not have worked continuously for two years), but the numbers exclude employees on fixed-term contracts for 12 weeks or less or on task contracts where the task is not expected to last more than 12 weeks. Section 188(2) applies to dismissal of over 10 workers. Where there are fewer than 10, it has been said that two or three days' consultation was useless (*TGWU v Nationwide Haulage Ltd* (1978)), an industrial tribunal decision. (Note that s 188(2) applies to all redundancy dismissals not just where 10 or more are sacked.) The government proposes to amend the legislation to make it operate only when 20 or more employees are dismissed for redundancy within a 90-day period and to replace 'at the earliest opportunity' with 'in good time', a less demanding standard but one which is found in the Collective Redundancies Directive.

Section 188 requires the employees to be at one establishment. The principal authority is *Barratt Developments Ltd v UCATT* (1978). Employers proposed to dismiss 24 construction workers across eight sites (out of their 14 sites). The EAT confirmed an IT's decision that since all sites were administered from one location, they formed one establishment. Therefore, the number of workers could be aggregated to bring what is now s 188(2) into play. Presumably one looks at the autonomy of the individual locations.

9.7.7   Establishment

9.7.8 Employer/employee	One technical matter is that associated employers do not constitute one employer for the purposes of the protective award. Therefore, one cannot aggregate employees of different but associated employers to trigger a larger protective award than would otherwise be given: *Green & Son (Castings) Ltd v ASTMS* (1984). This was so even though the three companies on the facts of this case shared accounting and personnel services and they were subsidiaries of a holding company (and so associated employers for other purposes).

The usual 16 hours per week rule does not apply in the definition of 'employee' for the purpose of consultation on redundancies.

9.7.9 Protective award	The remedy for non-compliance with the duty to consult is the award by an industrial tribunal of a protective award to individual employees on the application of the recognised independent trade union. The award, which is discretionary, orders the employers to pay remuneration based on the employees' normal working hours (ie excluding voluntary overtime) for the 'protected period' (s 189(3)). By s 189(4):

> '(t)he protected period –
>
> (a) begins with the date on which the first of the dismissals to which the complaint relates takes effect, or the date of the award, whichever is the earlier, and
>
> (b) is of such length as the tribunal determines to be just and equitable in all the circumstances having regard to the seriousness of the employer's default in complying with any requirement of s 188; but shall not exceed 90 days in a case (involving 100 or more employees), 30 days in a case (involving 10-90), or 28 days in any other case.'

Unions cannot obtain an injunction to oblige employers to consult (*Griffin v South West Water Services Ltd* (1994) (High Court)).

9.7.10 Compensation	The protective award is intended to be compensatory, not penal (*Talke Fashions Ltd v Amalgamated Society of Textile Workers & Kindred Trades* (1977)). The gravity of the employers' misconduct and the loss occasioned to the employees must be considered. The seriousness of the default is measured by the increased loss to the employees. In the *Barratt* case, above, the award was said to be based on the amount payable as wages or in lieu of notice which the employee would have obtained had consultation procedures been followed. Loss is therefore not calculated by reference to the financial loss suffered by the

employee during the protected period. Accordingly, money may still be payable despite the fact that the employees immediately obtained other jobs. Because the amount awarded is based on the 'just and equitable' criterion, an award of no compensation may be given. In *Amalgamated Society of Boilermakers v George Wimpey & Co Ltd* (1977) the EAT did not make an award where the employees were kept informed but the employers had not complied with the obligation to provide information in writing. Similarly, no award was made in *ASTMS v Hawker Siddeley Aviation Ltd* (1977) when the employers and union had agreed on the payment of wages in lieu of notice. The rule enforcing set off between the protective award and wages due or damages for breach of contract was abolished in 1993. Previously the sanction of the protective award was rendered nugatory where the award was wiped out by the payment of wages in lieu. Even after the change the compensation is not of such a level as to make the right effective to satisfy EC law. If the relevant Directive were directly effective, employees would be able to rely on it to gain compensation beyond the present limits. Those limits and the previous set off were condemned by the ECJ in *Commission of the European Communities v United Kingdom*, above. The sanctions were not adequate to deter employers.

A protective award is not granted where the employee is not ready and willing to work, joins industrial action, is dismissed (fairly) for a reason other than redundancy, unreasonably terminates her contract, is offered suitable alternative employment, or her contract is renewed and the renewal takes effect before or during the protected period (see s 191 of TULR(C)A).

9.7.11   Exclusions

The time limit is laid down in s 189(5):

9.7.12   Limitation period

'An industrial tribunal shall not consider a complaint under this section unless it is presented to the tribunal –

(a) before the proposed dismissal takes effect, or

(b) before the end of the period of three months beginning with the date on which the dismissal takes effect, or

(c) where the tribunal is satisfied that it was not reasonably practicable for the complaint to be presented within the period of three months, within such further period as it considers reasonable.'

The remedy for non-compliance with the award is an individual complaint to an IT: s 192.

9.7.13   Non-compliance

9.7.14	Comment	The protective award is a strange remedy in several respects. It is one enforceable by a trade union but paid to individual employees. What if one or more of those employees are not union members? Can they oblige the union for their workplace to undertake proceedings for their benefit? The answer is unknown. Moreover, while the right is one to consultation the remedy is not one to enforce consultation.
9.7.15	Notification	Employers have a duty to notify the Secretary of State for Employment in writing that they are proposing to dismiss for redundancy: s 193. The revised s 195 definition of redundancy applies to s 193. See para 9.7.1 above. Where the proposal is to make redundant 100 or more employees within 90 days at one establishment, the notification must take place at least 90 days before the first dismissal. If the proposal relates to 10 or more within a period of 30 days at one establishment, the notification must take place at least 30 days before the first dismissal. As with consultation with recognised independent trade unions there is a 'special circumstances' defence where it was not reasonably practicable for the employers to comply with the law on notification; if the excuse applies, the employers must 'take all such steps towards compliance with that requirement as are reasonably practicable in the circumstances': (s 193(7)). It is an offence punishable by a fine (currently up to £5,000) to fail to give notice: s 194(1). It is thought that the object of s 193 is to enable the government to have in place retraining schemes and job-placement opportunities. It would be interesting to know whether s 193 does actually have this effect. The definitions of eg 'establishment' and 'special circumstances' are as in the previous paragraphs. It should be noted that notifying the Secretary of State is a duty separate from that of consultation. Both obligations must be fulfilled.
9.7.16	Critique	Comments on consultation and notification:

- Provided employers do consult and notify, there is nothing to prevent employers from dismissing for redundancy many employees ('mass redundancy'). The laws on consultation and notification are, moreover, procedural, not substantive, in effect. Non-compliance does not stop sackings.

- Linked with consultation on redundancy there is the obligation to consult under the Transfer of Undertakings (Protection of Employment) Regulations 1981 (SI 1981/1794). For this obligation see Chapter 13.

- There is debate whether present law complies with EC norms, which is found in the Directive on the Approximation of Laws of the Member States relating to Collective Redundancies (EC 75/129 as amended by EC 92/56). The aims of the 1975 Directive are 'to ensure comparable protection for workers' rights in different Member States and to harmonise the costs which such protective rules entail for Community undertakings' (*Commission of the European Communities v UK* 1994 ECJ). The changes in the 1993 Act were necessitated by the two Directives. They came into force on 30 August 1993. In brief the following matters arise.

(a) English law gives the right to authorised representatives of independent trade unions, whereas the Directive places responsibility with employee representatives (ie trade unions need not be involved); the ECJ held in *Commission of the European Communities v UK* that English law did not match up to EC standards in this regard, for where there was no union, employers did have to negotiate with employees' representatives. The government proposes to amend the law to give employers the option of negotiating with either the union (where there is one) or with elected representatives of the employees. Those representatives may be ones elected solely for the purpose of negotiating on redundancies.

(b) The Directive applies when redundancies are contemplated, the UK legislation when they are proposed. English cases are divided on whether contemplating and proposing are the same concept or whether contemplating occurs before proposing. As a matter of language the latter construction is correct. The ECJ ruled in the *Commission* case, above, that English law fell short of EC standards in this respect. English law is brought into line by reading 'proposing' as 'contemplates'. The government when it enacted the consultation procedures in 1975 thought that they were complying with EC law. Interestingly the Directive expressly does not apply to public bodies. It is questionable whether British Coal is such an organisation, even pre-privatisation and in *Griffin v South West Water Services Ltd* (1995) Blackburne J held that a privatised utility was not a 'public administrative body' within the Directive (although it was an emanation of the State for the purposes of the doctrine of direct effect).

It is uncertain whether the Collective Redundancies Directive is directly effective. Some articles seem to be unconditional and sufficiently precise. It is also uncertain whether an action against the State for non-implementation would be properly brought by an individual or by a union. The issue of who are the workers' representatives within Articles 2 and 6 was said not to be unconditional and sufficiently precise in *Griffin*. This issue will no doubt be referred to the ECJ soon.

- Just as occurs with regard to redundancy payments tribunals cannot investigate the reason for the redundancy (*Association of University Teachers v University of Newcastle-upon-Tyne* (1987)). No judicial body can prevent redundancies by checking the managerial prerogative to dismiss. As will be seen in the chapter dealing with the calculation of redundancy payments the remedy for breach of the legislation is not re-employment in the same or similar job but pecuniary compensation. The remedy, therefore, does not prevent dismissals but puts a monetary tariff on them. Since most employers pay up without a tribunal hearing, there is not even satisfaction which some employees might get through having their complaint heard by a public body.

- The widened definition of 'redundancy' noted in para 9.7.1 above may lead to unforeseen problems. Consultation and notification requirements apply if dismissal is for a reason unconnected with the individual employee. Assume that the employers wish to cut the pay of their workers. They give each employee the requisite length of notice lawfully to terminate the contracts, and in the same letter offer re-engagement but with less pay. Within s 195 as amended there is dismissal not related to an individual employee. Therefore, consultation with any recognised independent union is a legal necessity. Certainly redundancies in the interests of efficiency fall within the new s 195. It would seem, however, that 'dismissal' within the Directive as amended does not include constructive dismissals such as may occur when employers suspend payment of their debts and the employees leave.

Redundancy Payments

Qualified employees dismissed by reason of redundancy have the right to claim in an industrial tribunal that they should be awarded a redundancy payment.

Introduction

Employees dismissed for misconduct lose this right. Misconduct includes industrial action:

Simmons v Hoover (1977).

Misconduct

There is a presumption of redundancy. Accordingly the burden of disproof is on the employers. The definition includes the closure of the business at the place the employee works and the diminution in the requirements of the business for the employee to do work of a particular kind:

Definition

Nelson v BBC (1977)

Vaux Breweries v Ward (1968)

Hindle v Percival Boats (1969)

Johnson v Notts CPA (1974)

Murphy v Epsom College (1985).

Employees lose their entitlement if they unreasonably reject an offer of suitable alternative employment. Suitability is judged objectively, reasonableness subjectively:

Suitable employment unreasonably refused

Taylor v Kent CC (1969)

Thomas Wragg v Wood (1976).

There is a statutory four-week trial period in the new job; however, if the employee is constructively dismissed there is a common law trial period of reasonable length in addition:

Trial periods

Air Canada v Lee (1979).

Employees under notice of redundancy have a right to reasonable time off work to seek employment or retraining.

Time off

Redundancy procedure

Employers must consult with authorised representatives of recognised independent trade unions at the earliest opportunity in the event of redundancies. The remedy is a protective award. There is a defence of special circumstances:

TGWU v Ledbury Preserves (1985)

Clarks of Hove v Bakers' Union (1978).

Present law may fall short of EC law because it requires the existence of a recognised independent trade union, whereas EC law speaks of consultation with employee representatives (ie there need be no union).

There is a duty on employers to notify the Secretary of State of mass redundancies.

The definition of redundancy in the context of the procedure for handling redundancies is wider than that in the earlier parts of this chapter. It covers dismissal for any reason not connected with the individual employee.

Chapter 10

Unfair Dismissal:
The General Approach

10.1 Introduction

In an unfair dismissal claim once the employee has shown that she is qualified and has been dismissed (Chapter 8) the burden switches to the employers to demonstrate a potentially fair (also called *prima facie* valid) reason for the dismissal. If they cannot do so, the employee wins. If they can do so, the question for the industrial tribunal is whether the dismissal was fair or not having regard to the size and administrative resources of the firm and equity and the substantial merits of the case. The issue of the remedy is considered in Chapter 12. The next chapter deals with particular instances of fair or unfair dismissal which do not fall within the general run of unfair dismissal (eg dismissal of a trade-union-related reason). Accordingly, in this chapter are considered two stages, the third and fourth, in a straightforward unfair dismissal application, the reason and the reasonableness – see the diagram at the start of Chapter 8. Also this chapter contains a discussion of the effect of an employee's request for written reasons for dismissal within s 53 of the Employment Protection (Consolidation) Act 1978, hereinafter EP(C)A.

10.1.1 'Unfair'

The denomination of this claim as 'unfair dismissal' must not be allowed to mislead. What the term really means is 'dismissal contrary to statute' just as wrongful dismissal is concerned with dismissal at common law. One must apply the law set forth in the statute, not simply say: 'Gosh! Didn't those employers dismiss unfairly!'

10.2 Written reasons

An employee who is dismissed is entitled to receive in writing the reason for her dismissal, provided that she has been continuously employed for two years.

10.2.1 Right

At common law there was no right to be informed of the reason for one's dismissal. By virtue of s 53 of EP(C)A an employee who is dismissed by her employers with or without notice or whose fixed-term contract is not renewed may request from them a statement in writing concerning the reason for dismissal. It should be noted that an employee who is constructively dismissed is not entitled to written reasons. There is a qualifying period of two years: Employment Act 1989, s 15. The employers must reply within

14 days if that is reasonably possible with the reason(s) for dismissal. There is no need for more than a brief statement. The employers need not add any reference as to why they believed the reason to be an acceptable one to use: *Harvard Securities plc v Younghusband* (1990). The statement may refer to documents such as letters already sent to the employee and it may be sent to a representative of the dismissed employee not to each employee individually: *Kent County Council v Gilham* (1985), a dinner ladies' case.

10.2.2   Unreasonable failure to provide reasons

If the employers unreasonably fail to provide reasons or the reasons are incomplete or false, the employee may complain to an industrial tribunal (IT). Until 30 August 1993 the law was that ITs had jurisdiction only if the employers unreasonably refused to provide reasons, but s 53(4) of EP(C)A was amended by TURERA. The application must be made within the notice period or within three months of the effective date of termination. The IT has a discretion to extend the time limit if it was not reasonably practicable to present the claim within those three months. If the claim is successful, the tribunal will award two weeks' pay. This remedy has been held to be a penal one and therefore under English canons of construction it is subject to strict interpretation. In *Lowson v Percy Main & District Social Club Institute Ltd* (1979) it was held that the employers did not unreasonably refuse the request where they did not communicate with their solicitors, but the company gave reasons when the solicitors realised that the request of the employee had not been satisfied. However, in *Brown v Stuart Scott & Co Ltd* (1981) it was reasonable not to provide reasons when the employers believed that they had not sacked the employee. If the written reasons are incomplete or false, the IT may investigate the true reasons.

10.2.3   Effect

The written statement is admissible as evidence in an IT: s 53(3). In an unfair dismissal claim an IT would not look favourably on employers who give one reason for the purposes of s 53 and another to defend the claim.

10.2.4   Critique

Controversy over s 53 has recently centred on the increase to two years of the qualifying period. The government's view was that the increase from six months brought the law on written reasons in line with that of unfair dismissal. There is, however, no necessary link between s 53 and s 54 (which states that every employee has a right not to be unfairly dismissed), for every employee surely ought to know the reason why she has been dismissed and that argument indeed applies even to workers employed for fewer than six months; and even if not qualified for unfair dismissal, surely the employee ought to be provided with a reason for the purposes of other claims.

Once the employee has proved that she is qualified and has been dismissed, the burden switches to the employers to show that they had a reason to dismiss.

10.3 Reason for dismissal

10.3.1 Definition and effect

To defend an unfair dismissal claim the employers must have a 'reason' for dismissal. The reason is 'the set of facts known to the employer or beliefs held by him which cause him to dismiss the employee': *Abernethy v Mott, Hay and Anderson* (1974). The knowledge of the employee is irrelevant. It is sufficient that the employers believe that they dismissed on a certain ground; they need not demonstrate that that ground was fully supported by all the evidence. The employers' motive is relevant in determining what was their true reason for dismissing. Sham reasons are disregarded. The reason given has to be the real reason, not necessarily the one provided by the employers. For example, if a Housing Association sack an employee on the grounds that his job has been taken over by the independent contractors, that reason may be a 'smokescreen' to hide the true reason, which might be that the employee pilfered property or spied on inhabitants of the block of flats. Where there are two or more reasons, the IT must define which was the ground that motivated the employers to sack (*Carlin v St Cuthbert's Co-operative Association Ltd* (1974)). In *Smith v City of Glasgow District Council* (1987) the House of Lords held that, where the employers put forward several reasons and one of them is not accepted, they must prove that that reason was not the principal reason. Accordingly, if they cannot show that the surviving reasons constituted the principal reason, they lose at this stage.

10.3.2 Reliance on reason

The law on reasons provided by employers is a little confusing. Basically employers cannot argue before the IT a reason which they did not write in the Notice of Appearance. However, if the different reasons are in truth simply different labels covering the same facts, the IT may determine that the real reason was pleaded. The usual example is that it may not be clear until the case is heard whether the facts give rise to redundancy or to a reorganisation falling within 'some other substantial reason'. *Hotson v Wisbech Conservative Club* (1984) illustrates the law. The employers' Notice of Appearance said that the employee was dismissed for 'inefficiency'. This reason is one of incapacity; in fact he was sacked for dishonesty ie for misconduct. The EAT held that the employers were not entitled to change their reason before the tribunal.

10.4	**After-discovered reasons**	If employers wrongfully dismiss a worker but between the sacking and trial discover a reason which would have justified them dismissing summarily, had they known of it, they have a defence to the action (*Boston Deep Sea Fishing & Ice Co v Ansell* (1888)). The law is to opposite effect in unfair dismissal. Employers cannot use an after-discovered reason to make fair an unfair dismissal (*W Devis & Sons Ltd v Atkins* (1977), one of the leading cases in UK employment law). The employee was dismissed for refusing to obey a lawful order. After dismissal the employers uncovered evidence that he had been dishonest. The House held that the employers could not rely on the subsequently discovered evidence to convert an unfair dismissal into a fair one. An example of the effect of *Devis v Atkins* is a prosecution of the employee for a crime committed during employment. If the employers reasonably believe that the employee committed the offence (eg theft), they may dismiss and, provided that an adequate investigation was carried out, the likelihood is that the dismissal will be fair. The fairness is not affected by a jury's post-dismissal finding that the employee was not guilty. The following points should, however, be noted.
10.4.1	Exceptions	• While a dismissal is not fair, the compensation may be reduced – even to nil – by the presence of a subsequently discovered reason. In *Devis v Atkins* itself the compensation was reduced to nothing because the employee had suffered no loss.

• Where the employee is dismissed and then she is refused the right to appeal through the company's complaints procedure, that refusal is taken into account in assessing the reasonableness of the dismissal, according to the House of Lords in *West Midlands Co-operative Society Ltd v Tipton* (1986). The House reconciled their decision with that in *Devis v Atkins* by saying that that authority related to after-discovered reasons justifying dismissal of the employee, whereas the refusal of the employers to permit the employee to start the grievance procedure related to the employers' conduct and was, therefore, a reason which had to be taken into account by the tribunal when determining the equity and substantial merits of the case. The Lords considered that the appeal process was part of the dismissal; ie dismissal did not for this purpose take place until the appeals procedure was exhausted. Evidence relating to the dismissal can be used if discovered in the appeal, but such evidence cannot be led if it relates to a different ground for dismissal. Yet the House held that the date of dismissal was the date when the employers fired the employee, not the date when they refused to start the appeal process (or the date when that process would have ended, had it started).

- Evidence relating to the particular reason (eg conduct) for dismissal may be taken into account even though it is uncovered after dismissal (*Tipton*). However, as we have seen, after-discovered evidence in relation to what would have been a potentially fair reason for dismissal is not admissible.

- Medical evidence which appears during an appeal against dismissal can be used (*National Heart and Chest Hospitals v Nambiar* (1981)). The law may be wider than this proposition.

  It may cover situations where the employee is kept on until the end of internal appeals and fresh information is discovered during the process. Evidence confirming the initial decision to dismiss may be led but not evidence which uncovers a different potentially fair reason to dismiss (*Monie v Coral Racing Ltd* (1981)).

- Matters occurring between the date of giving notice of dismissal and the date of its expiry can be looked at. Moreover, the fact that an appeal did not take place until after the effective date of termination does not matter when determining reasonableness (*Rank Xerox (UK) Ltd v Goodchild* (1979)).

- Evidence may be given of matters which the employers did not know but ought to have known at the time of dismissal 'if it was a proper case to carry out a further investigation and if they had carried out that investigation' (*W Weddel & Co Ltd v Tepper*, (1980), interpreting *dicta* of Viscount Dilhorne in *Devis v Atkins*).

Though the after-discovered reason cannot be used to render fair an unfair dismissal, there is nothing to prevent the employers from using that ground as a potentially fair reason on dismissal for that reason, ie the employers lose the first claim but win on any second claim by the employee, which could occur if she is reinstated by the IT.

10.4.2   Later dismissal

To defend a claim the employers must prove that they have a substantial reason justifying dismissal. If they cannot, the dismissal is unfair. If they can, the IT moves to the next stage, consideration of the reasonableness of the dismissal. Accordingly, though s 54 of EP(C)A proclaims that every employee has a right not to be unfairly dismissed, that right is defeasible.

10.5   Potentially fair reasons: burden of proof

| 10.5.1 | Five reasons | EP(C)A lays down five reasons which can justify dismissal: |

- conduct eg theft, fighting at work, absenteeism;
- capability or qualifications of the employee for performing the work she was employed to do eg incompetence. Illness by statute falls within this *prima facie* fair reason;
- redundancy;
- contravention of statute eg a delivery driver cannot do her job because she has lost her licence;
- some other substantial reason justifying dismissal of the employee from the post she held.

| 10.5.2 | Reason and reasonableness | There is a tendency to run together the issues whether the employers had a *prima facie* valid reason to dismiss and whether they acted reasonably but by statute the issues are separate and there is a different burden of proof, since in relation to the former the onus is on the employers but in relation to the latter there has been since 1980 no formal burden, the IT deciding by reference to all the circumstances. |

| 10.5.3 | Conduct (s 57(2)(b)) | Conduct cases are very much based on their own facts, but common instances include failure to obey lawful orders (such as refusing to sign a letter apologising to a customer), theft from the employers, doing 'foreigners' (ie using the company's materials on work other than the company's), violence at work, gross negligence and (gross) swearing. A refusal to work non-contractual overtime has been treated as misconduct in that the order was a reasonable one. Cases cannot be used as precedents. The same swear words may be acceptable on a building site between a tiler and her foreman but not between the master of ceremonies and the principal speaker at the Chancellor of the Exchequer's speech at the Guildhall in London. Similarly wearing a badge saying 'Lesbians ignite!' might be acceptable among university lecturers but not among audit clerks (*Boychuk v H J Symons Holdings Ltd* (1977)). |

| 10.5.4 | Capability or qualifications (s 57(2)(a)) | By s 57(4) capability includes 'skills, aptitude, health or any other physical or mental quality', while qualifications are defined as 'any degree, diploma or other academic, technical or professional qualification relevant to the position which the employee held'. A finding of incompetence may spring from one incident or from several. In *Taylor v Alidair Ltd* (1978) when the case was in the EAT Bristow J gave the following illustrations of situations where a single bad incident could make a dismissal fair: where the employee |

was 'the scientist operating the nuclear reactor, the chemist in charge of research into the possible effects of, for example, thalidomide, the driver of the Manchester to London express, the driver of an articulated lorry full of sulphuric acid'. The Court of Appeal endorsed those illustrations. The requirements eg of a driving licence need not be laid down in a written contract.

10.5.5 Redundancy (s 57(2)(c))

The term redundancy is defined as per s 81(2) of EP(C)A. Refer to the previous chapter.

10.5.6 Contravention of statute (s 57(2)(d))

This reason covers the situation when 'the employee could not continue to work in the position which he held without contravention (either on his part or that of his employer) of a duty or restriction imposed by or under any enactment' (s 57(2)(d)). An illustration is *Sandhu v Department of Education & Science* (1978). The Secretary of State dismissed the employee, a teacher, for being unsuitable. The dismissal was under his statutory powers. The claimant could not continue to work lawfully: he would have done so in contravention of statute. Therefore, the employers' reason fell within s 57(2)(d). In the discussion below of procedural fairness there is no special section dealing with contravention of a statute. The same principles as apply elsewhere govern procedural fairness in relation to this reason eg could the employers who dismissed a driver for not having a licence have put her on to different work?

10.5.7 'Some other substantial reason' (SOSR) (s 57(1)(b))

By statute and statutory instrument two forms of dismissal are deemed to be for a substantial reason. By s 61 of EP(C)A a temporary employee who is engaged to fill the place of a permanent worker who is pregnant or has been suspended on medical grounds will have been dismissed for a substantial reason if she is warned that her post is only temporary and she is then dismissed. By virtue of the Transfer of Undertakings (Protection of Employment) Regulations 1981 the employee is deemed to have been dismissed for a substantial reason where it is done for 'economic, technical or organisational reasons entailing a change in the workforce' when the undertaking is transferred. The Transfer Regulations are considered in Chapter 13.

10.5.8 Common examples

Outside s 61 and the Transfer Regulations certain situations have been seen as falling within the category of SOSR. These situations are noted below but the categories of SOSR are not closed.

- Pressure from customers

In *Dobie v Burns International Security Services (UK) Ltd* (1985) the employers provided security at Speke airport, Liverpool. The employee was a security officer. The airport authority refused to let him continue in employment after various incidents for which he allegedly was to blame. It should be noted that threatened or actual industrial action cannot be used by the employee as a potentially fair reason. See the next chapter.

• Reorganisations in the interest of efficiency

Redundancy dismissals fall within s 57(2)(c), above. If the statutory definition of redundancy is not satisfied, there may nevertheless be a *prima facie* valid reason within s 57(1)(b). It should be noted that a dismissal in this area as in others can be fair despite the fact that it was the employers who were in breach of contract. The test whether the reason is a substantial one has varied across the years. In *Robinson v British Island Airways Ltd* (1978) the EAT demanded a 'pressing business reason' but in *Bowaters Containers Ltd v McCormack* (1980) the change had to be merely 'beneficial' ie to the employers. The most authoritative case, *Hollister v National Farmers' Union* (1979), demanded a good, sound business reason. More recently, the EAT has suggested that the true test is a balancing one: were the employers reasonable in their belief that the advantage to them as reorganised outweighs the detriment to the employee (*Chubb Fire Security Ltd v Harper* (1983)). There is no need for the employers to demonstrate that the business reasons for the change were so pressing that unless the employee accepted the revised terms the enterprise would collapse (*Catamaran Cruisers Ltd v Williams* (1994)). Employers cannot simply say that the reorganisation was needful. They must act on reasonable information. For example, in *Orr v Vaughan* (1981) the employers accepted the recommendation of a bookkeeper that a certain beauty salon in which the employee worked should be closed down. The employers did not provide further evidence that it was that salon which was losing money. The EAT held that there had been no reasonable investigation of the needs of the business. The Tribunal said that the information had to be reasonably acquired. Presumably that phrasing indicates that the data need not be specially commissioned or too expensive to track down on a cost/benefit analysis. One important point about SOSR is demonstrated by the cases. The employers may have a potentially fair reason to dismiss even though their actions are in breach of contract. Moreover, an employee may be fairly dismissed despite her seeking to rely on the contractual position.

- Unilateral changes to contractual terms

  A refusal to accept new contract terms may amount to SOSR. In *R S Components Ltd v Irwin* (1973) NIRC the employees refused to accept a covenant in restraint of trade. The Court held that they were dismissed for SOSR. The firm's profits had been bitten into when some workers left to establish a competing company. The dismissals of the employees who refused were a substantial reason.

- Temporary workers

  In situations falling outside s 61 dismissal of those on temporary contracts may be for SOSR. In *North Yorkshire County Council v Fay* (1985) the expiry of a fixed-term contract of a teacher was a dismissal for SOSR when the employee knew that the job was temporary.

SOSR covers many other situations. An example is the dismissal of the wife where the husband is dismissed, their being engaged on a 'joint contract' as when they are club stewards. In *Saunders v Scottish National Camps Ltd* (1980) the Court of Session, the Scottish equivalent of the Court of Appeal, held that dismissal was for SOSR where the employers dismissed a homosexual employee in the belief that persons of such sexuality were more likely to interfere with children than heterosexuals. In one of the first important unfair dismissal cases a refusal by colleagues to work with an employee because she insisted on boasting about her sexual dalliance with a 'toyboy' was held to be some other substantial reason (*Treganowan v Robert Knee & Co Ltd* (1975)). The dismissal of an apprentice when the contract of apprenticeship expired is SOSR. The term also covers dismissal for unacceptable attendance record, even though the absence was caused by sickness.

10.5.9   Categories not closed

Criticisms of SOSR:

10.5.10   Commentary

- The meaning of 'substantial'

  Courts and tribunals have accepted that SOSR is satisfied by something less than a real need of the business. Only if the reason is 'trivial or unworthy', as the Court of Appeal put it in *Kent CC v Gilham* above, is it not substantial. This test is an easily satisfied one arguably not in line with the ordinary language meaning of 'substantial' and surely not in line with the intention of Parliament. Most reasons advanced for doing something as serious as sacking an employee are assuredly not trivial and not unworthy. Moreover, what is trivial? What is unworthy?

- Management description of a reason for dismissal has rarely been questioned. If the employers consider the reason to be important, it is 'substantial' (*Banerjee v City & East London AHA* (1979)). The reason is challengeable only on the basis of no evidence.

- Managerial prerogative

  In a well-known article Bowers and Clarke (1981) 10 ILJ 34 argued that the elasticity of SOSR meant that tribunals could preserve rule by management by holding the reason for dismissal to be SOSR. Yet one object of the unfair dismissal was to rein in managerial prerogative at the point of dismissal. It might have been helpful if Parliament had provided a definitive list of substantial reasons.

- The principal types of SOSR mentioned above are readily exploited by employers. If employers repudiate the contract and the employee accepts, there is a wrongful dismissal. However, there may not be an unfair dismissal. The employers may contend that the change was SOSR; therefore, the issue then turns on the fairness of the dismissal. One might have expected unfair dismissal to be more favourable to employees than wrongful dismissal, but that expectation may be disappointed.

10.6   Reasonableness

If the employers demonstrate a potentially fair reason the IT must determine whether the dismissal was fair or unfair, having regard to that reason and taking into account whether in the circumstances including the size and administrative resources of their undertaking and equity and the substantial merits of the case (s 57(3)) the employers acted reasonably. This section looks at various matters which an IT may consider when dealing with the fairness of the dismissal. It opens with a discussion of general matters, then looks at specific matters connected with particular potentially fair reasons. It must throughout be noted that matters relevant to one reason may well be relevant to another: to some extent the law on procedural fairness is applied to all the reasons. However, for the purposes of exposition it is convenient to divide up the various aspects of fairness and some issues, such as that of warnings, are closely linked to some reasons (eg a warning not to repeat conduct, a warning to improve standards) but not to others (eg if employers come under customer pressure to dismiss, a warning to the employee that they are under such pressure is hardly feasible). Three points of interpretation in s 57(3) are that 'equity' means not the rules and maxims of equity but 'common fairness', as Donaldson LJ put it in *Union of Construction, Allied Trades and Technicians v Brain* (1981). The second point is that s 57(3) directs the IT to concentrate on the behaviour of the employers, not on any injustice to the employee. The Lords emphasised this interpretation in *Devis v Atkins*, above. Finally, s 57(3) does not give tribunals much guidance on how to determine whether a dismissal was a reasonable one: A large amount of discretion is left in their hands, and the exercise of that discretion is reviewable only if the tribunal has misdirected itself in law or its decision is perverse. There is a serious possibility of inconsistent determinations.

In relation to the reason for the dismissal the employers need not know, for example, that the employee was incapable: it suffices that they believed on reasonable grounds that she was. This law is sometimes known as the rule in *British Home Stores Ltd v Burchell* (1980). There is a three-stage test:

10.6.1   Reasonable grounds

- Did the employers believe the reason?

- Did they have 'in mind reasonable grounds upon which to sustain that belief'?

- Did they carry out 'as much investigation into the matter as was reasonable in all the circumstances of the case'?

This test, which runs together the reason for and reasonableness of the dismissal, points up the issue of procedural fairness, which is discussed below. Accordingly, merely believing that the employee was incompetent is insufficient. There must be some objective grounds for that belief and the employers must reach the decision to dismiss in a fair manner eg after warnings about raising standards. The *Burchell* test originated in a case involving theft but has been widely applied and received the imprimatur of the Court of Appeal in *W Weddel & Co Ltd v Tepper*, above. Stephenson LJ added that the employers should not 'form their belief hastily without making the appropriate enquiries'. Nevertheless, *Burchell* remains a principle, rather than a law. It is not *per se* an error of law for an IT not to go through the test. It should also be noted that *Burchell* is irrelevant where the facts are clear, for example, that the employee had stolen the item or was entertaining a young lady in his office late at night.

Browne-Wilkinson J stated in oft-quoted words in *Iceland Frozen Foods v Jones* (1983):

10.6.2   *Iceland Frozen Foods v Jones* (1983)

'... the correct approach for the IT to adopt in answering the question posed by s 57(3) of the Act of 1978 is as follows: (1) the starting point should always be the words of s 57(3) themselves; (2) in applying the section an IT must consider the reasonableness of the employer's conduct, not simply whether they [the members of the IT] consider the dismissal to be fair; (3) in judging the reasonableness of the employer's conduct an IT must not substitute its decision as to what was the right course to adopt for that of the employer; (4) in many, though not all, cases there is a band of reasonable responses to the employee's conduct within which one employer might reasonably take one view, another quite reasonably take another; (5) the function of the IT, as an industrial jury, is to determine whether in the particular circumstances of each case the decision to dismiss the employee fell within the band of reasonable responses which a reasonable employer might have adopted.'

The 'reasonable responses test' has become standard. If these employers did dismiss and reasonable employers might have dismissed, the dismissal is fair. If the employers acted within the band of reasonable responses, their conduct was fair. For example, a dismissal for a second, though minor, job-related fraud is within the range of reasonable responses. It is immaterial that if the members of the IT had been the employers, they would have done more before dismissing. There are many cases to this effect. Steven Anderman's comment in *Labour Law* (1993) 2nd edn, p 141, is incisive. 'In effect the judiciary has read into the Act a self-denying ordinance which attempts to ensure that rather than imposing upon employers an objective notion of fairness in the interpretation of the statutory standard, it is to be limited to reflecting the lowest common denominator of acceptable managerial practice.'

10.6.3   Size

Size does matter. Section 57(3) directs the IT to consider the size and administrative resources of the employers. It may, for instance, be reasonable for one enterprise to dismiss but on the same facts it would be unreasonable for another undertaking to do so. It would not be reasonable for the owner of a corner-shop to provide several layers of appeals, whereas it might be reasonable for a chain of high street stores to provide an appeal structure. However, the ACAS Code of Practice, considered below, is expressed to apply to all businesses regardless of size, and under s 57(3) small firms must follow a procedure which is fair in the circumstances.

10.6.4   Guidelines

The Court of Appeal has instructed ITs not to act legalistically but with common sense (eg *Kent County Council v Gilham (No 2)*

(1985)). In *Duffy v Yeomans & Partners Ltd* (1994) the Court of Appeal said that: 'there is a grave danger that this area of law is becoming ever-sophisticated, and that there is an attempt to lay down matters which are no more than factors which an industrial tribunal should take into account in reaching its decision whether the employer acted reasonably in the circumstances of the particular case.' As the quote above from *Iceland Frozen Foods* demonstrates, ITs are to act as industrial juries (and therefore not as industrial courts). One effect is that the Employment Appeal Tribunal cannot correct IT decisions which are different on the same facts. Indeed, the Appeal Court has several times trenchantly rebuked the EAT for laying down guidelines for ITs to follow. Lawton LJ in the Court of Appeal in *Bailey v BP Oil (Kent Refinery) Ltd* (1980) stated: '... it is unwise for this court or the Employment Appeal Tribunal to set out guidelines and wrong to make rules and establish presumptions for industrial tribunals to follow or take into account.' Only if the EAT or the Court of Appeal can say there was an error of law or 'My goodness, that must be wrong' may they intervene (*per* May LJ in *Neale v Hereford and Worcester County Council* (1986)). The IT 'has to look at the question in the round and without regard to a lawyer's technicalities. It has to look at it in an employment and industrial relations context': *UCATT v Brain*, above. (It may surprise members of the Court of Appeal that their brethren have not always refrained from endorsing guidelines.) Since ITs must not substitute their own ideas for the employers' assessment of reasonableness, the term 'industrial jury' is something of a misnomer.

Particular matters: the importance of procedural fairness. Procedural fairness is a major concern of tribunals when considering whether a dismissal was fair. The question being asked is whether employers reached the decision to sack in a fair way. Did they, for example, issue a warning that they would for the next 'offence' dismiss the employee? Did they consult with the employee when considering whether to dismiss on medical grounds? There are hundreds of cases reported in the law reports or excerpted in journals such as *IDS Brief* and the *Industrial Relations Review and Report* which from 1995 has been renamed as *Employment Trends*, as well as thousands of unpublished transcripts from ITs and the EAT. There follows an outline of the topic with emphasis on only the more significant cases and on the relevant ACAS Code of Practice and the accompanying handbook. In the words of Lord Donaldson MR in *Piggott Bros & Co Ltd v Jackson* (1992): in deciding whether the employer acted reasonably or unreasonably in treating the employee's conduct an IT 'will

10.6.5   Importance of procedure

have to consider what alternative courses of action were open to the employer – should he, for example, not have dismissed at all or should he have taken further steps to persuade the employee to desist from such conduct and only have dismissed if that proved ineffective?'

10.6.6   Renewed emphasis

A series of decisions downgraded the importance of procedural fairness. Where a fair procedure had not been followed tribunals were encouraged to ask whether it would have made any difference to the question of dismissal. Employers could establish that a dismissal was fair despite an unfair procedure by showing that they would probably still have dismissed if a fair procedure had been followed. This approach was in effect overturned by the House of Lords in *Polkey v A E Dayton Services Ltd* (1988). It is now irrelevant whether or not the defect in procedure made a difference. The test is: was it reasonable for the employers, in the light of their knowledge at the time of dismissal, to adopt the procedure they did? (But see *Duffy* in the next paragraph.) The result is that tribunals once again place great emphasis on whether a fair procedure was followed before dismissal. So, for example, these procedural matters could make a dismissal unfair:

- Conduct – a dismissal for misconduct without giving the employee an opportunity to answer the allegations;

- Capability – a dismissal for poor performance without sufficient warnings and an opportunity to improve;

- Redundancy – a dismissal for redundancy without warning or consultation or without consideration of alternative jobs.

10.6.7   Exception

The House of Lords qualified the general rule by stating that if it was clear to the employers at the time of dismissal that following the proper procedure would have been *'utterly useless'* (emphasis supplied), failure to follow that procedure may be justified. (*Polkey* itself might have been such a case.) The Court of Appeal held in *Duffy v Yeoman & Partners Ltd* (1994) that employers need not actually make a decision not to consult. It is sufficient if a reasonable employer might not have consulted. This case looks like a return to the pre-*Polkey* law. It is also inconsistent with the decision of this Scottish EAT in *Robertson v Magnet Ltd (Retail Division)* (1993). Despite this qualification, the better view is that in *every* case of dismissal an employer should always follow a fair procedure. One illustrative case is *Charles Robertson (Developments) Ltd v White* (1995) where the employers' argument was that it would have been utterly useless to adopt a fair procedure because the employee had been caught stealing by a video camera.

Holland J said:

> 'each applicant was a well-established employee and each theft, while inexcusable as such, was not of the most heinous nature ... in either case, a disciplinary interview, so far from being useless, had a potential value as an aid to a balanced decision as to dismissal, and one that could be seen to be fair.'

The 'any difference' test will still be relevant to the question of remedies. If, for example, in a case of misconduct it is shown that, though the employer had not investigated the matter adequately, the employee was nevertheless 'guilty', compensation may be reduced.

10.6.8   Effect on remedy

The ACAS Code No 1 on Disciplinary Practice and Procedures (issued first in 1977) is supplemented by an ACAS advisory handbook *Discipline at Work* (1987). The advisory handbook complements the ACAS Code No 1 by giving more practical advice. It does not impose any binding legal obligations. It is an attempt to show what is good industrial relations practice. The handbook was to have been an ACAS Code but the then Secretary of State for Employment rejected it as being too legalistic and too difficult for small employers to use. ACAS Code No 1 operates in a different fashion. An industrial tribunal (but not a court) is empowered to take the Code's provisions into account when determining the fairness of a dismissal. However, non-compliance with the provisions of the Code will not automatically render a dismissal unfair. Compliance or non-compliance is one of the factors for consideration. The aim of a set of procedures is not primarily the imposition of sanctions but rather to ensure that employees are treated fairly and consistently. The importance of following proper procedures can become crucial in relation to a dismissal since the way in which the dismissal has been handled can be challenged before an industrial tribunal. Fairness in handling a dismissal will be judged by reference to whether the employer acted reasonably in all the circumstances. Failure to follow a proper procedure can make what is otherwise a dismissal for good cause an unfair dismissal. A checklist for handling a disciplinary matter is set out in the advisory handbook.

10.6.9   Code and handbook

Rules are necessary to advise employees of the kind of acts and behaviour which constitutes a breach of discipline. In the words of the advisory handbook:

10.6.10   Rules

> 'They set standards of conduct at work and make clear to employees what is expected of them.'

In the words of the ACAS Code para 7:

> 'Rules should be readily available and management

should make every effort to ensure that employees know and understand them.'

This paragraph reflects *Meyer Dunmore International Ltd v Rogers* (1978).

Each organisation will have varied requirements. Neither the advisory handbook nor the ACAS Code contains a universal set of rules. However, some factors will be common to all organisations.

10.6.11   Contents

The advisory handbook gives the following examples which might be appropriate in a small company:

- Timekeeping

  Are employees required to 'clock-in'? Clocking-on offences have led to fair dismissals provided that the rule was clear (eg *Dalton v Burton's Gold Medal Biscuits Ltd* (1974)). What rules apply to lateness?

- Absence

  Who authorises absence? Who approves holidays? Whom should employees notify when they are absent from work? When should notification of absence take place? When is a medical self-certificate sufficient? When will a doctor's certificate be necessary?

- Health and safety

  Are there special requirements regarding personal appearance or cleanliness eg length of hair, jewellery, protective clothing? Are there special hazards? Are there non-smoking areas? Is alcohol prohibited?

- Use of company facilities

  Are private telephone calls permitted? Are employees allowed to be on company premises outside working hours? Is company equipment generally available for personal use?

- Discrimination

  Is it clear that racial and sexual abuse or harassment will be treated as disciplinary offences? Is there a rule about clothing or uniform which is disproportionately disadvantageous to a racial group and which cannot be justified on non-racial grounds? Is there a rule requiring higher language standards than are needed for safe and effective performance of the job? Is there a requirement about mobility of employment which cannot be justified on operational grounds and is disadvantageous to one sex?

- Gross misconduct

  Are the kind of offences regarded as gross misconduct and

which could lead to dismissal without notice clearly specified?

The advisory handbook gives these examples of gross misconduct: theft, fraud, deliberate falsification of records, fighting, assault on another person, deliberate damage to company property, serious incapability through alcohol or being under the influence of illegal drugs, serious negligence which causes unacceptable loss damage or injury, serious acts of insubordination.

ITs may question the application of the rules to particular facts. For example, in *Ladbroke Racing Ltd v Arnott* (1983) the employers implemented a rule that employees were not permitted to place bets on pain of dismissal. Bets had certainly been placed but the breaches of the rule were minor and the employees did not gain any monetary advantages from their breaches. The Court of Session held that the employers had acted unreasonably. The case demonstrates that not even clear rules prevent the IT from investigating the fairness of the dismissal. | 10.6.12   Application

Furthermore, inconsistency of treatment may give rise to an unfair dismissal. If there is a rule that both employees will be dismissed if one clocks in the other but the rule has not been enforced in the past, dismissal is probably unfair should the firm decide on one occasion to apply the rule. Warnings that the rule is going to be enforced for the future should be used. Different outcomes may, however, be justified by the circumstances. For instance, where two employees are seen fighting at work, it may be reasonable to dismiss one but retain the other if the former has a worse disciplinary record than the latter. | 10.6.13   Inconsistency

Disciplinary rules can act as warnings. Therefore, in relation to fair procedure discussed below rules can replace warnings. The rule, however, still must cover what occurred and be applied. 'Liable to instant dismissal' does not mean 'will be dismissed' (*Meridian Ltd v Gomersall* (1977)). | 10.6.14   Interpretation

The ACAS Code of Practice's guidance on the form of disciplinary procedures is well established. Procedures should: | 10.6.15   Procedures

- be in writing;

- specify to whom they apply;

- provide for matters to be dealt with quickly;

- indicate the disciplinary actions which may be taken;

- specify the levels of management which have the authority

to take the various forms of disciplinary actions and ensure that immediate supervisors do not normally have the power to dismiss without reference to senior management;

- provide for individuals to be informed of specific complaints against them and to be given an opportunity to state their case directly to those considering disciplinary action before decisions are reached;

- give individuals the right to be accompanied, either by a trade union official where a trade union is recognised or by a fellow employee of their choice;

- ensure that any investigatory period of suspension is with pay (unless the contract of employment clearly provides otherwise) and specify how pay is to be calculated during such a period;

- ensure that, except for gross misconduct, no employees are dismissed for a first breach of discipline;

- ensure that disciplinary action is not taken until the case has been carefully investigated. (Any decision has to be taken on a basis of adequate facts, which in turn demands adequate investigation);

- ensure that individuals are given a written explanation for any penalty imposed;

- provide a right of appeal and specify the procedure to be followed and the action that may be taken by those hearing the appeal.

A case illustrating these points is *Charles Robertson (Developments) Ltd* (1995). Two employees were dismissed for theft of a small quantity of sweets from a stockroom. The store manager dismissed them without hearing their case and without advising them of their 'rights' under the ACAS Code including the right to be accompanied by a representative of their choice.

10.6.16   Enforcement

Implementing disciplinary action. The advisory handbook suggests that:

'Before deciding whether a disciplinary penalty is appropriate consider the employee's disciplinary and general record, whether the disciplinary procedure points to the likely penalty, action taken in previous cases, any explanations and circumstances to be considered and whether the penalty is reasonable.'

The advisory handbook suggests that the following procedure be adopted (and provides specimen disciplinary procedures suitable for adoption either by any organisation or by small firms in Appendix 3):

- 'In the case of minor offences, the individual should be given a formal oral warning and told that a note that it was given will be kept for reference purposes.'

- 'In the case of more serious offences or where there is an accumulation of minor offences the individual should be given a formal written warning.'

- 'If the employee has received a previous warning, further misconduct may warrant a final written warning or consideration of a disciplinary penalty short of dismissal' (including disciplinary transfer, disciplinary suspension without pay, demotion, loss of seniority, or loss of increment, provided these penalties are allowed for by an express or implied term of the contract of employment).

- There may be occasions when misconduct is considered not to be so serious as to justify dismissal but serious enough to warrant only one written warning which will be both the first and final.

- A final written warning should contain a statement that any further misconduct will lead to dismissal. If all previous stages have been observed, the final step will be dismissal.

It will be seen that a three-stage procedure is recommended before dismissal, namely: formal oral warning, first written warning, and final written warning. This does not, however, mean that three warnings must always be given before any dismissal is considered. There may be occasions when, depending on the seriousness of the misconduct involved, it will be appropriate to enter the procedure at stage 2 (written warning) or stage 3 (final written warning). There may also be occasions when dismissal without notice is applicable. Moreover, the fact that an employee is on a final warning does not mean that an employer is justified in dismissing an employee immediately. The circumstances must still be considered.

10.6.17   Stages

In order to follow such a procedure it is necessary for a company to indicate which types of misconduct will attract the various penalties. The types of misconduct can be grouped in order to indicate the likely disciplinary sanctions that will be imposed. Examples are set out below. (There is no guidance on this in the advisory handbook.)

10.6.18   Misconduct defined

- Written warning:

    (i)   lateness or bad timekeeping;

(ii)   unauthorised absence from place of work;

(iii)   less serious cases of negligence;

(iv)   minor incidents of insubordination or disorderly conduct;

(v)   poor performance of job duties;

(vi)   time wasting;

(vii)   minor breaches of safety regulations;

(viii) refusal or failure to carry out the legitimate instructions of a manager.

- Final written warning:

    (i)   repetition of an offence or the commission of a different offence after a first written warning has been given;

    (ii)   disciplinary offences of the type detailed above and of a sufficiently serious nature to warrant a more serious sanction than a first written warning.

- Dismissal:

    (i)   prolonged unauthorised absence after the issue of a final warning;

    (ii)   repetition of offences of a less serious nature when taken individually after a final warning and/or suspension.

- Dismissal without notice for gross misconduct:

    (i)   theft of property from the company or other employees while on company premises;

    (ii)   falsification of company documents whether or not for personal gain;

    (iii)   making false statement in regard to matters affecting employment;

    (iv)   assault or battery on site against any person;

    (v)   unauthorised use of company vehicles;

    (vi)   habitual or gross intoxication on company premises;

    (vii)   flagrant violation of safety rules;

(viii) deliberate damage to company property or the property of other employees;

(ix)   serious negligence.

Dismissal for gross misconduct should only take place after the normal investigation to establish all the facts. The employee should be told of the complaint and be given an opportunity to state his or her case and be represented.

One problem which has arisen is whether employers are entitled to move from oral to written warning etc where the warnings relate to different matters. There may be a warning for arriving slightly drunk and another for theft of paper clips. While the law is uncertain, it is thought that employers are entitled to add together such warnings; otherwise they do not get a rounded view of the employee's behaviour and competence. Another issue is that as a matter of good industrial relations practice and probably of law a warning should be wiped off the record after, say, six or 12 months.

10.6.19   Counting warnings

The ACAS Code makes it clear that provision should always be made in a disciplinary procedure for an appeal (ACAS Code para 10(k)). Employers should:

10.6.20   Appeals

• provide for appeals to be dealt with speedily;

• wherever possible, use a procedure which is separate from the general grievance procedure;

• wherever possible, provide for the appeal to be heard by an authority higher than that taking the disciplinary action;

• pay particular attention to any new evidence introduced at the hearing and allow the employee to comment on it;

• examine all the issues fully and do not be afraid to overturn a wrong decision;

• realise that the provision of an appeal is an indispensable part of any disciplinary procedure. It is as important as the need to have a full investigation of the facts and to give the employee a chance to put her side of the case.

The Court of Appeal in *Sartor v P & O European Ferries (Felixstowe) Ltd* (1992) stated that an appeal can retrospectively cure a bad first hearing, provided that it took the form of a full rehearing and that, if possible, representatives of the management should not be the same at hearing and on appeal. The employers' failure to comply with the contractual appeals procedure, however, makes the process void and is such a fundamental defect that the dismissal by that body is unfair

(*Cabaj v Westminster City Council* (1994)). The reasonableness of the employers' conduct is irrelevant.

10.6.21 Notification

Notification of disciplinary rules and procedures to employees. Employers are required to give employees a written statement of the main terms of employment together with a note of the disciplinary rules and procedure. See Chapter 4. On the issue of a written statement and disciplinary rules an employee should be required to give a receipt.

10.6.22 Absence

Procedures in cases of absence. ACAS in the advisory handbook gives guidance on the procedure for handling absences. A distinction is made between absences on grounds of ill-health (see later) and absence for reasons which may call for disciplinary actions. The following points are made by ACAS.

- Accurate record keeping is vital. The records should show:

  lateness and any reasons therefor;

  the duration of any absence and any reasons therefor.

  In this way management can pick up and deal with any problems at an early stage.

- Absences should be investigated promptly and the employee asked to give an explanation. In the absence of a good reason for absence the matter should be dealt with under the disciplinary procedure.

- The employee should be told what improvement in attendance is expected and warned of the likely consequences if this does not happen.

- If there is no improvement, the employee's age, length of service, performance, the likelihood of a change in attendance, the availability of suitable alternative work and the effect of past and future absences on the business should all be taken into account in deciding appropriate action.

  The advisory handbook gives separate guidance covering employees who fail to return from extended leave on the agreed date.

10.6.23 Incompetence

Dismissals on the basis of inadequate performance or lack of skill or competence should be handled differently from cases of misconduct. Part of the fault may be the employers' eg lack of adequate training or adequate supervision, lack of care in the recruitment and selection process. Normally one act of shoddy performance will not be sufficient to justify dismissal, but may be on the facts: *Alidair Ltd v Taylor* (1978) (bumping landing of aeroplane led to the employers losing confidence in the pilot).

The advisory handbook makes the following points.

- The standard of work required should be explained and employees left in no doubt about what is expected of them. Accurate job descriptions obviate disputes. (However, dismissal may be fair when a person high in the employers' hierarchy is sacked when she ought to have known of the standard.)

- The consequences of any failure to meet the required standards should be explained.

- Proper training and supervision are essential to the achievement of satisfactory performance. Appraisal systems may be useful as evidence.

- An employee should not normally be dismissed because of poor performance unless warnings and a chance to improve have been given. Consideration should be given to finding suitable alternative work (eg *Vokes Ltd v Bear* (1974)) but there is no requirement to create an alternative job (*MANWEB v Taylor* (1975), a case of general application). A warning in a case involving sub-standard work serves a different purpose from one given for misconduct. It can be used to show the employee how to improve on her performance.

How would you deal with the following? An employee was absent over two years with dizzy spells, anxiety, nerves, bronchitis, virus infection, cystitis, althruigia of the left knee, dyspepsia and flatulence. In the four quarters of one year she was absent for 20%, 27%, 22%, and 37%. Most if not all of the illnesses were covered by a doctor's note. She had received three warnings, and a final warning. Employers had followed their own procedure correctly. The GP whom the company employed thought that none of the sicknesses could be verified at the present time and that the employee did not seem to be suffering from any long-term illness, but of course he could not query the employee's own doctor's certificates. An industrial tribunal held the dismissal to be unfair, but the Employment Appeal Tribunal allowed the employers' appeal. The case is *International Sports Co Ltd v Thomson* (1980). They said that the employee had been fairly dismissed for absenteeism, a 'conduct' reason. Employers do not need to determine the *bona fides* of doctors' notes: no reasonable employer would have done that. There is no need for a formal medical examination where employee's complaints are intermittent and unconnected:

> 'What is required ... is, firstly, that there should be a fair review by the employer of the attendance record and the

10.6.24   Illness

reasons for it; and, secondly, appropriate warnings, after the employee has been given an opportunity to make representations.'

10.6.25   Relevance

In unfair dismissal cases sickness appears in two places.

- Because of sickness the contract of employment cannot be performed. In law this failure is called 'frustration'. Where there is frustration, employment has not been terminated by dismissal. Since there is no dismissal, there can be no unfair dismissal. See Chapter 7.

- Sickness may be a potentially fair reason for dismissal in the same way as redundancy and misconduct are. There has been a dismissal, and the employers are arguing that the dismissal was for sickness. If they show that reason, it is for the industrial tribunal to decide whether in all the circumstances of the case the employers acted fairly in dismissing the employee.

10.6.26   Consultation

The basic rule is to carry out such investigation as is reasonable. If the employers cannot be expected to wait any longer before dismissing, the dismissal will normally be fair (*Spencer v Paragon Wallpapers Ltd* (1977)). To decide this question employers should look at:

- the nature of the illness;

- the potential length of absence;

- the employee's personal circumstances;

- the urgency of filling the employee's post;

- the size and nature of the employers' firm.

Consultation will normally be a pre-requisite (*East Lindsey District Council v Daubney* (1977)). There is a need for 'sensitive consultation and discussion' with the employee. Consultation may well bring new facts to light. Employers should keep in touch with the employee so that they know the true position before dismissal. There is no duty on the employee to inform the employers of any progress (*Mitchell v Arkwood Plastics (Engineering) Ltd* (1993) EAT). The employers need not discover the true diagnosis of the employee's illness. It is sufficient that they know the medical position of persons in general with that ailment. Relying on the company doctor's report will usually not be sufficient, and the employers have no implied right to order an employee to submit to a medical examination by the company's doctor or by an independent practitioner. A doctor's note is not conclusive. In *Hutchinson v Enfield Rolling Mills Ltd* (1981) the employee was certified sick for one day but he was seen in Brighton at a union demonstration. It was held that he had been fairly dismissed. It is not by itself fair to sack where sick pay has run out, and it may be fair to dismiss even though sick pay has not run out (*Hardwick v Leeds Area Health Authority* (1975)). Requests for reports from the employee's doctor are regulated by the Access to Medical Reports Act 1988. This statute does not apply to reports from the company's own doctor. The Act permits employees to gain access to their own records and to comment on them.

Polkey emphasises the need for correct procedures eg to check the precise details of the illness and prognosis; give the employee the chance to state his or her case; keep in touch with the employee; ask the employee's GP when the employee may return to work. If there is any doubt about the reason for the employee's absence ask the employee to see the company doctor (if the employee refuses, the firm should warn her of dismissal); allow the employee to be accompanied by a TU representative, if there is one, or by a friend. It should be noted that it is immaterial that the employers caused the employee's illness. The tribunal must look at the fairness of the dismissal, not at the responsibility for the illness which led to the dismissal (*London Fire & Civil Defence Authority v Betty* (1994)). The employers accused the employee of racial discrimination and harassment of his colleagues. There were no grounds for these allegations. He fell ill and had a nervous breakdown. The EAT told the IT to consider procedural fairness and not investigate responsibility for the breakdown.

10.6.27   Other procedures

Consultation is not always necessary: eg there may be a risk to health of fellow employees; good eyesight in some jobs may be a necessity; there may be a need to cope with the Christmas rush or for the employee constantly to attend machines; or the employee may be medically unfit for (eg) work on North Sea rigs. The test of futility is objective.

10.6.28   Futility

A reasonable employer may instead of dismissing: eg put employee on to lighter work; put the employee in to a 'holding group'.

10.6.29   Redeployment

ACAS Advisory Handbook p 41 states:

10.6.30   Considerations

'If there is no improvement, employee's age, length of service, performance, the likelihood of a change in attendance, the availability of suitable alternative work and the effect of past and future absences on the business should all be taken into account in deciding appropriate action.'

On self-certification the *Handbook* suggests that:

'Where there is no medical advice to support frequent self-certified absences, the employee should be asked to consult a doctor to establish whether medical treatment is necessary and whether the underlying reason for absence is work-related.'

10.6.31   Redundancy

Polkey (1988) is itself a case where the employer selected the employee on the grounds of redundancy. The employee was employed by employers as one of four van drivers. The employers were losing money. They decided to reduce overheads by replacing the drivers with van salesmen and they had to act quickly. They sacked three of the drivers, including the employee, because they did not think they would be suitable salespeople. The employee was told he was being made redundant, handed a letter to that effect, and sent home. He complained that he had been unfairly dismissed. He supported his argument by saying that he ought to have been consulted or warned. There had also been no consultation with his union. The tribunals and the Court of Appeal ruled that since employers would have sacked him even if there had been consultation, the employee was fairly dismissed. However, the employee successfully appealed to the House of Lords. The Lords held that the rule which the courts had been following was incorrect. That rule was called the 'no difference' rule or the *British Labour Pump* rule. It was called the 'no difference' rule because it was said that a failure to follow the correct procedure did not make a dismissal unfair if it would have made no difference had the right procedure been adopted. It was called the *British Labour Pump* rule because the main case in which the 'no difference' rule was stated was *British Labour Pump Ltd v Byrne* (1979). In *Polkey* (1988) the House overruled the *British Labour Pump* rule.

10.6.32   *Polkey* (1988)

In *Polkey* the House of Lords restated the law. The task facing the industrial tribunal is to decide whether employers acted reasonably in dismissing, not whether justice was done. *Per* Lord Mackay:

'The subject matter for the tribunal's consideration is the employer's action in treating the reason as a sufficient reason for dismissing the employee. It is that action and that action only that the tribunal is required to characterise as reasonable or unreasonable. That leaves no scope for the tribunal considering whether, if the employer had acted differently, he might have dismissed the employee.'

One therefore has to look at the conduct of employers, not at whether employee has suffered any injustice. Did employers act reasonably?

- In deciding whether employers acted reasonably, the tribunal must consider whether they followed the correct procedure.

- The fact that employers would have dismissed anyway is irrelevant. One must look at what employers did, not what they might have done.

- 'In judging whether what the employer did was reasonable it is right to consider what a reasonable employer would have had in·mind at the time he decided to dismiss as the consequence of not consulting or not warning' (*per* Lord Mackay). For instance one must judge the dismissal against what a reasonable employer would have done. If a reasonable employer would have consulted and this employer did not, normally the outcome will be unfair dismissal.

- 'Normally' is used because there are exceptional situations where employers do act reasonably in dismissing without consultation. Various phrases have been used: 'complete waste of time', no possible 'explanation or mitigation', where the offence is 'heinous'. Lord Mackay in *Polkey* said:

  'It is quite a different matter if the tribunal is able to conclude that the employer himself, at the time of dismissal, acted reasonably in taking the view that, in the exceptional circumstances of the particular case, the procedural steps normally appropriate would have been futile, could not have altered the decision to dismiss and therefore could be dispensed with.'

The illustration often given of a futile procedure is an investigation after the employer saw the employee stab a fellow worker. Besides futile procedures being rare – and it might not be futile to investigate in the stabbing example: there may be provocation – futile procedures must be especially rare in redundancy cases, because (*Polkey* in the Court of Appeal):

  '... the system adopted for the selection of the individual for redundancy may be at the very centre of the inquiry when the tribunal comes to determine whether the employee has acted reasonably or unreasonably in treating redundancy as a sufficient reason for dismissing the employee concerned.'

Therefore, to defend an unfair dismissal claim successfully, employers must go through the correct procedures. Only exceptionally will they win if they do not do so, and this principle applies even though consultation would have made no difference to the result. With the *Polkey* approach employers lose more unfair dismissal cases than before unless they put their house in order. It is obviously worthwhile putting one's house in order to avoid eg bad publicity, the stigma of being branded a bad employer.

• What happens if employers would have dismissed had they gone through the correct procedure? As we have seen, they will normally lose the issue of liability for unfair dismissal. Nevertheless, compensation may be reduced if following the correct procedure would have made no difference. (It should be emphasised that compensation for a dismissal is unfair because of substantive (and not procedural) defects is not affected by this rule such as the selection of criteria for making individuals redundant.) Of the three remedies for unfair dismissal, reinstatement, re-engagement and compensation, the most likely award for an unfair redundancy is compensation. This is divided into two parts. The compensatory award may be reduced on the grounds that there has been no loss or that it is 'just and equitable' to award a lesser sum. The second part is the basic award, which is calculated according to the employee's age, weekly earnings, and the time he or she has worked for their employers. It cannot be reduced except for contributory fault eg misconduct, or for the sum which the employers have expended as a redundancy payment. Even if the tribunal awards no compensatory award, employers should be aware that they will face paying the basic award. From 1993 the maximum amount of the compensatory award is £11,000 in an unfair redundancy case. One cannot predict what percentage reduction a tribunal might make eg it could be 20% or it could be 100%.

10.6.33   Summary

To sum up, a dismissal on the grounds of redundancy may well be unfair if the rules of procedure have been broken. *Polkey* emphasises the need for a fair procedure. While it is true to say that a failure to adopt fair procedures will not *per se* lead to a finding of unfair dismissal, the chances are that it will. And the fact that employers win on one occasion because of special circumstances does not mean that they will win on the next occasion. Certainly a tribunal will be loath to hold a dismissal unfair if the substantial merits are with the employers and it will not require a perfect procedure, but it is no use trying to guess how a tribunal might react to an unfair procedure. It is worthwhile for legal purposes getting things right in the first place. Surely it is also worthwhile getting things right for industrial relations' reasons; good man/management relations; and reduced incidence of strikes.

10.6.34   Other options

As Lord Mackay said in *Polkey*:

'in the case of redundancy, the employer will normally not

act reasonably unless he warns and consults any employees affected or their representatives, adopts a fair basis on which to select for redundancy and takes such steps as may be reasonable to avoid or minimise redundancy by redeployment within his own organisation.'

Possible options include:

- a call for volunteers;

- the transfer of employee to another job (give employee a trial period in it);

- short-time working (NB could still be redundancy);

- a call for early retirement;

- possibly look for a job in the rest of the group.

In unfair redundancy cases the stress upon fair procedure takes two forms:

10.6.35 Procedure

- reliance on the Code of Practice; and

- stricter application than before of the steps laid down in *Williams v Compair Maxam Ltd* (1982) to see whether a fair procedure has been used.

The Code of Practice is like the Highway Code. It is not by itself law but may be taken into account by the industrial tribunal. Failure to comply with the Code does not necessarily mean that the dismissal was unfair but it is strong evidence that it was so. A failure to follow the Code may lead to the conclusion that a dismissal was unfair which, had the Code been followed, would have been fair. The Code does not have much to say specifically about redundancy, but the following principles may be drawn from it:

10.6.36 Code of Practice

- the rules should be written down. This ensures that employees know what they must do, and it reduces the chances of misunderstanding;

- the rules should be simple;

- the rules should not discriminate on the grounds of race, sex, or marital status;

- the rules should be generally available eg in the company handbook, on the notice board, given to employees when they join the firm as part of the written statement;

- special care should be devoted to those whose mother tongue is not English;

- if a rule is no longer applied, or has not been consistently applied, any change in practice should be told to the employees.

If the Code of Practice is followed, employers will usually win the case, but must still have a sufficient reason to dismiss and their decision to dismiss must be within the band of reasonable responses to the situation.

10.6.37   *Compair Maxam*

The much criticised case of *Compair Maxam* lays down the sort of procedure that firms ought to follow if they are to defend successfully a claim of unfair dismissal on the ground of redundancy.

- There should be no unfair selection procedure; eg retention of those who would in the opinion of management keep the company viable is a subjective criterion and therefore unfair. Criteria for selection should be reasonably objective and precise eg length of service, skill, attendance record, loyalty. Details of why particular marks had been given to individuals when assessing whom to select need not be disclosed. The relevant critieria differ from job to job, for example, in deciding which teacher to dismiss a governing body might take into account such criteria as exam results, ability to teach several subjects or one subject at several levels, academic qualifications and so on.

- Employers should make reasonable efforts to find an alternative job and consider alternatives to redundancy eg cutting costs in other ways. There is, however, no duty to offer the employee a job which came up after she had been dismissed (*Octavius Atkinson & Sons Ltd v Morris* (1989)). They should consult with employee and warn of impending redundancy. This is said to be one of the fundamentals of a fair procedure, though there is no duty to consult an individual employee where his or her union prohibits individual consultation. They should consult with the trade union. Both types of consultation are usually needed (*Huddersfield Parcels Ltd v Sykes* (1981) among other cases, but the Scottish EAT said in *Eaton Ltd v King* (1995) that consultation with individuals was not needed where there had been consultation with the union and the employees had been afforded the opportunity of commenting on the proposals to make them redundant), and both must take place before the final decision to make someone redundant, eg presenting the union with a list of those to be made redundant is not consultation. See the previous chapter for consultation with recognised unions pre-redundancy dismissals. There is no need for consultation in an emergency eg sudden loss of orders. Other possible reasons for not consulting include sabotage and demoralising the workforce. The latter reason,however, does not seem to be a good one: does not every redundancy lead to some demoralisation? It is suggested that employers should not rely on this reason for not consulting. An example of failure to consult occurs in a case where it was company policy not to consult with employees who were managers about dismissals. It was held that the dismissal was unfair.

Compair Maxam lays down guidelines, not rules. The guidelines do not always apply. The chances are that not all the guidelines have to be followed by small firms (though even so a small business may as well get procedure right). The industrial tribunal must look at how a reasonable employer would have treated this employee. The guidelines are helpful pointers in deciding that question. If the procedure for redundancy has been agreed with the trade union, there is less necessity to follow the guidelines. Despite the above, as the Employment Appeal Tribunal has said:

10.6.38   Guidelines

> 'it is not necessarily enough for an employer to say 'I adopted reasonable criteria' if after consulting as a reasonable employer would have done, different criteria leading to a different result might have been adopted.'

When the Court of Appeal has not specifically endorsed *Compair Maxam*, there are signs in the speeches in *Polkey* that the Lords are in favour of the approach, no matter how much the Scottish EAT disagrees with the guidelines.

Other points to remember include:

10.6.39   Further considerations

- Instead of compensation a tribunal in an unfair redundancy case might award re-engagement 'in employment comparable to that from which he was dismissed or other suitable employment'. The tribunal will take into account the wishes of the employee, practicability of re-engagement, and justice if the employee caused or contributed to the dismissal. As Lord Bridge said in *Polkey*:

  'In a case where an industrial tribunal held that dismissal on the ground of redundancy would have been inevitable at the time when it took place, even if the appropriate procedural steps had been taken, I do not ... think this would necessarily preclude a discretionary order for re-engagement on suitable terms ...'

- An employee may be unfairly dismissed even though by the time of the dismissal the employers have offered to dismiss another person instead.

- *Brown v Stockton-on-Tees BC* (1988) is important. Where a female employee is selected for redundancy because she needs maternity leave, the dismissal is for a 'reason connected with her pregnancy' and is automatically unfair. There is no need to see whether a reasonable employer would have done as this employer did. Therefore, employers must disregard the inconvenience of the fact that one of the potential persons to be made redundant is pregnant and will have to be off work.

- As stated above, the criteria for selection for redundancy must be free from bias on the grounds of race, sex and marital status eg if redundancies are based on the criteria of 'part-timers first', that may be discrimination if men form the full-time work force and women are the part-time employees.

10.6.40   Case-law effects

Unreported cases illustrating the effects of *Polkey* include:

- *Brown v Gavin Scott*

  The employers reorganised management structure to cut costs. They sacked the employee, the general manager of three shoe shops, without consultation. It was held that the dismissal was unfair. Consultation would not have been useless because a different solution might have emerged.

- *Mining Supplies v Baker*

  The employers decided to make redundant 29 manual workers. Negotiations were held with the union and volunteers were sought. There were insufficient volunteers and the union said that 'last in, first out' was the sole criterion which they were prepared to accept. The employers disagreed. They decided to discuss the matter with individual employees. The final choice came down between one with 19 years' service and one with 20. The company chose the former on the basis of 'what most fits the company's needs'. He was not told the reason why he was selected for redundancy. The Employment Appeal Tribunal followed *Polkey* to hold the dismissal unfair because the employers had not adopted a fair procedure. They said that on the basis of the facts of this case proper consultation would have required two weeks and they gave a compensatory award for those weeks.

- *GEC Energy Systems Ltd v Gufferty*

  The employers carried out work for X at a power station. X did not renew the contract. The employers served redundancy notices on their staff. They then entered into negotiations with the CEGB for work at another power station. The CEGB made it clear that fewer workers were needed. They identified the staff they wished to keep. The employee was not one of them. The employers did not say why they were not keeping the employee on. The redundancy was held to be unfair because:

(a)   no real attempt had been made to find the employee another job;

(b)   too little account had been taken of the employee's length of service, good record, and the difficulty he would find in obtaining employment elsewhere.

In this case, a full and skilled consultation process was required. Therefore the dismissal was unfair. *Polkey* was applied. The case was sent back to the industrial tribunal to assess compensation.

In order for a dismissal in a business reorganisation to be fair there must normally be discussion and consultation with the employees affected, to avoid misunderstanding and any possible injustice to an employee. However, the ultimate question is whether the employer has acted reasonably, not whether it is reasonable for the employee to accept new terms. An employee may be acting reasonably in refusing to accept eg because the new terms are disadvantageous to her yet the employer may be acting perfectly reasonably eg because pressing business needs demand that overtime has to be worked.	10.6.41 'Some other substantial reason'
Where a temporary employee is dismissed, the dismissal is not automatically fair so that if eg there is suitable alternative employment available, a failure to offer it may render the dismissal unfair.	10.6.42 Temporary workers
Dismissal at the behest of customers may be fair if the complaint is valid eg misconduct/incompetence on the employee's part subject to the usual safeguards of investigation and a fair hearing etc. If the commercial situation is such that the employer is forced to bow to the customer's wishes the employer must first try to resolve the situation in an alternative way eg changing the employee's workload to prevent contact/dissuading the customer.	10.6.43 Customer pressure

Unfair Dismissal:
The General Approach

By statute employees employed for two years or more are entitled to written reasons explaining their dismissal.

Written reasons

Employers must prove the reason which activated the dismissal:

Reason

Smith v City of Glasgow DC (1987).

Subject to exceptions fair reasons to dismiss discovered after dismissal are not acceptable though compensation may be reduced:

After-discovered reasons

Devis v Atkins (1977)

West Midlands Co-op v Tipton (1986).

There are five potentially fair reasons: capability (including illness), conduct, redundancy, illegality and 'some other substantial reason':

Potentially fair reasons

Taylor v Alidair (1978)

Hollister v NFU (1979).

    Conduct covers eg violence at work, theft from employers and gross negligence.

    Capability covers lack of skill and lack of an academic degree or professional qualification.

    Redundancy is defined as in the previous chapter.

    Illegality includes a delivery driver's loss of licence.

    'SOSR' is not defined in the statute. It includes a business reorganisation not amounting to redundancy and dismissal at the behest of customers.

Industrial tribunals decide fairness, having regard to the size and administrative resources of the firm and equity and the substantial merits of the case. Of importance is procedural fairness eg warnings, investigation:

Reasonableness

BHS v Burchell (1980)

Iceland Frozen Foods v Jones (1983)

Bailey v B P Oil (1980)

Polkey v Dayton Services (1988)

Spencer v Paragon Wallpapers (1977)

Williams v Compair Maxam (1982).

The tribunal may take into account ACAS's Disciplinary Practice and Procedure (a Code of Practice) as expanded by its advisory handbook *Discipline At Work*, which gives employers practical advice on avoiding unfair dismissal claims. It should be emphasised that even small workplaces are subject to the principles of procedural fairness, though such principles may be attenuated for the smallest of employers. The Code recommends the use of a series of warnings, but that procedure can be short-circuited depending on the nature of the incident. It should be recalled that tribunals are not subject to EAT rules and may reach inconsistent outcomes.

Chapter 11

Unfair Dismissal – Particular Problems

This chapter looks at various situations where dismissal is either 'automatically unfair' or 'automatically fair'. The term 'automatically unfair' means that the industrial tribunal does not investigate the reasonableness of the dismissal as it does with regard to the five potentially fair reasons such as conduct discussed in the previous chapter. 'Automatically fair' is the term given to reasons where the dismissal is fair without reference to the reasonableness of the dismissal. The term 'inadmissible reason' has recently been resurrected in the Trade Union Reform and Employment Rights Act 1993 (hereinafter TURERA). The topic of 'industrial pressure' in the context of unfair dismissal is also noted.

11.1 Introduction

By s 152(1) of the Trade Union and Labour Relations (Consolidation) Act 1992, (TULR(C)A), it is unfair to dismiss an employee if the reason or principal reason for the dismissal was that:

11.2 Automatically unfair

- she was or proposed to become a member of an independent trade union (TU) (s 152(1)(a)); it need not be shown that she intended to join any particular union;

- had taken part or proposed to take part in the activities of an independent TU at an appropriate time (s 152(1)(b)); or

- was not a member of any TU, or of a particular TU; or of one of a number of particular TUs, or had refused or proposed to refuse, to become or remain a member (s 152(1)(c)).

The IT looks at the employers' state of mind, not just at 'but-for' causation (*CGB Publishing v Killey* (1995)). This decision is out of line with the law on racial and sexual discrimination.

Section 146, which deals with action short of dismissal, is dealt with below but the two claims are similarly phrased (eg 'appropriate time'). Cases on one are used on the other. There are also laws aimed at preventing dismissal or action short of dismissal for refusing to make payments to charity (in lieu of union dues).

Protection is given only to employees, whereas the International Labour Organisation's Convention No 98, the Right to Organise and Collective Bargaining, applies to all workers. There are the usual exceptions such as share fishermen.

11.2.1   (In)dependence

The difference in wording between point 1 on the one hand and points 2 and 3 on the other should be noted (para 11.2, above). The third point applies to any TU, independent or not. Points 1 and 2 require the union to be independent. The definition of 'independent' is discussed in Chapter 14 below. Section 152(1)(a) and (b) form part of the protection given to employees who wish to associate together: they are part of the laws guaranteeing freedom of association. Section 152(1)(c), however, is part of the present government's attack on the closed shop. However, it is not restricted to closed shop situations but covers non-members wherever.

11.2.2   Activities

Dismissal for taking part in the activities (a phrase which is not defined in the statute) of an independent TU includes the dismissal of an activist by her present employers for the disruption she caused in her previous job (*Fitzpatrick v British Railways Board* (1991)). Other activities include attendance at union meetings (eg *British Airways Engine Overhaul Ltd v Francis* (1981)), acting as a shop steward (*Driver v Cleveland Structural Engineering Ltd* (1994)) and attempting to recruit new members (eg *Lyon v St James Press Ltd* (1976)). Leading a strike is taking part in the activities of a trade union (*Britool Ltd v Roberts* (1993)). However, actually taking part in industrial action is not an activity of an independent TU and if it were, it would not take place at an appropriate time; instead, the IT may not hear and determine the case, subject to exceptions. See automatically fair reasons below. It was suggested in *Lyon* that acts which were wholly unreasonable, extraneous or malicious would not be protected but these dicta have not as yet been applied.

11.2.3   Criticised cases

Two cases have come in for criticism. In *Carrington v Therm-A-Stor Ltd* (1983) employees were dismissed when the union sought recognition from the employers. The Court held that they had been dismissed, not for their own union activities, but as it were for the union's union activities. For the right to apply employees have to be dismissed for what they do, not for what the union does. Therefore since s 152 was not fulfilled, they were unprotected. In *Chant v Aquaboats Ltd* (1978) an employee was dismissed for organising a petition complaining about safety at work. He was a member of a union. The EAT held that his complaint did not fall within s 152. What he did was not taking part in union activities for the TU had not invited him to organise the petition; and he was not a TU official. The union was not involved. Therefore, the activities were not those of a TU but of himself. This outcome was not affected by the fact that a union official had approved the petition.

The phrase 'appropriate time' in s 152(1)(b) means by sub-section (2) time outside the working hours or time within working hours which 'in accordance with arrangements agreed with or consent' given by his employers, the employee may· take part in the activities of a TU. Consent may be implicit: *Marley Tile Co Ltd v Shaw* (1980). The Court, however, held that the implication was not to be made when the employers simply kept silent when they were informed that a union meeting was to be held in working hours. In *Zucker v Astrid Jewels Ltd* (1978) the EAT held that the employee's talking about the advantages of union membership when working was taking part in a union's activities at an appropriate time because the employers had not prohibited talk during work. As that case also shows, lunch-times and tea-breaks are appropriate times even though the employee is paid for them. In *Burgess v Bass Taverns Ltd* (1994) the EAT held that a shop steward talking at an induction couse for trainee managers was taking part in union activities at an appropriate time.

11.2.4 Appropriate time

Schedule 7 para 1 of TURERA deems a contravention of s 152(1) to be an inadmissible reason. There is no qualifying period or age limit: s 154 of the TULR(C)A as rewritten by Schedule 7 para 1 of TURERA. There are special rules on compensation which are discussed in the next chapter. Three matters require mention here.

11.2.5 Procedure

- Where the unfair dismissal falls within s 152, the IT when assessing compensation takes into account the contributory conduct of the employee but not if her conduct

  'constitutes a breach or proposed breach of a requirement:

  (a) to be or become a member of any TU or of a particular TU or one of a number of particular TUs;

  (b) to cease to be, or refrain from becoming a member of any TU or of a particular TU or one of a number of particular TUs; or

  (c) not to take part in the activities of any TU or of any particular TU or of one of a number of particular unions': s 155(2).

- Awards may be made against third parties for the reason specified in para 11.2.9 below.

- An applicant under s 152 may apply to an IT for interim relief within seven days of the effective date of termination: s 161. Where the dismissal is for a reason falling within s 152(1)(a) or (b) the IT cannot proceed unless there is a document in writing signed by an authorised official of the independent TU of the employee who is a member or was proposing to become a member, stating that at the date of dismissal the employee was or proposed to become a member of that union and there seem to be reasonable grounds for supposing that the reason for dismissal was the one alleged. If it is likely that s 152 has been breached, the IT asks the employers to reinstate the employee in the same job or re-engage her in a similar job. If the employers do not attend the hearing or they are unwilling to reinstate or re-engage the complainant, the IT must make an order for the continuation of her contract of employment, by which her employment rights (eg pay, seniority, pension) are retained until settlement or resolution of the dispute. If the employers do not comply with the reinstatement or re-engagement, the IT must make an order for the continuation of the employee's contract and order compensation on the usual 'just and equitable' basis, 'having regard

  (i)   to the infringement of the employee's right to be reinstated or re-engaged in pursuance of the order; and

  (ii)   to any loss suffered by the employee in consequence of the non-compliance': s 166(1).

  If the employers do not comply with the order to continue the employment contract, the IT determines the amount of pay owing, if non-payment is the breach; if the non-compliance is other than non-payment, the IT orders the employers to pay compensation on the 'just and equitable' basis, having regard to the employees loss occasioned by the non-compliance.

11.2.6   Burden of proof

If the employee does not have the two years' continuous service for an ordinary unfair dismissal claim, she must prove that she was dismissed for a reason falling within s 152 (*Smith v Hayle Town Council* (1978)). (If she has that qualifying period, the burden is on the employers (same case).) If she can show the s 152 reason, the burden of proof switches to the employers (see *Maund v Penwith District Council* (1984)).

As well as protection from dismissal on TU grounds, employees (with the usual exceptions such as share fishermen) have a right not to have 'action short of dismissal' taken against them: s 146(1) of TULR(C)A. The action short of dismissal is one based on the same grounds (with amendments to the wording) as s 152. The action must be taken 'for the purpose of' the grounds listed. One looks at the employers' purpose, not at the effect on the employee (*Gallacher v Department of Transport* (1994) CA). Refusing to promote a union official because he did not possess proven managerial experience but to get that experience he would have to give up his full-time union job did not fall within s 146(1). The employers' purpose was to ensure that only those with appropriate experience were promoted. Neill LJ said that 'purpose' connoted 'an object which the employer desires or seeks to achieve'. Action short of dismissal means treating the employee less favourably than another employee would be treated on the relevant ground, such as when an employee who took part in a union meeting is denied promotion but one who did not is granted it. A case is *NCB v Ridgway* (1987). The employers refused to apply a wage increase which they had negotiated with the Union of Democratic Miners to members of the National Union of Mineworkers. On a complaint the Court held that the employers' conduct constituted action short of dismissal. The Court held that the employers' conduct was aimed at deterring NUM members from remaining in their union, and that within s 146 the action was taken against the union members as individuals. Section 146 also covers penalising employees for seeking to be or for being a member of a TU and penalising them for taking part in TU activities at appropriate times. 'Penalising' means putting the employee at a disadvantage, and covers the refusal of a car-park space (*Carlson v Post Office* (1981)). Non-renewal of a fixed term contract is not action short of dismissal: it is a dismissal because of the definition of 'dismissal' found in the 1992 Act and its precursors (*Johnstone v BBC Enterprises Ltd* (1994)). Since the applicant had waived his right to unfair dismissal, he had no remedy.

By s 148(2) the IT is instructed to disregard pressure exercised by calling, organising, procuring or financing industrial action such as a strike. By s 148(3), as inserted by TURERA s 13, the IT is directed to consider only evidence that the employers' purpose was to further a change in the relationship with all or any class of their employees if there is evidence of that and evidence of a purpose which falls within s 146. In other words

11.2.7 Action short of dismissal

11.2.8 Pressure and purpose

s 146 has been severely restricted. The aim of s 13 is to reverse two Court of Appeal cases, *Associated British Ports v Palmer* (1993) and *Associated Newspapers Ltd v Wilson* (1993), which had held that it was action short of dismissal when employees were given 'sweeteners' to make them sign personal contracts (ie ones which had no place for the union) when those who refused to sign did not get the extra money. In fact the decisions were reversed by the House of Lords in 1995, thereby rendering the amendment otiose. Lord Bridge held that 'action' short of dismissal did not include an omission to give a benefit to union members. The new s 148(3) provides that if the employers' action was one which no reasonable employer would take, the IT may then investigate whether there was action short of dismissal within s 146.

11.2.9	Procedure and remedy

There is the usual time limit of three months from the date of the last action short of dismissal, or if it was not reasonably practicable for the complaint to be made within that time, within a reasonable further period (s 147). The burden of proving the purpose for which action was taken lies on the employers: s 148(1). If the IT upholds the complaint, it makes a declaration and may award compensation (which is not financially limited by statute):

> 'such as the tribunal considers just and equitable in all the circumstances having regard to the infringement complained of and to any loss sustained by the complainant which is attributable to the action which infringed his rights' (s 149(2)).

'Loss' covers, for example, frustration felt on failing to join a union.

Mitigation must take place, industrial pressure is disregarded, and contributory fault may reduce the compensation (s 149(4)–(6)). A third party who put pressure on the employers to make the employee join a TU may be joined (by either the complainant or the employers) as party to the proceedings and ordered to pay compensation: s 160. See the last section of this chapter for analogous provisions on industrial pressure and joinder in the context of unfair dismissal.

11.2.10	Selection for redundancy on union grounds

By s 153 of the 1992 Act, where an employee is redundant but she is selected for redundancy on a ground specified in s 152 (1) (above) eg TU activities, the dismissal is deemed to be unfair. Redundancy is defined as in Chapter 9. From 30 August 1993 there has been no qualifying period for this right.

11.2.11	Unfair selection

The law used to be that if employers selected for redundancy in contravention of a customary arrangement or agreed procedure, the dismissal was automatically unfair unless the employers had a special reason justifying departure from the custom or procedure: s 59(1)(b) of EP(C)A, as renumbered by TURERA. This law was abolished by the Deregulation and Contracting Out Act 1994, s 36(1). The general law of unfair dismissal now applies. Failure to follow the procedures laid down in a collective agreement may well result in the dismissal being unfair.

TURERA 1993; s 24(1), substitutes with effect from 1994 a new s 60 into EP(C)A. By it dismissal is automatically unfair if the reason or principal reason for it was for the first five of the following reasons:

11.2.12   Pregnancy/childbirth

- pregnancy or any reason connected with pregnancy;

- childbirth or any reason connected therewith;

- the use of maternity provisions;

- incapability of working following childbirth if she has a medical certificate stating that 'by reason of disease or bodily or mental disablement' she is incapable of working after maternity leave, dismissal taking place within four weeks of the end of her leave;

- in consequence of a requirement or recommendation in relation to the right to return after maternity; and

- redundancy within the maternity leave period and s 38 of EP(C)A has not been complied with (offering her a suitable alternative vacancy).

The revision of s 60 occurred as a result of the Pregnant Workers Directive (92/85). This measure is based on the Framework Directive (89/391) on health and safety. Voting on health and safety matters is by qualified majority voting, and opposition by the UK can be thereby overridden. In fact, the government abstained on the vote.

By s 24(2) of TURERA the reasons except for the last one are deemed to be 'inadmissible' reasons. By s 24(3) the qualifying period for unfair dismissal is disapplied in relation to an inadmissible reason. The claim of the applicant in *Webb v EMO Air Cargo (UK) Ltd* (1993) could now be brought under the amended s 60. However, a refusal to employ on the grounds that the candidate was pregnant cannot be brought because s 60 applies to dismissal, not refusal to employ.

11.2.13   No qualifying period

| 11.2.14 | Written statement | As a supplementary to the new s 60 of EP(C)A TURERA s 24(4) adds a new sub s (2A) to s 53 of EP(C)A to give a woman a right to a written statement of the ground of dismissal if she is dismissed while she is pregnant or while she is on maternity leave after childbirth. There is no need for her to make a request and there is no minimum length of continuous service. This provision came into force in 1994. |

11.2.15   Dismissal for assertion
            of statutory right

Section 29 of TURERA inserts a new s 60A into EP(C)A. By it with effect from 30 August 1993:

'(1) The dismissal of an employee by an employer shall be regarded for the purposes of this Part as having been unfair if the reason for it (or, if more than one, the principal reason) was that the employee –

(a) brought proceedings against the employer to enforce a right of his which is a relevant statutory right; or

(b) alleged that the employer had infringed a right of his which is a relevant statutory right.

(2) It is immaterial for the purposes of subsection (1) whether the employee has the right or not and whether it has been infringed or not, but, for that subsection to apply, the claim to the right and that it has been infringed must be made in good faith.

(3) It shall be sufficient for subsection (1) to apply that the employee, without specifying the right, made it reasonably clear to the employer what the right claimed to have infringed was.

(4) The following statutory rights are relevant for the purposes of this section, namely -

(a) any right conferred by –

(i)   this Act, or

(ii) the Wages Act 1986,

for which the remedy for its infringement is by way of a complaint or reference to an industrial tribunal;

(b) the right conferred by section 49 (minimum notice);

(c) the rights conferred by the following provisions of the Trade Union and Labour Relations (Consolidation) Act 1992, namely, sections 68, 86, 146, 168, 169 and 170 (deductions from pay, union activities and time off).'

Section 146 of TULR(C)A is dealt with above under the heading 'trade union grounds'. 'This Act' in s 60A(4)(a)(i) is EP(C)A. Therefore, assertions of unfair dismissal and redundancy are covered.

A dismissal under s 60A is deemed to be an inadmissible reason and there is no qualifying period or minimum hours of work. Selection for redundancy because the applicant has asserted a statutory claim is automatically unfair.

11.2.16   No qualifying period

Section 60A reflects a growing concern with the penalisation of persons who brought eg claims that action short of dismissal had been taken against them and they had complained to an IT in consequence of which they had been actually or constructively dismissed. This concern found expression in the Offshore Safety (Protection against Victimisation) Act 1992 (which is repealed by TURERA but widened beyond the narrow situation covered by that Act).

11.2.17   Victimisation

Schedule 5 to TURERA gives employees protection against dismissal in health and safety matters. It inserts a new s 57A into EP(C)A. By it with effect from 30 August 1993:

11.2.18   Health and safety

'(1) The dismissal of an employee by an employer shall be regarded for the purposes of this Part as having been unfair if the reason for it (or, if more than one, the principal reason) was that the employee –

(a) having been designated by the employer to carry out activities in connection with preventing or reducing risks to health and safety at work, carried out, or proposed to carry out, any such activities;

(b) being a representative of workers on matters of health and safety at work, or a member of a safety committee –

(i) in accordance with arrangements established under or by virtue of any enactment, or

(ii) by reason of being acknowledged as such by the employer,

performed, or proposed to perform, any functions as such a representative or a member of such a committee;

(c) being an employee at a place where –

(i) there was no such representative or safety committee, or

(ii) there was such a representative or safety committee but it was not reasonably practicable for the employee to raise the matter by those means,

brought to his employer's attention, by

reasonable means, circumstances connected with his work which he reasonably believed were harmful or potentially harmful to health or safety;

(d)   in circumstances of danger which he reasonably believed to be serious and imminent and which he could not reasonably have been expected to avert, left, or proposed to leave, or (while the danger persisted) refused to return to, his place of work or any dangerous part of his place of work; or

(e)   in circumstances of danger which he reasonably believed to be serious and imminent, took, or proposed to take, appropriate steps to protect himself or other persons from the danger.' There is a defence to this head of liability that the employee had taken or intended to take steps which were so negligent that a reasonable employer would have dismissed; if so the dismissal is fair.'

These provisions derive from the so-called 'framework' Directive (89/391) on health and safety. There are similar provisions covering detriment short of dismissal on the grounds in s 22A of EP(C)A inserted by TURERA.

11.2.19   No qualifying period

Dismissal under s 57A(1)(a) and (b) is deemed to be an inadmissible reason. There is no qualifying period in any part of s 57A. A special award is made (see Chapter 12) where para (a) or (b) is contravened. A selection for redundancy on either ground is deemed to be automatically unfair, and interim relief is available. Action short of dismissal on health and safety grounds is also compensated on the 'just and equitable' basis with the usual deductions, but there is no maximum limit on compensation.

11.3   Automatically fair

Where Parliament has stated that the reason for the dismissal is an automatically fair one, the tribunal cannot deal with the case even though the employee is qualified and has been dismissed.

11.3.1   Industrial action/ lock-out

Dismissal during industrial action/lock-out was originally designed to keep ITs out of collective disputes. It has, however, been successively altered with the result that its original purpose has been seriously undermined. Calls have been made that dismissals during industrial action should be heard and if ITs get involved in the merits of strikes, so be it. If this exception does not apply the IT has jurisdiction to hear and determine the cause in the ordinary way as detailed in the last chapter: see *TNT Express (UK) Ltd v Downes* (1993). If s 238 is inapplicable the IT, *Downes* holds, may investigate any justification for the industrial action.

By s 238(1) of TULR(C)A, an IT may not investigate whether at the time of dismissal the employee was taking part in official industrial action such as a strike or the employers were conducting a lock-out, provided that all employees involved were dismissed and none was re-engaged within three months of dismissal. To s 238(1) there is an exception. A claim for unfair dismissal may be heard if not all 'relevant employees' have been dismissed or only some have been re-engaged within the three months: s 238(2). The tribunal must now consider the claim: the effect of s 238(2) is not to make the dismissal automatically unfair. It may be reasonable to dismiss some strikers, but to keep others. In other words normal unfair dismissal law governs. That law includes the deduction for contributory fault. If the industrial action is not endorsed or authorised by a TU (under s 20(2) of TULR(C)A), ie if it is unofficial, no employee may apply for a remedy for unfair dismissal: s 237. Industrial action is not unofficial if none of the employees is a member of a TU. If the action was official but the union has repudiated it, it does not become unofficial until the end of one working day after repudiation: s 237(4) ie the workers have a day's grace before s 237(1) applies. If s 238 does apply so that the IT has jurisdiction, the limitation period is six months from the date of dismissal, or if it was not reasonably practicable to bring a claim within that period, within such time as the IT considers reasonable: s 239(2). A person is not taking part in a strike if she has communicated her intention to return.

11.3.2   Effects

For the purposes of ss 237–238 strike, industrial action and lock-out are undefined. There is a definition of strike found in TULR(C)A 1992, s 246, which, it appears, applies to ss 237–238. A strike is 'any concerted stoppage of work'. In Schedule 13, para 24, of the Employment Protection (Consolidation) Act 1978, which defines it for the purposes of continuity of employment, a lock-out is the closure of the workplace, suspension of work or the employers' refusal to continue to employ some employees. It seems that a breach of contract is not necessary. Industrial action covers work-to-rule, go-slows, and even withdrawal of voluntary overtime (ie there is no need for a breach of contract) (*Faust v Power Packing Casemakers Ltd* (1983)). Therefore, even though the employees are not in breach of contract, they lose the protection of employment law. In *Rasool v Hepworth Pipe Co Ltd* (1980), however, taking part in an unauthorised mass meeting during working hours, the meeting being held to consider employees' views on forthcoming wage negotiations, did not constitute industrial action (rather it was taking part in TU activities but at an

11.3.3   Definitions

inappropriate time: see above). No pressure was being put on the employers. An individual protest is a strike according to the much criticised EAT decision of *Lewis v E Mason and Sons* (1994). A refusal to drive a lorry from Wales to Edinburgh in winter because it did not have an overnight heater was held to be industrial action. His refusal to obey a lawful order constituted such action. The EAT said that the issue of whether industrial action was occurring was an issue of fact for the IT, and the present finding of the IT was not perverse. At the time of that decision the TULR(C)A definition did not apply. Nevertheless, it cannot be said that there was *concerted* action. It is suggested that in this context 'taking-part in' means 'participating with others in'. Industrial action is a collective not individual matter. (It is also suggested that the order was unlawful.) According to *Manifold Industries Ltd v Sims* (1991) – there are contrary cases – the test for deciding whether an employee was taking part in the action is objective. It is irrelevant whether the employers knew that she was participating. A belief that the employee was on strike but she was not does not excuse the employers (*Thompson v Woodland Designs Ltd* (1980)).

11.3.4   'Taking part'

'Taking part' in action is also determined objectively. It does not matter what the employee's motive was. In *Coates v Modern Methods and Materials Ltd* (1982) the employee was taking part in a strike even though her reason for joining in was that she was afraid of abuse from her colleagues if she did not. A person off sick is not taking part in a strike (*Hindle Gears Ltd v McGinty* (1985)). General expression of support for a strike by a sick employee does not mean that he is taking part in the action. However, an employee who is on strike but becomes ill remains on strike for the purposes of ss 237–8 (*Williams v Western Mail and Echo Ltd* (1980)). The employees must be actually participating in action; it is insufficient that a strike has been threatened (*Midland Plastics Ltd v Till* (1983)). The taking part in the action relates to the time of the dismissal. *Lewis*, above, can also be criticised on this point too. A threat of industrial action, that no employee would come to work on the following day, was held to be industrial action, at the time when the employee was dismissed, but surely a threat of action is not the same as action, as indeed *Midland Plastics* had held. A surprising case is *McCormick v Horsepower Ltd* (1981). An employee was dismissed for redundancy. He had earlier refused to join a picket line. Since he had been dismissed, the IT had no jurisdiction.

11.3.5   Action or activity?

If the employees' conduct does not amount to a strike or other industrial action, it may constitute a union activity, in which case the protection afforded between s 152(1) of TULR(C)A comes into play. If so, the employees have greater protection than in a normal unfair dismissal claim. A mass meeting is instanced as not being industrial action (even though production is stopped) but being a union activity. The line is fine.

'Relevant employees' in relation to industrial action are by s 238(3):

11.3.6   Relevant employees

> 'those employees at the establishment of the employer at or from which the complainant works who at the date of his dismissal were taking part in the action'.

The definition excludes employees who have died, retired or resigned. Therefore, if a co-worker has to return to work before the claimant was dismissed, she does not count as a relevant employee for the purposes of s 238(2). The effect is that employers can wait and see who comes back, then sack all those still out, no doubt the ones whom they consider to be trouble-makers. It seems, furthermore, that the dismissals of those taking part in action can take place at any time up to the end of the IT hearing. If all those taking part are dismissed before then, they are 'relevant employees' (*P & O European Ferries (Dover) Ltd v Byrne* (1989)). This Court of Appeal decision may not accord with the legislative intent. In relation to lock-outs, 'relevant employees' are defined, again in s 238(3), as those directly interested in the dispute, a term which includes those who have returned to work (*Campey & Sons v Bellwood* (1987)). Therefore, this definition is wider than that in respect of industrial action. Another difference is that in relation to a lock-out, there is no restriction as to establishment, whereas in respect of industrial action the relevant employees must work at the same establishment as the employee. 'Establishment' is undefined. The effect of 'establishment' may be demonstrated thus. Assume that during a recession a firm is faced with the need to cut the workforce. As a reaction to proposed cuts employees at two factories, one in London, one in Norwich, go on strike. The employers can now close one of the plants, say London, without fear of unfair dismissal claims despite the fact that the employees at the other establishment are still on strike. For a discussion of 'establishment' in the context of handling redundancies, see Chapter 9.

By s 238(4), an offer of re-engagement under s 238(2) is defined as an offer by the employers, their successors or associated employers to re-engage the employee:

11.3.7   Offer of re-engagement

> '... either in the job which he held immediately before the

date of dismissal or in a different job which would be reasonably suitable in his case.'

A job offer remains suitable even though it is treated as the second stage in disciplinary procedures (*Williams v National Theatre Board Ltd* (1982)). Since the employees turned down that offer, they had no claim. The Court of Appeal also held that there is an offer within the sub-section when the offers vary in the terms and conditions. The Court opined that job offers with seriously reduced terms would not be within s 238(4). There can be an offer of re-engagement within s 238(2) even though the employers did not know that they had previously dismissed an employee for taking part in industrial action (*Bigham v GKN Kwikform Ltd* (1992)). (This situation can happen in large firms.) An advertisement to the world does not constitute an offer.

11.3.8	Exceptions

Section 237(1) and s 238(2) do not apply if the reason or principal reason for dismissal was the health and safety ground found in s 57A of EP(C)A and the maternity ground found in s 60 of the same Act: TURERA, para 76–77 of Schedule 8. Section 57A was added by the 1993 Act: s 60 was substituted for the old s 60 by the same statute with effect from October 1994. Sections 57A and 60 are discussed above.

11.3.9   Critique: comments on ss 237–238

The law makes (*per* Waite J in *Hindle Gears Ltd v McGinty* (1985)):

'... the process of dismissal of a striking workforce into something like a game of hazard on which the winner takes all, in which defeat or victory turns on the fall of a single card.'

It has become so encrusted with exceptions that everything depends on interpretation. Is what is happening a strike or other industrial action? If so, ss 237 apply; if not, the dismissal may be for trade union reasons with the result that the dismissal is automatically unfair and the employers have to pay an increased level of compensation. The problem is exacerbated by the fact that 'strike' is left undefined and by the fact that the issue whether there is 'industrial action' is a question of fact for the tribunal, and the EAT cannot intervene which of two tribunals holding diametrically different views is correct where the issue is deemed to be one of fact. The latter rule has been said judicially not to be in accord with the development of orderly industrial relations.

The protection from claims which ss 237–8 provide applies even though the employers have provoked the strike. The TURERA gives employees some protection where the industrial action was a response to health and safety matters but outside of that area employees have no claim. For employees the position is made even worse by the provision on lock-outs. The employer can lock the employees out for whatever reason and thereby avoid any unfair dismissal liability. If, for example, the employers cut wages, the employees refuse to accept the cuts and in return the employers lock them out and then dismiss them, the IT has no jurisdiction. When Rupert Murdoch sacked 5,500 workers for refusing to move from Fleet Street to Wapping, the dismissals could not be challenged.

Sections 237–8 apply no matter the reason the employers had for dismissing. There is no reason to show that the industrial action was the activating cause. It is sufficient that industrial action or a lock-out was taking place at the date of dismissal. This point reinforces the second point above, about employers' provoking a strike, then dismissing the employees without fear of legal sanction.

One anomaly can be demonstrated by reference to *Faust v Power Packing Casemakers Ltd*, above. Employers sacked employees for refusing to work voluntary overtime. The refusal was linked to a pay claim. Since the workers were taking part in industrial action at the time of dismissal, the IT had no power to hear their claim for unfair dismissal. If, however, the employers had dismissed just one employee for the refusal, only she being in dispute over pay, she no doubt would have won a claim for unfair dismissal. One person cannot act in concert or in combination as appears to be necessary before ss 237–8 apply. Yet the sole difference is that on the actual facts of *Faust* three were dismissed; on the hypothetical facts only one was. Why should numbers make a difference? When s 238 was first drafted, the answer was: to keep ITs away from the merits of collective disputes. With the changes to s 238 (and the enactment of s 237) that argument is no longer fully sustainable.

The Committee of Experts of the International Labour Organisation in 1989 condemned the precursor of s 238 on the grounds that it deprived employees of their right to challenge the fairness of their dismissal before a judicial body in breach of the Convention No 87, 1948, on Freedom of Association and Protection of the Right to Organise.

Dismissal on grounds of national security is automatically fair: Schedule 9, para 2(1) to the Employment Protection (Consolidation) Act 1978.

11.3.10   National security

With regard to any unfair dismissal claim in considering whether employers acted fairly in dismissing, ITs cannot take

11.4   Industrial pressure

into account the fact that the sacking was brought about by industrial pressure such as a strike or the threat of one: s 63 of EP(C)A. An example is *Colwyn Borough Council v Dutton* (1980). Trade union members refused to act as crew to the claimant when he drove a dustbin lorry. They considered that he drove dangerously. The IT could not take into consideration his colleague's action.

11.4.1   Joinder

Section 160 of TULR(C)A, noted above, permits the claimant or employers to join unions as parties to proceedings where the employers were induced to dismiss the employee as a result of actual or threatened strike or other industrial action where the pressure was exercised because the employee was not a member of any or any particular TU or of a number of particular unions. The IT can order compensation to be paid by the union.

Unfair Dismissal – Particular Problems

It is automatically unfair to dismiss an employee on grounds of union membership/non-membership, union activities at appropriate times, selectively on union grounds, for reasons of pregnancy or childbirth, or because she deals with health and safety matters:

Fitzpatrick v BRB (1991)

Carrington v Therm-A-Stor (1983)

NCB v Ridgway (1987).

The rights to become a member and to take part in activities apply only in relation to independent unions, whereas the right not to be dismissed for not being or refusing to become a member applies to both independent and sweetheart unions. 'Appropriate times' include after work. 'Last in, first out' (LIFO) may be a customary arrangement. An agreed procedure may be a system to which the parties have impliedly given their consent.

The rights not to be dismissed for asserting a statutory right and for health and safety reasons were introduced in 1993.

Automatically unfair

It is automatically fair to dismiss employees during a strike, other industrial action, or a lock-out except when the action is official and either not all relevant employees have been dismissed or there has been selective re-employment within three months of the dismissal:

Faust v Power Packing (1983)

Coates v Modern Methods (1982).

Management prerogatives have been progressively widened on this point throughout the 1980s and early 1990s. It should be noted that there is no longer any protection for unofficial strikes, even when their colleagues have been selectively re-engaged.

Hindle Gears v McGinty (1985)

Dismissal is automatically fair even though the employers have provoked the action.

The aim behind the law was to prevent tribunals' being concerned with the merits of industrial disputes, but the amendments to the law have undermined this purpose.

National security is an automatically fair reason.

Automatically fair

Industrial pressure

Tribunals must not in unfair dismissal claims take into consideration industrial pressure such as a strike. However, employees and employers may join the party organising the pressure and that party may be ordered to pay the compensation:

Colwyn BC v Dutton (1980).

Chapter 12

Redundancy Payments and Unfair Dismissal Remedies

This chapter deals with the remedy where an employee is statutorily redundant and where an employee is unfairly dismissed. The law is found in the Employment Protection (Consolidation) Act 1978 (EP(C)A) as amended.

12.1 Coverage

These are calculated according to a set formula which is dependent on the employee's normal working hours and remuneration.

12.2 Redundancy payments

Redundancy payments are calculated according to a statutory formula (Schedule 4 to EP(C)A): the week's pay up to £205 x the number of years of continuous employment to a maximum of 20 x a multiplier based on the age of the employee, that multiplier being $1^1/_2$ for each full year the employee is over 41, 1 for each year between 22 and 40 and $6^1/_2$ for each year between 18 and 21, and only the best 20 years are counted. The sum of £205 may be changed by the Secretary of State for Employment but no variation was made in 1993. Examples:

12.2.1 Calculation

- Assume the employee is 63 earning £275 per week and has worked continuously for the employers for 37 years. Only 20 years are counted. Work backwards 20 years from 63. Therefore, the years the employee was 43 to 63 count. For years over 41 the multiplier is $1^1/_2$. Only £205 out of the £275 count. The calculation is £205 x 20 x $1^1/_2$ = £6,150. As can be seen, the figures of £205, $1^1/_2$ and 20 are the maximum under statute; accordingly £6,150 is the maximum redundancy payment. There is no deduction for contributory fault.

- Assume the employee is aged 45 and is earning £185 per week. She has been working continuously for the employers for 10 years. She has worked 4 full years above 41; assume she has worked 6 full ones below 41. Therefore, the sum is £185 x 4 x $1^1/_2$ plus £185 x 6 x 1. Note that the fact that she is over 41 does *not* mean that her pay up to the maximum is multiplied by $1^1/_2$. It is the years over 41 which count.

  It should be noted that unlike when calculating the basic award for unfair dismissal, years of employment under 18 do not count for redundancy payments. If the employee is aged 64, one twelfth is deducted from the payment for each month the employee is over 64. (No claim is possible if the employee is over the normal retiring age if it is lower than 65; if there is no such age, the limit is 65.) If the employers give the employee a redundancy payment without an industrial tribunal being involved, they must give her a written statement demonstrating how they calculated the amount. If no statement is given, the employee may request one in writing, specifying a date at least one week away by which the employers must reply. The maximum week's pay and the maximum total seem small in modern conditions, especially in the light of the fact that only employees with 20 or more years' continuous employment over the age of 41 and earning £205 can obtain the maximum.

12.2.2   Week's pay

The calculation of the week's pay is stated in Schedule 14 to EP(C)A. Where the express or implied terms of the contract of employment (and not practice unless there has been a contractual variation) determine the number of hours or the minimum number, the employee is said to have normal working hours. This concept is also used when calculating whether the applicant has sufficient hours to satisfy the qualifying period for rights such as redundancy payments. The amount of week's pay is dependent in this instance on the normal working hours. If an employee works 37 hours per week, the week's pay is that remuneration for those hours. Overtime causes problems. What happens if the employee receives basic pay for 37 hours but extra pay for overtime? The principal authority is *Tarmac Roadstone Holdings Ltd v Peacock* (1973). The Court held that only if overtime was compulsory on *both* sides was it to be counted towards the week's pay. An employee was paid a basic wage for 40 hours, but he regularly worked an extra 17 hours per week overtime. He had to do the overtime if offered, but the employers did not contractually have to offer it. Therefore, overtime was not compulsory on both sides and was not counted when calculating the week's pay. That pay was based on the 40 hours he was contractually obliged to do. Under Schedule 14 his 'week's pay' was less than he received as pay per week ie a statutory not a common-sense definition applies. The effect is to reduce the redundancy payment to which an employee would otherwise be entitled.

12.2.3   Non-time workers

With regard to piece-workers, 'week's pay' is calculated by reference to the normal hours of work multiplied by the average hourly rate of pay (excluding overtime payments) in the 12 weeks preceding the last complete week before the calculation date. A similar calculation is made for shift-workers (whose hours may also need to be averaged) and those who have no normal working hours such as double-glazing salespeople and lecturers. One point of interest with regard to the categories of employees mentioned in this paragraph is that the 12-week period must consist of weeks in which the employee earned money. The effect can be dramatic. If a firm is going to make workers redundant it may well reduce pay towards the date of dismissal eg a piece-worker may find that there are fewer pieces to be made. Yet the week's pay is calculated according to the average of the last 12 weeks of work. If no work is performed with the result that no remuneration is earned, that week is not counted, and the week immediately preceding the 12 is substituted. If the employee has worked for fewer than 12 weeks of work with her present employers, then if continuity of employment is preserved with her previous employers, weeks worked for the latter count.

'Remuneration' in Schedule 14 includes contractual bonuses and commission, including incentive bonuses (see *British Coal Corp v Cheesbrough* (1990)). By para 9 of Schedule 14 if bonuses are annual payments a proportionate amount is included in the week's pay. *Ex gratia* bonuses such as at Christmas are excluded: *Skillen v Eastwoods Froy Ltd* (1967). Expenses are included if the sum paid on them by the employers exceeds the amount spent by the employee: *S & U Stores Ltd v Wilkes* (1974), but note that this situation may be a fraud on the revenue rendering the contract illegal and void. Compulsory service charges which are divided up among staff constitute pay: *Tsoukka v Potomac Restaurants Ltd* (1968), but tips paid by the customer direct to the employee are not, because they are not payments from the employers: *Palmanor Ltd v Cedron* (1978). The value of payments in kind eg a company car and free lodgings are not included: *S & U Stores* (above). Holiday pay is excluded because its payment relates to remuneration during employment, not to payment during normal *working* hours. State benefits are excluded.

12.2.4 Remuneration

Pay means gross pay. 'Week' ends on a Saturday unless pay is calculated weekly when the week ends on the day when the employee is paid.

12.2.5 Week ending

Which week's pay is the relevant one is determined by looking at the 'calculation date' as defined in para 7 of Schedule 14. Normally this date is the last day of work, but it is the date on which the statutory minimum period of notice would have expired (ie s 49 of EP(C)A applies: see above, Chapter 7), if the employers dismissed with insufficient contractual notice. This provision ensures that pay rises after dismissal but before the statutory period of notice has elapsed are taken into account.

12.2.6 Calculation date

12.3   Unfair dismissal

Unlike redundancy payments, unfair dismissal need not be redressed by money. There is the possibility that the ex-employee may get her job back.

12.3.1   Possible remedies

In the straightforward unfair dismissal claim there are three possible remedies: reinstatement, re-engagement, or compensation. The industrial tribunal must consider the remedies in that order ie reinstatement is meant to be the primary remedy. The remedies are not cumulative. The successful claimant receives only one remedy, not a medley of them. By s 68(1) of EP(C)A the IT has the duty of explaining what reinstatement and re-engagement are and it must ask whether the applicant wishes the tribunal to order one of these remedies. Reinstatement and re-engagement are together sometimes called re-employment. That term will be used to cover both orders. If re-employment is ordered, continuity is preserved and the weeks between dismissal and order count. The law is laid down in the Employment Protection (Continuity of Employment) Regulations 1993 (SI 1993/2165), which apply where the IT has ordered re-employment and where an ACAS conciliation officer has blessed a settlement between the parties. Conciliation settlements under the Trade Union Reform and Employment Rights Act 1993 also preserve continuity. If there is no order or ACAS intervention, continuity is, it seems, preserved by EP(C)A, Schedule 13 para 9(1)(c): *Ingram v Foxon* (1984). See Chapter 8, paras 8.5.7 and 8.5.15.

12.3.2   Reinstatement (s 68 of EP(C)A)

A tribunal may order the employers to reinstate the employee. Reinstatement means that the employee is restored to her pre-dismissal job. She retains all the benefits (eg pension, length of service and pay including increments) in that job. She is treated as not having been dismissed: s 69(2). Accordingly, benefits such as pay increases which she would have received, had she not been dismissed, are given to her. Another consequence is that since she is treated as not being dismissed, she has to relinquish any money she did receive from her employers such as an *ex gratia* payment. Any money she received from new employers during the period between dismissal and reinstatement is deducted.

12.3.3   Unreasonable refusal

If the employers are ready to reinstate but the employee refuses the offer unreasonably, the basic award may be reduced: s 73(7A).

12.3.4   Re-engagement

An order for re-engagement is one by which the employee is placed into 'employment comparable to that from which he was dismissed or other suitable employment', the terms so far as reasonably practicable being as favourable to him as if he had been reinstated: s 69(4). As with reinstatement, rights are preserved. The IT must specify the name of the employers, the nature of employment, the rate of pay, any arrears of pay, any right which must be restored to the employee including any pension and seniority rights, and the date by which the employers must comply with the order. Without these specifications the order is invalid. Since the order puts the employee into the position she would have been in, had she not been dismissed, she is awarded pay she lost out on between dismissal and re-engagement (*City and Hackney Health Authority v Crisp* (1990)).

The IT first inquires whether the claimant wishes to be re-employed. If so, it determines whether to order reinstatement; if it decides that it will not, it determines whether to order re-engagement. When considering either order the IT must consider (the first of these would be better phrased as a pre-requisite):

12.3.5 Re-employment: procedure (s 69 of EP(C)A)

- the wishes of the claimant (eg she may not want to be re-employed because of a personality clash);

- the practicability of re-employment; and

- whether she caused or contributed to her dismissal: if she did, the IT must inquire whether it is 'just' to order re-employment. Contributory fault is the same concept as that used in awards of compensation for unfair dismissal (see below). Therefore, the fact that the employee contributed to a large degree can preclude reinstatement but the IT may instead order re-engagement without full back-pay.

A failure by an IT to follow this process does not render the order null and void, but the EAT can set aside the decision if there is a possibility of injustice (*Cowley v Manson Timber Ltd* (1995) CA). The Court said that any other ruling would be inconvenient.

Discussion in the cases centres around whether it is practicable for the employers to reinstate. 'Practicable' is quite a strong word. It does not mean 'expedient' (*Qualcast (Wolverhampton) Ltd v Ross* (1979)). Impracticability is not impossibility. In the Court of Appeal case of *Port of London Authority v Payne* (1994) it was held in accordance with this proposition that employers did not have to call for members of the workforce to take voluntary severance. The burden of proof is on the employers. In *Payne* the Court said that IT should take into account the commercial judgment of the management and that employers should not have to investigate 'every possible avenue which ingenuity might suggest'. The following factors have been held to make it impracticable to re-employ:

12.3.6 'Practicable'

- opposition to re-employment from the workforce: *Coleman v Magnet Joinery Ltd* (1975) (eg re-employment would lead to a strike (*Langston v AUEW (No 2)* (1974));

- breakdown of a personal relationship such as where the firm has few employees (*Enessy Co SA v Minoprio* (1978)). Lord McDonald in the Scottish EAT said that an IT should not force re-employment on small employers who were reluctant to take back the employee unless there was powerful evidence that the order would succeed;

- taking back the employee would mean the dismissal of another (*Freemans plc v Flynn* (1984)).

It may also be impracticable if the employee would have been made redundant in the period between dismissal and re-employment if she had still been employed. Unfitness is another reason. The lack of a vacancy does not make it impracticable to re-employ.

12.3.7   Permanent replacement

If the employers have taken on a permanent replacement, the IT may not take that situation into account when determining the practicability of the re-employment unless the employers can show:

- it was not practicable to arrange for the dismissed employee's work to be done except by a permanent replacement (s 70(1)); or

- the replacement was engaged after the lapse of a reasonable time without the dismissed employee having contacted them to say that she wished to be re-employed, and it was no longer practicable to arrange for her work to be done except by the replacement (s 71(4)).

12.3.8   Practicability as defence

The issue of practicability in s 70(1) may be raised both when the IT is considering which remedy to award and when dealing with total non-compliance (para 12.3.9) below.

12.3.9   Additional award

Sanction for non-compliance (s 71 of EP(C)A)

If employers refuse to have the employee back the IT must make an award of compensation in the normal way considered in the next section and may make an award of additional compensation, usually called an 'additional award': s 71(2). This award is between 13 and 26 weeks' pay with a minimum and maximum, or between 26 and 52 weeks' pay with a minimum and a maximum if the reason for dismissal was racial or sexual discrimination. 'Week's pay' was defined above when considering redundancy payments. The maximum week's pay is the same as that in respect of the basic award (at present £205). The current (from 1 June 1993) limits are £5,330 minimum to £10,660 maximum in sex and race cases, and £2,665 minimum to £5,330 maximum for other ones. The additional award is not tied to the loss suffered by the employee. It is a penal, deterrent remedy: *George v Beecham Group* (1977). The additional award will not be granted if the employers can prove that it was not practicable to comply with the order: s 71(2)(b). However, s 71(2)(b) is disapplied where the dismissal was for an inadmissible reason as defined in s 57A(1)(a) and (b): para 6 of Schedule 5 to the Trade Union Reform and Employment Rights Act 1993: s 57A was inserted by the same Act and inadmissible reason is defined in the previous chapter. This reference to practicability has been criticised for giving employers two bites of the cherry. They can raise it pre-order and post-order. It might be said that the second occasion gives the employers opportunity to raise matters which have arisen since the order, but it is not so restricted. A possible way of reconciling the contentions of 'two bites' and 'only post-order' and one which has come to be accepted in the cases is this: when considering whether to order re-employment, statute tells the IT to have regard to practicability, whereas at the present stage impracticability is a full defence ie at the first stage the IT can potentially hold that the re-employment may be impracticable but still order it, whereas under s 71 impracticability provides the employers with an excuse or justification for non-compliance with the order: *Timex Corp v Thomson* (1981), which has been followed by the EAT.

The award of compensation which the IT must make is subject to a deduction if the employee has unreasonably prevented the order being complied with. The unreasonable prevention is treated as failure to mitigate: s 71(5).

12.3.10   Unreasonable prevention

If the employers comply only partly with the order, the IT must order such compensation as it thinks fit, having regard to the employee's loss. The maximum, currently £11,000, may be exceeded 'to the extent necessary to enable the award fully to reflect the amount specified as payable under s 69(2)(a) or (4)(d) ...': s 71(1A) as inserted by s 30(2) of the Trade Union Reform and Employment Rights Act 1993. Section 69(2)(a) and (6)(d) relate the payments which the complainant might reasonably have expected to have but for dismissal between the date of termination and re-employment. Accordingly pay arrears and the loss of other benefits can be recompensed even if the normal statutory maximum is exceeded.

12.3.11   Partial compliance

It should be noted that ITs have no jurisdiction to put the employee physically back into her workplace. The sanction for

12.3.12   No specific performance

non-compliance is monetary. Specific enforcement is not an option. Moreover, the 'additional award' is just that – it is awarded on top of the basic and compensatory awards.

12.3.13   Critique

Reinstatement is sometimes called 'the lost remedy' see Dickens *et al* (1981) 10 ILJ 160. Since the inception of unfair dismissal it has been seen as the primary remedy: the IT is instructed to consider it first. Since 1975 (before then re-employment could only be recommended) the IT has been empowered to order the employers to reinstate. Nevertheless, the proportion of employees who actually get their job or a similar one back through the tribunal system is low, about 1% of cases heard. (There were 72 cases of orders for re-employment in 1993–4.) This figure is substantially below that obtained outside the tribunal system through arbitration and mediation, often involving trade unions.

12.3.14   Primary remedy's failure

The following reasons have been suggested for the low rate of re-employment.

- tribunals have not insisted on re-employment being impracticable: see P Lewis (1982) 45 MLR 384;

- legalism in tribunals has led to the importation of concepts from the common law. The common law set its face against the specific enforcement of contracts of personal service. Since the chair is a lawyer and the parties are often represented by lawyers, IT proceedings may be imbued with common law principles. The IT is searching, it is said, for an agreement to reinstate;

- employees may not wish to be re-employed. They may fear victimisation, and there was until recently no remedy for dismissal on grounds of assertion of statutory rights (see s 60A of EP(C)A, inserted by s 29 of the 1993 Act): the employee has to make another (normal) unfair dismissal claim. One reason for not wanting re-employment is that the employee may have a new job. These reasons do explain a good part of the failure of re-instatement to fulfil expectations that it would be the primary remedy. Nevertheless, it is suggested that in large firms there should be little problem in re-employing workers, and that employers would not find their authority undermined substantially by taking employees back when they have been unfairly dismissed. It might also be said that the remedy will be more correlative with the right than is presently the case.

12.3.15   Compensation

If neither reinstatement nor re-engagement is ordered, the IT considers the award of compensation. In a normal unfair dismissal case both a basic and a compensatory award are granted: s 72. The median award for these in 1992–3 was £2,616. In 1993–4 it was £2,773. There may be an extra 'additional award', which was considered above. In the event of a dismissal for a trade union reason, a special award is given. The basic, compensatory, and special awards will be discussed in that order. Where there is an inadmissible reason for dismissal (see the previous chapter), there is a new special award unless the complainant does not request the IT to make an order for re-employment or the case falls within s 73(2) (see para 12.3.17 below): Trade Union Reform and Employment Rights Act 1993, para 7 of Schedule 5, inserting s 72(2) into the 1978 Act.

This award is calculated in the same way as a redundancy payment except that full years of continuous employment under the age of 18 count. As with redundancy payments there is a one-twelfth deduction for each month the employee is over 64. The basic award is £2,700 if dismissal was for an inadmissible reason. For the minimum in trade union cases see 'particular provisions' below at para 12.3.18.

12.3.16   Basic award: calculation (s 73)

By EP(C)A s 73(7B) misconduct which was uncovered after dismissal may be used to reduce the basic award (though it cannot be used to make an unfair dismissal fair (*W Devis & Sons Ltd v Atkins* (1977)). The IT may make a 100% deduction in respect of an after-discovered reason. The basis on which the statute directs the IT to make a percentage deduction is the 'just and equitable' one. The award is reduced only if it is just and equitable so to do. The effect is that there is no need to show that the misconduct caused or contributed to the dismissal (*cf* the compensatory award, below). Neither this deduction nor the following one applies if the dismissal was for redundancy: sub-section (7C), unless the dismissal was unfair on grounds of selection for redundancy for trade union reasons.

12.3.17   Deductions

Contributory fault can reduce the award. By 'contributory fault' is meant misconduct known to the employers pre-dismissal which contributed towards them dismissing. Where the employers dismiss two employees, not knowing which stole money from them, no deduction is made for contributory fault for it has not been proved that the individual employee contributed to his dismissal.

If the employee unreasonably refuses an offer of reinstatement, this award may be reduced by a just and equitable amount (s 73(7A)). The award is not reduced by failure to accept an offer of re-engagement.

Redundancy pay is deducted (s 73(9)) whether the payment was under the State scheme detailed in Chapter 9 or under a private one. If the basic award is totally extinguished by this deduction, the excess is deducted from the compensatory award.

If the employers make an *ex gratia* payment to compensate the employee for losing her right, that sum may be (but need not be) set off against the basic and compensatory awards.

It should be noted that there is no power to reduce the basic award where the applicant has not mitigated her loss.

12.3.18   Particular provisions

Where the dismissal is unfair because the employee was dismissed on trade union grounds (s 152) or was selected for redundancy on trade union grounds (s 153), the basic award is one of not less than £2,700, subject to a deduction for contributory fault in relation to the s 153 reason: s 156(1),(2), of the Trade Union and Labour Relations (Consolidation) Act 1992. There is no deduction for any 'fault' in reaction to being or not being a union member. This sum is in addition to the special award. What are trade union grounds was discussed in the previous chapter. The £2,700 minimum applies to dismissal on health and safety grounds with the normal deduction for contributory fault.

The maximum basic award is of two weeks' pay where the employee has been made redundant and unreasonably refuses an offer to renew the contract or one of suitable alternative employment or unreasonably terminates the contract during the trial period: s 73(2). 'Week's pay' is defined above.

12.3.19   Comment

It is sometimes said that the basic award represents compensation for the loss of an employee's proprietary rights in her job. Certainly the sum is not based on actual economic loss, but it is a small amount to pay to buy out proprietary rights (the present maximum is £6,150) and since 1980 there has been no irreducible minimum below which the award may not go.

12.3.20   Compensatory award

Unlike the basic award the compensatory award is determined by reference to what the employee lost. It is subject to a statutory maximum, which is currently £11,000. The additional award is extra to this financial limit. The employee has to demonstrate loss: *Adda International Ltd v Curcio* (1976). However, the EAT has said that the IT should not hide behind the burden of proof when determining loss: *Barley v Amey Roadstone Corp Ltd (No 2)* (1978). The amount need not be as scrupulously proved as it is in a High Court action for personal injuries. If the loss is nothing, a nil compensatory award is given. If, for example, a dismissal is unfair because of lack of consultation, but the employee would have been dismissed anyway if there had been consultation, the remedy is just for the length of time consultation would have taken. The Law Society's Employment Law Committee in 1995 suggested that if the maximum had been increased in line with inflation it would now be £46,000; a sum more apt to deter than one of £11,000. It has been proposed that there should be no financial limit in the hope that employers would amend their dismissals procedure and that employees would obtain true compensation.

The fundamental rule of compensatory award is laid down in s 74(1):

12.3.21   Just and equitable

> '... the amount of the compensatory award shall be such amount as the tribunal considers just and equitable in all the circumstances, having regard to the loss sustained by the complainant in consequence of the dismissal in so far as that loss is attributable to action taken by the employer.'

Behaviour subsequent to dismissal is not taken into account when determining what is just and equitable. Therefore, breach of the implied duty of confidentiality after termination of employment is irrelevant (*Soros v Davison* (1994)).

The employee who suffers no loss receives no compensation: it is not unjust to award a nil payment. The assessment is (*British United Shoe Machinery Co Ltd v Clarke* (1978)):

> '... often a difficult question, but one which the industrial tribunal in their capacity as an industrial jury are well suited to answer, and in respect of which they will not go wrong if they remember that what they are trying to do is to assess the loss suffered by the claimant, and not to punish the employer for his failure in industrial relations.'

On the facts no compensation was given because the employee would have been made redundant even had there been consultation. The EAT held that where a dismissal for redundancy was unfair because of a failure to consult and it was uncertain whether he would or would not have been retained if consultation had taken place, the IT should assess the probability of his being retained as a percentage and then use that percentage to determine the loss attributable to the employers within s 74(1) (*Dunlop Ltd v Farrell* (1993)). Where, however, unfairness resides not in procedural unfairness but in substance (in this case the employers had artificially narrowed the pool from which to select for redundancy), the IT should not reduce the award in such a way (*Steel Stockholders (Birmingham) Ltd v Kirkwood* (1993) (Scottish EAT)). In other words one does not now inquire whether the employee would have been selected in any event. It must be said that the line between procedure and substance is not pellucid.

12.3.22   Statutory maximum

The £11,000 maximum is applied only after deductions (considered below) have been made (*Walter Braund (London) Ltd v Murray* (1991)).

12.3.23   *Norton Tool* (1973)

When assessing compensation ITs must not simply award a global sum but must refer to heads of compensation (*Norton Tool Co Ltd v Tewson* (1973)). The Court laid down several heads.

12.3.24   Loss to hearing date

The IT looks at the complainant's loss of earnings net of tax and national insurance up until the time of the hearing. This sum is based on the actual loss, not on 'week's pay' as defined above. Accordingly, overtime pay and tips are included. If there is a dispute as to the correct remuneration, the issue is decided by the IT even though the dispute is a contractual one. Having determined the loss the IT deducts money earned elsewhere ie mitigation applies. (It has been said that if the employee obtains employment before the hearing but loses it, compensation should cover only the period between the dismissal and the fresh job (*Courtaulds Northern Spinning Ltd v Moosa* (1984)), provided that the new employment is better paid than the old (*Fentiman v Fluid Engineering Products Ltd* (1991)). If the pay is the same or less, the loss under this head runs to the date of the hearing with deduction for pay from the new employers. If the pay is the same or less, the loss under this head runs to the date of the hearing with deduction for pay from the new employers (*Ging v Ellward (Lancs) Ltd* (1978)). If the employee earns money from a source other than his employers during the notice period, however, that sum will not be deducted (*TBA Industrial Products Ltd v Locke* (1984)). This rule was said to be in accord with good industrial relations practice. (If, however, the employee substantially exceeds his pay from the employers, that sum is deducted, for that mitigation is said to be good industrial practice.) Contrariwise if the employers dismiss with pay in lieu of notice, that sum is deducted (*Addison v Babcock FATA Ltd* (1987)). *Ex gratia* payments on unfair dismissal are deducted (*Horizon Holidays Ltd v Grassi* (1987)), unless the payment would have been given to the employee, had the dismissal been fair (*Roadchef Ltd v Hastings* (1988)). The law on payments during the notice period and *ex gratia* payments cannot be said to be settled (see also 12.3.33).

Expenses and perks are covered as losses reasonably incurred as a result of dismissal eg in the case of a dismissed University lecturer the cost of buying the *Times Higher Education Supplement:* s 74(2). Losses of contractual benefits such as membership of a private health insurance scheme, a low-interest mortgage, a company car if private use was allowed are included. Unfortunately for employees, legal expenses are not covered by this head.

12.3.25   Expenses and perks

The IT chooses a multiplier based on the amount of time after the date of hearing the employee's losses may continue. For example, the fact that the dismissal leads to depression and anxiety can be taken into account by the tribunal in determining how long the employee would take to get back into work (*Devine v Designer Flowers Wholesale Florist Sundries Ltd* (1993)). The cut-off point is when the illness is no longer attributable to the employers' action, for after that date it is no longer just and equitable to award compensation. If the IT finds that the employee would have stayed in the job after the normal retiring age, compensation can extend to that extra period. This multiplier (see tort law where the same principle applies) is affected by any relevant factors such as whether the employee might have left the labour market, whether there were suitable job opportunities in the vicinity. It is possible, having regard to such factors, that an IT can find that the former employee will never work again. The multiplier is, as in the previous head, affected by perks (see above). If the employee who was unfairly dismissed would have been dismissed anyway because eg redundancies took place shortly after dismissal, the sum awarded will be low. The IT is under an obligation to explain how it reached the multiplier (*Qualcast*, above). Except for the statutory maximum there is no limit on the sum which can be awarded under this head. For example, in *Morganite Electrical Carbon Ltd v Donne* (1988) the EAT held that future loss covering 82 weeks was not wrong or perverse. If the employee would find it more difficult than the average one to obtain work, the sum will be increased. An example which has occurred is where the employee had defective vision. When calculating both losses no account is taken of insurance moneys paid on termination. The same principle applies in the law of tort. Invalidity benefit is classified as an insurance benefit and so is not deducted from either the loss to the date of the hearing or future loss (*Hilton International Hotels (UK) Ltd v Faraji* (1994)).

12.3.26   Future loss

12.3.27	Accelerated receipt	As with wrongful dismissal there may be a deduction for accelerated receipt in respect of this head of compensation.
12.3.28	Accrued rights	Accrued rights covers such matters as the loss of the period of continuous employment. The employee has to start building the length of service necessary to qualify for rights such as unfair dismissal. Similarly, the employee will have to build up notice periods. It is normal practice to award a nominal sum of £100 under this head: *S H Muffett Ltd v Head* (1987). Loss of pension rights are also recompensed, often by reference to a report prepared by the Government Actuary's Department which sets out various ways of assessing loss.
12.3.29	Manner of dismissal	Compensation may be awarded for the way in which the employee was dismissed if she lost (some of) her employability as a result: *Vaughan v Weighpack Ltd* (1974). No award is, however, made for distress or demotivation. The law was summed up in the *Norton Tool* case: 'Loss does not include injury to pride or feelings.'
12.3.30	Deductions	Even if the loss has been substantial, little or no compensation may be awarded if it would be unjust or inequitable to award a figure which truly compensates the employee.
12.3.31	Contributory fault (s 74(6))	Once the IT has determined the amount of compensation available by adding together moneys due under the *Norton Tool v Tewson* heads of compensation, it may deduct part or the whole of that sum for action of the employee which caused or contributed to her dismissal. The standard of proof is on the balance of probabilities. The proportion is determined on the 'just and equitable' basis. If there is a deduction under the general principle in s 74(1) (for example, because the applicant's employment would have ceased anyway shortly after the date on which he was unfairly dismissed), the amount of that deduction should be taken into account when calculating contributory fault compensation under s 74(6) (*Rao v Civil Aviation Authority* (1994)). There have been conflicting decisions, but it seems that if there is contributory fault, the basic and compensatory awards need not be reduced by the same percentage, though the EAT thought in *RSPCA v Cruden* (1986) that a difference would be justifiable only in exceptional circumstances. The most recent authority is *Charles Robertson (Developments) Ltd v White* (1995). With regard to the basic award, s 73(7B) permits a just and equitable reduction on account of the applicant's conduct. That conduct need not have caused or contributed to the dismissal. In respect of the compensatory award, however, s 74(6) is restricted to conduct which caused or contributed to the dismissal. The EAT upheld

an industrial tribunal's decision to reduce the compensatory award by 100% on the ground that the employees by stealing a small amount of sweets had caused their dismissal, but to reduce the basic award by only 50% because of the employers' failure to adopt a fair procedure on dismissal. The Court of Appeal said the effect of the law in *Rao*, above, may be that different percentages may occur for 'The deduction which is just and equitable under s 73(7B) is not the same as that which is just and equitable under s 74(6)'. The IT looks at the proportion with a broad-brush approach, considering all the circumstances. One point of interpretation should be noted. 'Fault' is necessary. Therefore, if the employee was not at fault, there is no contributory fault. *Morrish v Henlys (Folkestone) Ltd* (1973) was mentioned in Chapter 4. The employee was told to falsify accounts. This order was unlawful. Accordingly he did not contribute to his dismissal when he refused to 'cook the books'. Another example is that when an employee is dismissed during an official strike, then in cases where the IT does have jurisdiction to hear the application (see the previous chapter), the participation in the action is not contributory fault. If it were, so holding would defeat the purpose of the provision (*Courtaulds Northern Spinning Ltd v Moosa* (1984)). However, the EAT in *TNT Express (UK) Ltd v Downes* (1993) held that *Moosa* was wrongly decided. 'Fault' does, however, cover incapability to do the job where the employee could have put it right (*Sutton and Gates (Luton) Ltd v Boxall* (1979)), and it includes situations where the employee is not in breach of contract (*Nelson v BBC (No 2)* (1979)). ITs must consider only the fault which led to the dismissal and not any other faults of the employee (*Hutchinson v Enfield Rolling Mills Ltd* (1981)). There can be contributory fault even though the dismissal was a constructive one (*Polentarutti v Autokraft Ltd* (1991)). Deduction for payment in lieu of notice is made after the deduction for contributory fault; in other words full credit is given for this sum (*Derwent Coachworks v Kirby* (1995)), though there are contrary authorities.

In an after-discovered reason case (the *Devis v Atkins* scenario) the contributory fault provision does not apply because the employee's behaviour did not cause or contribute to her dismissal. Instead the compensatory award is reduced on the grounds that the sum is given on the 'just and equitable' basis under s 74(1), quoted above (para 12.3.21). It has been argued that the House was incorrect to award nil compensation on the grounds that s 74(1) says that the IT *shall* award compensation but that argument does not take into account the following words of the sub-section. It may be just and equitable to award nothing.

12.3.32   After-discovered reason

12.3.33	*Ex gratia* payment	If the employers make an *ex gratia* payment, it seems that this amount should be deducted from the compensatory award as reduced by contributory fault, not from the compensatory award before the fault deduction (*Clement-Clarke International Ltd v Manley* (1979)). (There are contrary cases.) There is therefore no difference in this respect between contractual payments such as pay in lieu of notice and non-contractual ones.
12.3.34	Illness	It has been said that only rarely will ill-health justify a deduction (*Slaughter v C Brewer & Sons Ltd* (1990)). Section 74(6) speaks of 'action of the complainant'. Is ill-health 'action'? If, however, the sickness renders the employee incapable of working, there may be a deduction in accord with the general 'just and equitable' ground noted in 12.3.21.
12.3.35	Mitigation (s 74(4))	The compensatory award may be reduced by the employee's failure to mitigate. Mitigation means the same as at common law (see para 7.2.16, above). The employee must take reasonable steps to find a new job. The onus of proof lies on the employers to disprove that the employee took reasonable steps (*Bessenden Properties Ltd v Corness* (1974)). It has been held that to refuse an offer of reinstatement by one's employers is a failure to mitigate, but it was decided in *Seligman and Latz Ltd v McHugh* (1979) that non-use of a grievance procedure did not constitute a failure to mitigate. In *Lock v Connell Estate Agents* (1994) the EAT held that non-use of the internal appeals procedure did not constitute a failure to mitigate for the applicant is not under a duty to make the defendants change their minds, though there are some several contrary *dicta*. The sum involved in the mitigation calculation is determined by considering how long the employee would have been out of work if she had mitigated; it is not done by reducing the compensatory award by a percentage (*Smith, Kline and French Laboratories Ltd v Coates* (1977)). Expenses such as moving house to get a new job in an attempt to mitigate are part of the employee's loss, for which she is compensated. Mitigation does not apply to the basic award except when the employee unreasonably refused re-employment (see 12.3.3).
12.3.36	Recoupment	By the Employment Protection (Recoupment of Unemployment Benefit and Supplementary Benefit) Regulations (SI 1977/674) the IT does not deduct from the sum payable for loss to the date of the hearing the amount paid in income support or unemployment benefit. The IT orders the employers not to pay over compensation for loss to the date of the hearing to the employee. The Department of Employment then serves on the employers what is called a 'recoupment notice' instructing

them to pay the Department the sum of unemployment benefit/income support which the employee has received. The employers then pay over the remainder to the employee. The effect is that she gets only what she has lost financially. If the employee did not receive any such State benefit, the Regulations do not apply.

In relation to that part of the compensatory award which covers loss of future earnings, over whatever period the IT decides to make the award, the employee is disqualified from unemployment benefit and income support.

12.3.37   Disqualification

Compensation in unfair dismissal cases tends to be on the low side. The median award is the equivalent of a few months' wages (£2,616 in 1992–3): it is not enough to deter dismissals.

12.3.38   Comment

The special award is a sum paid in addition to the basic and compensatory award where the dismissal is for a trade union reason. What is a trade union reason was discussed in the previous chapter. As stated above, the minimum basic award in such circumstances is currently £2,700. If the employers comply with the order to reinstate, no special award is given.

12.3.39   Special award

By s 158 of the Trade Union and Labour Relations (Consolidation) Act 1992 the special award is 104 weeks' (actual) pay where reinstatement is requested but not granted subject to a minimum of £13,400 and £26,800 maximum; where an order for re-employment under s 71(2)(a) of EP(C)A is made but not complied with, this award consists of 156 weeks' (actual) pay, subject to a minimum of £20,100 with no maximum. 'Actual' is in brackets because the 'week's pay' is calculated according to Schedule 14 to EP(C)A detailed above but there is no maximum weekly sum (ie the present £205 limit does not apply).

12.3.40   Calculation

The employers have a defence if they can prove that it is not practicable to comply with the order to reinstate or re-engage.

12.3.41   Impracticable

Once the special award is calculated, it is subject to deductions where the employee has unreasonably prevented the re-employment order being complied with, or has rejected an offer of reinstatement, or has contributed to the dismissal (this deduction is made where it is just and equitable to do so (s 158(4)), and is approaching retirement (the one-twelfth deduction for each month over 64, as above). Failure to join a union is not to be treated as contributory fault. The fact that a permanent replacement has been engaged is irrelevant as to practicability unless the employers show that it was not practicable to continue, for the employee's job to be done, without engaging a replacement: s 158(6).

12.3.42   Deductions

| 12.3.43 | Joinder | The union may be joined as defendant to the claim by either the employee or the employers. Compensation may be awarded against it (s 160). Similar provisions apply if dismissal is for an inadmissible reason: new s 75A of EP(C)A, inserted by TURERA 1993. |
| 12.3.44 | Action short of dismissal | Action short of dismissal (see the previous chapter) is recompensed under the terms of s 149 of the 1992 Act by the IT's having regard to the 'just and equitable' basis. There is no maximum. |

Redundancy Payments and Unfair Dismissal Remedies

These are calculated according to a statutory formula dependent on length of continuous employment, age, and week's pay. Pay is capped at £205 pw. 'Pay' excludes non-compulsory overtime:

Tarmac Roadstone v Peacock (1973).

Redundancy payments

A tribunal may award reinstatement (same job), re-engagement (comparable job) or compensation. Compensation comprises of the basic and compensatory award, the latter comprising money for loss to the date of hearing, future loss, loss of accrued rights, and compensation for the manner of dismissal. It is subject to deductions for contributory fault and failure to mitigate. An additional award is granted for failure to comply with a re-employment order. A special award is granted for dismissal on trade union grounds or for dismissal for an inadmissible reason. Criticism is made of the low level of reinstatement and compensation.

Unfair dismissal

Practicability: *Coleman v Magnet Joinery* (1975)

Compensatory award: *Norton Tool v Tewson* (1973)

Future loss: *Morganite v Donne* (1988)

Accrued rights: *Muffett v Head* (1987)

Manner of dismissal: *Vaughan v Weighpack* (1974)

Fault: *Sutton & Gates v Boxall* (1979)

Mitigation: *Seligman v McHugh* (1979)

The following is a rapid summary of the financial limits in unfair dismissal cases with effect from 1 June 1993.

Summary of financial limits

	Minimum £	Maximum £
Basic award	-	6,150
Basic award where dismissal for redundancy but offer of re-employment unreasonably refused	-	410
Compensatory award	-	11,000
Additional award	2,665	5,330
Additional award where dismissal on sex or race grounds	5,330	10,660
Compensation for not complying fully with order to re-employ	-	11,000
TU grounds/ inadmissible reason		
Basic award	2,700	6,150
Compensatory award	-	11,000
Special award		
Re-employment sought but not granted	13,400	26,800
Re-employment ordered but not complied with	20,100	no limit

The financial limit for redundancy payment is £6,150.

Chapter 13

Transfer of Undertakings

The topic of transfer of undertakings has been reserved for separate consideration because of its complexity. It is a textbook case of the influence of EC on domestic law, and because EC law·in this area is ever-changing, so is English law.

To understand the topic one must grasp that there are several overlapping 'layers' of law. If one layer is for some reason inapplicable one should look at the next layer. This chapter deals with the common law, the English statutory law pre-EC (which still exists) and the EC law both as part of English law as a result of the Transfer of Undertakings (Protection of Employment) Regulations 1981 (TUPE) (SI 1981/1794) and as a result of decisions of the European Court of Justice (ECJ). A flow-chart is provided.

Relevant Transfer?

↓

Economic, technical or
organisational (ETO)
reason?
+ entailing changes in workforce?

No   Yes

Unfair dismissal   = Some other
substantial reason

Remedies   Reasonable?

Yes   No

No claim   Unfair
dismissal

Remedies

13.1.3   Recent changes

The reader should also be aware of the significant changes in this aspect of law made by the Trade Union Reform and Employment Rights Act 1993:

- TUPE was previously restricted to undertakings in the nature of a commercial venture. Section 33(2) abolishes that restriction. Non-profit making bodies and charities are now covered. Before the coming into effect of these changes a school reorganisation whereby two schools were closed and then re-opened as one did not fall within TUPE, and dimissed teachers had to rely on the Directive. Prior UK law was held to be in breach of the Acquired Rights Directive (77/187) in this respect in *Commission of the European Communities v United Kingdom* (1994) ECJ.

- By s 33(4), new paras (4A) and (4B) are inserted into TUPE, Reg 5, with the effect that the rights and obligations are not transferred if the employee objects to being employed by the transferee employers: instead her contract is terminated, but she is not to be treated as being dismissed by the transferors. She had no right to claim unfair dismissal and redundancy payments. The surprising effect is that the employee is given a right to object, but if she exercises that right, she is dismissable and, if dismissed, has no remedy. This amendment attempts to bring UK law into line with EC law as laid down in *Katsikas v Konstantinidis* (1993). In this case the ECJ held that an employee was not transferred without her consent. She need not give notice or state the reason for her leaving. Controversially it was held by the EAT in *Photostatic Copiers (Southern) Ltd v Okuda* (1995) that TUPE does not apply when the employee is unaware of the fact of transfer and the identify of the transferees, for how otherwise does he know that he can object? The criticism is that TUPE normally acts for the employee's benefit and will not do so if the employers do not inform the employee of the transfer. Since the Regulations are to be read purposively (ie to protect employees), this case is incorrect, a conclusion which is fortified by an understanding of one of the aims of the Regulations, the *automatic* transfer of obligations from the old to the new employers.

- There are other minor changes affecting the scope of TUPE, the non-transfer of occupational pension schemes and the duty to consult with unions (there are also changes to the procedure for handling redundancy found in the Trade Union and Labour Relations (Consolidation)

Act 1992, provisions which are in some respects parallel to consultation of a transfer).

- Section 94 of the Employment Protection (Consolidation) Act 1978 (EP(C)A) which dealt with the change of ownership of a business in the context of redundancy payments is abolished as otiose. Because of these changes care must be taken when referring to old decisions.

These amendments came into effect on 30 August 1993 and are not retrospective.

At law an employee could not be compelled to serve a new master, and the new master was not compelled to continue to employ the employee: *Nokes v Doncaster Amalgamated Collieries Ltd* (1940). The employee had no rights against the transferees, only against the transferors, who might be insolvent.

13.2 Laws

Common law survives where statute, statutory instrument, and EC law relating to transfers do not apply. Where those laws do not apply, the employee may well have a claim for a redundancy payment. A purchase of shares does not change the identity of the employer. The company remains the company.

13.2.1 Common law

From 1963 parliament intervened to protect employees in the event of the transfer of a business. The most important provision is para 17(2) of Schedule 13 to EP(C)A. This sub-para was discussed in Chapter 8.

13.2.2 Paragraph 17(2)

Directive 77/187 on the approximation of the laws of the Member States relating to the safeguarding of employees' rights in the event of transfer of undertakings, business or parts of businesses was grudgingly enacted by the government in TUPE. If TUPE falls short of EC standards in the Directive, an applicant can rely on the Directive where it is unconditional and sufficiently precise in an action against an emanation of the State (ie the Directive is only vertically directly effective). An employee cannot rely on the Directive against a non-State employer. TUPE must also be construed in conformity with the Directive. For a general discussion of the effect of EC law see Chapter 2. The Directive is often known as the Acquired Rights Directive. Another name is the Business Transfers Directive. At the time of writing negotiation is under way on revising the Directive to ease problems on insolvency of the transferor employers, to remove sub-contracting from its scope, to facilitate its application to cross-border takeovers, to provide joint and several liability for the transferors and transferees, and to oblige employers to consult 'in good time'.

13.2.3 The influence of EC law

Member States are to be given the option to exclude employers who normally employ fewer than 50 employees from the scope of the Directive.

13.2.4   TUPE

The basic thrust of TUPE can be summarised thus. In the event of a relevant transfer the contract of employment is automatically transferred from the old to the new employers (therefore, if the applicant was not employed by the transferors, neither the Directive nor the Regulations apply (*Gale v Northern General Hospital NHS Trust* (1994) CA; similarly, collective agreements are transferred. A dismissal connected with a transfer is automatically unfair unless the employers have an economic, technical or organisational reason for dismissing. Perhaps the principal criticism of TUPE is that they do not operate on a transfer by share purchase which is the main method by which businesses are transferred in the UK. TUPE does not apply because the employers remain the same in formal terms, though the effect on employees may be the same as when the Regulations do apply: both the workers in the enterprise as it existed before the change of ownership and the workers in the purchasing firm may be adversely affected by the takeover. The Regulations do not apply to employees who ordinarily work outside the UK (Reg 13). An agreement to contract out of the Regulations is void: Reg 12.

13.2.5   Relevant transfer

TUPE applies only to transfers of an undertaking, or part of one, which take place by sale, other disposition, or operation of law. 'Other disposition' includes the contracting out of a service such as the cleaning of a hospital, as well as the situation where a company is dissolved and the employees continue working for the former directors and sole shareholders. The undertaking must be transferred as a going concern. No property need be transferred. Regulation 2(1) provides that 'undertaking' includes trade or business. It is possible that the use of the term 'undertaking' means that the contracting out of one piece of work on one occasion will not result in a transfer within TUPE. The ECJ has said that the Directive applies when the undertaking is transferred and retains its identity (*Spijkers v Gebr. Benedik Abattoir CV* (1986)). It is sufficient that the activities performed immediately before and immediately afterwards are the same. It applies even though only one employee is transferred (*Schmidt v Spar – und Leihkasse der früheren Ämter Bordesholm, Kiel und Cronshagen* (1995) ECJ). It does not matter that the part transferred is merely ancillary to the main business. English cases have reiterated the law on para 17(2), Schedule 13 to EP(C)A, about the difference between transfer as a going concern and transfer of the assets only (see Chapter 8). The Regulations are construed to give effect to the Directive (*Kelman v Care Contract Services Ltd* (1995)), a decision of the EAT which summarises present law. The usual point must be made: the words of English law must not be distorted. The Regulations used to be restricted to transfers in the nature of a commercial venture but as a result of *Dr Sophie Redmond Stichtung v Bartol* (1992) the law was widened in 1993 to cover such an undertaking. See further 13.2.7 below. The type of factors which are important in para 17(2) such as goodwill may be also important under the Regulations but the important issue remains 'whether, having regard to all the circumstances, the economic entity identified prior to the transfer can be found after the transfer ... Not has the same business continued in existence nor has the goodwill been transferred?' (*per* Morison J in *Council of the Isles of Scilly v Brintel Helicopters Ltd* (1995)). A transfer of only fixtures and fittings was held not to be a transfer of an undertaking in *Robert Seligman Corp v Baker* (1983). Whether there has been a transfer is one of fact. If the applicant was employed in a part of a group of companies which was not transferred when other parts were, he is not protected by the Regulations (*Michael Peters Ltd v Farnfield* (1995)). The Regulations do, however, apply to a person who was employed in a transferred part but who continued to work for the receivers of the transferors for some time after the transfer (*Sunley Turriff Holdings Ltd v Thomson* (1995)). In the latter case the Scottish EAT held that it was immaterial that the transferees and receivers were mistaken about the effects of the contractual position.

Regulation 3(1) states that the transfer must be from one person to another. There is normally no difficulty in demonstrating that this has occurred. Difficulty has arisen at the ECJ level about the termination or forfeiture of a lease where the owners retake possession and then grant a lease to new lessees. There has been held to be a transfer both where the employees were dismissed on the expiry of the lease by the old lessees (*Daddy's Dance Hall A/S v Foreningen af Arbejdsledere i Danmark* (1989)) and where they were dismissed after expiry of the lease (*P Bork International A/S v Foreningen af Arbejdsledere i Danmark* (1989)). Franchise arrangements have caused difficulty in the ECJ and English courts, but depending on the facts the Directive and Regulations can apply: (*Landsorganisationen i Danmark v Ny Molle Krø* (1989)). The last case emphasises that the Directive applies where there has been a change of employers; it does not matter that there has been no change of owners. Regulation 3 was amended in 1993 to ensure that leases and franchises are covered. There need be no transfer of property and the transfer can take place on a

13.2.6   Leases: franchises

series of transactions. For example, in *Bork* all the employees were dismissed when the lease on a factory expired. The purchasers of the freehold of the factory then engaged more than half of them. The ECJ held that the directive applied despite there being negotiations between the old employers and the new ones.

13.2.7   Privatisation

Much has been written on the application of TUPE to privatisation. The abolition of the rule that the part transferred had to be in the nature of a commercial venture partly resolves the issue. Collecting dustbins may well not be in the nature of a commercial venture but that fact is now irrelevant. One remaining difficulty is that if a firm or local council contracts out of a function, there is no transfer of the undertaking or part of it eg *Hadden v University of Dundee Students' Association* (1985). The students' union contracted out the catering to an outside firm. The firm took on the complainant. The union then took back the catering and the firm dismissed her. The EAT held that TUPE did not apply; all that the firm had done was to perform their contract with the union. There was no transfer. It may be that on different facts (the EAT took into account the considerations that the firm was paid a management fee and took a percentage of the profits) a different decision would be reached. Furthermore, perhaps the case cannot stand with EC law. The latest ECJ case on this point, *Rask v ISS Kantineservice A/S* (1993), says that there is a transfer where an identifiable economic entity is transferred: the legal form of the transaction is irrelevant. It does not matter that the part transferred is ancillary to the main business but certainly there need be no transfer of goodwill or even of assets. It even does not matter that the service is to be performed for a fixed fee. This case seems to block government efforts to contract out for the employees' transfer is caught by the Directive and it cannot save money by contracting out. A transfer of further education colleges from local authority control to that of corporations was, it was conceded, a relevant transfer. The High Court in *Kenny v South Manchester College* (1993) held that there was a transfer within the Acquired Rights Directive when, as a result of competitive tendering, prison education was transferred from a county council to the defendants, even though there was no transfer of assets, and even though there was no direct transfer from the council to the new providers. Applying *Sophie Redmond* the EAT held in *Wren v Eastbourne BC* (1993) that a transfer of services as a result of compulsory competitive tendering fell within TUPE. The change was simply one of contractors. A transfer of a privatised cleaning contract from one contractor to another is within the Regulations even though no equipment, material, or goodwill was transferred (*Dines v Initial Health Care Services Ltd* (1995)). The Court of Appeal held that an economic unit had been transferred. It did not matter that the cleaning service was handed back to the hospital and on the next day given to the second contractors for, as EC cases demonstrate, a transfer may take place in two stages. Moreover, it was immaterial that there was no contract between the two employers. Similarly a transfer of school cleaning services from a local authority's direct service organisation to governors when a school obtained grant-maintained status was a transfer within the Directive (and after the removal of the non-commercial venture exception is within the Regulations) (*Governors of Highams Park School v Odger* (1994)). Similarly a transfer of paediatric and neonatal services from two district health authorities to an NHS trust was a transfer within the Regulations: *Porter v Queen's Medical Centre* (1993) High Court. The fact that the services were carried out in a different way did not prevent there being a transfer; nor did it matter under the relevant English statute providing for the transfer there were no contractual rights and liabilities. The transfer was nevertheless one by law and therefore 'legal' within the Directive. TUPE also applies to the 'contracting in' of services as occurs when a council contracts out a function to a company, the company goes into liquidation, and the council resumes the service (*Council of the Isles of Scilly v Brintel Helicopters Ltd*, above).

The application of the Regulations to the practice of 'hiving down' is one area where in respect of employees' rights English law is in advance of EC laws. Hiving down occurs when the receiver or liquidator sells (or tries to sell) a unit of a business which is insolvent. The employees remain in the service of the bankrupt firm. Their services are provided to the buyers through a wholly-owned subsidiary of the bankrupt firm. The buyers now can select which employees they wish to engage. Before the Regulations the employees' rights lay against the insolvent firm and through them against a State-run fund where redundancy payments were claimed (in other respects they were unsecured creditors). The Transfer of Undertakings (Protection of Employment) (Amendment) Regulations 1987 (SI 1987/442) operate to safeguard the rights of the employees now working for the wholly owned subsidiary. By Reg 4 the transfer to the subsidiary is deemed not to take effect until immediately before either the transferee company ceases to be a wholly-owned subsidiary of the transferors (this provision does not apply in the event of a winding up) or the business is transferred by the transferee company to another person. The

13.2.8 Hiving down

effect is that where the hiving off is successful, the employees remain in the employment of the company which is parent to the wholly-owned subsidiary until the business is transferred to the buyer. They are then automatically transferred to the subsidiary and thence to the buyers.

13.2.9   Transfer of contract

Where there is a relevant transfer, the contract of employment of an employee employed by the transferors immediately before the transfer is not terminated by the transfer; instead the contract is treated as if it were made with the transferee employers (Reg 5(1)). No transferee need be identified at the time of the transfer for the Regulations to apply (*Harrison Bowden Ltd v Bowden* (1994)). One looks with hindsight to see what happened. Rights and duties under that contract are transferred, and the transferees become liable for anything, except criminal liability, done or incurred by the transferors. Liability is not joint between the transferors and transferees. In *Stirling DC v Allan* (1995) the Court of Session held that the Regulations were clear on this point. The Directive provided for the transfer of obligations. Member States were given the option to provide for joint liability but the UK did not take up that option. Among matters transferred are continuity of employment and an accrued right not to be unfairly dismissed by the transferors (*Green-Wheeler v Onyx (UK) Ltd* (1993)). However, the employee may make a claim for unfair dismissal against transferees (see below) but the employers may have a defence. If it is uncertain against whom the claim should be brought the claimant may complain against both. The IT will decide against whom the claim should be brought.

13.2.10   'Immediately before'

Where the employee was dismissed before the date of the transfer for a reason unconnected with the transfer, the dismissal may or may not be unfair depending on normal principles (see Chapter 10). It is not automatically unfair. For a case where there was held to be no connection, see *Longden v Ferrari Ltd* (1994), where the EAT upheld an IT decision that the receivers dismissed the employees because of pressure from the bank and not at the behest of the purchasers, despite the fact that the transferees had told the receivers which workers they wished to retain. Michael Rubenstein ([1994] IRLR 151) commented that: 'It must be strongly arguable that selection for retention and non-selection are two sides of the same coin, and that the EAT's holding ... opens the door to abuse.' The rights and duties under the contract are not transferred because the employee was not employed at the moment of transfer: *Secretary of State for Employment v Spence* (1987), where a three hours' gap prevented transfer, even though the three hours were on the same date. This decision was approved *obiter* by the House of Lords in *Litster v Forth Dry Dock and Engineering Co Ltd* (1990). In *Litster* there was collusion but the case applies generally (*Harrison Bowden Ltd v Bowden*, above, and *Ibex Trading Co Ltd v Walton* (1994)). In *Spence* at 11 am there was no work. The employees were dismissed. The purchasers of the business took over at 2 pm, apparently not knowing of the sackings. They re-employed the whole workforce. Since there had been no transfer, the employees' rights were against the old employers (only), but they were insolvent and accordingly the employees' redundancy payments had to be made by the State. The decision worked in favour of these employees who wanted redundancy payments, not the continuance of work. The new employers were not liable to make these payments. They would have been liable had there been a transfer. The Lords in *Litster* approved the ruling in *Spence* on the grounds that the old employers and the new did not collude with the aim of selling off the business at an advantageous price without the employees. *Spence* has been heavily criticised. One point is that the Regulation speaks of 'date': why should 'date' be read as 'moment'? The employees did end employment and restart on the same date. Furthermore, the factual basis of the ruling in *Spence* may be questioned. The old employment folded at 11 am because the contractors with whom the old employers had done 80% of its business had withdrawn, but by 2 pm the new employers had signed an agreement with the contractors. There may not have been actual collusion between the old and the new employers but something fishy may have occurred.

13.2.11   Date of transfer

For the purposes of Reg 3(1) the date of the transfer is when the transferees take over, not the time when the legal process of a sale (or other transfer) is completed. The transfer occurs (*Daddy's Dance Hall*):

'... as soon as there is a change ... of the natural or legal person responsible for operating the undertaking who, consequently, enters into obligations as an employer towards employees working in the undertaking, and it is of no importance to know whether the ownership of the undertaking has been transferred.'

13.2.12   *Litster*

If the contract of employment has been terminated for a reason connected with the transfer before the date of transfer the dismissal is automatically unfair: *Litster*. The employees were dismissed an hour before the transfer. The transferors were in receivership. A new company was established to take over the business but it did not wish to take on the transferors' employees. It wished to use workers from elsewhere who would work for less wages than the employees. Those employees claimed for unfair dismissal. Were they employed 'immediately before' the transfer? Since the employees were dismissed one hour before the transfer one might be permitted to think that TUPE did not apply, applying *Spence*. The House of Lords held, however, that the dismissals were for a reason connected with the transfer. Regulation 8(1) applied. Rights under the employment contracts were transferred to the transferees. The Lords said that the Regulations had to be read in conformity with the EC Directive as interpreted by the ECJ in *Bork International*. Regulation 5 applies now not just to those who were employed at the date of the transfer but also to those who would have been so employed if they had not been unfairly dismissed within the circumstances prescribed in Reg 8 (see below). The Lords stated that the Regulations were intended to protect employees who would not be protected if employers could dismiss without incurring liability. The effect is to stop evasion of the Regulations. In *Spence*, however, there was no attempt at evasion.

13.2.13	Transfer of what?	Where there has been a relevant transfer, all rights, powers, duties and liabilities of the transferors arising under or in connection with the contract of employment are transferred to the transferees (Reg 5(2)(a)). On the facts of *Litster* the claims for unfair dismissal were against the new company, not the old. It is thought that Reg 5(2) transfers not just contractual but statutory and tortious duties too. The transfer of tort duties was mentioned in *Spence* (possibly, vicarious liability is not transferred). If the working of the English Regulations ('in connection with') is too narrow to include statutory obligations, the Directive, Article 3(1), will operate, and Reg 5(2)(a) must be interpreted in conformity with it. The effect is that claims for breach of contract (eg arrears of pay) and for personal injury are transferred and the transfer takes place without the consent of the employee. For the position where she objects, see para 13.1.3 . However, criminal liabilities such as breaches of the Health and Safety at Work Act 1974 are not transferred (Reg 5(4)). The effect of Reg 5 is often described as a statutory novation of the contract. It is as if the employment contract had from the start been made with the transferees. It has been held that the protective award is not transferred: *Angus Jowett & Co Ltd v NUTGW* (1985). Continuity is preserved.

13.2.14 Dismissal or ineffective?

If there is a dismissal in connection with the transfer, two interpretations are possible. First, the dismissals are void. Therefore, the contract is not terminated by the dismissal and the employee remains in employment with the transferees. There is support for this approach in *Bork International* and in

Lord Oliver's speech in *Litster*. The second view is that the dismissal does terminate the contract: all the Regulations do is to say which employers are liable. The second approach is more in line with English thinking. *Litster* however preserves continuity and the transfer of the contract in any event.

TUPE, Reg 5(5), states that an employee has the right to terminate her contract without notice if a substantial change is made to her conditions of work and that change is to her detriment. A change only in the identity of her employers does not give her this right unless the change was in all the circumstances a significant one to her detriment. The effect of the opening part of Reg 5(5) is to preserve the employee's right to resign when there has been a substantial change in her employment (ie constructive dismissal). So if an employee's pay is reduced after and because of the transfer, there is a constructive dismissal. Regulation 8(1), below, applies, and the dismissal is automatically unfair. The defence in Regulation 8(2) does not apply because even if there is an economic, technical or organisational reason there is no change in the workforce. By Reg 5 the transferees will be liable.

13.2.15   Substantial change

Regulation 5(5) seems to apply even though the change is not one to the contract of employment, eg there may be a change to promotion prospects, or to prospects for continued employment.

13.2.16   Non-contractual benefits

Regulation 5 does not operate to transfer occupational pension schemes: Reg 7(1), as it now is. However, that restriction has been narrowed to old age, invalidity and survivors' benefits: s 33(5) of the Trade Union Reform and Employment Rights Act 1993, inserting a new Reg 7(2) into TUPE. Other matters such as contractual benefits on redundancy are now transferred.

13.2.17   Occupational pensions

A dismissal is automatically unfair if the reason or principal reason for it was the transfer or a reason connected with it: Reg 8(1). There will be no transfer within this provision when the employees are dismissed at a time when no purchaser of the business could be identified or no certainty that any sale of the business would occur (*Ibex Trading Co Ltd v Walton* (1994)). If the employers demonstrate that the reason or principal reason was (Reg 8(2)):

13.2.18   Regulation 8

'an economic, technical or organisational reason entailing changes in the workforce of either the transferor or the transferee before or after a relevant transfer.'

If this defence applies (the burden of proof being on the employers), the employers' reason is treated as one of the potentially fair reasons, some other substantial reason, and the industrial tribunal has to consider s 57(3) of the Employment Protection (Consolidation) Act 1978 ie was the dismissal fair taking all the circumstances including procedural fairness (such as consultation) and the size and administrative resources of the employers into account? (See Chapter 10.) The deeming of the dismissal to be 'some other substantial reason' does not affect claims for redundancy payments (*Gorictree Ltd v Jenkinson* (1984)). For the remedy for unfair dismissal see the previous chapter.

13.2.19   Connection with transfer

There is no restriction as to the time beyond which a reason cannot be connected with the transfer. As long as there is a link, a dismissal years later suffices. If the dismissal is not in connection with the transfer, the normal law of unfair dismissal applies.

13.2.20   'ETO'

A dismissal for an economic, technical or organisational reason (often called an 'ETO') may nevertheless be a redundancy (*Gorictree Ltd v Jenkinson* (1984)). Pressure put by the purchasers on the transferors to dismiss the workforce before the transfer is not an ETO on the grounds that TUPE is meant to protect employees and 'economic' must be read *ejusdem generis* with technical or organisational ie it must relate to the conduct of the business, not to its attractiveness to purchasers (*Wheeler v Patel* (1987)). A dismissal of employees at the request of the transferees is not an economic reason. However, the term is not restricted to situations in which those dismissed would have been dismissed anyway, had there been no transfer (*Trafford v Sharpe & Fisher (Building Supplies) Ltd* (1994)). There is no definition in the Regulations or elsewhere in employment law of these terms. 'Economic, technical or organisational' is a phrase taken direct from the Directive with no attempt made to fit it into UK domestic law. An example of transferee employers successfully claiming an ETO reason is *Porter v Queen's Medical Centre*, above. A reorganisation at a hospital which led to new specialisms being demanded of consultants was an ETO reason entailing changes in the workforce. The plaintiffs' contracts of employment terminated when notice given by their (transferor) employers elapsed.

13.2.21   'Entailing changes'

It used to be thought that 'entailing changes in the workforce' meant that the number of employees or their functions had to change. In a significant decision the Court of Appeal in *Berriman v Delabole State Ltd* (1985) held that Reg 8(2) does not apply where there was a change to an employee's contract to his disadvantage. The number of workers did not change. The employers' aim was to standardise the contracts of their workers after a transfer, an aim which might be laudable. However, the reduction in the employee's terms and conditions (a cut in his pay) was a constructive dismissal which he did not accept. It was automatically unfair. The Court said that 'entailing changes in the workplace' encompassed both a change in the overall numbers or a change in the functions of the employees. A change of pay was therefore not a change in the workforce. A change in numbers meant a change in the number of staff, not a change where one employee is replaced by another. The Court looked to the purpose of the Directive, which was to preserve employees' rights including 'their existing terms of service' on a transfer. If the transferees seek instead to get the transferors to dismiss the employees, *Litster* applies. An example of a change in functions is *Crawford v Swinton Insurance Brokers Ltd* (1990). A clerk was asked to become an insurance salesperson. The EAT held that Reg 8(2) applied. There was a change in the workforce because the employers needed one clerk less and one salesperson more.

It appears that the claim for unfair dismissal must be made by an employee who is qualified to bring the complaint. Therefore, rules such as the qualifying period of two years' continuous employment would seem to apply. However, in *Milligan v Securicor Ltd* (1995) it was held that an employee could claim for unfair dismissal even though he did not have two years' employment. The EAT reasoned that the Directive to which the Regulations were related was intended to protect employees in the event of a transfer and any inconsistent English law was to be struck down. The EAT granted leave to appeal. The case is out of line with orthodoxy and it has previously been stated by the EAT that the two-year qualifying period applies: see *Macer v Abafest Ltd* (1993) and *Harrison Bowden Ltd v Bowden* (1994). See Chapter 8 for these rules.

13.2.22   Qualifications

Regulation 10 of TUPE imposes on employers, whether transferors, transferees or both, a duty to inform and consult with independent trade unions which they recognise in the event of a transfer. The procedure for handling redundancies dealt with in Chapter 9 applies only to the employers who dismiss. Another difference is that the duty to consult in Regulation 10 applies even though no one is to be made redundant. As a result of the decision in *Commission of the European Communities v UK*, above, the government is considering ways of making English law attain European standards. The ECJ said that EC-wide law on this matter had to be comparable among Member States and had to impose

13.3   Trade unions

similar costs on employees across the Community. While the government has set its face against the compulsory recognition of unions and the establishment of works councils, changes are imminent.

13.3.1   Information

Information must be provided to the union's representatives about the fact of transfer, when it will take place, the reasons for it; about the 'legal, economic and social implications' for those employees who will be affected; about the measures which will be taken in relation to those 'affected employees'. That term includes not just those who will be transferred but anyone who may be affected by the transfer or measures taken in connection with it: Reg 10(1). The independence of trade unions is discussed in Chapter 14. A representative is an official or other person authorised to carry out collective bargaining: Reg 2(3). If it is the transferors who are under the duty to consult, the transferees must give them the relevant information: Reg 10(3). The law on handling redundancies is narrower than TUPE for only in the latter must there be information about the legal, economic and social complications of the transfer. What are legal, economic and social implications is unclear.

13.3.2   When?

The information must be given 'long enough before a relevant transfer to enable consultations to take place'. There are no minimum time limits as there are in the procedure for handling redundancies (see Chapter 9). Certainly information need not be given at the stage when there are only proposals for transfer: it would appear that it need be given only when the parties are agreed on the transfer. The Directive speaks of the fact of transfer, not of proposals for transfer. The position is otherwise in the law on handling redundancies. In this respect the law is more pro-employees in redundancy dismissals than is the right discussed here.

13.3.3   Consultation

Where the employers will be taking measures with regard to the affected employees, they must consult with union representatives 'with a view to seeking that agreement to measures to be taken'. The words in inverted commas were added by s 33(6) of the 1993 Act to Reg 10(5). The employers must consider the union's objections and reply to them, giving reasons for rejections. The employers need inform only the union which they recognise. Therefore, the transferees need not inform the union of the transferees' workplace. The Directive is not, however, limited to recognised unions. It applies to employees' representatives or, if none, the employees themselves. The EC Commission took proceedings against the UK for not fully implementing the Directive. The ECJ ruled in

Commission of the European Communities v UK (1994) that UK law fell short of the EC standard. There had to be a method of designating representatives of employees when the employers did not recognise a union. The government proposes to give employers a choice to negotiate with the union or elected representatives (who could be elected solely for this purpose).

Regulation 10(7) gives employers a 'special circumstances' defence of apparently the same width as on the law on handling redundancies (Chapter 9). If there are such circumstances making it not reasonably practicable for the employers to inform or consult they must take all reasonably practicable steps to comply with their duties. The burden of proof of special circumstances and all reasonably practicable steps is on the employers.

13.3.4   Special circumstances

Enforcement is by the union bringing a claim to an industrial tribunal: Reg 11(1). The claim must be made within three months of the completion of the transfer: Reg 11(8). The remedy is a just and equitable sum to a maximum of four weeks' pay: Reg 11(11) as amended by the 1993 Act, s 33(7)(a). The Tribunal is instructed to have 'regard to the seriousness of the failure of the employer to comply with his duty'. There no longer is any set off for the protective award: Reg 11(7) as amended by s 33(7)(b). The repeal of this set of provisions may encourage unions to use TUPE more, though the sanction remains derisory. The protective award discussed in Chapter 9 is of more significance than this exceptionally weak remedy. The small size is a breach of the Directive, which, like all legally enforceable Directives, must be accompanied by an adequate remedy (*Commission of the European Communities v UK* above). The previous set off and the present financial limit were condemned.

13.3.5   Sanction

By Regulation 6, 'any collective bargain agreed by the transferor shall have effect as if made by the transferee'.

13.3.6   Collective agreements

Finally, if an undertaking or part of an undertaking is transferred and it retains an identity distinct from the remainder of the transferees' business, any recognition of a union by the transferors is transferred to the transferees: Reg 9. However, the transferees may resile from recognition whenever they wish in the usual way. Moreover, there is no enforcement mechanism provided in Reg 9. Unions must rely on industrial muscle to retain recognition. And if the identity is not preserved, Reg 9 is inapplicable. The effect is that if the transferred part of the undertaking is merged with the transferees' business, there is no transfer of recognition.

13.3.7   Recognition

Transfer of Undertakings

At common law contracts of employment could not be transferred, but the 1981 Transfer of Undertakings (Protection of Employment) Regulations operate on a relevant transfer to preserve continuity of those employed immediately before the transfer and rights and duties under the contract are transferred. A dismissal in connection with the transfer is automatically unfair unless the employers have an economic, technical or organisational reason entailing changes in the workforce, in which case the dismissal is potentially fair. The transfer need not be in the nature of a commercial venture.

Laws

Dr Sophie Redmond Stichtung v Bartol (1992)

　　Leases and franchises may be transferred.

Daddy's Dance Hall (1989)

Ny Molle Krø (1989)

　　Privatisation continues to cause problems to English courts and tribunals.

Wren v Eastbourne BC (1993)

Porter v Queen's Medical Centre (1993)

Dines v Initial Health Care Services Ltd (1994)

　　Criminal liability, protective awards and some aspects of occupational pensions are not transferred.

　　An 'ETO' includes a redundancy.

Litster v Forth Dry Dock (1990)

Berriman v Delabole Slate (1985).

There is a duty to inform union representatives about the transfer and a duty to consult 'with a view to seeking agreement to measures to be taken'. Collective agreements are transferred, as is recognition where the identity of the part transferred is preserved. Since there is no duty under English law to continue recognition of unions, this provision can be easily circumvented. The ECJ ruled in *EC Commission v UK* (1994) that the government had failed to satisfy the standards of the EC in several respects including restricting consultation to situations in which there was a recognised union.

Trade unions

Chapter 14

Trade Unions

This chapter considers the definition of trade unions, their legal status, history and independence, recognition by employers, the right to information for collective bargaining purposes, various rights to time off and the political fund. The next chapter deals with the internal affairs of unions (ie the relationship with their members). The final chapter deals with some aspects of collective bargaining and industrial action. Some of this material may be differently ordered on your course.

14.1 Coverage

This section looks at trade union, special register bodies and employers' associations.

14.2 Definition

The Trade Union and Labour Relations (Consolidation) Act 1992 (TULR(C)A), s 1, defines a trade union for the purposes of the Act as:

14.2.1 By statute

'an organisation (whether temporary or permanent) –

(a) which consists wholly or mainly of workers of one or more descriptions and whose principal purposes include the regulation of relations between workers of that description or those descriptions and employers or employers' associations; or

(b) which consists wholly or mainly of –

(i) constituent or affiliated organisations which fulfil the conditions in paragraph (a) (or themselves consist wholly or mainly of constituent or affiliated organisations which fulfil those conditions); or

(ii) representatives of such constituent or affiliated organisations, and whose principal purposes include the regulation of relations between workers and employers or between workers and employers' associations, or the regulation of relations between its constituent or affiliated organisations.'

The definition is important because trade unions have various benefits and are subject to various burdens as this and the following chapters show. There are some 300 unions.

The principal authority is *Midland Cold Storage Ltd v Steer* (1972). Though the definition covers temporary bodies, it did not include an *ad hoc* committee of shop stewards. The Court held that the body's function was not the regulation of employment relations but the organisation of industrial action. It was formed for the purpose of blacking a company, and even though it was an organisation of workers (it consisted of shop stewards of various unions and it had a convenor and a secretary), it did not constitute a union because its purpose was not that stated in s 1(a). As long as the principal purpose is the regulation of employment relations, it does not matter that the union does not perform all possible purposes of a union, that the (express) objects of the organisation do not include the regulation of such relations, or that it does not have the industrial muscle to carry out collective bargaining fully (*BAALPE v NUT* (1986)). There is no minimum number of members.

14.2.2   Federations

The definition of 'union' covers a federation of unions, the best known union being the International Transport Workers Federation (see eg *NWL Ltd v Woods* (1989)). For this reason the Trades Union Congress, the TUC, is thought to be a union.

14.2.3   Workers

The definition in s 1 refers to 'workers'. This term is wider than that of 'employees' but it does not cover all persons who in ordinary language perform work. By s 296 of TULR(C)A 'workers' include employees and all those who agree to perform personally a service for another person, but not those whose relationship with the person who engaged their service is that of professional and client. Because of the definition authors are not workers because they do not come under a duty to perform services (*Writers' Guild of Great Britain v BBC* (1974)) and the Law Society is not a union because the relationship of solicitor and client is one of professional and client (*Carter v The Law Society* (1973)).

14.2.4   Special register bodies

Certain bodies do seek to regulate employment relations but their principal purpose is not such regulation but the maintenance of professional standards of practice. The two main organisations are the British Medical Association and the Royal College of Nursing. There are 13 other bodies. These are called 'special register' bodies. The main advantage of being on the register is that like trade unions the bodies' rules and purposes are not affected by the restraint of trade doctrine (see below). No more organisations may be added to the register.

14.2.5   Employers' associations

By s 122(1) of TULR(C)A an employers' association is:

'... an organisation (whether temporary or permanent) - (a) which consists wholly or mainly of employers or individual owners of undertakings of one or more descriptions and whose principal purposes include the regulation of relations between employers of that description or those descriptions and workers or trade unions ...'

The definition also covers constituent and affiliated organisations just as the definition of 'trade union' does. The Certification Officer keeps a list of employers' organisations. Unlike trade unions these associations may be (but need not be) companies. If the association is unincorporated, it is treated as a quasi-corporate body just as a union is.

TULR(C)A, s 10(1), states:

'A trade union is not a body corporate but –

> (a)   it is capable of making contracts;
>
> (b)   it is capable of suing and being sued in its own name, whether in proceedings relating to property or founded on contract or tort or any other cause of action; and
>
> (c)   proceedings for an offence alleged to have been committed by it or on its behalf may be brought against it in its own name.'

Therefore, a union is not a company and indeed by s 10(3) cannot be registered as a company, a friendly society or an industrial and provident society. The side-note to s 10 reads: 'quasi-corporate status of trade unions' ie unions are not companies but have some of the rights and obligations of them.

14.3   Legal status of unions

Section 12(1) vests union property (including its records) in trustees in trust for the union. In this respect TUs differ from unincorporated associations such as clubs where the property is held on trust for the members. If the trustees act unlawfully, a union member may apply to the High Court for various orders including the removal of the trustees and the appointment of receivers. Such orders took place in the Miners' strike 1984–5, though at that time the Court's power was not found in statute as it is now. The Commissioner for the Rights of Trade Union Members may assist the member in such proceedings.

14.3.1   Trusts

Despite s 10(1), a TU does not have sufficient legal personality to suffer injury to its reputation. Accordingly it cannot sue for libel: *Electrical Electronic Telecommunications and Plumbing Union v Times Newspapers Ltd* (1980). O'Connor J said that not merely was a union not a company it was not to be treated as a company. Therefore, it did not have the requisite personality. However, it had earlier been held that unions could sue for defamation.

14.3.2   Libel

14.4   Restraint of trade

By s 11(2) of TULR(C)A 'no rule of a trade union is unlawful or unenforceable by reason only that it is in restraint of trade'. This sub-section is self-explanatory.

14.4.1   Purposes

By s 11(1) of the same statute:

> '... the purposes of a trade union are not, by reason only that they are in restraint of trade, unlawful so as - (a) to make any member of the trade union liable to criminal proceedings for conspiracy or otherwise, or (b) to make any agreement or trust void or voidable.'

There is a possibility that even this wide provision might be outflanked by the common law. In *Edwards v SOGAT* (1971) Lord Denning MR postulated that individuals had a right to work exercisable against TUs (though not against employers or the State). If so union purposes which conflicted with this right to work could be struck down as being in restraint of trade. What interferes with an individual's right to work also is contrary to the doctrine of restraint of trade. Little has been heard of this notion since Lord Denning retired.

14.5   Listing

The Certification Officer (CO) keeps a list of TUs: s 2(1), TULR(C)A. Membership of this list is voluntary. The list comprises of those unions which were on a list kept in 1974, together with any union which the CO since put on the list. Unions may apply to the CO for putting on the list. The CO must put the name on the list if he is satisfied that the organisation is a trade union, that the form containing the body's rules, officers, address, and name has been duly completed, and that the organisation's name is not the same as another union or so similar to another as likely to deceive the public: s 3. There is also a charge. There are some 300 unions on the list. Listing is not a condition for an organisation's being classed as a trade union.

14.5.1   Advantages

The advantages of listing are these:

- membership of the list is evidence that the body is a TU (s 2(4));

- listing is a prerequisite of a certificate of independence: s 6(1);

- tax relief is available on income and gains applied for provident benefits.

For present purposes the second point is the most important. Listing is a step towards the certificate and only if a union is independent does it and its members enjoy certain rights.

The CO may remove the name of a body from the list if it is no longer a union and must remove it if so requested or if he is satisfied that the organisation no longer exists: s 4. There is an appeal to the Employment Appeal Tribunal against refusal to list and removal from the list: s 9(1). Surprisingly the appeal may be on a question of fact, not just of law: s 4(4). (The same applies to the certificate of independence.)

Certain rights and privileges are given only to trade unions which are independent. Organisations of workers which are not independent of employers are sometimes called 'sweetheart (or house) unions' or staff associations, though a staff association can take on so much of the mantle of a TU that it becomes independent.

14.6   Independence

By s 5 of TULR(C)A an independent trade union is a TU which:

> '(a) is not under the domination or control of an employer or group of employers or of one or more employers' associations, and (b) is not liable to interference by an employer or any such group or association (arising out of the provision of financial or material support or by any other means whatsoever) tending towards such control.'

In s 5(b) 'liable to interference' means 'vulnerable to, or at the risk of, interference': *Squibb UK Staff Association v CO* (1979). The test is not whether the TU is likely to suffer interference in practice but whether intervention may occur. On the facts of *Squibb* the union was not independent. Although the employers did not at present interfere in the running there was the possibility it might do so later. Indeed the union could not continue without employers' involvement.

The CO determines whether the TU is independent. He has set out various criteria, which were accepted in *Blue Circle Staff Association v CO* (1977).

- History

  If the union was set up by management or with management help, it is unlikely for some time to be classified as independent. Nevertheless, it can after a while grow apart from the employers so that it no longer is vulnerable to influence. On the facts of *Blue Circle* the staff association was not independent. It originated as a management tool ('a sophisticated instrument of personnel control') and was not free from 'paternal control'.

- Membership

  If a union is formed which recruits only among employees

of one company, it is not likely to be independent. As with all these guidelines this one is not a condition of independence. For example, the NUM (National Union of Mineworkers) is independent despite its recruiting only among employees of British Coal.

- Financial aspects

  If a union receives a subsidy from the employers it is unlikely to be independent.

- Facilities

  If the employer provides amenities such as free phones the union may not be independent. In *Squibb* the employers provided free offices, free internal mail, and time off with pay. The Court held that the union was not independent.

- Collective bargaining

  The lack of 'robustness' in negotiation on industrial matters is a mark of non-independence.

- Internal affairs

  In *Blue Circle* the employers nominated the chair of the Joint Central Committee. This ability demonstrated that the union was liable to interference. In *Government Communications Staff Federation v CO* (1993) the EAT held the federation to be liable to interference because the Director of GCHQ could withdraw his approval for its existence.

The Union of Democratic Mineworkers satisfied these factors and was granted a certificate of independence after the miners' strike. It is not always easy for breakaway factions to be credited with independent status.

14.6.4   Procedure

A TU desirous of independence applies to the CO for a certificate: s 6(1). The union must be a listed one (see above). The CO makes 'such enquiries as he thinks fit' and takes into account 'any relevant information submitted ... by any person', including rival unions. The CO then uses the criteria just stated to determine whether the union is truly independent. An appeal against refusal of a certificate is to the EAT and may be as to fact or as to law (s 9). The EAT heard the case *de novo* and may take into account information which the CO did not know. Only a union aggrieved by the refusal of a certificate may appeal. A TU which dislikes the grant of a certificate to another union may not appeal. The CO may revoke the certificate 'if he is of the opinion that the union is no longer independent' (s 7). Again there is an appeal on fact or law to the EAT. There is nothing to stop a union which has been refused a certificate to apply again. The CO may give the union advice in his reasons for refusing the certificate as to how it can gain the certificate.

Once issued the certificate:

> '... is conclusive evidence for all purposes that a trade union is independent; and a refusal, withdrawal or cancellation of a certificate of independence ... is conclusive evidence for all purposes that a trade union is not independent.' (s 8(1))

Where an issue arises in any court, IT, the EAT, ACAS or the Central Arbitration Committee as to independence, the matter is stayed until the issue is resolved by the CO: s 8(4).

Independence is important on a number of grounds. Only independent TUs have the rights to:

- obtain information for collective bargaining purposes;

- appoint health and safety representatives;

- be consulted on redundancy and on the transfer of undertakings.

Only members of independent TUs have the right to engage in TU activities and to time off work for union duties and activities. They must not have action short of dismissal taken against them on trade union grounds.

Recognition may be defined as the situation in which employers undertake to negotiate with TUs on collective bargaining issues 'to any extent': s 180(3) of TULR(C)A. A union may be recognised for one, some or all purposes. Being recognised for one purpose does not mean that the union is automatically recognised for all purposes. The acquisition, retention and widening of recognition is a matter of custom and practice, the arrangements often reached after years of contention and sometimes of industrial action. There may be a trade dispute over recognition. If so, ACAS may employ its officers to help a settlement to be reached. Recognition may be the outcome of an express agreement or of an implied arrangement (such as occurred when a firm consulted with the union about the allocation of work, job security, and discipline), but merely allowing the union to represent members eg at disciplinary hearings is insufficient: *USDAW v Sketchley Ltd* (1981). Since recognition is voluntary, so is de-recognition, of which there were a number of incidents in the 1980s. It is thought that the number of employees whose employers recognised unions fell from two-thirds to a little over a half between 1980 and 1990.

14.6.5   Effect

14.6.6   Advantages

14.7   Recognition

Sometimes derecognition is partial in that unions are deprived of only some of their roles.

14.7.1	Voluntary nature	There used to be a way in which unions could by law extend recognition to new workplaces but that procedure was abolished in 1980 as not being compatible with the British tradition of voluntarism and with the present government's desire to rein unions in. Because there is no legal enforcement of recognition, employers can withdraw from agreements recognising unions at will. The National Coal Board could break an agreement to give exclusive recognition to the National Union of Mineworkers without incurring legal liability (*NCB v NUM* (1986)). Both collective agreements in general and recognition agreements in particular cannot be visited by legal sanctions if broken. It is Labour Party policy to enforce recognition when a majority of the workforce desire it.
14.7.2	Illustration	The most important case remains *NUGSAT v Albury Bros Ltd* (1979). Recognition by an employers' association of which the firm was a member did not mean that the firm recognised the union. Recruitment of a small number of employees, a letter to the firm about pay, and one meeting did not constitute recognition. Negotiations which may lead to recognition do not constitute recognition.
14.7.3	Transfer Regulations	There is a reference in the general law to recognition in the Transfer of Undertakings (Protection of Employment) Regulations 1981 SI 1981/1794 whereby the transferee employers must continue to recognise unions recognised by the transferors where the transferred undertaking or part of an undertaking is transferred as a unit and is not merged with the transferees' trade or business.
14.7.4	Advantages	Only independent recognised unions have various rights eg to be consulted on redundancies and transfers of undertakings, to obtain information for collective bargaining and to appoint safety representatives. Only members of recognised independent TUs have various rights to time off work. Information for collective bargaining and time off are discussed next. Information and consultation and redundancies and transfers have been discussed above (Chapters 9 and 13 respectively).
14.8	**Collective bargaining information: duty to provide**	By s 181(1) of TULR(C)A:

'... an employer who recognises an independent trade union shall, for the purposes of all stages of collective bargaining about matters, and in relation to descriptions of workers in respect of which the union is recognised by him, disclose to representatives of the union, on request, the information required by this section.'

The union must therefore be independent and recognised. Recognition means recognition at the date of the request. Subsequent derecognition is irrelevant. The right extends only to those issues on which the employers recognise the union (*R v CAC ex p BTP Tioxide Ltd* (1981)) ie this right cannot be used to broaden the matter in respect of which the union is recognised. 'Representatives' means TU officials and others authorised by the TU to carry on collective bargaining such as shop stewards. The aim behind the legislation is to smooth the way towards collective agreements.

By s 181(2):

'... the information to be disclosed is all information relating to the employer's undertaking which is in his possession, or that of an associated employer, and is information -

(a) without which the trade union representatives would be to a material extent impeded in carrying on collective bargaining with him, and

(b) which it would in accordance with good industrial relations practice that he should disclose to them for the purposes of collective bargaining.'

It is difficult to understand how a TU could be materially impeded in bargaining one year if it never had the information in previous years for in those years it was presumably not materially impeded!

14.8.1   Included matters

In determining what is to be disclosed, reference may be made to the ACAS Code of Practice no 2 'Disclosure of Information to Trade Unions for Collective Bargaining Purposes' 1977. The Code invites negotiators to take into account the subject-matter of the bargaining, the issues, the level of negotiations (eg are they at factory or company level?), the firm's size and its type of business. Among matters which might be raised are pay and benefits, conditions of service (eg redundancy, promotion and appraisal), manpower (eg turnover, planned changes to equipment), performance such as productivity and financial matters including assets and liabilities. Research which is now somewhat aged shows that rare were the occasions on which TUs obtained information about non-labour costs, redundancy proposals and profits. The Code has the same legal status as other ACAS Codes. It is not law but tribunals may consider it.

14.8.2   Code of Practice

Collective bargaining is defined in s 178(1) as negotiations relating to or connected with a collective agreement which is:

'any agreement or arrangement made by or on behalf of one or more trade unions and one or more employers or employers' associations and relating to one or more of the matters specified in s 178(2).'

14.8.3   Collective bargaining

Section 178(2) states:

'the matters referred to above are –

(a)   terms and conditions of employment, or the physical conditions in which any workers are required to work;

(b)   engagement or non-engagement, or termination or suspension of employment or the duties of employment, of one or more workers;

(c)   allocation of work or the duties of employment between workers or groups of workers;

(d)   matters of discipline;

(e)   a worker's membership or non-membership of a trade union;

(f)   facilities for officials of trade unions; and

(g)   machinery for negotiation or consultation, and other procedures, relating to any of the above matters, including the recognition by employers or employers' associations of the right of a trade union to represent workers in such negotiation or consultation or in the carrying out of such procedures.'

(The same list appears in relation to the definition of trade dispute as a defence to claims in tort in respect of industrial action: s 244(1). See the final chapter.) The list while lengthy does not cover everything in relation to which a union might be recognised eg investment plans for the next decade.

14.8.4   Exemptions

Disclosure is not permitted where it would breach national security or a statute, where there would be a breach of confidentiality, where it relates to an individual (unless she consents to disclosure), where disclosure would cause 'substantial injury' to the undertaking 'for reasons other than its effect on collective bargaining', or where the information was created in connection with legal proceedings (s 182(1)). By s 182(2)(b) employers are not required to compile information if doing so 'would involve an amount of work or expenditure out of reasonable proportion to the value of the information in the conduct of collective bargaining'. Employers need not provide the original documents. The obligation is fulfilled by providing material which satisfies the obligation. An example of confidentiality is *Civil Service Union v Central Arbitration Committee* (1980). A firm put in a tender when the government was contracting out cleaning. The cost of contracting out was on a form marked 'In confidence'. The information it was held could not be disclosed. The Code of Practice suggests:

'... substantial injury may occur if, for example, certain customers would be lost to competitors, or suppliers would refuse to supply necessary materials, or the ability to raise funds to finance the company would be seriously impaired as a result of disclosing certain information.'

The Code states that the burden of proof is on the employers. It might be said that this embargoed information is the sort of data which would be most useful to a TU wishing to promote the interests of its member *vis-à-vis* their employers.

The remedy is long-winded. The union complains to the Central Arbitration Committee (CAC). The CAC refers it to ACAS if there is a reasonable likelihood that the matter can be resolved by conciliation. If there is no such likelihood or conciliation fails, the CAC hears and determines the complaint, giving reasons. If the complaint is well-founded, the CAC so states and specifies a period longer than a week by the end of which the employers must disclose the relevant information. If by the end of that time the data has not been divulged, the TU may present a further complaint to the CAC. Again the CAC considers and determines the complaint, giving reasons for their rulings. If the further complaint is well-founded, the CAC so states. At the same time or after presenting the further complaint, the TU may claim before the CAC that their members specified in the claim should receive the terms and conditions in their contracts requested in the claim. If the employers comply with the request for information, the whole claim falls. If, however, they do not, the CAC after hearing both sides may order the employers to observe the terms and conditions specified in the claim or such other terms and conditions as the CAC considers appropriate. The new terms and conditions become part of the employees' contract (and are enforced in the normal way) until superseded or varied by a collective agreement, by a later award of the same type, or by an agreement between the employers and employees covered, provided in the last case that the change is favourable to the employees. The right and the remedy are out of kilter. There is no remedy that the union is to be provided with the information, and the CAC cannot prescribe what the employers must disclose in future negotiations. One interesting matter is that there is no appeal from the award of new terms and conditions. The long-winded nature of the procedure is shown by the fact that CAC Awards are made many months after the annual negotiations about which the TU has complained have been settled. The complaints procedure is not much used. There are about 20 references a year to the CAC. The highest ever figure was 37 in 1993. This right to information, which was established in 1975, has not been limited by the present government, perhaps because the remedy is tortuous and the

14.8.5   Redress

uptake small. An alternate view is that the information makes unions moderate their demands.

14.8.6   Other statutes

Besides information which must be supplied for collective bargaining there are also duties on employers to provide information to safety representatives and to employees covered by occupational pension schemes. Information about redundancies (Chapter 9) and transfers of undertaking (Chapter 13) have already been considered. The Employment Act 1982 states that companies employing more than 250 workers must include in their annual report a statement about action taken to inform and consult with their employees. It seems that this provision is more honoured in the breach than in the observance.

14.9   Time off

Parliament has provided several rights to time off – for trade union duties and activities, health and safety representatives, public duties and ante-natal care.

14.9.1   Time off for trade union duties and training (paid)

By s 168(1) of TULR(C)A 1992:

'... an employer shall permit an employee who is an official of an independent trade union recognised by the employer to take time off during his working hours for the purpose of carrying out any duties of his, as such an official, concerned with - (a) negotiations with the employer related to or connected with matters falling within s 178(2) (collective bargaining) in relation to which the trade union is recognised by the employer, or (b) the performance on behalf of the employees of the employer of functions related to or connected with matters falling within that provision which the employer has agreed may be so performed by the trade union.'

Section 178(2) is set out above. Since the right is one to paid time off during working hours, the employee has no right to pay for performing union duties at other times or indeed to payment in lieu. Employers must also permit the official to undergo industrial relations training which is relevant to the performance of his collective bargaining duties mentioned in s 168(1) and which is approved by her TU or the TUC: s 168(2). By s 168(3):

'... the amount of time off ... and the purposes for which, the occasions on which and any conditions subject to which time off may be so taken are those that are reasonable in all the circumstances having regard to any relevant provisions of a Code of Practice issued by ACAS.'

The relevant Code of Practice is No 3, 'Time off for Trade Union Duties and Activities' 1991 (SI 1991/968). The Code notes that if the TU representative's constituents are undertaking industrial action but she is not, it may be reasonable to give her time off and that, as a matter of good industrial relations, management should consider giving facilities such as premises to hold meetings in order that TU officials can more easily perform their duties. In *Adlington v British Bakeries (Northern) Ltd* (1989) the Court of Appeal held that a preparatory meeting fell within the business for which time off was available. The test of reasonableness is the same as that found in unfair dismissal, the 'range of reasonable responses' test: *Ministry of Defence v Crook* (1982). The Court of Appeal held in *Thomas Scott & Sons (Bakers) Ltd v Allen* (1983) that it was unreasonable for all eleven shop stewards to have time off at the same time, while the EAT said in *Wignall v British Gas Corp* (1984) that it was reasonable to refuse time off when the worker had already had 12 weeks off.

The right is to time off with pay (*cf* the next right to time off): s 169(1). In the case of pieceworkers and others whose pay varies with the amount of work done the amount is calculated by reference to 'the average hourly earnings' of the employee:

    14.9.2 With pay

> '... or if no fair estimate can be made of these earnings, the average hourly earnings for work of that description of persons in comparable employment with the same employer or, if there are no such persons, a figure of average hourly earnings which is reasonable in the circumstances.' (s 169(3))

Earnings can include voluntary overtime (*cf* the definition of week's pay in Schedule 14 to EP(C)A: Chapter 12).

The remedy for not allowing time off or not paying for it is a complaint to an industrial tribunal within three months of the failure or if the IT was satisfied that it was not reasonably practicable for the complaint to be presented within that period, within such further period as the IT considers reasonable. If the complaint is upheld, the IT makes a declaration if the breach is one of failure to allow time off and may award compensation on the 'just and equitable' basis, 'having regard to the employer's default in failing to permit time off ... and to any loss sustained by the employee ...' (s 172(2)). If the complaint is of non-payment the IT must order the employers to pay the sum due. The IT can order the employers to provide time off in the future.

    14.9.3 Remedy

Section 170(1) of TULR(C)A states:

    14.9.4 Time off for trade union activities (unpaid)

> 'an employer shall permit an employee of his who is a member of an independent trade union recognised by the employer in respect of that description of employee to take

time off during his working hours for the purpose of taking part in - (a) any activities of the union; and (b) any activities in relation to which the employee is acting as a representative of the union.'

The amount, purposes, occasions and conditions of time off must be reasonable having regard to the ACAS Code of Practice: s 170(3). Time off does not cover activities consisting of industrial action: s 170(2). The remedy is a complaint to an IT within three months or a reasonably practicable period. The IT must make a declaration if the complaint is well-founded. It may make an award of compensation on the 'just and equitable' basis, having regard to the employers' default and the employee's loss. Again, the employers cannot be ordered to give a certain amount of paid time off for activities to take place after the declaration is granted. It should be noted that s 170 unlike s 168 is not restricted to time off for collective bargaining purposes. In *Menzies v Smith & McLaurin Ltd* (1988) the employee applied for paid time off for training. The EAT held that the subjects of the training were not connected with collective bargaining: they involved issues relating to import controls and North Sea oil. The matters did, however, fall within s 170 as being union activities. The Code of Practice instances attendance of union conferences and of emergency meetings. Though time off under s 170 is without pay there is nothing to prevent the parties reaching a contract to provide for pay. If a TU official cannot get paid time off within s 168, unpaid time off within s 170 may nevertheless be available. One interesting case is *Luce v Bexley LBC* (1990). The EAT held that lobbying against the Education Reform Act 1988 was a political, not a TU, activity. Therefore, union officials could not get time off despite the lobbying being about a matter which concerned all teachers and organised by the TUC.

14.9.5 Time off for health and safety representatives (paid)

Health and safety representatives of recognised trade unions have a right to reasonable time off with pay to perform their functions. The right extends to training to do their jobs. The law is laid down in the Safety Representatives and Safety Committee Regulations 1977, SI 1977/1500. If the employers already provide a course, a representative may be lawfully denied time off to attend a TUC-sponsored course on the same subject. The remedy for refusing time off is compensation assessed on the 'just and equitable' basis. The remedy for failing to pay for the time off is the amount which should have been paid. In neither case is there a statutory limit. The restriction to trade unions has been heavily criticised for some years; and it should be remembered that recognition can be withdrawn at any time without legal sanction.

The aim behind the time off provisions is to improve industrial relations and as for time off for health and safety representatives to improve workplace safety. There are also rights to time off without pay (though the work must be proportionally reduced) for public duties such as being a JP and members of police authorities (the Employment Protection (Consolidation) Act 1978, s 29); time off with pay for ante-natal care (s 31A of EP(C)A, inserted by the Employment Act 1980) – the aim of this provision is to reduce perinatal mortality; and time off with a maximum of two-fifths of a week's pay as defined in Schedule 14 to EP(C)A when an employee is under notice of dismissal for redundancy and is refused time off (s 31 of EP(C)A). In the last case if the employee is given time off but not paid for it, the amount which should have been paid is awarded subject to the maximum of two-fifths of a week's pay. In the case of ante-natal care the remedy for refusing time off is the amount which would have been paid; if the employers fail to pay for the time off, the remedy is the amount which should have been paid. There are no statutory limits on either award. As for public duties the award is of compensation assessed on the 'just and equitable' basis with no limit. There is no qualifying period for any of the rights to time off.

In a famous case, *Amalgamated Society of Railway Servants v Osborne* (1910), the House of Lords decided that TU funds could not be used for political objects eg to pay salaries to Labour MPs. The Trade Union Act 1913 reversed this ruling. It stated that union moneys could be used for any purpose mentioned in the TU's constitution but that such moneys had to be donated from a separate fund, the political fund. In 1984 the Conservative government introduced the law that TU members must be balloted every 10 years to see whether they desired or not to maintain a fund. The law is now found in TULR(C)A, Chapter VI, as amended by the Trade Union Reform and Employment Rights Act 1993 (TURERA). Some 50 unions have such funds.

A special fund must be established to hold money to be expended on political matters: ss 71(1), 82(1). Before one can be established there must have been a 'political resolution' approving political objects as objects of the union: s 71(1)(a). Union rules must provide for exemption from payment of any member objecting to contributing: s 71(1)(b). Contribution to the fund must not be a condition of membership: s 82(1)(d). A union cannot finance political objects out of its general fund, nor can it transfer money from its general to its political fund. It may be that political fund money can be spent on general

14.9.6   Other leave requirements

14.10   Political fund

14.10.1   Basic law

objects, at least if the rules so permit. The Commissioner for the Rights of Trade Union Members may assist members to bring actions against their union for using funds for political ends not in accordance with the statute.

14.10.2   Political objects

Political objects are defined in s 72(1) as expending money:

'(a)   as any contribution to the funds of, or on the payment of expenses incurred directly or indirectly by, a political party;

(b)   on the provision of any service or property for use by or on behalf of any political party;

(c)   in connection with the registration of electors, the candidature of any person, the selection of any candidate or the holding of any ballot by the union in connection with any election to a political office;

(d)   on the maintenance of any holder of a political office;

(e)   on the holding of any conference or meeting by or on behalf of a political party or of any other meeting the main purpose of which is the transaction of business in connection with a political party;

(f)   on the production, publication or distribution of any literature, documents, film, sound recording or advertisement the main purpose of which is to persuade people to vote for a political party or candidate or to persuade them not to vote for a political party or candidate.'

By s 72(4) 'political office' connotes the office of MP, MEP, member of a local authority or any position within a political party. 'Service' in (b) would seem to cover the loan of staff. (e) covers the annual Labour Party Conference. Money spent on the Labour Party's headquarters was for a political purpose (*Richards v NUM* (1981)) (s 72(1)(b) expressly covers such expenditure: before 1984 it was for the CO to determine if such expenditure was for a political purpose). 'Maintenance' includes finance for research facilities: *ASTMS v Parkin* (1984). Campaigning at general election time against cutbacks in public services was political (*Paul v NALGO* (1987)).

14.10.3   Protected property

Where there is a political fund, the money in it cannot be used to satisfy a judgment against the union but it can be sequestered to pay a fine for contempt of court. In the jargon the fund is 'protected property'.

14.10.4   Voting

By s 73(1) a political resolution must be approved in a vote on a ballot of the members. Voting must be by marking a paper in a fully postal ballot, not by show of hands. All union members (except overseas ones) are entitled to vote on the continuance of a fund; overseas ones are entitled to vote where a resolution has expired. A simple majority is needed. A new resolution is needed every 10 years: s 73(3). The ballot must be held in accord with rules approved by the CO: s 76(1). TULR(C)A as amended by TURERA lays down detailed rules about the appointment of an independent scrutineer, the entitlement to vote, voting, counting by an independent person (who may be the scrutineer), and the scrutineer's report on the ballot. Perhaps the main provisions are s 77(3) and (4). By s 77(3):

> 'Every person who is entitled to vote in the ballot must - (a) be allowed to vote without interference from, or constraint imposed by, the union or any of its members, officials or employees, and (b) so far as is reasonably practicable, be enabled to do so without incurring any direct cost to himself.'

By s 77(4):

> '... so far as reasonably practicable, every person who is entitled to vote in the ballot must - (a) have a voting paper sent to him by post at his home address, and (b) be given a convenient opportunity to vote by post.'

Since 1988 a workplace ballot has not been possible. The vote must be fully postal. Those who may vote must not be just those who currently contribute. Only overseas members can be excluded from the vote.

A member of the TU may apply to the CO or the High Court (which deals with breaches of statute) when the union has not acted in accord with the rules for a political ballot approved by the CO. The time limit is one year from the day of the announcement of the result of the ballot (TULR(C)A ss 79-81). If the application is made to the Court, the Court may issue an 'enforcement order', instructing the union to hold the ballot properly to remedy the defect, or to desist from doing a specified act. The CO has no such power. There is an appeal from the CO to the EAT.

14.10.5 Remedy

A person who does not wish to contribute to the political fund is exempted: s 82(1)(b). The union must tell the members that they have a right to be exempted: s 84(2). A person cannot be refused admission to the union on the ground that she is unwilling to contribute to the political fund. By s 82(1)(c):

14.10.6 Non-contributors

> '... a member shall not by reason of being so exempt - (i) be excluded from any benefits of the union, or (ii) be placed under a disability or a disadvantage as compared with other members of the union (except in relation to the control or management of the political fund) ...'

The main case is *Birch v NUR* (1950). An exempted member complained that the union's national executive committee had stripped him of his office of branch chair because he did not pay the political levy. The judge held that his removal was unlawful. The CO ruled unlawful a provision that a non-contributing member paid five-thirteenths of one penny each week which was refunded in a lump sum every quarter (*McCarthy v APEX* (1979)). It is also unlawful for unions to charge higher subscriptions to members who do not pay the political fund than those who do. If the employers operate a check-off system for union dues, they cannot refuse to operate a check-off for those union members who do not pay the levy: s 86. Non-payment of the political fund is often called 'contracting out'. The present government has at times suggested that the law should be changed so that members have to 'contract in' to the fund but as yet this proposal has not been enacted. It might be argued, however, that the present law on balloting is unfair to those who wish to pay. Why should they be denied the opportunity of contributing to the levy by fellow members who do not wish to contribute? After all, non-contributors are protected against discrimination.

14.10.7 Lapse

Where the political resolution lapses because a ballot has not been held within 10 years or it has been defeated, the TU must stop collecting money for the fund. Any money collected after the lapse must be refunded. No money can be added to the fund (except interest on the sum). The union may transfer the whole or part of the political fund to another fund or it can freeze the fund in the hope that a later vote may revive it.

14.10.8 Comment

In 1984 the government introduced the provision about the ballot's having to be held every 10 years. It believed that the re-ballots would lead to fewer political funds than before, the effect being that TUs' financial support for the Labour Party would haemorrhage. In fact unions which had political funds successfully retained them in the mid-1980s and a few unions which did not have them ran successful ballots to establish them, the argument being that unions should be able to speak on political matters affecting their membership especially because the definition of 'political' was a wide one covering eg campaigns against government cutbacks. One contention was that trade unionists who vote for the Conservatives – and about one-third of them do – should not stifle the expression of views by their colleagues, and the link with the Labour Party was played down though there is nothing to prevent unions supporting the Conservatives or Liberal Democrats. The 'crunch' may come in the mid-1990s when the unions face the second ballot under the 1984 provisions. The restrictions on political funds do not apply to companies. It has seemed unfortunate to the present writer that he could not contract out of subsidising one political party when buying food, beer and new houses!

Trade Unions

Trade unions are organisations of workers the principal purpose of which is the regulation of employment relations:

Midland Cold Storage v Steer (1972).

The association need not be permanent and need not have industrial muscle.

Definition

Unions are quasi-corporate bodies able to make contracts, sue and be sued, and to be prosecuted. They cannot, however, sue for libel:

EEPTU v Times Newspapers (1980).

Legal status

Unions' rules and purposes are not in restraint of trade. It has been postulated that unions' rules may be struck down on the basis that they interfere with an individual's right to work.

Restraint of trade

Unions may be placed on the Certification Officer's list.

Listing

Unions free of employers' control and not liable to interference have various rights:

Squibb v CO (1979)

Blue Circle v CO (1977).

The Certification Officer investigates the union's history, membership, finance, facilities, role in collective bargaining and internal affairs.

The rights include being consulted on collective redundancies and on the transfer of undertakings and to receive information for collective bargaining purposes.

Independence

Employers' recognition of unions is not supported by statute:

NUGSAT v Albury Bros (1979).

Recognition

Recognised independent unions must be given information for collective bargaining purposes. Some matters are exempted:

R v CAC ex p BTP Tioxide (1981).

Collective bargaining information

Time off

Union officials must be given reasonable time off with pay for aspects of collective bargaining for which the union is recognised. Members have a right to time off without pay for union activities:

Adlington v British Bakeries (1989)

Luce v Bexley LBC (1990).

Political fund

Unions wishing to expend money on political objects must establish a separate fund in a fully postal ballot. Non-contributors must not be discriminated against.

Paul v NALGO (1987)

Birch v NUR (1950).

Political objects include the maintenance of MPs and campaigns against cuts in public services.

Voting must be fully postal and must be held every 10 years. There are detailed rules on balloting and counting.

Chapter 15

Trade Union Governance

This chapter considers freedom of association, the legal status of the rule-book and various rights of an applicant for membership and of a member against her trade union (TU) whether arising under contract, public law or statute. It concludes with discussion of elections for certain union positions with the linked members' rights such as to be a candidate. In relation to freedom of association the reader is also directed to action short of dismissal and dismissal on trade union grounds discussed in Chapter 11.

Various international treaties state that individuals have a right to form organisations such as trade unions. Examples are Article 20 of the Universal Declaration of Human Rights 1948 and Article 11 of the European Convention on Human Rights. The International Labour Organisation (ILO), an arm of the United Nations, has Conventions on this topic which states may ratify. The European Social Charter 1961 and the EC Social Charter 1989 both upheld the freedom of association. These treaties are not, however, binding on the UK until ratified and once ratified they can be denounced. The repeal of the Fair Wages Resolution and of the Truck Acts involved the denunciation of two Conventions of the ILO.

The ILO has found the UK to be in breach of its international obligations. Examples include the abolition of collective bargaining for teachers and the banning of unions at GCHQ. A majority of the European Court of Human Rights held in *Young, James and Webster v UK* (1981) that Article 11 of the Convention was broken when the employers dismissed employees in a closed-shop situation despite Article 11 stating only that employees had a freedom to associate, not to leave unions. It is arguable that the law on unjustifiable discipline is contrary to Article 11. Choice of moving workplace or rejoining a union is not (*Sibson v UK* (1993)).

The UK does not ban the formation of unions except that the police cannot join unions and workers at GCHQ would be in breach of their contracts if they did so. Members of the armed forces may join but they must not participate in union activities which conflict with their service duties. Section 137 (first introduced in 1990) of TULR(C)A prohibits employers' refusing to employ persons on the grounds of TU membership

15.1 Introduction

15.2 Association and dissociation

15.2.1 International standards

15.2.2 Membership and non-membership

or of non-membership. It was held by the EAT in *Harrison v Kent County Council* (1995) that a refusal to re-employ an applicant who had previously been a shop steward and had displayed anti-management attitudes breached s 137. It was a question for the IT whether a refusal to employ because of his union activities was a refusal to employ because he was a TU member. Mummery J said that:

'... a divorce of the *fact* of membership and the incidents of membership is illusory ... membership of a union means more than the bare fact that a person ... holds a union membership card. Participation in the activities of a union is one of the ways in which membership of a union is manifested ... '

The government equated the rights to membership and to non-membership. Previously these had been seen as totally different. Membership supported collective bargaining, which was considered a good thing. Non-membership undermined it; therefore, it was a bad thing. Employers can still refuse to employ union members who are classified as trouble-makers. The right in s 137 extends to cover a requirement that a person should donate money to a charity if she did not wish to subscribe to a union. Such donations were one way in which unions sought to get round the 'free rider' problem - persons who took advantage of benefits obtained by unions such as increased pay but did not pay union dues. The remedy is a complaint to an industrial tribunal (IT) within three months of the employers' refusal or if it was not reasonably practicable for the complaint to be presented within that period within a reasonable time of the end thereof. The burden of proof is on the applicant. If the complaint is well-founded, the IT makes a declaration and may make an award of compensation calculated as for the tort of breach of statutory duty with a maximum the same as that of the compensatory award for unfair dismissal. Compensation for injured feelings may be awarded. The IT may make:

'... a recommendation that the respondent take within a specified period action appearing to the tribunal to be practicable for the purpose of obviating or reducing the adverse effect on the complainant of any conduct to which the complaint relates.' (s 140(1)(b))

15.2.3   Joinder

If the individual or employers claim that the latter were induced to act by pressure which a TU exercised on them 'by calling, organising, procuring or financing a strike or other industrial action, or by threatening to do so' (s 142(1)), the IT must join the union to the action if requested before the hearing of the complaint and may join it if made after the start of the hearing but before its conclusion. The IT may order compensation to be paid wholly or partly by the union: s 142(2).

Complementary to s 137 are ss 144-5 of TULR(C)A. By s 144:

15.2.4   Goods and services

'a term or condition of a contract for the supply of goods or services is void in so far as it purports to require that the whole, or some part, of the work done for the purposes of the contract is done only by persons who are, or are not, members of trade unions or of a particular trade union.'

By s 145(1): ·

'... a person shall not refuse to deal with a supplier or prospective supplier of goods or services on union membership grounds.'

'Union membership grounds' means grounds where there is a requirement that persons working under the contract are or are not members of any TU or any particular TU. Section 145 gives rise to a right in persons with whom there is a refusal to deal and those who may be 'adversely affected' by breach of s 145: s 145(5). Violation is actionable as a breach of statutory duty and the defences to that tort are available to this action.

Section 137 marks the culmination of the government's attacks on one form of union security, the closed shop. The right applies to pre-entry closed shops (ie ones in which individuals for employment must be a member of a certain TU or TUs before the employers can consider them suitable for the jobs). There is now no legal support for pre- or post-entry shops, even if the employers do not wish to upset existing arrangements in order to support good industrial relations. Two points of interpretation of s 137 should be noted. It applies only to refusal on grounds of membership of a TU. If the member is turned down because she is an activist, she has no right. Membership without activity is not totally meaningful. (In *Discount Tobacco and Confectionery Ltd v Armitage* (1990) recourse to a TU official asking him to help determine her terms and conditions was a function of membership, not an activity. This case would seem to be incorrect as a result of *Associated Newspapers Ltd v Wilson* and *Associated British Ports v Palmer* (1995).) Similarly, it would seem that s 137 would not apply to refusals of employment on the grounds that the applicants had participated in industrial action. The second point is that s 137 has a tendency to upset settled industrial relations practices. If the employers wish to bargain collectively only with one or a small number of unions, their wish is undermined by persons joining other unions. It is uncertain whether the decisions of the Lords in the '*Associated*' cases will affect *Harrison v Kent CC*, above.

15.2.5   Pre-entry closed shop

15.3   Union rules

The union rule-book is both a constitution for the union and a contract between the trade union (TU) and the member. Traditionally parliament has not intervened but there are now several members' rights against unions which supersede contrary rules. Statutory remedies are coming to be of more importance than contractual rights. In one instance there is an implied term:

> 'In every contract of membership of a trade union ... a term conferring a right on the member, on giving reasonable notice and complying with any reasonable conditions, to terminate his membership of the union shall be implied' (s 69 of the Trade Union and Labour Relations (Consolidation) Act 1992 TULR(C)A).

What is reasonable is not defined.

15.3.1   Judicial intervention

Accordingly it is for the judges to determine how long reasonable notice is and which conditions are reasonable. Besides statutory changes judges have a powerful role to play in the control of union rule-books through the construction of the rules and the application of natural justice. It has been argued that the judiciary lean too far in favour of maverick individuals at the expense of union collectivism. Judicial intervention was justified by Lord Denning MR in *Breen v Amalgamated Engineering Union* (1971) on the ground that:

> '... the rules are in reality more than a contract. They are a legislative code ... This code should be subject to control by the courts just as much as a code laid down by parliament itself.'

After a consideration of the interpretation of rule-books this section looks at common law and statutory intervention. Common law terms remain important for statute may not cover the issue.

15.3.2   Construction

It is the dual legal role of the union rule-book which underlies the judges' approach to it. As a contract it must be construed as such. If there is, for example, no power to expel expressly stated, contractual rules on implied terms govern. As a code the rules are subject to administrative law such as the doctrines of *ultra vires* and natural justice. Cutting across the contractual and administrative law approaches is the knowledge that often rule-books are drafted without legal help. Taking a strict, contractual approach to interpretation may not be in tune with what the drafters believed they were writing. A cynic might say that the courts adopt whichever mode gives an anti-trade union result. The most authoritative case, *Heatons Transport (St Helens) Ltd v Transport and General Workers Union* (1972), went beyond a strict construction to see whether at common law the union was vicariously liable for the actions of its shop stewards. To decide that question the House investigated custom and practice when the contract ie the rule-book was silent. It is arguable that the courts take a broad approach to the rules when they are investigating constitutional matters (eg is the union vicariously liable?) and a narrow one where the matter involves individual members (eg has the union the power to suspend a member?).

Since membership of a TU gives rise to a contract, a member deprived of her rights under the contract may claim in the ordinary courts that her contract has been broken by the TU. Legal aid may be available. The normal remedies are available, damages or injunction or both. A declaration may be awarded. The courts have said that, absent a rule, there is no common law power in a TU to expel. Therefore, if a union wishes to expel a member, there must be a rule and the union must apply that rule including any procedure under it: see eg *Hiles v Amalgamated Society of Woodworkers* (1968). There are many cases dealing with whether unions had power under their rules to perform various functions. Going through all the cases would be piling Pelion on Ossa. A small sample of what may be called classic cases follows.

15.3.3   Contract

- *Hopkins v NUS* (1985)

  A levy on members to support the National Union of Mineworkers was not allowed by the rules and an injunction was granted. However, the expenditure of this levy was lawful because the union's objects clause permitted it to spend money on the improvement of conditions and the protection of all members of the union. Since coal was transportable in ships crewed by the National Union of Seamen it was arguable that financial support to the NUM was lawful.

- *Lee v Showmen's Guild of Great Britain* (1952)

  A member was fined by a union committee for engaging in unfair competition. The Court held that what he had done did not constitute such competition. That is, the Court held that it could intervene where there was no evidence to support the finding of unfair competition.

- *Esterman v NALGO* (1974)

  Templeman J ruled that a committee was wrong to hold that refusing to participate in a strike was '... conduct which, in the opinion of the branch committee, renders her unfit for membership'. He held that the courts could prevent unlawful discipline and not just intervene when the action had been taken. It should be noted that the court intervened despite the subjective phrasing ('in the opinion of ... ') of the clause. The basis of Templeman J's ruling was that no reasonable tribunal could have come to the conclusion that it did: to discipline members for not taking part in industrial action when only 41% had voted in favour.

These cases demonstrate the courts' power to control discipline and expulsion through interpretation of the rule-book. Not even subjectively phrased rules such as that in the last case escape review. Besides control in these ways the Courts' power to rule on implied terms give judges power to give effect to their policies. For example, in *MacLelland v NUJ* (1975) it was held that members had to be given reasonable notice of important meetings.

| 15.3.4 | Further examples |

The Courts have tended to intervene if the union has, in their view, misinterpreted the relevant rule. In *Kelly v NATSOPA* (1915) the Court held that a union was wrong to hold that taking a part-time job was 'conduct prejudicial to the union's interests'. In *MacLelland v NUJ* above, the Court held that a member had been improperly disciplined for failing to attend a union meeting. He had turned up and signed in but had not stayed for the whole duration. It was held that what he had done was enough to constitute attendance. Accordingly, the union did not by contract have the power to discipline him. The Courts have strongly upheld the principle that their jurisdiction must not be ousted by the rules of domestic tribunals on the one hand yet on the other they have shown leeway to rules which are couched in wide language such as one whereby a member may be expelled for engaging in conduct which in the view of the national executive committee is prejudicial to the interests of the union.

| 15.3.5 | Remedies |

Courts are restricted to damages and remedies which prohibit action in reliance on the rule but they cannot enforce the rules by ordering specific performance: *Taylor v NUM (Yorkshire Area)* (1984). The Court could not order the holding of a ballot required by the rules. There is no statutory limit on damages in contractual actions against unions.

| 15.3.6 | Exhaustion of internal remedies |

One particular instance of judicial control is whether a member must follow a union rule that internal remedies must be exhausted before she can go to the courts. In *White v Kuzych* (1951) the Privy Council held that internal remedies such as an appeals process had to be gone through first but judges in later cases have stated that such a rule cannot oust the jurisdiction of the court though a good reason must be given for non-exhaustion (eg *Leigh v NUR* (1970) and *Radford v NATSOPA* (1972)). This non-ouster is supported by s 63 of TULR(C)A.

Any union rule or judge-made rule calling for the exhaustion of internal remedies is void if a member or ex-member has applied to the TU for a determination of the matter and no determination has been made within six months of the submission. Section 63 overrides contrary union rules, but it is arguable that it does not overrule the law in cases such as *Leigh v NUR* ie before the six months have elapsed the non-ouster principle still applies. If the rule were phrased not merely that internal remedies must be exhausted but there was no appeal from union decisions a *fortiori* it would be void as contrary to public policy: *Lee v Showmen's Guild of Great Britain*, above, and s 63 of TULR(C)A.

It is not yet clear whether a Court can intervene to prohibit proceedings before a decision has been reached. Among cases upholding such jurisdiction are ones from the 1984-5 miners' strike. In *Taylor v NUM (Derbyshire Area)* (1984) the Court prevented the application of disciplinary rules on the grounds that, since the strike was not official because it had been called in breach of the rules, disciplining for not taking part was illegal. In *Clarke v Chadburn* (1985) disciplining was unlawful because the rule had not been validly adopted. More recently, however, the Court of Appeal stated in *Longley v NUJ* (1987) that in advance of a determination the Courts will be loath to intervene.

15.3.7   Intervention pre-decision

There has been a debate especially in recent years whether the company law rule in *Foss v Harbottle* (1843) applies to unions. By that rule a member of a company cannot, subject to exceptions, bring an action for redress of harm done to the company partly because the company alone is the 'proper plaintiff' to remedy harm to itself and partly because the Court will not restrain something which the company might ratify. One exception is that a company cannot ratify an *ultra vires* act. Since that act is unlawful, it cannot be made lawful by ratification. The latest discussion appears in *Taylor v NUM (Derbyshire Area) (No 3)* (1985). The judge, Vinelott J, said in relation to a claim that the area officers should refund the £1.7m they had spent on the miners' strike on the grounds that they had acted in breach of their fiduciary duties to the union in supporting an unlawful strike:

15.3.8   *Foss v Harbottle* (1843)

> '*Foss v Harbottle* applies to a union but does not bar the right of an individual to an action joining the union and its officers as defendants and claiming that a particular application by the union and its officers was *ultra vires* ... and requiring the officers to make good the loss to the union. Being *ultra vires* the misapplication cannot be ratified by any majority of the members.'

The astute reader may be asking herself why a company law concept is applied in Labour Law. After all parliament has stated not just that a TU is not a company but is not even to be treated as one: see s 10(1) and (2) of TULR(C)A. The position remains uncertain whether *Foss v Harbottle* applies and if so whether the exceptions apply. On the facts the judge held that the courts will not grant an injunction if it will not serve a useful purpose. Certainly *Foss v Harbottle* does not apply where the wrong is done not to the union/company but to the member in her capacity as a member. The wrong is so done when the union fines or expels her.

15.3.9   Natural justice

Besides contract the Courts intervene on the grounds of natural justice. These rules, *nemo judex in sua causa* and *audi alteram partem*, are the same as those found in public law courses: 'no one shall be plaintiff and judge' and 'hear the other side.' Natural justice is distinct from contract. Contract cannot be used to exclude natural justice: *Radford v NATSOPA* above. It should be recalled that natural justice is concerned with procedure, not with substance. The fact that the decision was unjust is irrelevant if the way in which it was reached was just.

15.3.10   Bias

The most famous case on bias is *Roebuck v NUM (Yorkshire Area) (No 2)* (1978). Mr Scargill, President of the union, sued a newspaper for libel on its behalf. The plaintiffs, who were union members, gave evidence for the paper. Mr Scargill claimed that one plaintiff had contradicted in court what he had told the union's solicitors out of court and the editor had divulged union correspondence to the paper's lawyers. The behaviour was in his opinion detrimental to the interests of the union. The area council, which was chaired by Mr Scargill, said that the conduct was detrimental. It referred the issue to the area executive council, which was also chaired by Mr Scargill. It recommended suspension of the members. The area council, again chaired by Mr Scargill, confirmed the decision. The Court said that Mr Scargill had acted as 'the complainant, the pleader, the prosecutor, the advocate and the chairman.' The proceedings were tainted with the appearance of bias and so were contrary to natural justice. It should be noted that, as perhaps occurred in this case, there need not be actual bias. It is sufficient if there is a semblance of bias, a real possibility of prejudice. It is obviously difficult to provide totally bias-free persons where a union official is accusing a member of breach of a rule and another official forms the tribunal, but the courts have taken a broad approach and not struck down decisions easily. There is authority for the proposition that it is not always the law that a person cannot sit at first instance and on an appeal in the same matter, at least where the union rules so permit.

A union member is entitled to receive notice of the misconduct alleged and to be given enough time to defend herself: eg *Stevenson v United Road Transport Union* (1977). No notice need be given if everyone involved knows the nature of the charge. She is still entitled to answer the allegations.

The Courts have said that the right to be heard does not extend to the right to be legally represented: *Enderby Football Club v Football Association* (1971) (not a TU case). It may be that an appeals system is not a requirement of natural justice, and there are conflicting cases whether a defect at first instance may be cured on appeal. The width of natural justice varies from case to case.

The contractual method of controlling unions' decisions can work only where there is a contract. If an applicant for membership is turned down there is no contract in existence. There are statutory rules relating to turning individuals away on sexual and racial grounds and as we shall see statutory rules on the right to membership of a union. At common law Lord Denning MR in the non-TU case of *Nagle v Feilden* (1966) said on interlocutory motion that individuals had a right to work. He applied his doctrine to unions in *Edwards v SOGAT* (1971), *obiter*, on the grounds that the closed shop interfered with the worker's right to work when the union refused to readmit him, and there may be life in his doctrine. If so, the Courts would have power to strike down union rules concocted out of spite or whimsy which interfered with this right. However, as stated in the previous chapter, the doctrine seems to have quietly died since his retirement.

Courts have said that they have jurisdiction to strike down rules which are illegal at common law. In *Drake v Morgan* (1978) it was said *obiter* that a rule providing for the repayment of fines of members convicted of illegal picketing was unlawful. Doing so is nowadays statutorily illegal: TULR(C)A, s 15.

It is unlikely nowadays that expulsion from a TU will lead to the loss of a job, whereas a dismissal by definition means that an employee no longer has a job. Yet union rules are more strictly controlled by judges than are sackings. The principles of natural justice do not apply to ordinary master and servant cases. A radical might say that the difference represents the judges' class bias. They favour capitalists, employers, at the expense of labour, unions. When Lord Denning spoke in favour of the individual against the big battalions, he was not speaking of an employee against her employers but of a member against her TU.

15.4 'Bridlington': the principles

Trade unions meeting at the Trades Union Congress at Bridlington, Yorkshire, agreed a set of principles regulating recruitment at the workplace. The principles are non-contractual. Principle 5, which was renumbered Principle 3 in 1993, states:

> 'no union shall commence organising activities at any establishment or undertaking in respect of any grade of workers in which another union has a majority of the workers employed and negotiate terms and conditions, unless by arrangement with that union.'

Principle 2 prohibits unions from accepting applicants who are or recently have been members of a union affiliated to the TUC without making enquiries of that union. The notes to the Principles are of equal standing with the Principles. Principle 1 note (e), which is now part of the new Principle 3, states that no union shall enter into a sole negotiating agreement or any arrangement whereby other unions would lose their rights of recognition or to negotiate unless those unions concur. In the event of a dispute the TUC's Disputes Committee has jurisdiction and TUC unions must obey its rulings. For example, the Committee may order a union to surrender its newly recruited members in a workplace to a union which has already organised part of the workplace. In 1956 the TUC recommended to its affiliates that they should adopt a model rule in their rule-book to the effect that national executive committees could terminate an employee's membership on giving six weeks' notice where termination was to enforce a ruling of the Disputes Committee. A member's challenge to the model rule on the grounds that it infringed natural justice and public policy failed in *Cheall v APEX* (1984). Terminations to give effect to the rule were adjudged lawful provided that the expulsion fell within the Committee's jurisdiction and was authorised by the rule-book. (It is interesting to note that the member was not given a hearing, yet the Lords held that the rules of natural justice were not contravened: see the previous section.) The European Commission on Human Rights held that there was no contravention of Article 11 of the European Convention on Human Rights, freedom to associate, at least where there was no closed shop. The final sanction for refusing to apply to the Bridlington principles is expulsion from the TUC. The Electrical Electronic Telecommunication and Plumbing Union (EEPTU) was expelled in 1988 for failing to implement two awards by the Disputes Committee. There was acrimony when it was readmitted to the TUC in September 1993.

The Trade Union Reform and Employment Rights Act 1993, s 14, substitutes new ss 174–177 into the Trade Union and Labour Relations (Consolidation) Act 1992. The heading is 'right to membership of trade union'. The old ss 174–177 provided members with a right not to be unreasonably excluded or expelled from a TU, a right granted originally in the Employment Act 1980, ss 4–5. The new sections widen that right, which applied only when there was a closed shop. The old ss 174–17 are repealed. So the right to membership of a TU replaces the right not to be unreasonably excluded or expelled from a TU. The right does not replace the common law right to sue for breach of contract. One might have thought that the 1993 Act was needed less now because of the swift decline of the closed shop in the 1980s.

By s 174(1) an applicant or member must not be excluded or expelled from a TU except as detailed below. Exclusion includes the situation where:

'... an individual's application for membership of a trade union is neither granted nor rejected before the end of the period within which it might reasonably have been expected to be granted.' (s 177(2)(a))

Expulsion includes where:

'... an individual ... under the rules of a trade union ceases to be a member of the union on the happening of an event specified in the rules.' (s 177(2)(b))

The latter provision will take effect if there is a rule that membership lapses if fees have not been paid for a certain time. Should this occur, there is a right against the TU unless one of the defences (or perhaps better put exceptions) apply. However, expulsion does not cover the situation where the member resigns as a protest against policy. In other words, there is no doctrine of constructive expulsion.

The exceptions are found in s 174(2):

'The exclusion or expulsion of an individual from a trade union is permitted by this section if (and only if) –

(a) he does not satisfy, or no longer satisfies, an enforceable membership requirement contained in the rules of the union;

(b) he does not qualify, or no longer qualifies, for membership of the union by reason of the union operating only in a particular part or particular parts of Great Britain;

(c) in the case of a union whose purpose is the regulation of relations between its members and one particular employer or a number of

15.4.1   Right to membership

15.4.2   Definition

15.4.3   Exceptions

particular employers who are associated, he is not, or is no longer, employed by that employer or one of those employers; or

(d)   the exclusion or expulsion is entirely attributable to his conduct.'

(b) covers the National Union of Mineworkers' areas, each of which is a separate union. (c) permits single employer unions. Since it is not restricted to independent TUs 'house' unions can exclude or expel those protesting against the 'sweetheart' relationship without infringing this right.

| 15.4.4 | 'Enforceable' requirement | By s 174(3) a requirement is 'enforceable' if it 'restricts membership solely by reference to one or more of the following criteria: |

'(a)   employment in a specified trade, industry or profession;

(b)   occupational description (including grade, level or category of appointment); and

(c)   possession of specified trade, industrial or professional qualifications or work experience.'

There is not much room for the application of the Bridlington principles. Accordingly the statute gives an impetus to predatory unions. Inter-union disputes may increase with a concomitant threat to industrial relations. Section 174(3) does, however, safeguard craft unions.

| 15.4.5 | 'Conduct' | Conduct is negatively part-defined in s 174(4) to exclude: |

'... his being or ceasing to be, or having been or ceased to be -

(i)   a member of another trade union;

(ii)   employed by a particular employer or at a particular place; or

(iii   a member of a political party.'

It further excludes conduct covered by the right not to be unjustifiably disciplined by a TU (s 65 of TULR(C)A), on which see the next section. Nevertheless, this subsection does permit a union to refuse to admit to membership a person who is in arrears of subscription with another union.

| 15.4.6 | Remedy | The remedy is a little complex. The complainant makes a claim to an industrial tribunal within six months of the exclusion or expulsion, or if it was not reasonably practicable to bring the complaint within that period within a reasonable further time. If the complaint is well-founded, the IT makes a declaration. The complainant may now apply for compensation either to the IT if the complainant has been admitted or re-admitted to |

the TU; otherwise the claim is to the Employment Appeal Tribunal ie in this instance the EAT has original jurisdiction. This claim is made not before four weeks and not after six months from the date of the declaration. Compensation is awarded on the 'just and equitable' basis with reduction for contributory fault. (Fault has included applying for a job with employers whom he knew had a closed shop agreement: 15% was deducted.) The maximum compensation is 30 times the current limit on a week's pay for the purpose of calculating the basic award in unfair dismissal (£205) plus the maximum compensatory award (£11,000) ie £17,150 currently. Where the claim is determined in the EAT there is a minimum award of £5,000. This minimum is not reduced by any contributory fault. Appeals lie on points of law from the IT to the EAT. (Under the old right there was no minimum where the individual was admitted or re-admitted but there was where she was not (£2,700), and there was an appeal on a point of fact. The old law also had a maximum of £27,810 where she was not admitted or re-admitted.)

Depending on one's viewpoint the new right may be seen as an extension of the policy of statutory regulation on unions in an effort to destroy them through undermining their autonomy or as safeguarding individuals when they are oppressed by collective bodies. Unions argue that as voluntary bodies they should be able to control who can become members. The new law is wider than common law under which a union could exclude a person for any reason and could specify any qualifications for membership, provided that the rule was not arbitrary: on the last point see *Nagle v Feilden*, above para 15.3.13. Section 14 is akin to the widening of the law against unjustifiable discipline created in s 3 of the Employment Act 1988 now found in s 65 of TULR(C)A and expanded by s 16 of TURERA. The effect of the new ss 174–7 would appear to be the destabilisation of management-union agreements. Employers will have to deal with more unions, and some unions may be subject to undermining; perhaps breakaway unions will be encouraged. One side-effect may be that firms which have entered into single-union deals may find their agreements upset. A few years ago one might have commented that the destruction of single-union deals was not in accord with government policy which sought during Labour administrations to diminish inter-union disputes and during the early Conservative era to reduce complexity in industrial relations by encouraging single-union deals in the hope that Japanese and US

15.4.7   Comment

companies would come to greenfield sites but present policy is to destroy collective bargaining and this right is another brick in the wall. It would be amusing if the government policy backfired as it did with regard to the political fund and unions became less complacent with recruiting new members than previously. The Rules were amended in November 1993 to comply with the legislation. The model rule mentioned in 15.4 is no longer efficacious. The sole reasons for exclusion or expulsion are those stated in s 174, which is quoted in 15.4.3.

15.4.8   Overlap

Encouraging or advising a union not to accept an applicant may amount to unjustifiable discipline, which is discussed next.

15.5   Unjustifiable discipline

Section 3 of the Employment Act 1988 created a right not to be unjustifiably disciplined. This right is now found in ss 64-65 of TULR(C)A as expanded by s 16 of TURERA. This right is in addition to any contractual action. The two main provisions in the extended s 65(2), which defines the types of conduct in relation to which an employee is unjustifiably disciplined, are s 65(2)(a):

'... failing to participate in or support a strike or other industrial action (whether by members of the union or by others), or indicating opposition to or a lack of support for such action';

and the new s 65(2)(g):

'... resigning or proposing to resign from the union or from another union, becoming or proposing to become a member of another union, refusing to become a member of another union, or being a member of another union.'

(a) applies even though the majority of members have voted in favour of the action. Unions have criticised strongly this provision as an attempt to undermine the power of collective action. (g) can be seen as another step towards the undermining of the closed shop whereby employees had to be members of the union before performing a job. The definition of unjustifiability in s 65(2) is wide, but it is exhaustive and does not cover all kinds of conduct a union might adopt in relation to a member.

The Committee of Experts of the International Labour Organisation felt that the precursor of s 64 contravened Convention no 87 on Freedom of Association and Protection of the Right to Organise (1949). However, the government in 1993 widened the scope of s 65 and has not responded to criticism from the Committee.

15.5.1   'Disciplined'

By s 64(2) being 'disciplined' by a TU means that a determination has been made or purportedly made under the union's rules or by an official of the union, or by a number of persons including an official that:

'(a)   he should be expelled from the union or a branch or section of the union;

(b)   he should pay a sum to the union, to a branch or section of the union or to any other person;

(c)   sums tendered by him in respect of an obligation to pay subscriptions or other sums to the union, or to a branch or section of the union, should be treated as unpaid or paid for a different purpose;

(d)   he should be deprived to any extent of, or access to any benefits, services or facilities which would otherwise be provided or made available to him by virtue of his membership of the union, or a branch or section of the union;

(e)   another trade union, or a branch or section of it, should be encouraged or advised not to accept him as a member; or

(f)   he should be subjected to some other detriment ...'

An example of (d) is suspension from the union.

'Detriment' is undefined. It might be interpreted as it is in the discrimination field as 'putting under a disadvantage'. A recommendation that a member be disciplined is not a determination: *TGWU v Webber* (1991). Specifying that a person was on a strike-breaker in a circular is a detriment, at least when the union intends to cause embarrassment.

Two defences are given in s 65. If the individual asserts that the union, an official or a trustee of it is breaking or proposes to break a requirement imposed by the rules, any other agreement or by statute and the assertion is false and known by the individual to be false, discipline is not unjustified: s 65(6). The second exception occurs when the union would have penalised the member irrespective of her conduct which falls within s 65(2) and the union acted solely on the reason falling outside s 65(2).

15.5.2   Defences

The remedy for breach of the right is an application to an industrial tribunal: s 66(1). The claim must be presented within three months of the determination unless the IT finds that it was not reasonably practicable for the claim to be brought within that period or that the delay was attributable to an appeal against the determination, in which cases the individual has such further period as the IT considers reasonable: s 66(2). Whether the applicant was appealing depends on the substance of the facts, not on the form. If the claim is well-

15.5.3   Remedy

founded the IT so declares: s 66(3). If a claim is successful, the member cannot also succeed in a claim under the new s 174 of TULR(C)A, the right to be or not to be a union member (discussed in the previous section): s 66(4) of that Act as substituted by para 50 of Schedule 8 to TURERA 1993; however, common law remedies are unaffected.

15.5.4   Compensation

If the IT declares that the complaint was well-founded, the applicant may ask for compensation: s 67(1). Any fine is repayable. Application is made to the EAT if:

'(a)   the determination infringing the applicant's right not to be unjustifiably disciplined has not been revoked; or

(b)   the union has failed to take all the steps necessary for securing the reversal of anything done for the purpose of giving effect to the determination ...'
(s 67(2)).

Otherwise the claim is to the IT. The claim is made between four weeks and six months after the declaration: s 67(3). The four week period gives the TU a chance to change its decision. Compensation is awarded on the 'just and equitable' basis: s 67(5). The union must put the member back into the position she was in before the discipline even though she could herself have restored the position (*NALGO v Courtney-Dunn* (1991)). The applicant must mitigate her loss: s 67(6). The sum must be reduced if the member caused or contributed to her disciplining: s 67(7). Nowadays after the calculation has been made, s 67(8) operates to fix a minimum and a maximum. The minimum in a case heard originally by the EAT under s 67 is the same as that found in the revised s 176 of TULR(C)A, now £5,000. There is no minimum in an IT case. The maximum is the aggregate of 30 times the maximum 'week's pay' (£205) and the maximum compensatory award (£11,000) ie £17,150. In *Bradley v NALGO* (1991) the EAT awarded the then minimum. The remedy was compensatory, not punitive. The complainants, who had been expelled for not participating in a strike, did not have their job prospects diminished because of their expulsion. The protection for non-strikers against their union should be compared with the lack of protection for strikers against their employers.

15.5.5   Sex and race

Unions may not exclude discipline or expel members on sexual or racial grounds: Sex Discrimination Act 1975, s 12; Race Relations Act 1976, s 11. Unions may, however, reserve seats for women when to do so would preserve an irreducible minimum of women to serve on the union's executive.

Parliament has imposed the requirement that votes be held for the posts of various union officials including members of the national executive, except those who merely provide factual or legal information.

By s 46 of TULR(C)A, first enacted in 1984, elections committee must be held for various union posts, namely, the president, general secretary, member of the (principal) executive (committee) and any post by virtue of which a person is a member of the executive. Since 1988 it has not mattered whether the executive committee member had a vote and since that date ballots must be fully postal. It is interesting to note that the worst instance of corruption, the Electrical Trades Union in the late 1950s and early 1960s involved postal voting.

> 'Member of the executive means a person who may attend and speak at some or all of the meetings of the executive, otherwise than for the purpose of providing the committee with factual information or with technical or professional advice ...' (s 46(3))

An example might be a solicitor. Elections need not be held for the posts of president or general secretary if she is not a voting member of the executive, or an employee of the TU holds the position under the rules for under 13 months, *and* has not within the 12 months preceding the engagement held either position. Re-elections must take place within five years. The Act overrides contrary union rules. There are exceptions for newly formed unions (s 57) and those within five years of retirement (s 58). The principal executive committee, which the 1992 Act renamed the 'executive', is the one which, under whichever name, is the body which runs the TU on a day-to-day basis (s 119). Accordingly, a committee which deals with conditions of employment is not such a body: *Paul v NALGO* (1987), a decision of the Certification Officer. Generally speaking, unions accept the legitimacy of elections for the national executive.

By s 47(1), 'no member of the trade union shall be unreasonably excluded from standing as a candidate'. Exclusion is not unreasonable if the union excludes all persons of a class to which the individual belongs (s 47(3)), the usual example being Communists. The Certification Officer upheld a rule that candidates could not stand for office when they could not complete the term of office before retirement. 'No candidate shall be required, directly or indirectly, to be a member of a political party' (s 47(2)). The union must not discriminate on the grounds of sex or race, but it may reserve posts on elected committees for members of one gender (Sex Discrimination Act 1975, s 49).

15.6   Ballots

15.6.1   Principal executive

15.6.2   Candidature

| 15.6.3 | Election addresses and scrutineers | There are various stringent requirements in relation to addresses (s 48) and the independent scrutineer of the election (s 49 as extended by TURERA). For example the scrutineer's name must be notified to the voters. |

15.6.4 Constituencies

Section 50 governs the entitlement to vote. Unions may exclude (all) members who are out of work, (all) in arrears of dues, or (all) apprentices, trainees, students or new members: s 50(2). Entitlement to vote may be restricted by reference to:

'(a) a class determined by reference to a trade or occupation;

(b) a class determined by reference to a geographical area; or

(c) a class which is by virtue of the rules of the union treated as a separate section ...' (s 50(3))

Overseas members may be excluded.

15.6.5 Voting and counting

Voting is by marking a ballot paper: s 51(1). Therefore, other forms such as by show of hands are unlawful. Indirect voting eg at a delegate conference is outlawed. The paper is sent and returned by post 'so far as is reasonably practicable': s 51(4). In the jargon voting is 'fully postal' – the paper is sent out and returned by post. This law was enacted in 1988: previously a workplace ballot was lawful. By s 51(3):

'... every person who is entitled to vote at an election must –

(a) be allowed to vote without interference from ... the union or any of its members, officials or employees; and

(b) so far as is reasonably practicable, be enabled to do so without incurring any direct cost to himself.'

The union may state that candidates are on an official 'slate': *Paul v NALGO* (1987). Counting must be done fairly and accurately, though an inaccuracy is disregarded 'if it is accidental and on a scale which could not affect the result of the election': s 51(5). (Unions are under a duty to keep accurate lists of members: now s 24 of TULR(C)A.) The outcome of the election may be determined by a 'first-past-the-post' system or by the single transferable vote method. There are detailed provisions in relation to the scrutineer's report: s 52 as broadened by TURERA, ss 1–2. Counting must be done by independent persons: s 51A as inserted by s 2 of TURERA.

15.6.6 Remedy

A member or a candidate may apply to the Certification Officer (CO) or the High Court for a declaration that her rights have been infringed. The CROTUM may aid the Court proceedings. By s 56(4):

'... where the court makes a declaration it shall also, unless it considers that to do so would be inappropriate, make an enforcement order; that is, an order imposing on the union one or more of the following requirements –

(a)   to secure the holding of an election in accordance with the order;

(b)   to take such other steps to remedy the declared failure as may be specified in the order;

(c)   to abstain from such acts as may be so specified.'

Breach of an enforcement order is contempt of court punishable by an unlimited fine or imprisonment or both. If the application is to the CO, he is limited to making a declaration. If the complaint fails before the CO, the member may still apply to the Court, but if the union fails, it has no such right. Even if the CO has not determined the complaint, the aggrieved individual may bring proceedings in court (*Lenehan v UCATT* (1991) (Hoffmann J)). Complaints to the CO have been rare. There were no decisions by him in 1992.

The statutory rules on ballots are additional to union rules. If the union rule-book is not followed there is a breach of the contract of membership eg in *Taylor v NUM (Yorkshire Area),* above, the question was whether or not the failure to ballot members on the 1984-5 strike was a breach of the rules.

15.6.7   Additional to common law

There used to be provisions dating from 1980 permitting the Secretary of State for Employment to provide funds for TU ballots (s 115 of TULR(C)A) and giving independent TUs the right to use employers' premises for secret ballots (s 116) but these were abolished by s 7 of TURERA. No funds are available after 31 March 1996. Between now and then funding is reduced by one quarter per year. Section 116 was repealed as otiose. Statutory ballots now must be fully postal. There is nothing to prevent unions and employers reaching arrangements with regard to facilities for non-statutory ballots such as those for elections to the post of shop steward. The TUC was originally very much against the provision of State funds for balloting in union elections, before industrial action and before continuing political funds, seeing it as an encroachment on union autonomy, a 'sweetener' for the bitter pill of government regulation. The position changed; since unions had to hold elections, money for them had to come from somewhere. The squeeze on union finances caused by a reduction in membership in the 1980s led to a shift towards acceptance of State funds. The withdrawal of funds for stationery, printing and postage will hit some unions hard. State funding was seen by the government as part of the policy

15.6.8   Funds and premises

of 'giving unions back to their members' ie getting rid of unrepresentative officials. The statutory stipulation that ballots must be held but funding will not be provided does not look evenhanded.

Trade Union Governance

Refusal to employ on the grounds of TU membership or non-membership is unlawful. TUs may be joined and have to pay compensation:

Young, James & Webster v UK (1981).

Association and dissociation

Union decisions and rules are controlled through contract law and natural justice principles. There is discussion whether the rules may be unenforceable when conflicting with 'the right to work', whether they may be struck down for illegality, and whether *Foss v Harbottle* applies:

Hopkins v NUS (1985)

Lee v Showmen's Guild (1952)

Leigh v NUR (1970)

Taylor v NUM (Derbyshire Area) (no 3) (1985)

Roebuck v NUM (Yorkshire Area) (1978)

Stevenson v URTU (1977)

Edwards v SOGAT (1971).

Union rules

TUC-affiliated unions strive to avoid poaching; however, there is a right to membership of trade unions which undermines the Bridlington principles. Statute prohibits the exclusion and expulsion from unions, subject to exceptions. The exceptions include an enforceable membership requirement such as that the union recruits only in one industry and the worker does not work in it.

'Bridlington'

There is a statutory right not to be unjustifiably disciplined by a TU. This includes a fine for not participating in strikes despite a majority in favour.

TGWU v Webber (1991)

Bradley v NALGO (1991).

Unjustifiable discipline

Fully postal ballots must be held for elections to the union's principal executive committee. Members have a right to stand as candidates. There are technical rules relating to the holding

Ballots

of ballots. State funding for ballots is being phased out, and independent unions are no longer entitled to use employers' premises for ballots. The repeal of the latter legislation is consistent with the move towards fully postal voting.

Chapter 16

Industrial Action

This chapter considers the law on collective agreements between unions and management, the effect of industrial action such as strikes on individual contracts of employment, unions' liability· in respect of tort (including remedies against them and their representatives), and picketing. Use of the law has increased over the last decade and the government has increased the range of possible plaintiffs.

16.1 Coverage

The law relating to collective agreements has changed substantially over the past 25 years. Originally they were not contracts for the reason that they were not intended to be legally binding. The Industrial Relations Act 1971 created a presumption that they were legally binding but that presumption was rebutted by a clause to the effect that the agreement was not contractual, a TINA LEA clause ('this is not a legally enforceable agreement'). It is thought that there was only one agreement 1971–1974 which was legally enforceable. After 1974 collective bargains reverted to their common law status (now TULR(C)A 1992, s 179). There have been calls over the past decade for collective agreements to be legally enforceable (eg the Green Paper, *Industrial Relations in the 1990s*, 1991, Cm 1604, which noted that most of the rest of the EC had legally enforceable agreements) but as yet no change has been made. Unions continue to bear an antipathy towards law and lawyers, and that antipathy would be worsened by employers' suing them for breach of contract. Nowadays unions may wish to see legal enforceability, which would provide a brake on the movement towards derecognition and individual contracts.

16.2 Collective agreements

For a large part of the period 1909–1979 there were various 'props' or auxiliary mechanisms supporting collective bargaining. Wages councils provided minimum wages in various industries; there was a procedure whereby agreements could be 'extended' across industries. The government from 1979 withdrew these props, the final one, Wages Councils, being abolished in 1993. There remains support for ending industrial action eg ACAS may be involved: see Chapter 2. Government policy is 'to move pay determination away from centralised collective bargaining and make it more responsive to local needs' (White Paper, *People, Jobs and Opportunities*, Cm 1810, 1992, para 4.4). Fewer than half the workforce is now

16.2.1 Auxiliary support

covered by collective agreements, a decline from the three-quarters in 1980.

| 16.2.2 | Individual contract |

Despite the agreements between unions and management not being legally enforceable, provided that the terms are appropriate they may be incorporated into individual contracts of employment: see Chapter 4. As there stated there is a special way for embodying 'no strike' clauses.

| 16.2.3 | Breach |

Disputes over changes to collective agreements may lead to industrial action, which can thus be seen as a normal part of industrial relations. Since collective agreements are not legally enforceable, judicial remedies are not available for breach. Leaving aside the coal industry there has been a general decline in the number of strikes over the last twenty years.

16.3 Effect on employment contract

Industrial action will almost certainly breach individual contracts of employment despite both parties not contemplating or desiring that outcome.

| 16.3.1 | Breach |

A contract of employment has been described as a wage-work bargain. The employee agrees to work in return for a wage. In contractual terms there is an implied term that the employee will be ready and willing to work. This term is a condition, breach of which provides the employers with the election to terminate the contract (ie dismiss) or to treat it as continuing; in either option the employers may claim damages in the ordinary courts. In practice employers rarely sue employees who are likely to be 'men of straw' and legal action is likely to exacerbate industrial relations. An exceptional case is *NCB v Galley* (1959), discussed in Chapter 4. Dismissal may not be an option if the employee is skilled. It cannot be said that law and practice are consistent. The problem lies in the law's deeming the contract to have terminated when the strike was merely a 'blip' in a long-term relationship. This lack of fit is made worse by the law that any type of industrial action, a strike, a go-slow, or work-to-rule is almost certainly a breach of contract. Even when the employees keep strictly to the works rules, the Court of Appeal held that they had broken the implied duty to co-operate with their employers in the running of the business: *Secretary of State for Employment v ASLEF (No 2)* (1972). Not every worker realises that she has no legal redress if she is dismissed while on strike. This rule applies even though the industrial action was provoked by the employers. The courts have said that there is no breach of contract where the employees give notice that they are terminating employment, but the ending of the relationship is not what they want: they want improved terms, not no job.

Lord Denning MR suggested in *Morgan v Fry* (1968) that giving notice merely suspended the contract for the duration of the action but his idea was rejected in *Simmons v Hoover Ltd* (1977) as being inconsistent with employment protection law, which is predicated on there being a repudiation of the contract. Therefore, action remains a breach of contract. All industrial action can be seen as a breach of the implied duty of co-operation. This duty is a fundamental one. Therefore, action is repudiatory of the contract of employment. A strike notice is thus notice of a breach of contract and not, as Davies LJ suggested in *Morgan v Fry*, a notice of termination and an offer to work on different terms and conditions. It is hard to agree with persons who say there is a right to strike in the UK. And the contractual rules apply even if it is the employers who provoked the dispute. If, however, employees resigned lawfully to put pressure on employers, there is no breach of contract (*Boxfoldia Ltd v NGA 1982* (1988)). Giving notice of industrial action, however, does not prevent a breach from occurring.

Three effects of industrial action on the contract should be noted. First, a dismissal for taking part in a strike is misconduct and accordingly the employee cannot claim a redundancy payment: see *Simmons v Hoover Ltd*, discussed in Chapter 9. A protect against redundancy leads to the loss of redundancy payments! Secondly, unless there is selective re-engagement in an official strike dismissal is fair for unfair dismissal purposes: see Chapter 11. Even if those who participate in industrial action are immune from liability (see below), they will still be liable for breach of contract. Employees can therefore be lawfully dismissed for taking part in a lawful strike. Thirdly, as was seen in 4.9.11, employers can deduct or stop pay for industrial action.	16.3.2 Other effects
No order for specific performance of a contract of employment may be made and no injunction restraining a breach of or threatened breach of such a contract may be granted where the effect in either case would be to oblige the employee to do work or attend at any place for the purpose of doing work: s 236 of TULR(C)A.	16.3.3 No specific performance
There are various restrictions on strikes. Most apply only to specific categories of workers eg police. There is a statutory tort of inducing a prison officer to withdraw services or commit a breach of discipline found in s 127 of the Criminal Justice and Public Order Act 1994. Two apply more broadly. By the Emergency Powers Act 1920 as amended in 1964 the	**16.4 Restricted strikes**

government may proclaim a state of emergency lasting for a month when

'... events of such a nature and on so extensive a scale as to be calculated, by interfering with the supply and distribution of food, water, fuel or light, or with the means of locomotion, to deprive the community or any substantial proportion of the community of the essentials of life... '

have happened or are immediately threatened. The government may make regulations under the Act as it most famously did in the three-day week of the early 1970s. The regulations must not make it a crime to take part in a strike or to persuade others peacefully to join in.

Section 240(1) of TULR(C)A states:

'A person commits an offence who wilfully and maliciously breaks a contract of service or hiring, knowing or having reasonable cause to believe that the probable consequences of his so doing, either alone or in combination with others, will be –

(a)   to endanger human life or cause serious bodily injury; or

(b)   to expose valuable property, whether real or personal, to destruction or serious injury.'

Malice is irrelevant. The offence is triable only summarily with a maximum imprisonment of three months or a fine up to level 2 on the standard scale (presently £100) or both. There seems never to have been a prosecution under s 240 or its predecessors. No doubt it could cover strikes by doctors and nurses. The most obvious candidates for inclusion are firefighters.

One outcome of the Industrial Relations Act 1971 was a decision not to imprison individual TU members or organisers. In prison they could be presented as martyrs and gain public support. The present government has throughout sought not to imprison trade unionists for this very reason. Using s 240 would destroy its policy. As far as is known no prosecution has ever been brought under this section, even though it has existed since 1875.

16.4.1   Post Office Act

An example of the criminalisation of a strike in a specific industry is s 58 of the Post Office Act 1953, which makes it an offence wilfully to delay or procure the delay of a postal packet. Individuals do not have *locus standi* to ask for an injunction to restrain industrial action which gives rise to such a crime. The Attorney-General in his discretion may bring a relator action. In *Gouriet v UPOW* (1978) the Attorney-General refused to seek an injunction to stop the defendants inducing their members to boycott post to South Africa. The Lords held that no injunction could be sought to stop breaches of the criminal law by a member of the public in the absence of special damage or the infringement of her private rights.

It should also be noted that there may be offences during sit-ins. Besides criminal damage and other 'normal' crimes, criminal law penalises several forms of trespass: see Pt II of the Criminal Law Act 1977. Conspiracies to commit these crimes are ones contrary to s 1 of the same Act.

16.4.2   Sit-ins

Students often find difficulty in tackling problems involving industrial action. The law looks unmanageable. Certainly it is complex and it depends on the interrelationship between common law and statute. The way to deal with the law is to do what the courts do and adopt a sequential view:

16.5   Liability for action

- do the employers have a common law cause of action?

- if so, does statute give immunity from tort?

- if so, is that immunity removed by statute?

    These are also rules on pre-strike ballots. Remedies must be considered after establishing liability. Trade unions are nowadays liable to the same extent as individuals subject to a maximum limit on damages.

This economic tort is the principal one committed in industrial disputes. The classic definition is that of Jenkins LJ in *D C Thomson & Co Ltd v Deakin* (1952): the employers must show

16.5.1   Inducing breach

> '... first, that the person charged with actionable interference knew of the existence of the contract and intended to procure its breach; secondly, that the person so charged did definitely and unequivocally persuade, induce or procure the employees to breach their contracts of employment with the intent mentioned; thirdly that the employees so persuaded, induced or procured did in fact break their contracts of employment; and fourthly, that the breach of the contract forming the alleged subject of interference ensued as a necessary consequence of the breach of the employees concerned of their contracts of employment.'

The Lords approved this statement in *Merkur Island Shipping Corp v Laughton* (1983).

16.5.2   Direct form

The simplest form of this tort may be represented thus:

(E = employee, Rs = employers, TU = trade union or organiser or other person). Between E and Rs there is a contract of employment.

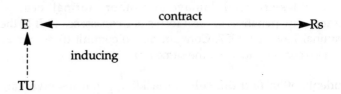

The TU induces the employee to break her contract with the employers. This form of the tort is sometimes known as 'direct inducement'.

16.5.3   Indirect form

A second form, indirect inducement, arises where TU puts pressure on suppliers to or distributors of the Rs with whom TU is in dispute. The TU is seeking to boycott or 'black' Rs. This activity is sometimes known as 'secondary action'. Primary action occurs when employees put pressure on their own employers.

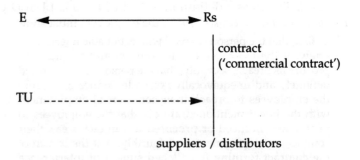

TU is inducing a breach of contract between Rs and suppliers/distributors to put pressure on Rs to improve E's terms and conditions. All the suppliers and distributors may bring actions. The procuring of the breach of contract constitutes the unlawful means necessary for the indirect form of the tort.

16.5.4   Example

In the second form of the tort there must be unlawful means. An illustration of indirect inducement is *Torquay Hotel Co Ltd v*

Cousins (1969). TU brought pressure on suppliers (of oil) to stop deliveries to Rs with whom TU was in dispute. The pressure was that TU would call out its members at suppliers if suppliers did not stop deliveries ie members at suppliers would breach their contracts of employment if suppliers did not breach their commercial contract with Rs. This demand constituted unlawful means for the purposes of this tort. The majority were of the opinion that there was a breach induced by the defendant. A *force majeure* clause in the contract between the suppliers and the employers simply excused the suppliers from liability for breach of contract: it did not mean that there was no breach. In the indirect form it is accepted that interference is sufficient. It should be noted that in the tort of interference with contract of business unlawful means must be proved for both the direct and the indirect forms even though the tort seems to have developed in response to the narrowness of the present tort where breach has to be demonstrated.) Unlawful means include the commission of a tort such as trespass, nuisance, or inducing breach of statutory duty.

Jenkins LJ said that the defendants must intend to procure breach. A judge at Sheffield County Court (that is, the judgment is not binding) held, however, in *Falconer v ASLEF* (1986) that it sufficed that the plaintiff was a member of a foreseeably affected class, a passenger on British Rail with whom the defendants were in dispute. (He won damages for two nights accommodation in London.) Intent was unnecessary. If, however, the defendants do not realise that there is a possibility of their action inducing the breach, this tort is not committed.	16.5.5 Constituents: intent
Jenkins LJ said in *Thomson v Deakin* that defendants would be liable only if they knew of the contract's terms. This requirement has been watered down. It suffices that they know of the contract; they no longer need to know of the terms. Wilful blindness as to terms suffices. There is nothing to stop well-advised employers sending details of contracts to TU and officials. In *Merkur Island* above, the defendants knew the terms of the contract, a time charter, because they had a copy of it. The House of Lords, however, agreed with the Court of Appeal that the defendants must be deemed to have been aware of the contract. The case involved interference with business (see 16.5.19) but the torts are the same on this point.	16.5.6 Knowledge
The dispute must lead to a breach of contract in the direct form of this tort. If there is no breach induced, there is no tort. This requirement was widened in *Prudential Assurance Co v Lorenz*	16.5.7 Breach

(1971) to cover breach of an equitable duty. TU induced members not to pass insurance premiums they had received to Rs. Not doing so was breach of their (equitable) duty to account. The court held that TU was to be forbidden to induce breaches of this duty. However, the Court of Appeal in a non-labour case thought that this tort did not exist or at least there was no tort of inducing a breach of trust. There is no tort if the contractual term is void for illegality. There is no tort of inducing a person not to enter into a contract – a contract must exist before a person may be induced to break it.

| 16.5.8 | Inducement |

The Courts distinguish inducement from advice. A statement of fact is not inducement: *Thomson v Deakin*. In *Camellia Tanker SA v ITF* (1976) inducement was stated to cover 'pressure, persuasion, or procuration'. Telling members of the progress of negotiations did not constitute inducing them to break their contracts. It is, however, an inducement where the third parties are ready and willing to act in brach of their contract with the employers.

| 16.5.9 | Cause |

It must be proved that the TU's acts did cause the suppliers/distributors not to perform their contract with Rs: *Thomson v Deakin*. On the facts of the case the plaintiff could not prove that another firm's decision not to supply them with newsprint was occasioned by the union's inducing its members at the firm to join in industrial action.

| 16.5.10 | Unlawful means |

Unlawful means are required for the 'indirect' variant of this tort. They may be a breach of contract, or tort, or some other form of civil liability. Trespass in order to change tyres at a motor show has been held to be unlawful means. Presumably a crime is sufficient, though cases are in conflict. In the words of Lord Denning MR in *Torquay Hotel Co Ltd v Cousins*:

> 'a trade union official is only in the wrong when he procures a contracting party directly to break his contract or when he does it indirectly by unlawful means.'

A breach of statutory duty is unlawful means: *Meade v Haringey LBC* (1979). Whether such a breach occurs is a matter of construction of the statute: *Lonrho Ltd v Shell Petroleum Ltd (No 2)* (1982) and *Associated British Ports plc v TGWU* (1989). (It should be noted that the statutory protection covers inducing breach of contract, not inducing breach of statutory duty.)

The requirement of unlawful means distinguishes this tort from the situation in *Allen v Flood* (1898), where the House of Lords held that it was not a tort to oblige a third party to act in such a way as to affect the plaintiff detrimentally, even when the defendant intended to injure the plaintiff.

An example of a breach of contract being unlawful means is *Emerald Construction Co Ltd v Lowthian* (1966). TU called out its members at Rs. Rs worked for a firm which had subcontracted work to them. Rs fell behind and they were in breach of contract with the firm ie TU had induced Rs to break the contract with the firm by inducing Rs' workers to breach their contracts. The workers' breach was the unlawful means for this form of inducing breach of contract. An interesting point is that the workers were in fact independent contractors for, and not employees of, Rs.

16.5.11   Illustration

Potentially, justification is a defence to inducing breach of contract (and presumably to inducing breaches of equitable and statutory obligations) but it has succeeded in only one case, *Brimelow v Casson* (1924). The Court held the tort to be justified when chorus girls were induced to go on strike for more pay, the alternative being to become prostitutes. In an early case the House of Lords held that defendants were liable despite their acting simply in furthering their aspirations and were not activated by malice (*South Wales Miners' Federation v Glamorgan Coal Co Ltd* (1905)). A protest against a wage cut did not fall within the defence of justification. Perhaps in modern times this defence could be read more broadly than 70 and more years ago. More recent is *Greig v Insole* (1978), the world series cricket case, where it was held that the motives of the International Cricket Council did not justify the procuring of breaches of contracts between individual cricketers and the Packer group.

16.5.12   Justification

In *Rookes v Barnard* (1964) the House of Lords held that there was a tort of intimidation. It covered not just a threat of violence but also a threat to break a contract or to commit some other unlawful act. A union said that its members would withdraw labour if a non-unionist was not dismissed by his employers. They did dismiss him. The dismissal was lawful because it was with the correct length of notice. Accordingly, the tort of inducing breach of contract did not apply for no contract was broken. The Lords held that the union had acted tortiously. It threatened to act in breach of contract; namely, in breach of a no-strike clause in a collective agreement. (Counsel had, surprisingly to modern readers, conceded that the clause was legally binding.) Exemplary damages were awarded.

16.5.13   Intimidation

16.5.14	Criticism	Leaving aside the exemplary damages point *Rookes v Barnard* has been severely criticised. Controversy has centred on the invention of this tort. The last similar case dates from 1793 and the facts related to threats of violence. One might have thought that the tort had died out or it was narrowly drawn, but the Lords really created a novel tort. The effect was that since at that time the tort was not one covered by a statutory immunity, TU organisers were liable; yet TU members would not have been liable had they gone on strike, because the immunity attached to breaches of contract (ie breaches of contract attracted immunity, but the threats to break contracts did not).
16.5.15	Meaning of intimidation	The boundaries of the tort are hard to see. Cases are rare. Certainly a line is drawn between intimidation and advice, and it seems that the threat must be one which is powerful enough 'to induce the other to submit' (*per* Lord Denning MR in *Morgan v Fry* (1968)). A threat to take lawful action is not intimidation. Possibly justification is a defence.
16.5.16	Interference	Interference with contract and interference with business or trade. Interference with contract has been accepted fairly recently as a tort, and there have been intimations that there exists a tort of 'interference with the trade or business of another person by doing unlawful acts', as Lord Diplock put it in *Merkur Island Shipping Corp v Laughton* above. This possible tort would be a 'super tort' or the genus of which inducing breach of contract is a species. Similarly, intimidation would be a species of this tort. Lord Reid in *J T Stratford & Son Ltd v Lindley* (1965) considered that the tort of inducing breach of contract was not restricted to breaches of contract. Lord Denning MR in *Torquay Hotel Co Ltd v Cousins*, above, said *obiter* that the tort of interfering with contract existed and the House of Lords recognised its existence in *Merkur Island* and *Hadmor Productions Ltd v Hamilton* (1983). The tort is aimed at protecting the commercial expectations of the parties.
16.5.17	Width	The parameters of the tort of interference with contract were laid down by Lord Denning MR in *Torquay Hotel*.

> 'First there must be interference in the execution of a contract. The interference is not confined to the procurement of a breach of contract ... Second, the interference must be deliberate. The person must know of the contract, or, at any rate, turn a blind eye to it and intend to interfere with it ... Third, the interference must be direct.'

Whether the interference is direct or indirect, the

interference must be by unlawful means. On the facts of *Torquay Hotel* Lord Denning MR held that the suppliers would not be liable for failure to supply if failure was caused by an industrial dispute. Since there was no breach of contract, there could be no tort of inducing breach of contract, but the present tort fitted the facts.

The tort of interference with trade or business, the existence of which is established, it is thought, would extend beyond interference with contracts, for no contract need exist. The predominant purpose to injure is necessary (*Barretts and Baird (Wholesale) Ltd v IPCS* (1987)). The mere fact of interference was insufficient. This decision, however, is only a first instance one. Further clarification is needed. This case is also inconsistent with the *Falconer v ASLEF*, above at 16.5.5, which did not require an intent to injure. *Falconer* in turn is inconsistent with *Deakin*. There must also be unlawful means. The nature of those means has been substantially debated by the House of Lords in non-employment cases. It seems that in this tort both the direct and indirect interference forms must have unlawful means. In the *Barretts* case the judge thought that breaches of their own contracts of employment by the workers constituted unlawful means but this proposition has been doubted. A breach of statutory duty has been said to be unlawful means for this tort.

16.5.18   Interference with business

In *Middlebrook Mushrooms Ltd v TGWU* (1993) the employers dismissed workers who protested against their wages being cut. The ex-employees 'picketed' local supermarkets, trying to discourage shoppers from buying the company's produce. The Court of Appeal held that the leaflets handed out by the pickets were not aimed at inducing breaches of contract between the shopkeepers and the company. There was no direct interference with contracts. The pickets were seeking to persuade shoppers not to buy. The shoppers had no contract with the company. No doubt the effect hoped for would be that the supermarket owners would not place orders with the company. The possible tort was one of indirectly inducing the shopowners not to enter into contracts in the future. Being of the indirect form unlawful means were necessary. Since none were used, there was no tort. Neill LJ opined that when employers sought injunctions against unions and their members, the Court should take into account Article 10 of the European Convention on Human Rights, the right to freedom of speech.

The width of the tort is uncertain and is best viewed through the cases.

16.5.19   Cases

- *Brekkes Ltd v Cattel* (1972)

  The tort is committed when there is interference with an expectation that a contract will be made.

- *Hadmor Productions*

  A television station had a licence to broadcast but was not contractually obliged to do so. The union threatened to ask its members at the station not to broadcast programmes made by the plaintiffs. The Lords held that there was an expectation that the plaintiffs' programmes would be broadcast, which was broken.

- *Merkur Island*

  The International Transport Workers Federation has for a long time tried to increase pay for seafarers by attempting to bring pressure on shipowners to pay union rates. The plaintiffs' ship was 'blacked'. Tugmen and lock-keepers refused to aid the boat's leaving port. There was an exemption clause in the charterparty that there would be no liability 'in the event of loss of time due to boycott of the vessel in any port ... by shore labour or others.' Therefore, there was no breach of the term that voyages would be made with utmost despatch. Nevertheless, there was an interference with contract. The unlawful means were procuring the tugmen and lock-keepers to break their contracts of employment.

  The existence of this tort of interference with trade or business by unlawful means is significant because it is not one of the torts rendered lawful in trade disputes, as discussed in the next section of this book. It has the potential to swallow up the other economic torts. If breach of contract is unlawful means for this tort, businesses affected by industrial action will be able to sue those on strike for loss, and there is no statutory immunity.

16.5.20   Conspiracy

Civil conspiracy is 'the agreement of two or more to do an unlawful act or to do a lawful act by unlawful means' (*Mulcahy v R* (1868) *per* Willes J). A conspiracy to injure is different. It does not require an independent wrong and it occurs where the predominant purpose is to injure the plaintiffs, not to advance the defendants' legitimate interests. Pecuniary loss must be caused. An unlawful means conspiracy will also amount to interference with trade or business by unlawful means. It was said that the first type also required the defendants to intend to injure the plaintiffs: *Lonrho*, above. However, the House decided that a person was liable without having the predominant purpose of injury to the plaintiff in a conspiracy to use unlawful means: *Lonrho plc v Fayed* (1992). Lord Bridge said:

'Where conspirators act with the predominant purpose of injuring the plaintiff and in fact inflict damage on him, but do nothing which could have been actionable if done by an individual acting alone, it is the fact of their concerted action for that illegitimate purpose that the law, however anomalous it may now seem, finds a sufficient ground to condemn their action as illegal and tortious. But when conspirators intentionally injure the plaintiff and use unlawful means to do so, it is no defence for them to show that their primary purpose was to further their own interests.'

Unlawful acts include crimes (which amount to torts: *Lonrho v Shell Petroleum*, above) and torts. It is debatable whether breach of contract is unlawful for this purpose. Unlawful means include an agreement to cause loss with the intention to injure the plaintiffs (*Huntley v Thornton* (1957)). Members of a district committee were liable when they expelled a TU member out of spite. Any strike involves an agreement with the purpose of injuring the employers, the plaintiffs. There is debate whether a breach of contract constitutes unlawful means in this tort. Potentially all strikers are liable for the tort of conspiracy. However, this variant of the tort is not committed where the predominant purpose of the defendants is to promote a legitimate interest (*Mogul SS Co v McGregor, Gow & Co* (1892)). If causing injury, not promoting the union's interests, is the predominant purpose, there is a conspiracy to injure (*Quinn v Leathem* (1901)). Since that case union objectives have been held to be legitimate. The most famous case is *Crofter Hand Woven Harris Tweed Co v Veitch* (1942) where it was decided that a closed shop was a legitimate purpose. Also legitimate are pressure to oblige employers to start employing union members (*D C Thomson & Co Ltd v Deakin* (1952)) and to get rid of a colour bar (*Scala Ballroom (Wolverhampton) Ltd v Ratcliffe* (1958)).

16.5.21 Economic duress

The House of Lords suggested in *Universe Tankships Inc of Monrovia v ITWF* (1983) that economic duress made a contract void with the effect that money paid under coercion was recoverable. The Lords said that though the statutory immunity discussed next does not directly apply to economic duress, industrial action which amounted to duress would be immune on the same basis as if economic duress constituted an economic tort rendered immune by s 219 of TULR(C)A.

16.5.22 *Allen v Flood* (1898)

The existence of this tort is seemingly inconsistent with one of the classic cases of the common law, *Allen v Flood* (1898), that action done with the purpose of injuring another was not tortious *per se*.

16.6   Immunity

English law has for many years granted the organisers of industrial action an immunity from liability in tort. Continental parts of the European Union generally have a right to strike, sometimes enshrined in the Constitution.

16.6.1   Definition

Section 219(1) and (2) of TULR(C)A read:

'(1) An act done by a person in contemplation or furtherance of a trade dispute is not actionable in tort on the ground only –

(a)   that it induces another person to break a contract or interferes or induces another person to interfere with its performance, or

(b)   that it consists in his threatening that a contract (whether one to which he is a party or not) will be broken or its performance interfered with, or that he will induce another person to break a contract or interfere with its performance.

(2) An agreement or combination by two or more persons to do or procure the doing of an act in contemplation or furtherance of a trade dispute is not actionable in tort if the act is one which if done without any such agreement or combination would not be actionable in tort.'

The side-note to s 219 reads: 'protection from certain tort liabilities'. Perhaps terminology should change from immunity to protection.

Nowadays a union has the same immunity as an individual. It is no longer totally immune. Note that (1)(a) and (b) cover any contract, not just contracts of employment as was once the case. The aim was to protect secondary action but that aim has been frustrated by the withdrawal of the immunity from such action.

16.6.2   Effect

'Not actionable in tort'. Section 219(1) and (2) protect persons who would otherwise be tortfeasors from liability in tort. It does not protect from other forms of liability, notably criminal law and breach of contract. Furthermore, protection is limited to the torts specified. There is no protection from other torts such as breach of statutory duty, trespass, and harassment. There has been controversy over the meaning of 'not actionable'. What it means is that in relation to the torts mentioned no one is allowed to sue. Otherwise put, the activity is rendered lawful. What is made lawful is not unlawful means for another tort such as interference with trade by unlawful means. Therefore, although there is no direct protection against this tort, there is indirect protection from liability.

The immunity from conspiracy in s 219(2) requires brief discussion. It does not make lawful conspiracies to commit unlawful acts for those acts are actionable if done by one person. It only renders immune conspirators who use unlawful means. If, however, the unlawful means are rendered immune, there is no tort of conspiracy to use unlawful means.

16.6.3 Conspiracy

Section 244(1), which defines 'trade dispute', is restricted to 'workers and their employer'. By s 244(5) 'worker' means:

16.6.4 Workers and their employers

'(a) a worker-employed by [his] employer; or

(b) a person who has ceased to be so employed if his employment was terminated in connection with the dispute or if the termination of his employment was one of the circumstances giving rise to the dispute.'

The employers against whom the workers are taking industrial action must in law be their employer. The corporate veil will not be pierced: *Dimbleby & Sons Ltd v NUJ* (1984). Employers can establish a company between them and their suppliers/distributors. A strike against the wrong firm will lose the immunity it would have had, had it been against the right firm. It is not easy to find always who the employers are. The shift from national to company bargaining weakens this part of the immunity. A dispute between a union and the employers where the workers are not involved no longer attracts the immunity. The International Transport Workers' Federation's lengthy campaign against ships flying flags of convenience is not protected because there is no dispute between the crew and the shipowners.

The restriction to 'workers and their employer' means that disputes between two sets of workers are not protected. Therefore, demarcation disputes no longer attract immunity, unless there is a dispute too with the employers. Employers may find it difficult to avoid involvement. A dictum of Lord Diplock in *Dimbleby* above, that demarcation disputes between employees employed by the same employer are immune when disputes between employees alone are not, should presumably be read in this light.

16.6.5 Worker and worker

There must be a dispute. It need not be a full-blown one. A dispute 'exists wherever a difference exists, and a difference can exist long before the parties become locked in combat' (*per* Lord Denning in *Beetham v Trinidad Cement Ltd*((1960)). The term is widened by s 244(4):

16.6.6 Dispute

'... an act, threat or demand done or made by one person or organisation against another which, if resisted, would have led to a trade dispute with another, shall be treated as being done or made in contemplation or furtherance of a trade dispute with that other, notwithstanding that because that other submits to the act or threat or accedes to the demand no dispute arises.'

Accordingly if the employers cave in to the claim on presentation thereof, there is nevertheless a dispute. This in fact occurred in *Hadmor Productions* mentioned earlier. There will, however, be no dispute attracting the immunity where it has been settled. Similarly, there is no dispute where employees were happy to be paid less than other workers.

16.6.7	Golden formula

'In contemplation or furtherance of a trade dispute.' This phrase is often known as the 'golden formula'. A trade dispute is defined in s 244(1) as a:

'... dispute between workers and their employers which relates wholly or mainly to one or more of the following -

(a)   terms and conditions of employment, or the physical conditions in which any workers are required to work;

(b)   engagement or non-engagement, or termination or suspension of employment or the duties of employment, of one or more workers;

(c)   allocation of work or the duties of employment between workers or groups of workers;

(d)   matters of discipline;

(e)   a worker's membership or non-membership of a trade union;

(f)   facilities for officials of trade unions; and

(g)   machinery for negotiation or consultation, and other procedures relating to any of the above matters, including recognition by employers or employers' associations of the right to a trade union to represent workers in such negotiation or consultation or in the carrying out of such procedures.'

Only the matters listed attract immunity.

16.6.8	Wholly or mainly

The term 'relates wholly or mainly' should be noted. It is a closer link than that formerly required, which was that the dispute be connected with one of the listed matters. In *Mercury Communications Ltd v Scott-Garner* (1984) a dispute was held to be relating wholly or mainly to upholding British Telecom's monopoly, not relating wholly or mainly to the threat to jobs at British Telecom. The action was not immune. It would have been immune before the change. However, in *Wandsworth LBC v National Association of Schoolmasters* (1993) the Court of

Appeal held that a boycott of standard assessment tests was one brought about by an increased workload for teachers. Accordingly, it was concerned with their terms and conditions of employment. It was not wholly or mainly one relating to a protest against educational policy. The decision which motivation is predominant places a substantial power in the hands of the courts.

The restriction to the matters listed is meant to limit lawful strikes to those which are non-political. An example of industrial action which fell on to the 'political' side is *BBC v Hearn* (1977). Television technical staff threatened not to transmit the FA Cup Final to South Africa as a protest against apartheid. The TU argued that there was a term in its members' contracts that they should not be contractually obliged to transmit broadcasts to South Africa as long as apartheid continued. The Court held that at the time of the action this issue had not arisen ie the workers were not striking to enforce this term in their contracts. Accordingly, none of the matters in s 244(1) was the subject of dispute, and there was no immunity. If there had been a dispute as to contractual terms there would have been a dispute, and indeed the Court was willing to go further to include disputes about practices which were not contractually binding. But the ratio of the case demonstrates that the mere fact that there is threatened action does not bring the immunity into play. There must be a difference over a listed matter. The House of Lords has said that industrial action is not simply converted into a trade dispute by the union's arguing that the way to resolve the matter is to include it as a term in the employees' contracts (*Universe Tankships Inc of Monrovia v International Transport Workers' Federation* (1983), *obiter*). No protection is afforded to these situations: where unions act out of 'ruffled dignity' (*Huntley v Thornton*, above); inter-union rivalry leading to annoyance with the plaintiffs (*Stratford v Lindley*, above) and an *ad hominem* attack on a person who criticised the TU (*Torquay Hotel v Cousins*, above).

16.6.9   Trade

According to Lord Loreburn in *Conway v Wade* (1909) 'contemplation' is when 'a dispute is imminent and the act is done in expectation of and with a view to it', and 'furtherance' is when 'the dispute is already existing and the act is done in support of one side to it'. An act done when a dispute is only a possibility is not done in contemplation of it. Similarly, boycotting a contractor who drove through a picket line is not action taken in furtherance of a trade dispute for the dispute was at an end. The boycott came too late to attract the immunity. Preparation by the union is not by itself in

16.6.10   Contemplation or furtherance

contemplation of a dispute. Where a union official sought to find out about employers' wage bills and weekly sales, no immunity to inducing breach of contracts of employment was available because no dispute was imminent. Where, however, a union told its members not to co-operate with a private contractor, it was held that the act was in contemplation of a dispute. The line is fine. If the defendants honestly believe that what they are doing is in furtherance of the dispute, that is sufficient. The Courts have no power to withdraw immunity on the ground that the acts were too remote from the dispute or that it is commercially impossible to comply with the demand (*NWL Ltd v Woods*, above, *Express Newspapers Ltd v McShane* (1980) and, *Duport Steels Ltd v Sirs* (1980), a famous trilogy of cases).

16.6.11   Political strikes

This paragraph considers strikes against the government. As stated above, a line is drawn between trade and political disputes. A strike against the government may appear to be political. However, in industrial relations the government may have a role not just as the formulator and enforcer of policy but also as employers. What about action against a pay freeze? There is no difference on this point between government and other employers. The immunity applies. For example, in *Sherard v AUEW* (1973) the union threatened a strike against a pay standstill. Since other employers could also impose a pay freeze, the government was treated in the same way as ordinary employers. The Courts have gone further. If denationalisation threatens jobs, a protest strike against it is immune (*General Aviation Services (UK) Ltd v TGWU* (1974)). However, protests against more general government policies such as the passing of the Industrial Relations bill is not immune (*Associated Newspapers Group Ltd v Flynn* (1970)). A 'day of action' against economic policy was not immune (*Beaverbrook Newspapers Ltd v Keys* (1980)). The Court of Appeal held in *London Borough of Wandsworth v National Union of Schoolmasters/Union of Women Teachers* (1993) that a boycott of school assessment tests was related wholly or mainly to workload or working hours and therefore was a trade dispute. Since 1982 action is not protected unless it is 'wholly or mainly' related to one of the listed matters. This phrase means then more disputes are political after 1982 than before because though the matter might have been connected with a listed subject, it is not wholly or mainly relating to it. Part of the government's strategy was to restrict the width of the immunity.

16.7   Impermissible purpose

Lawful strikes can be rendered unlawful by impermissible purpose. By ss 222–225 of TULR(C)A industrial action for several reasons is not protected by the immunity. Action against employers to enforce union membership is not protected: s 222. This provision is part of the attack on the closed shop. It is not, however, restricted to situations where a closed shop exists. By s 223:

'... an act is not protected if the reason, or one of the reasons, for doing it is the fact or belief that an employer has dismissed one or more employees in circumstances such that by virtue of s 237 (dismissal in connection with unofficial action) they have no right to complain of unfair dismissal.'

This provision was introduced in 1990. It reinforces the position of employers who have dismissed unofficial strikers. Interlocutory injunctions restraining the industrial action are available.

See Chapter 11 for dismissals for unofficial strikes. Section 224 deals with secondary action, which is discussed separately below. Action is not protected if it involves pressure on employers to impose a term in a contract that their suppliers or distributors should recognise unions: s 225. Action is not immune if only one of the reasons for the dispute relates to s 222 or s 225.

Secondary action is defined in s 224(2) as:

16.8   Secondary action

'... when ... a person –

(a) induces another to break a contract of employment or interferes or induces another to interfere with its performance, or

(b) threatens that a contract of employment under which he or another is employed will be broken or its performance interfered with, or that he will induce another to break a contract of employment or to interfere with its performance, and the employer under the contract of employment is not the employer party to the dispute.'

The effect is to outlaw industrial action in solidarity with other workers. Some people view the curtailment of such strikes as a body blow to unions' perceptions of their role. To get round the prohibition of sympathy strikes union officials have to try and convert the industrial action into primary action; that is, to involve other employers in the dispute and then call out the employees.

Before 1980 TUs had immunity where they undertook industrial action against one employer in order to bring pressure on another. The Employment Act 1980 reduced the

16.8.1   Former immunity

width of the immunity. The law was complex and criticised for so being. Instead of reformulating it the government abolished the immunity for secondary action in 1990. There is an exception, which is more nominal than real, for peaceful picketing, which is considered below.

16.9   Strike ballot

For acts done by unions to be immune, a ballot is necessary. The government's stated aim was to oblige unions to adopt 'proper democratic procedures' (*Industrial Relations in the 1990s*, 1991). This section of the book does not apply to industrial action which is unofficial ie not union-backed. Such industrial action remains protected. Acts done by a TU, even a TU which is not recognised, to take part in industrial action are not immune without a ballot: s 226(1). This provision was introduced in 1984. Most ballots have been in favour of striking. For instance, in 1992 90% of Uotes were in favour. A sample voting paper must be sent to the employers not later than three days before the ballot and notice of the ballot must be given to them not less than seven days before the vote: s 226A, inserted by s 18 of the Trade Union Reform and Employment Rights Act 1993. This provision gives the employers more time to react to the call for industrial action. Pre-strike ballots are now an accepted part of the industrial scene, and ballots to end action are becoming common. There is a Code of Practice on 'Trade Union Ballots on Industrial Action', 1991, which courts and tribunals may take into account. (The Code is out of date in that it does not incorporate changes made by the 1993 Act.) Some parts of the Code do not have a statutory footing: for example, it suggests that the internal disputes settlement procedures should be exhausted before a ballot is arranged. A new Code is expected in late 1995.

16.9.1   Loss of immunity

If this process does not take place, immunity is lost from those employers but not otherwise. A union has to appoint an independent scrutineer in order to retain any immunity: s 226A inserted by s 20 of TURERA. TUs must inform the relevant employers of the outcome as soon as reasonably practicable: s 231A, inserted by TURERA s 19. (There need be no scrutineer where there are fewer than 50 members entitled to vote.) To secure immunity ss 227–232 must be complied with. There must be a majority in favour (s 232 relates to ballots of overseas members).

16.9.2   Entitlement to vote

Those entitled to vote are those who:

'... it is reasonable at the time of the ballot for the union to believe will be induced to take part ... in the industrial action in question, and no others' (s 227(1)).

If those entitled to vote are denied the opportunity, the ballot is invalid. A simple mistake, however, does not invalidate the ballot. Independent contractors who personally do work or perform services must be allowed to vote.

The basic rule as to voting constituencies is that separate ballots must be held for each workplace: s 228(1). The aim is to prevent gerrymandering to produce a militant constituency out of several workplaces where moderates are in the majority. There is a complicated exception in s 228(3), the thrust of which is that there can be just one ballot for employees of one occupational description who work in different places. A ballot may be held covering employees of different employers if it is reasonable for the unions to believe that there is a common factor (*University of Central England v NALGO* (1993)). Surprisingly there must even be a ballot where the union consists of other unions only and has no individual members (*Shipping Co Uniform Inc v ITF* (1985)).

16.9.3   Voting

Voting is by marking a paper: s 229(1). Papers so far as is reasonably practicable must be sent out and returned by post (with the exception of merchant seamen): s 230(2) of TULR(C)A, as inserted by s 17 of TURERA. The effect is that workplace and semi-postal ballots no longer attract any statutory immunity (and this is so despite the fact that some unions achieve a higher turn-out of voters in workplace ballots than in fully postal ones). The Code of Practice on Trade Union Ballots on Industrial Action, revised version, 1991, suggests that the union gives members a fortnight to vote when second class post is used. This recommendation undercuts unions' necessity to act very promptly or members' interest will wane rapidly. Postal ballots will hold back fervour. The paper must specify who may call the industrial action: s 229(3). It must contain either or both of the following:

> '... a question (however framed) which requires the person answering it to say, by answering "Yes" or "No", whether he is prepared to take part or, as the case may be, to continue to take part in a strike'; or

> '... a question (however framed) which requires the person answering it to say, by answering "Yes" or "No", whether he is prepared to take part or, as the case may be, to continue to take part in industrial action': s 229(2).

Both questions must be put if both forms of action are proposed (*Post Office v Union of Communication Workers* (1990) CA). If both questions are put, a majority in either suffices for that type of action; the fact that altogether the votes against action outweigh those in favour is irrelevant (*West Midlands Travel Ltd v Transport and General Workers' Union* (1994) CA).

The paper must also contain the following words: 'If you take part in a strike or other industrial action, you may be in breach of your contract of employment': s 229(4). This phrase has come to be known as the 'health warning'. No explanation must be added to this written declaration (even if the action will not amount to a breach!). However, the union may provide a separate leaflet detailing its stance and commenting on s 229(4). The aim behind this sub-section is to dampen enthusiasm for industrial action. By s 229(1)(A) inserted by TURERA the name of the scrutineer must be on the ballot paper except for constituencies of fewer than 50 members (s 226C inserted by TURERA). Ballot papers must also be consecutively numbered.

16.9.4	No interference	There must be no interference from the union of its members or officials in the vote: s 230(1). The voting must be in secret and the votes must be fairly counted, though inaccuracies are disregarded if they do not affect the outcome: s 230(4). Secret voting by post is the government's response to traditional methods of voting in TUs – by show of hands, at mass meetings, at the workplace, at a branch meeting.
16.9.5	Information	All persons entitled to vote must be told of the result including 'yes' and 'no' votes and spoilt ballot papers: s 231. Employers must be told as soon as reasonably practicable: s 231A, inserted by TURERA. If not the defendants lose immunity totally.
16.9.6	Non-provision	Immunity is in relation to the relevant employers (only) forfeited if the employers are not informed of the industrial action: s 234A, inserted by s 21 of TURERA. The notice must specify those employees ('so that he can readily ascertain them'), state whether the action will be continuous or not (such as a series of one-day strikes), and state that the notice is given for the purposes of s 234A. The effect of s 234A is to permit employers to know which employees are covered by the notice of industrial action. The obligation includes a duty to inform employers of the names of individuals when there is no other means of disclosing who is affected (*NATFHE v Blackpool and the Fylde College* (1994)). If the action is discontinuous, the union must inform the employers of the dates of the action: the effect is that random dates to maximise disruption cannot be chosen. Notice must be given within the period from the ballot to the seven days before the action. This provision is perhaps the most controversial one in TURERA for employees may be susceptible to nobbling and may be victimised. Forewarned is forearmed.
16.9.7	Call to action	The calling of industrial action must be by a 'specified

person' (s 233) ie the one mentioned in s 229(3) above. There must have been no call for industrial action before the ballot. The ballot is not effective after four weeks: s 234. It will, however, be valid for 12 weeks if a court order prohibiting the action is set aside. In *Post Office v Union of Communications Workers*, above, the Court of Appeal held that a ballot in September 1988 did not render lawful a strike in September 1989 even though there had been industrial conflict in the interim. The effect of s 234 and s 234A is to give unions little time for the outcome of the ballot to be utilised. If the action is not called by the correct person, immunity is lost.

'The citizen's right of action' and the member's right.

By s 235A inserted by TURERA any individual (a term which normally excludes a company) may make a claim for an order to the High Court if a TU or another person has done an unlawful act to induce a person to take part in industrial action and the effect of the action does or is likely to prevent, delay or reduce the quality of goods or services to him. 'Unlawful' includes actionability in tort. But the tort need not be actionable at the suit of the plaintiff, and it includes the situation where the member's right discussed next is infringed. It does not matter that the person was not entitled to receive the goods or services. No loss need be caused. The sort of person who could bring this action is the plaintiff in *Falconer v ASLEF*, above at 16.5.5. The order requires the TU to desist from inducing persons to participate in industrial action. Inducement is done by the TU if it is 'authorised or endorsed' by the union within s 20(2)–(4) of TULR(C)A. New s 235B, creates a new institution, the Commissioner for Protection against Unlawful Industrial Action, to assist individuals. The Commissioner's functions resemble those of the Commissioner for the Rights of Trade Union Members discussed in Chapter 2 which see (eg the provision of legal representation). As with the CROTUM the appointment, pay etc of the CPUIA are governed by ss 266–71 of TULR(C)A as amended by TURERA, Schedule 8 paras 79–84. Assistance can be given only against unions, not individuals: s 235B(2) In her first report (for 1993–4) covering her first seven months, the Commissioner received one request for legal assistance, which she granted, but in fact the assistance was not required. The present CROTUM is also the CPUIA (or COPAULIA).

Employers may not wish to resort to law for fear of inflaming the situation. This right undercuts that desire. It is thought that an injunction will not help resolve industrial disputes.

16.10   Citizen's and member's right

16.10.1   Citizen's

16.10.2	Member's right

Section 235A refers to 'unlawful' acts. Besides tortious acts, which are not immune, 'unlawful' means a breach of s 62 of TULR(C)A as amended by Schedule 8 para 47 of TURERA. By s 62(1), a TU member:

> '... who claims that members of the union, including himself, are likely to be or have been induced by the union to take part or continue to take part in industrial action which does not have the support of a ballot may apply to the court for an order.'

The order requires the TU to ensure that there is no inducement to members to participate in action. Acts are those of the TU if authorised or endorsed under s 20(2)–(4). Persons working for the Crown are deemed to be employees for the purpose of defining industrial action ('a strike or other industrial action by persons employed under contracts of employment': s 62(7)).

16.10.3	Comment

The new action does not apply to lock-outs. It does not apply when firms cut back services or reduce standards: one cannot sue BR for withdrawing trains. Unions and management will not be able to deal with disputes themselves. The law in Chapter 16.9 and 16.10 are part of the government's plan to decrease strikes and union power by increasing the number of requirements for a lawful industrial action. The member's action is in addition to any contractual right she may have under the union's rulebook: see. for example, *Taylor v National Union of Mineworkers (Yorkshire Area)* (1984).

16.11   Vicarious liability

A union may be responsible in law for the actions of its officials including shop stewards. Vicarious liability for the economic torts, the ones normally involved in industrial action, is laid down in statute. Otherwise the common law applies.

16.11.1	Statute

By s 20(1) of TULR(C)A:

> '... where proceedings in tort are brought against a trade union:
>
> (a)   on the ground that an act –
>
> > (i)   induces another person to break a contract or interferes or induces another person to interference with its performance, or
> >
> > (ii)   consists in threatening that a contract (whether one to which the union is a party or not) will be broken or its performance interfered with, or that the union will

induce another person to break a contract or interfere with its performance, or

> (b) in respect of an agreement or combination by two or more persons to do or to procure the doing of an act which, if it were done without
>
> any such agreement or combination, would be actionable in tort on such ground,

> then, for the purpose of determining in those proceedings whether the union is liable in respect of the act in question, that act shall be taken to have been done by the union if, but only if, it is to be taken to have been authorised or endorsed by the trade union in accordance with the following provisions.'

By s 20(2):

16.11.2 'Authorised or endorsed'

> '... an act shall be taken to have been authorised or endorsed by a trade union if it was done, or was authorised or endorsed –

> (a) by any person empowered by the rules to do, authorise or endorse acts of the kind in question, or

> (b) by the principal executive committee or the president or general secretary or

> (c) by any other committee of the union or any other official of the union (whether employed by it or not).'

In (c) 'other official' includes a shop steward even though union rules do not allow her to call a strike ((c) was added in 1990). The next sub-section makes the union liable for the acts of a group of persons and individuals within that group where a union official was a member of the group and the purposes of the body included the organising of industrial action. This rule was also added in 1990.

An illustration of s 20(2) occurred in the unreported High Court case of *British Railways Board v National Union of Rail, Maritime and Transport Workers* (1992). Members of a staff committee set up by a collective agreement between the plaintiffs and defendants were not union officials. Therefore, industrial action led by these people was unofficial. The outcome was that a strike in their favour after they has been dismissed was unofficial and therefore impermissible under s 223 (see 16.7, above).

If the act was authorised or endorsed under s 20(2)(c) it can be repudiated by the executive, president or general secretary provided they repudiate as soon as they know of the facts:

16.11.3 Repudiation

s 21(1). The repudiation must be in writing and the TU:

'... must do its best to give individual written notice of the fact and date of repudiation, without delay —

(i)   to every member of the union who the union has reason to believe is taking part, or might otherwise take part, in industrial action as a result of the act, and

(ii)   to the employer of every such member... ' (s 21(2)).

This statement must be included:

'Your union has repudiated the call (or calls) for industrial action to which this notice relates and will give no support to unofficial industrial action taken in response to it (or them). If you are dismissed while taking unofficial industrial action, you will have no right to complain of unfair dismissal' (s 21(3)).

Section 21(2) and (3) became part of the law in 1990. Repudiation ceases to be effective if the executive, president or general secretary acts inconsistently with it (eg by nodding and smiling at shop stewards who are carrying on the action). If within three months (TURERA, Schedule 7 para 17) of the purported repudiation a person who is party to a commercial contract seeks confirmation of it and who has not previously been given written confirmation, the repudiation is ineffective if repudiation is not 'forthwith confirmed in writing' (s 21(6)). Commercial contracts are defined to exclude contracts of service and contracts to perform work or services personally. The whole thrust of this law is to make unions centralise their decision-making process.

16.11.4   Nods and winks

Section 21 is the government's response to what it sees as unions' encouragement of unofficial strikes. Unions may not wish to show their hand but by nods and winks encourage members to take unofficial action. Section 21 ensures that unions take control, the sanction being damages in tort up to the maximum stated in the next section of this book. Section 21 is otiose, for as the Court of Appeal held in *Express and Star Ltd v NGA (1982)* (1986), a union is liable for contempt when it encourages members to strike unofficially, even though that contempt is based on disobedience to an order based on a tort covered by s 20.

16.11.5   Common law

Section 20 applies to only the economic torts and to contempt proceedings based on breach of an injunction in respect of these torts. With regard to other torts the common law in *Heatons Transport (St Helens) Ltd v TGWU* (1972) applies.

There is a limit on the amount of damages which may be awarded against a TU in tort. If there are fewer than 5,000 members, the maximum is £10,000; 5,000–25,000 members: £50,000; 25,000–100,000 members: £125,000; and more than 100,000 members: £250,000: s 22. These limits have remained static since they were introduced in 1982. This maximum applies to each action, not each dispute. If a dispute gives rise to 10 suits by employers, each employer can sue up to the maximum. These maxima do not apply to tort actions concerning personal injury through negligence, nuisance or breach of duty, property and product liability under the Consumer Protection Act 1987. The maximum can be exceeded by adding interest to the damages. By s 23 certain TU funds are 'protected property' which cannot be used to pay damages. These include the provident and political funds. Property which is 'protected' cannot be used for paying damages whether the claim is brought in tort or otherwise.

16.12   Damages

For many years before 1982 unions were not liable in tort. When the law was changed, the government thought that if there was no limit, TUs would quickly be made bankrupt. The narrowing of the immunities and the technicalities of the ballot may lead to increased losses to union funds.

16.12.1   Effect of changes

Section 22 is limited to tort. Unlimited fines remain available for contempt of court. For example, the National Graphical Association was fined £675,000 for contempt in 1984. There is no limit on the amount payable by individuals.

16.12.2   Width of law

Holding the ring is the jargon phrase for this area of law. The courts are meant to act as do umpires in boxing. Their decisions may, however, affect the outcome of industrial action.

16.13   Injunctions

Most cases against TUs never reach trial. Courts therefore rarely have to consider damages against unions. TU officials are likely to be 'men of straw'. What employers and other affected individuals want is an interlocutory injunction to stop the industrial action. This type of prohibitory order is granted by the High Court pre-trial and may be granted *ex parte*, the aim being to preserve the status quo pre-trial. Since, however, few trade dispute cases reach trial, it is the grant of this order which in practice is important. The union, if injuncted, will find it hard to re-motivate its members when the interlocutory injunction is lifted. The employers will argue that they will suffer financial loss if the remedy is not awarded. One major problem for unions is that they are not always represented at the grant of these orders. Affidavit evidence is not available, and proceedings need not take place in open court in the day

16.13.1   Effect

time. The remedy can be granted over the telephone.

16.13.2   Financial loss

Generally, judges grant interlocutory injunctions if plaintiffs have an arguable case: *American Cyanamid Co v Ethicon Ltd* (1975). The courts have strongly held to the principle that at this stage of the proceedings there must be no 'mini-trial' on the merits. Merits are for the full trial. Because employers can point to pecuniary loss as a result of industrial action and TUs cannot point to such damage if the injunction is granted, employers usually gain this relief despite the fact that support for action may disappear over time, a matter which has not yet been considered properly by the courts. If the remedy is granted, plaintiffs have to give an undertaking to pay damages at full trial if they lose then, but this promise is nugatory because full trials are rare and TUs cannot calculate their losses in economic terms. In the words of Lord Diplock in *NWL Ltd v Woods* (1979) the 'practical realities' are that the grant of an interlocutory relief 'is tantamount to giving final judgment against the defendants'. One factor for consideration by the court has been said to be the public interest (*Associated British Ports v TGWU* (1989) CA), a point not dealt with by the Lords. No account has so far been taken of the public interest behind the freedom to strike.

16.13.3   *Ex parte*

Parliament has sought in s 221 to defuse TU anger at the grant of prohibitory orders. By s 221(1):

'... where –

(a) an application for an injunction ... is made to a court in the absence of the party against whom it is sought or any representative of his; and

(b) he claims, or in the opinion of the court would be likely to claim, that he acted in contemplation or furtherance of a trade dispute, the court shall not grant the injunction ... unless satisfied that all steps which in the circumstances were reasonable

have been taken with a view to securing that notice of application and an opportunity of being heard with respect to the application have been given to him.'

This sub-section thereby restricts *ex parte* orders. The effect is to put the likelihood of the defence's success into the balance.

16.13.4   Consideration

Section 221(2) reads:

'... where –

(a) an application for an interlocutory injunction is made to a court pending the trial of an action; and

(b) the party against whom it is sought claims that

he acted in contemplation or furtherance of a trade dispute, the court shall, in exercising its discretion whether or not to grant the injunction, have regard to the likelihood of that party's succeeding at the trial of the action in establishing any matter which would afford a defence to the action under section 219 (protection from certain tort liabilities) or section 220 (peaceful picketing).'

Section 221(2) is a consciousness-raising provision.

If it is probable that the defendants have a s 219 or s 220 defence the remedy is refused: *NWL Ltd v Woods*, above. Section 221(2) does not apply if there are immediate threats to health and safety (*Beaverbrook Newspapers Ltd v Keys* (1980)) or the fundamental rights eg freedom of the press (*Express Newspapers*, above).

Since s 221(2) applies only in relation to those economic torts mentioned in s 219, in relation to the other torts the *American Cyanamid* test applies. In a restraint of trade case, *Lansing Linde Ltd v Kerr* (1991), however, the Court of Appeal said that *American Cyanamid* did not apply with full force where trial was unlikely. Since trial is unlikely in industrial matters, this statement may require reconsideration: otherwise the courts have been acting in error for 15 years. Contrariwise Lord Diplock in *NWL Ltd v Woods* said that the courts retained a residual discretion to grant an interlocutory injunction even when the immunities apply if the action would be 'disastrous' to employers and the community. There are similar suggestions in other cases, but no judge has as yet relied on them.

16.13.5 Application

Breach of injunction is penalised by punishment for contempt of court and sequestration of the defendant's assets. Contempt, at least if it is wilful, is punishable by a fine or imprisonment (up to two years) or both at the court's discretion. There is no maximum limit on the fine. No union property is exempt. An example is *Austin Rover Group Ltd v AUEW* (1985). The judge held that the general secretary of the TU should have done something to help implement an order that the TU should not issue any instruction to take industrial action. No fine was ordered because the breach was not serious. Arthur Scargill was fined £1,000 in 1984. Substantial fines have been ordered in other cases against TUs. In *Richard Read (Transport) Ltd v NUM (South Wales Area)* (1985) the defendants were fined £50,000.

16.13.6 Contempt

If sequestration is ordered, commissioners seize the defendant's assets. Obstruction of them is a contempt. Money can then be used to pay fines. The TU's accountants must cooperate.

16.13.7 Sequestrati

Trustees can be removed if they attempt to save union assets from sequestration: *Clarke v Heathfield (No 2)* (1985).

16.14   Picketing

Picketing is a form of protest during disputes, whether industrial or not, whereby demonstrators seek one or more of several objectives: to communicate the fact that they are in dispute, to seek support for their action, and to stop replacement labour. What is sometimes known as secondary picketing occurs when others join in to bring pressure on the employers who are parties to the primary dispute or where employees picket other than at their place of work. The restriction to one's place of work was intended to deter flying pickets. Picketing can give rise to offences and to civil liability.

16.14.1   Crime

Besides offences such as criminal damage, assault and battery, and offences contrary to the Public Order Act 1986 (such as s 3, affray), certain offences classically may occur. Note also ss 11-16 of the 1986 Act which deal with public demonstrations and processions. The Criminal Justice and Public Order Act 1994 inserted s 4A into the Public Order Act 1986 to create the offence of intentional harassment. A person will be liable if she shouts insulting words at a non-striker with intent and causes another person harassment, alarm or distress.

16.14.2   Breach of the peace

Breach of the peace occurs when a person behaves in such a way as to be likely to cause, or does cause, a breach of the peace. That person can be a picket, the persons picketed or anyone else. In *Piddington v Bates* (1960) Lord Parker CJ held that a constable was acting lawfully when he limited the number of pickets to two at the entrance to a factory when he contemplated a breach of the peace as a real possibility. As the case demonstrates, the accused is guilty even though he did not use or threaten violence. In *Kavanagh v Hiscock* (1974) a policeman had reason to believe that a breach of the peace might occur if he did not clear all pickets from the entrance to a hospital. The Court held that he was justified in doing as he did. Pickets have no right to stop vehicles, even ones which contain replacement labour. The police have a right to stop vehicles carrying pickets miles away from the site if they apprehend a breach of the peace: *Moss v McLachlan* (1985). Again the police could use this power to prevent any pickets reaching the site. Going through a police cordon constitutes a breach of the peace.

16.4.3   Obstruction

Obstruction of the highway is now found in s 137 of the Highways Act 1980. The wilful obstruction of the free passage without lawful authority or excuse is a crime. Whether the offence occurs is dependent on the duration and place of the obstruction, its purpose, and whether there was an actual obstruction rather than a potential one: *Nagy v Weston* (1965). There is no right to stop vehicles: *Broome v DPP* (1974).

Public nuisance is a common law crime is committed when free passage is blocked by pickets, but it is thought that picketing *per se* does not amount to public nuisance. Forty pickets walking in a circle at an entrance to a workplace was a public nuisance: *Tynan v Balmer* (1967). Picketing a person's home is also a nuisance: *Thomas v NUM (South Wales Area)* (1985) *per* Scott J.

16.14.4   Nuisance

Section 51(3) of the Police Act 1964 creates the offence of obstructing a police constable in the execution of his duty. Duty includes the prevention of trouble at a picket-line. If the protesters object to what the constable is doing when she tells them to go home, this offence may have been committed. Obstructing a constable is not an arrestable offence but a police officer may arrest without warrant when she reasonably apprehends a breach of the peace: she may well so apprehend when she is obstructed.

16.14.5   Obstructing a constable

By s 241(1) of TULR(C)A:

16.14.6   Watching or besetting

'... a person commits an offence who, with a view to compelling another person to abstain from doing or to do any act which that person has a legal right to do or abstain from doing, wrongfully and without legal authority –

(a)   uses violence to or intimidates that person or his wife or children or injures his property;

(b)   persistently follows that person about from place to place;

(c)   hides any books, clothes or other property owned by or used by that person, or deprives him of or hinders him in the use thereof;

(d)   watches or besets the house or other place where that person resides, works, carries on business or happens to be, or the approach to any such house or place; or

(e)   follows that person with two or more other persons in a disorderly manner in or through any street or road.'

The crime is punishable by a fine not exceeding £2,000 or 6 months' imprisonment or both. This crime was created in 1875 but very rarely used until the 1984–5 miners' strike. The fine was substantially increased in 1986 as a result of the strike and the crime was made an arrestable offence in that year.

'Wrongfully' means that the act must be tortious

16.14.7   'Wrongfully'

independently of the crime: *Ward, Lock & Co v OPAS* (1906) and *Thomas*, above. Therefore, if the picketing is lawful, there is no crime under this section. The contrary decision in *J Lyons & Sons v Wilkins* (1899) is nowadays regarded as incorrect. 'Intimidates' covers 'putting persons in fear by the exhibition of force ... or the threat of violence' (*Jones* (1974)). There is no need for violence against the person. Violence against property suffices. James LJ suggested in *Jones* that 'harsh words' would also constitute 'intimidates': *sed qu*. Scott J held in *Thomas*, above, that mass picketing amounted to intimidation for the purposes of this offence. 'Watches or besets' covers sit-ins. The offence is not restricted to the industrial context but has been used against an anti-roads protester. As criminal law students will remember, agreements to commit torts are generally not criminal (Criminal Law Act 1977, ss 1, 5) but agreements to commit crimes are conspiracies eg an agreement to attack a non-striker is an offence and remains so even if done in contemplation or furtherance of a trade dispute.

| 16.14.8 | Effect of civil immunity |

Even if the picketing is rendered civilly lawful by s 219 of TULR(C)A it can still be a crime contrary to s 241: *Galt v Philp* (1974), a Scottish case. The High Court of Justiciary held that a work-in amounted to watching or besetting. In other words watching or besetting can be committed not only by persons outside the premises but inside too.

| 16.14.9 | Effect on tort |

The fact that this crime has been committed does not *per se* mean that the defendants are tortiously liable: *Thomas v NUM (South Wales Area)*, above.

| 16.14.10 | Bail conditions |

As a condition for bail magistrates may impose a condition that the defendant shall not picket or demonstrate to support the dispute in connection with which he was arrested: *Mansfield J ex p Sharkey* (1984). The magistrates' condition did allow the defendant to picket his usual workplace. A person may receive a more severe sentence for breach of bail conditions than for the offence for which he or she was arrested.

| 16.14.11 | Police role |

Various discretions such as that of arrest are left in the hands of the police. These discretions have been criticised by civil libertarians as leaving too much power in the hands of the police. The arrest of pickets may worsen an industrial dispute.

| 16.14.12 | Civil law |

Other torts may occur such as interference with business by unlawful means (*Thomas*, above) and trespass to land, as occurred when the defendant, a union official, addressed a meeting on the employers' premises without permission, but the following are the more important ones.

The tort of private nuisance is committed when the defendant unlawfully interferes with the plaintiff's use or enjoyment of her land. Scott J in *Thomas*, above, held that interference with an individual's right to use the highway was a private nuisance. Mass picketing was held to constitute this tort in *Thomas*, above. Working miners were unlawfully harassed by striking ones, who were prohibited from blocking vehicles and people from entering premises. The correctness of this decision awaits a judgment by the Court of Appeal, and the proposition has been condemned as judicial legislation. Even if picketing is peaceful, it can be this tort where the defendants did not restrict their activity to the communication of information (*Mersey Dock and Harbour Co v Verrinder* (1982)).

16.14.13   Private nuisance

Scott J in *Thomas* thought that there was a tort of harassment actionable at the suit of those being picketed, but his decision was doubted by Stuart-Smith J in *News Group Newspapers Ltd v SOGAT 1982* (1987) In a non-employment case the Court of Appeal said that there is a tort of harassment. Public nuisance (see above) is also tortious.

16.14.14   Harassment

Use of the highway except for passing and repassing is trespass to the highway: *Hickman v Maisey* (1900). Special damage is required. Only owners of the highway may sue.

16.14.15   Trespass to highway

Section 220 of TULR(C)A gives immunity from civil and criminal liability to pickets in several situations. By s 220(1):

16.14.16   Immunity

'... it is lawful for a person in contemplation or furtherance of a trade dispute to attend –

(a)   at or near his own place of work; or

(b)   if he is an official of a trade union, at or near the place of work of a member of the union whom he is accompanying and whom he represents, for the purpose only of peacefully obtaining or communicating information, or peacefully persuading any person to work or abstain from working.'

This sub-section is to the effect that flying pickets and persons joining the picket line but not employed by the employers in dispute have no immunity. The narrow width of the protection afforded by this sub-section was demonstrated in the Wapping dispute. Closure of newspaper offices near Fleet Street and their transfer to Wapping resulted in illegal picketing at Wapping: the employees had never worked there; therefore, they were not 'at or near' their place of work. Picketing their former workplace would have no effect because the employers no longer were there.

'(2) If a person works or normally works –

    (a)   otherwise than at any one place; or

    (b)   at a place the location of which is such that attendance there for a purpose mentioned in subsection (1) is impracticable;

his place of work for the purposes of that subsection shall be any premises of his employer from which he works or from which his work is administered.

(3) in the case of a worker not in employment where –

    (a)   his last employment was terminated in connection with a trade dispute; or

    (b)   the termination of his employment was one of the circumstances giving rise to a trade dispute

in relation to that dispute his former place of work shall be treated for the purposes of subsection (1) as being his place of work.

(4) A person who is an official of a trade union by virtue only of having been elected or appointed to be a representative of some of the members of the union shall be regarded for the purposes of subsection (1) as representing only those members; but otherwise an official of a union shall be regarded for those purposes as representing all its members.'

Section 220(4) permits national officials to picket with others.

16.14.17 Secondary picketing

Secondary picketing is lawful if the pickets are at their own place of work. By s 224(1) secondary action which is lawful picketing is protected. Section 224(3) defines lawful picketing as:

'... acts done in the course of such attendance as is declared lawful by section 220 (peaceful picketing) –

    (a)   by a worker employed (or, in the case of a worker not in employment, last employed) by the employer party to the dispute; or

    (b)   by a trade union official whose attendance is lawful by virtue of subsection (1)(b) of that section.'

It should be remembered that by s 244 trade dispute is defined as one between workers and their employer. Picketing against other employers is unlawful. This type is sometimes called 'sympathy picketing'. Unfortunately, this action also goes by the name of secondary picketing sometimes. The question to ask is: where was the defendant picketing? An example of s 224 is this. Persons picket a factory. Lorry drivers bringing supplies from a firm to the employers turn back. Section 224 means that the pickets will not be liable, provided they do not go beyond what is permitted by s 220. Picketing the place where the lorries are based is unlawful.

Picketing is permissible within s 220(1) only in industrial disputes, only for the purposes mentioned, and only in respect of torts concerning attendance; torts beyond attendance are not rendered immune; and pickets cannot prevent persons entering premises (*Tynan v Balmer*, above) or stop vehicles (*Broome v DPP*, above). 'At or near' covers picketing at the entrance to a private industrial estate on which the employers' factory was sited (*Rayware Ltd v TGWU* (1989)). If the pickets had been closer, they would have been trespassing. The 1991 version suggests that if there is a choice as to places to picket, picketing should take place only at the closest spot for only there is 'at or near'. If their place of work has closed down, pickets cannot picket at the new workplace: *News Group*, above, the Wapping case – they cannot lawfully picket anywhere effectively.

16.14.18 Width of immunity

Immunity in the statute is not limited to a maximum number of pickets. In other words mass picketing is not *per se* unlawful. However, the Department of Employment's Code of Practice on Picketing 1980, revised 1991 (SI 1991/476), states that mass picketing may be tortious and recommends not more than six pickets at each entrance, adding that 'frequently a small number will be appropriate'. Scott J in *Thomas* thought that mass picketing constitutes intimidation and that six was the correct maximum. He stated that large numbers were unnecessary for peaceful persuasion. The Code has therefore had an effect on the law, though its legal status is solely that it is admissible in evidence and may be taken into account by a court, an IT or the CAC: s 207(3) of TULR(C)A. It should be noted that the Code does not affect the police's right mentioned in 16.14.2 to limit the number of pickets. Certainly mass picketing may tend to show that the protestors' purpose is not that of attendance for peaceful communication, but this remains a matter of evidence, not substantive law: *per* Lord Reid in *Broome v DPP*.

16.14.19 Numbers

The Code also states that picketing should not stop 'the operation of essential services, such as police, fire, ambulance, medical and nursing services', nor should it interfere with public health eg water purification. The law, however, states that peaceful picketing is lawful. Perhaps surprisingly it

16.14.20 Code on essential services

advises that TU members should not be disciplined or expelled for crossing picket lines. In this respect breach of the Code may help to demonstrate that the union member has been unjustifiably disciplined (see Chapter 15).

16.14.21   Critique

The narrowness of lawful picketing is striking. It is difficult to say that there is a right to picket in English law because the legality of picketing is hedged around with restrictions. For example, as the Code of Practice puts it, a picket may not 'attend lawfully at an entrance or exit from any place of work which is not his own, even if those who work there are employed by the same employer or covered by the same collective bargaining arrangements'.

The inability of pickets to stop vehicles and then communicate peacefully with the drivers is a major drawback of the legislation for pickets. The basic structure of the law was laid down in 1875 when there were no cars or lorries. In a traditional phrase the legislation was drafted for the horse-and-buggy era. Individuals walking to work can be communicated with; drivers cannot. The inability perhaps exacerbates any existing tendency to violence at the picket line. It is hard to credit that even as good a judge as Lord Reid thought in *Broome v DPP* that pickets' rights were the same as hitchhikers. It is arguable that official pickets, clearly so marked, in an official dispute should be allowed peacefully to communicate their message. In practice, sometimes the police do hold up traffic to allow pickets to pass on their message. It is only when this discretion is exercised that there is a 'right' to picket.

The Code of Practice has influenced the development of the law despite its not being a statute. Such 'soft law' or 'legislation by the back-door' is disliked by democrats. Criticism is especially strong on the limit of six per entrance and the attempt to prohibit picketing of so-called essential services: there is no ban on strikes in the essential services; if the government wishes to prohibit them, it should do so by statute. (One interesting point in conclusion is that the 'citizen's right of action' mentioned above was originally to have covered only essential services. It was widened between the Green Paper 'Industrial Relations in the 1990s', Cm 1602, 1991, and the Act.)

Industrial Action

Agreements between managements and unions are not normally legally binding but may affect the individual's contract.

Collective agreements

Industrial action is normally a breach of contract:

Simmons v Hoover (1977).

The courts have been astute to find that even working to rule is a breach of contract – the implied term to cooperate in the smooth running of the employers' business.

Effect on employment contract

Various statutes criminalise effects of action.

The Emergency Powers Act 1920 as amended is the principal statute.

Restricted strikes

Unions and others may be liable for various torts including inducing breach of contract, intimidation, interference with contract, and conspiracy. There is also a tort of breach of statutory duty and possible ones of inducing breach of an equitable obligation and interference with trade or business. (The last three are not immune from liability.) The possibility of economic duress arising is noted:

Thomson v Deakin (1952)

Torquay Hotel v Cousins (1969)

Rookes v Barnard (1964)

Hadmor Productions v Hamilton (1983)

Merkur Island v Laughton (1983)

Crofter Hand Woven Tweed v Veitch (1942)

Universe Tankships v ITWF (1983).

Liability for action

TULR(C)A s 219 provides immunity from most of the usual economic torts where action is taken in contemplation or furtherance of a trade dispute (the 'golden formula'):

Mercury v Scott-Garner (1984)

BBC v Hearn (1977).

Immunity

Impermissible purpose	Some strikes otherwise immune no longer attract immunity eg to enforce union membership. Pressure on employers to recognise a union by imposing a term in the contract to that effect is not allowed.
Secondary action	The former rules on secondary action have been abolished except in relation to the effects of picketing. Picketing at one's workplace remains lawful even though the effect is to hit suppliers and distributors.
Strike ballot	A fully-postal strike ballot is needed to keep the immunity for official action. The rules, which are technical, require eg the appointment of an independent scrutineer.
Citizen's and member's rights	An individual has a right of action to restrain tortious strikes. The TURERA 1993 creates the Commissioner for Protection against Unlawful Industrial Action to assist such actions.
Vicarious liability	By statute a union is liable for actions authorised or endorsed by the relevant officers or not repudiated by them.
Damages	Generally unions are liable only up to a specified sum; for example, a union with more than 100,000 members is liable to a maximum of £250,000 in relation to each employer. There is no limit on fines for contempt of court.
Injunctions	Employers gain interlocutory injunctions subject to statutory restrictions. Breach is a contempt of court and may lead to sequestration: *NWL v Woods* (1979).
Picketing	Criminal offences and torts abound in relation to picketing. Peaceful picketing at one's place of work for the purpose only of communicating information is rendered lawful by statute. Bail conditions may be imposed: *Piddington v Bates* (1960) *Thomas v NUM* (1985) *ex p Sharkey* (1984).

Recommended Reading List

Trade Union Immunities, Cmnd 8128, 1981

Democracy in Trade Unions, Cmnd 8778, 1983

Trade Unions and their Members, Cm 95, 1987

Removing Barriers to Employment, Cm 655, 1989

Unofficial Action and the Law, Cm 821, 1989

Industrial Relations in the 1990s, Cm 1602, 1991

**Official Publications -
all published by HMSO**

David Blanchflower and Richard Freeman, *Did the Thatcher Reforms Change British Labour Market Performance?* (Centre for Economic Performance, 1993)

Paul Davies and Mark Freedland, *Labour, Legislation and Public Policy* (Clarendon, 1993)

Simon Deakin and Frank Wilkinson, *The Economics of Employment Rights* (Institute of Employment Rights, 1991)

Linda Dickins, *Whose Flexibility?* (Institute of Employment Rights, 1991)

(Donovan) *Report of the Royal Commission on Trade Unions and Employers' Associations*, Cmnd 3623 (HMSO, 1968)

K D Ewing, C A Gearty and B A Hepple (ed), *Human Rights and Labour Law* (Mansell, 1994)

Charles G Hanson, *Taming the Trade Unions* (Macmillan, 1991)

John Hendy, *A Law unto Themselves: Conservative Employment Laws* (Institute of Employment Rights, 3rd edn, 1993)

Lord McCarthy (ed), *Legal Intervention in Industrial Relations* (Blackwell, 1991)

Lord Wedderburn (ed), *Labour Law in the Post-industrial Era* (Dartmouth, 1994)

Simon Deakin, 'Equality under a Market Order' (1990) 19 Industrial Law Journal 1

Modern labour law

Keith Ewing, 'Swimming with the Tide' (1993) 22 Industrial Law Journal 165

Patricia Fosh et al, 'Politics, Pragmatism and Ideology' (1993) 22 Industrial Law Journal 14

Sandra Fredman, 'The New Rights' (1992) 12 Oxford Journal of Legal Studies 24

Debra Morris, 'The Commissioner for the Rights of Trade Union Members' (1993) 22 Industrial Law Journal 104

U Mückenberger and S Deakin, 'From Deregulation to a European Floor of Rights' (1989) 3 Zeitschrift für Ausländisches und Internationales Arbeits – und Sozialrecht 153

Nigel Tremlett and Nitya Banerji, *The 1992 Survey of Industrial Tribunal Applicants* (Employment Department, 1994)

Lord Wedderburn, 'Freedom of Association and Philosophies of Labour Law' (1989) 18 Industrial Law Journal 1

EC Law

European Commission, *European Social Policy – a Way Forward for the Union* (COM (94) 333, 1994)

Ruth Nielsen and Erica Szyszczak, *The Social Dimension of the European Community* (Handelshojskolens Forlag, 2nd edn, 1993)

Catherine Barnard, 'A Social Policy for Europe' (1992) 8 International Journal of Comparative Labour Law and Industrial Relations 15

Brian Bercusson, 'The European Community's Charter of Fundamental Social Rights for Workers' (1990) 53 Modern Law Review 624

Brian Bercusson, 'The Dynamic of European Labour Law After Maastricht' (1994) 23 Industrial Relations Journal 1

Barry Fitzpatrick, 'Community Social Law after Maastricht' (1992) 21 Industrial Law Journal 199

Bob Hepple, 'The Implementation of the Community Charter ...' (1990) 53 Modern Law Review 643

Josephine Shaw, 'European Community Judicial Method' (1990) 19 Industrial Law Journal 228

Discrimination

Evelyn Ellis, *European Community Sex Equality Law* (Clarendon,

1991)

Bob Hepple and Erica Szyszczak (eds), *Discrimination: the Limits of Law* (Mansell, 1992)

Simon Honeyball, *Sex, Employment and the Law* (Blackwell, 1991)

Neil Millward, *Targeting Potential Discrimination* (EOC, 1995)

Aileen McColgan, *Pay Equity* (Institute of Employment Rights, 1994)

Chris Docksey, 'The Principle of Equality ... under Community Law' (1991) 20 Industrial Law Journal 258

Barry Fitzpatrick, 'Equality in Occupational Pensions' (1991) 54 Modern Law Review 271

Anthony Lester and Dinah Rose, 'Equal Value Claims and Sex Bias in Collective Bargaining' (1991) 20 Industrial Law Journal 163

Christopher McCrudden, 'The Effectiveness of European Equality Law' (1993) 13 Oxford Journal of Legal Studies 320

Sarah Moore, 'Justice Doesn't Mean a Free Lunch' (1995) 20 European Law Review 159

Michael Rubenstein, 'Sexual Harassment' (1992) 21 Industrial Law Journal 70

Mark Freedland, *The Contract of Employment* (Clarendon, 1976)   **Terms**

Francis Gurry, *Breach of Confidence* (Clarendon, 1984)

Hugh Collins, 'Market Power, Bureaucratic Power, and the Contract of Employment' (1986) 15 Industrial Law Journal 1

Bob Hepple, 'A Right to Work?' (1981) 10 Industrial Law Journal 65

Bob Hepple, 'Restructuring Employment Rights' (1986) 15 Industrial Law Journal 69

Simon Honeyball, 'Employment Law and the Primacy of Contract' (1989) 18 Industrial Law Journal 97

Richard Kidner, 'Vicarious Liability: For Whom Should the "Employer" Be Liable?' (1995) 15 Legal Studies 47

Christine Mogridge, 'Illegal Employment Contracts' (1981) 10

Industrial Law Journal 23

Brian Napier, 'Aspects of the Wage-Work Bargain' [1984] Cambridge Law Journal 337

Roger Rideout, 'The Contract of Employment' [1966] Current Legal Problems 111

Roger Rideout, 'Confidentiality or Protection of Trade Secrets?' (1986) 15 Industrial Law Journal 183

Jean Warburton, 'The Employment of Home Workers' (1984) 13 Industrial Law Journal 251

Termination

Hugh Collins, *Justice in Dismissal* (Clarendon, 1992)

Linda Dickins *et al*, *Dismissed* (Basil Blackwell, 1985)

Cyril Grunfeld, *The Law of Redundancy* (Sweet & Maxwell, 3rd edn, 1989)

Roy Lewis and Jon Clark, *The Case for Alternate Dispute Resolution* (Institute of Employment Rights, 1993)

John McMullen, *Business Transfers and Employee Rights* (Butterworths, 2nd edn, 1992)

John Bowers and Andrew Clarke, 'Unfair Dismissal and Managerial Prerogative' (1981) 10 Industrial Law Journal 34

Hazel Carty, 'Dismissed Employees: the Search for a more effective Range of Remedies' (1989) 52 Modern Law Review 449

Hugh Collins, 'The Meaning of Job Security' (1991) 20 Industrial Law Journal 227

Keith Ewing, 'Remedies for Breach of the Contract of Employment' (1993) Cambridge Law Journal 405

Patrick Elias, 'Fairness in Unfair Dismissal' (1981) 10 Industrial Law Journal 201

Keith Ewing and Andrew Grubb, 'The Emergence of a New Labour Injunction?' (1987) 16 Industrial Law Journal 145

Humphrey Forrest, 'Political Values in Individual Employment Law' (1980) 43 Modern Law Review 361

Sandra Fredman and Simon Lee, 'Natural Justice for Employees' (1986) 15 Industrial Law Journal 15

Paul Goulding, 'Injunctions and Contracts of Employment' (1990) 19 Industrial Law Journal 98

Elizabeth Macdonald, 'Contractual Damages for Mental Distress' (1994) 7 Journal of Contract Law 134

John McMullen, 'Takeovers, Transfers and Business Re-organisations' (1992) 21 Industrial Law Journal 15

John McMullen, 'Frustration of the Contract of Employment and Statutory Labour Law' (1986) 49 Modern Law Review 785

John McMullen, 'The Resurgence of Proceduralism in Unfair Dismissal Law' (1988) 51 Modern Law Review 651

Patrick Elias and Keith Ewing, *Trade Union Democracy, Members' Rights and the Law* (Mansell, 1987)

Trade Unions

Sheldon Leader, *Freedom of Association* (Yale, 1992)

Gillian Morris and T J Archer, *Trade Unions, Employers and the Law* (Butterworths, 2nd edn, 1993)

Ferdinand von Prondzynski, *Freedom of Association and Industrial Relations* (Mansell, 1987)

Stephen Dunn *et al*, 'Special Edition – Workplace Industrial Relations in Transition' (1993) 31 British Journal of Industrial Relations 169

Stephen Dunn and David Metcalf, *Trade Union Law Since 1979: Ideology, Intent, Impact* (Centre for Economic Performance, 1994)

Stephen Dunn and Martyn Wright, *Managing Without the Closed Shop* (Centre for Economic Performance, 1993)

Keith Ewing, 'Trade Union Recognition' (1990) 19 Industrial Law Journal 209

Howard Gospel and Paul Willman, 'Disclosure of Information: the CAC Approach' (1981) 10 Industrial Law Journal 10

Sheldon Leader, 'The European Convention on Human Rights, the Employment Act of 1988 and the Right to Refuse to Strike' (1991) 20 Industrial Law Journal 39

Paul Smith *et al*, 'Ballots and Union Government in the 1980s' (1993) 31 British Journal of Industrial Relations 365

Richard Townshend-Smith, 'Refusal of Employment on Grounds of Trade Union Membership or Non-membership' (1991) 20 Industrial Law Journal 102

Industrial action

Simon Auerbach, *Legislating for Conflict* (Clarendon, 1990)

Keith Ewing, *The Right to Strike* (Clarendon, 1991)

Jane Elgar and Bob Simpson, *The Impact of the Law on Industrial Disputes in the 1980s* (Centre for Economic Performance, 1992)

Jane Elgar and Bob Simpson, *Union Negotiators, Industrial Action and the Law* (Centre for Economic Performance, 1993)

Roger Welch, *The Right to Strike: a Trade Union View* (Institute of Employment Rights, 1991)

Simon Auerbach, 'Legal Restraint of Picketing' (1987) 16 Industrial Law Journal 227

J Kodwo Bentil, 'Improper Interference with Another's Business or Trade Interest as a Tort' (1993) Journal of Business Law 519

Hazel Carty, 'Intentional Violation of Economic Interests' (1988) 104 Law Quarterly Review 250

Patrick Elias and Keith Ewing, 'Economic Torts and Labour Law' (1982) Cambridge Law Journal 321

Keith Ewing, 'The Right to Strike' (1986) 15 Industrial Law Journal 142

Gillian Morris, 'Industrial Action in Essential Services: the New Law' (1992) 21 Industrial Law Journal 89

Gillian Morris, 'Industrial Action: Public and Private Interests' (1993) 22 Industrial Law Journal 194

Peter Wallington, 'Injunctions and the Right to Demonstrate' (1986) Cambridge Law Journal 86

Peter Wallington, 'Some Implications for the Policing of Industrial Disputes' (1987) Criminal Law Review 180

Index

A

action short of dismissal   11.2.7, 11.2.9,
12.3.44, 14.6.6
additional award   12.3.9
Advisory Conciliation and
   Arbitration Service   1.3.12, 2.3.1
   advice   2.3.1
   arbitration   2.3.1
   codes of practice   2.3.1
   conciliation   2.3.1
appeals in unfair dismissal   10.6.20
arbitration   1.3.2, 2.3.1,
2.3.2
associated employer   8.5.5

B

ballots:
   see Industrial action,
basic award   12.3.15-12.3.19
Bridlington rules   15.4-15.4.8

C

Central Arbitration Committee   2.3.2, 14.8.5
Certification Officer   2.2.2, 2.3.4,
14.5, 14.5.2,
14.6.3-14.6.5
citizen's right   16.10.1, 16.10.3
claim in time   8.3.9, 8.3.10
closed shop   1.3.2, 1.3.12,
1.3.21, 1.3.26,
15.2.5
Codes of Practice   2.3.1, 2.3.3, 6.11,
10.6.9, 10.6.10,
10.6.15, 10.6.35,
10.6.36, 14.8.2,
16.14.19-16.14.21
collective agreement   1.3.9, 1.4,
4.9.35-4.9.42,
4.10.1, 13.2.4,
13.3.6, 16.2-16.2.3
collective bargaining   1.22, 1.3.2,
1.3.3, 1.3.5,
14.8.3, 15.2.2
Commission for Racial Equality   2.3.3
Commissioner for Protection
   against Unlawful Industrial
     Action   1.3.22, 2.3.5
Commissioner for the Rights of
   Trade Union Members   1.3.22, 2.3.5
compensatory award   12.3.15,
12.3.20-12.3.38
Conciliation Officer   2.3.1
conspiracy   16.5.20
constructive dismissal   7.2.9, 8.4.1,
8.6.3-8.6.6,
9.5.1, 13.2.15

continuity of employment   4.6.2, 8.3.2,
8.5-8.5.13
   arrangement or custom   8.5.18
   pregnancy   8.5.18
   sickness or injury   8.5.18
   strike   8.5.2
   transfer of business   8.5.10-8.5.12,
13.2.2
   transfer of undertakings   8.5.13
contract of employment   3.1
   illegality   3.1, 4.9.22
   industrial action   4.9.11
   incorporation   4.9.35-4.9.42
   no-strike clause   4.9.38, 16.2.2
   terms   4.7-4.10.2
   written statement   1.3.20, 4.6-4.6.10
custom   4.9.7, 4.9.43

D

damages   4.8.15
   trade union   16.12-16.12.2
   wrongful dismissal   7.2.11-7.2.17
directives   2.4.2-2.4.9,
5.2.5, 13.2.3

discrimination
   advertisements   6.5.2
   direct   6.4.3-6.4.11
   enforcement   6.7-6.7.4
   equal pay:
     see Equal pay
   genuine occupational
     qualifications   6.6-6.6.3
   indirect   6.4.12-6.4.20
   justifiable   6.4.20
   marital status   6.3.2
   nationality; national origins   6.3.3
   pregnancy   6.6.5
   race   1.3.12, 3.1.1,
6.1-6.3, 6.3.3-6.4.9,
6.4.12-6.4.21,
6.4.8-6.6.1, 6.6.3,
6.6.4, 6.6.7,
6.7-6.8.4, 15.5.5
   segregation   6.4.24
   sex   1.3.12, 1.3.17,
1.3.20, 2.4.2, 2.4.8,
3.1.1, 3.5.2, 5.1.1,
5.1.18, 5.3, 6.1-6.3.2,
6.4-6.6.2, 6.6.4-6.6.6,
6.6.8-6.9.2, 15.5.5
   sexual harassment   6.4.10, 6.4.11,
6.5.3, 10.6.11
   victimisation   6.4.23
   dismissal   3.1, 4.10.3, 7.2-7.2.29,
8.1.1, 8.6-8.6.6,
10.6.18, 11.1-11.2.6
     asserting statutory right   11.2.15, 11.2.16

cause | 7.2.5-7.2.7
common law | 7.2
fixed-term contract | 8.6.2
frustration | 7.1.2-7.1.10
mutual agreement | 7.1.13-7.1.17
repudiation | 7.2.9
statute | 7.2.25
summary | 7.2.5
wrongful | 7.2.8-7.2.22
duress | 16.5.21
duties
on employee | 4.9.21-4.9.32
on employer | 4.9.10-4.9.20

E
economic duress | 16.5.21
effective date of termination | 8.4-8.4.2
Employers' Associations | 14.2.5
Equal Opportunities Commission | 2.3.3
equal pay | 2.4.5, 2.4.7,
2.4.8, 5.1-5.3,
6.4.3, 6.9, 6.9.1
collective agreement | 5.1.15
comparator | 5.1.3
equal value | 5.1.3, 5.1.9-5.1.13,
5.2.4
equality clause | 4.9.44, 5.1.2
genuine material difference | 5.1.14-5.1.17, 5.2.8
job evaluation study | 5.1.3, 5.1.7, 5.1.8
red-circling | 5.1.14
same employment | 5.1.6
European Community law | 1.3.15, 1.3.17,
2.1.1, 2.4-2.4.9,
5.2-5.2.9, 13.2.3

F
faithful service | 4.9.25-4.9.29
fixed term contracts | 4.5, 7.1.11, 7.1.12,
8.3.8, 8.4.1, 8.6.2
freedom of association | 15.2-15.2.2
frustration | 3.1, 7.1.2-7.1.10

I
illegality
contract | 4.4-4.4.6, 4.9.22
unfair dismissal | 10.5.6
ill-health:
see Sickness
immunity
economic torts | 16.6-16.6.11
picketing | 16.14.16-16.14.19
incapability | 10.5.4
independent contractors | 3.2.1, 3.2.2, 3.2.3,
3.3.3, 3.3.4, 3.3.6,
3.3.15, 3.4.1, 3.4.9,
3.5.4, 3.5.8, 3.6, 3.8
inducing breach of contract | 16.5.1-16.5.12

industrial action | 1.2.1, 1.3.18,
1.3.25, 2.4.9, 4.9.11,
11.3.1-11.3.9, 15.2.3,
16.3-16.14.21
ballot | 1.3.9, 1.3.21, 1.3.22
golden formula | 1.3.1, 1.3.21,
16.6.7-16.6.11
immunity | 16.6-16.6.11
notice | 1.4
political strike | 16.6.11
suspension of contract | 16.3.1
trade dispute | 16.6.9-16.6.11
industrial tribunal | 2.1.1, 2.2, 2.2.1,
3.6, 4.6.5
information for collective
bargaining purposes | 14.8-14.8.6
injunction | 4.8.13, 4.8.14,
7.2.23-7.2.27,
16.13-16.13.5
interference with contract | 16.5.16, 16.5.17
interference with trade
or business | 16.5.16, 16.5.18,
16.5.19
intimidation | 16.5.13-16.5.15

L
listing | 14.5-14.5.2

M
misconduct
redundancy payments | 9.2-9.2.3
unfair dismissal | 10.5.3, 10.6.8,
10.6.11, 10.6.18

N
normal retiring age | 5.2.1, 8.3.5
notice period | 1.3.5, 3.1.1,
4.9.46, 7.2-7.2.4,
7.2.11, 7.2.12
notification of collective
redundancies | 9.7.15, 9.7.16

O
office holders | 3.2.1, 3.5.1, 3.5.2

P
picketing | 1.3.21, 1.3.26,
16.14-16.14.21
civil liability | 16.14.12-16.14.15
code of practice | 2.3.1,
16.14.19-16.14.21
criminal liability | 16.14.1-16.14.10
immunity | 16.14.8,
16.14.16-16.14.19
secondary | 16.14.17
political fund | 1.3.2, 14.10-14.10.8
political strike | 16.6.11